Creativity and Captivity

American Society of Missiology
Monograph Series

Series Editor, James R. Krabill

The ASM Monograph Series provides a forum for publishing quality dissertations and studies in the field of missiology. Collaborating with Pickwick Publications—a division of Wipf and Stock Publishers of Eugene, Oregon—the American Society of Missiology selects high quality dissertations and other monographic studies that offer research materials in mission studies for scholars, mission and church leaders, and the academic community at large. The ASM seeks scholarly work for publication in the series that throws light on issues confronting Christian world mission in its cultural, social, historical, biblical, and theological dimensions.

Missiology is an academic field that brings together scholars whose professional training ranges from doctoral-level preparation in areas such as Scripture, history and sociology of religions, anthropology, theology, international relations, interreligious interchange, mission history, inculturation, and church law. The American Society of Missiology, which sponsors this series, is an ecumenical body drawing members from Independent and Ecumenical Protestant, Catholic, Orthodox, and other traditions. Members of the ASM are united by their commitment to reflect on and do scholarly work relating to both mission history and the present-day mission of the church. The ASM Monograph Series aims to publish works of exceptional merit on specialized topics, with particular attention given to work by younger scholars, the dissemination and publication of which is difficult under the economic pressures of standard publishing models.

Persons seeking information about the ASM or the guidelines for having their dissertations considered for publication in the ASM Monograph Series should consult the Society's website—www.asmweb.org.

Members of the ASM Monograph Committee who approved this book are:

Margaret Guider, OSF, Associate Professor of Missiology, Boston College School of Theology and Ministry

Bonnie Sue Lewis, Professor of Mission and World Christianity, University of Dubuque Theological Seminary

RECENTLY PUBLISHED IN THE ASM MONOGRAPH SERIES

Mary Carol Cloutier, *Bridging the Gap, Breaching Barriers: The Presence and Contribution of (Foreign) Persons of African Descent to the Gaboon and Corisco Mission in Nineteenth-Century Equatorial Africa*

Creativity and Captivity

Exploring the Process of Musical Creativity amongst Indigenous Cosmopolitan Musicians (ICMs) for Mission

Uday Balasundaram

FOREWORD BY
Michael Rynkiewich

American Society of Missiology Monograph
Series vol. 51

☙PICKWICK *Publications* • Eugene, Oregon

CREATIVITY AND CAPTIVITY
Exploring the Process of Musical Creativity amongst Indigenous Cosmopolitan Musicians (ICMs) for Mission

American Society of Missiology Monograph Series 51

Copyright © 2021 Uday Balasundaram. All rights reserved. Except for brief quotations in critical publications or reviews, no part of this book may be reproduced in any manner without prior written permission from the publisher. Write: Permissions, Wipf and Stock Publishers, 199 W. 8th Ave., Suite 3, Eugene, OR 97401.

Pickwick Publications
An Imprint of Wipf and Stock Publishers
199 W. 8th Ave., Suite 3
Eugene, OR 97401

www.wipfandstock.com

PAPERBACK ISBN: 978-1-7252-6576-9
HARDCOVER ISBN: 978-1-7252-6577-6
EBOOK ISBN: 978-1-7252-6578-3

Cataloguing-in-Publication data:

Names: Balasundaram, Uday, author. | Rynkiewich, Michael, foreword.

Title: Creativity and captivity : exploring the process of musical creativity amongst indigenous cosmopolitan musicians (ICMs) for mission / by Uday Balasundaram ; foreword by Michael Rynkiewich.

Description: Eugene, OR: Pickwick Publications, 2021 | American Society of Missiology Monograph Series 51 | Includes bibliographical references and index.

Identifiers: ISBN 978-1-7252-6576-9 (paperback) | ISBN 978-1-7252-6577-6 (hardcover) | ISBN 978-1-7252-6578-3 (ebook)

Subjects: LCSH: Ethnomusicology. | Church music. | Missions—music.

Classification: ML3007 B35 2021 (print) | ML3007 (ebook)

Cover illustration by Sujatha E. Balasundaram.

11/30/21

To God the Father, Jesus Christ the Son, and the Holy Spirit,
Bezalel, and for creatives everywhere,
Called
Commissioned
Anointed
Appointed, and
Charged, to
Inspire,
Imagine,
Illumine, and
Interrogate
The systems and structures of the world,
And thereby, to
Build up the Church for mission
In the context of the *creatio Dei*
In this world and the next—

Be a better creative . . . your creative best is yet to come.

Contents

Foreword by Michael Rynkiewich | ix
Preface | xi
Acknowledgments | xiii
Introduction | xv

1. Introduction | 1
2. Musical Creativity | 27
3. New Spaces | 56
4. Creative Mission | 84
5. Creative Being: Embodiment | 109
6. Creative Construction: Enactment | 152
7. Creative Performance: Expression | 185
8. Theorizing ICM Identity for Mission | 211

Appendix A: Musical Creativity and Missiology | 233
Appendix B: Adaptation of Csikszentmihalyi's (1988, 1997, 1999)
  Systems Model of Creativity for ICMs in Mission | 236
Appendix C: Creative Construction: Toward the Development
  of a Sonic Theology | 237
Appendix D: C3M—Covenant Creative Communities for Mission | 255
Appendix E: MUHANA Ashram | 258
Appendix F: Community Transformation through the Arts (CTA) | 262
Appendix G: Estuary Cultures: A Way for Church Movement | 263
Appendix H: Questions for Witnessing Artists | 271
Bibliography | 275
Index | 299

Foreword

NEITHER JESUS NOR THE early church ever thought it necessary that the Christian movement be tied to one language. If it were so, then perhaps Aramaic should have had the priority since it is the language that Jesus spoke, the thought patterns of his teachings and parables. Indeed, when they sang a hymn after the Passover dinner, they sang in Aramaic.

Perhaps Greek had a claim since all the holy writings are in that language, and the emerging theology employed those concepts and rhetoric. Greek was more widespread, but only because of the conquests of Alexander, and thus it resonated also as an imperial language. Or, perhaps Latin had a claim to be the language of the church since the incubator of the early church was the Roman Empire. John of the Apocalypse might have had something to say about that. Indeed, Latin did become the language of the Roman church, but then at the expense of many local Christianities, Celtic Christianity among them.

The truth is that never was there a time in God's creative mission on earth that one style of evangelism, one model of the people of God, nor one form of expression of worship in art and music was the order of the day, except by imperial decree either from outside the church or, too often, from within. Even the Apostle Paul presented himself and his gospel in different personas, speaking different languages, following different customs—becoming all things to all people in order that he might win some. Paul used empire to follow the trails of diaspora in order to find the interstitial spaces between established groups. In Paul's notion of creative mission, Christianity became an urban religion, even a diaspora religion, and its expression took on a cosmopolitan flavor.

In this book, Uday Balasundaram explores the variety of expressions in today's aesthetics of worship, particularly in the creation and performance of music. Drawing on the anthropological concept of the "indigenous cosmopolitan," he probes the tensions between Christianity as a rooted religion at home in one culture, language, and hymnody, and Christianity as a routed religion traveling between cultures and languages. Sometimes the journey is easy and sometimes there is resistance, but always there is a creative flow of something new, where the gospel for the world becomes the gospel for our people.

Uday asks: Who are these people who are able to express in music the fruit of the Spirit, the love, joy, and peace of following Christ in resonances that speak to the local while avoiding invasive forms of Western music? Who is able to resist the hegemonic tendencies of the universal church while faithfully representing the indigenous experience of God's love in Jesus Christ? At the same time, how are some musicians able to transcend the boundaries to reach other followers of Christ? Their creativity wrestles with categories of indigenous, diasporic, and cosmopolitan, yet they connect with their audiences.

God's inherent creativity, seen at the very beginning, is not muted when, as we near the end, Revelation 7:9 clearly tells us that the new song is sung in many verses that gather up the experiences of so many different people around the world. Uday represents an "indigenous cosmopolitan" himself, and presents several case studies of others. These creative artists, musicians, and worship leaders are thoroughly embedded and competent in one language and music, and yet precisely because of their authenticity, they are able to cross boundaries in order to tell the story of God's persistent insistent appeal to all of humanity to return to God's loving arms.

This is the story of our globalizing world where some live in indigenous communities, some live in diaspora communities, and some are thoroughly at home in a cosmopolitan world; and, this is important, some are able to move back and forth effortlessly between these communities with their different contexts, languages, worldviews, and Christianities. As I once sat having tea in the heart of a great Indian city, there were around me students from all over the country and abroad, who gathered in this non-judgmental space for tea, conversation, and music. Theirs is a search for meaning, for self, and for reliable relationships. The music is sometimes old and sometimes bold, but they are in a setting where they can be attuned to God's call. Beyond that, the music also plays in South Africa, Australia, and Peru, precisely because it emerges from a creative being engaged in the creative activity of mission on behalf of a multi-dimensional God who is calling multi-faceted people on a journey toward the community of God.

Michael Rynkiewich
May 2020

Preface

THE RADICAL REORGANIZATION OF cultural boundaries in the wake of globalization has led to new identities that emerge "in-between" and extend "beyond" perceptions of nation, race, ethnicity, and class. The concept of "indigenous cosmopolitanism" describes those who do not entirely forsake indigenous identity, but concurrently desire participation in broader relational networks. Indigenous Cosmopolitanism refers to hybridity that emerges in the negotiation of identity amid the interstitial passages between the binaries of colonial and postcolonial logics of power. Indigenous cosmopolitanism is a way of being that is pertinent for a vast majority of musicians whose music and audiences are not limited to a local geographical area. Rather, the ways in which these musicians conceive, produce, and mediate their music, as well as ways in which they invite others to participate in their music takes place in the context of transnational spatial and temporal relational networks.

The purpose of this monograph is to explore the ways in which Christian indigenous cosmopolitan musicians understand and practice their musical creativity for mission. The thesis is as follows: Christian indigenous cosmopolitan musicians for mission (ICMs, hereafter) understand themselves as participating in the creativity of God, and by implication, become channels of the creative activity of God through their musical creativity as they create fresh ways to build the church for mission with others.

The book is arranged in two main sections. Following the preface, chapter 1 serves as introduction. The first main section consists of Chapters 2–4. Here I deal largely with the conceptual and theoretical bases for musical creativity, new spaces, and creative mission respectively. In the second section, chapters 5–7, I explore data from interviews with key informants.

In chapter 8, I summarize issues of method and analysis, discuss missiological implications, and share some concluding thoughts for mission. The following table offers a visual layout of the chapters:

Organization of Chapters

Chapter 1—Introduction		
Chapter 2 Musical Creativity	Chapter 3 New Spaces	Chapter 4 Creative Mission (Framework: MFTC)
Chapter 5 Creative Being	Chapter 6 Creative Enactment	Chapter 7 Creative Performance
Chapter 8—Conclusion		

Acknowledgments

I THANK ALMIGHTY GOD, whose patience and guidance I experienced firsthand through the hand of my academic mentor, Dr. Michael Rynkiewich, "Mike," and my committee members, Dr. Lalsangkima Pachuau, who provided deep insight, constructive critique, and early help in articulating my thesis, and Dr. Jay Moon for the excellent introspective questions at my defense. I also want to extend my indebtedness to the faculty, staff, and students of Asbury Theological Seminary, especially the E. Stanley Jones School of World Missions and Evangelism and the Advanced Research Program office.

At the risk of not mentioning the names of several whom I would like to thank personally, I make especial mention of Dr. Terry C. Muck for guiding my initial Area Study when I was yet trying to articulate the notion of "area" and what it meant for researching music in a global era, Dr. George Hunter III for going ahead with teaching to a class of one in the Spring of 2008 as well as for help in applying theories of rhetoric to music, Dr. Arthur McPhee and Evelyn McPhee for their genuine and ongoing friendship and for their investment in my life and my family as we refined the thesis for the dissertation proposal, and Dr. Eunice Irwin for encouraging critical thinking in the intersection of music, missional identity, and contextual theology.

I also want to thank the pastoral team, elders, members-at-large and especially those of the worship ministries of Loudonville Community Church, Albany, New York, for prayers and support as I worked on my dissertation while serving on staff at the church and beyond. Thank you to our Christ Church family in Lexington, Kentucky and the many friends, family, particularly, Sanjay for continually challenging me to put my thoughts into sustainable action, and supporters around the world who strengthened us through prayer and financial giving along the way. I am extremely grateful to the several artists, worship teams, and especially to my Key Informants for their time, insight, and inspiration. On a more personal note, thank you to my mother, Pramila Balasundaram, quintessential artist and entrepreneur, whose creativity and cutting-edge work with the intellectually disabled over the last thirty years and community based rehabilitation strategies through the arts among some of the world's most neglected, continues to be an inspiration.

I am ever indebted and grateful to our Lord for the unique creative presence that sustained and energized every single day of the doctoral journey through the unflinching and ever-present love and support of my wife, Sujatha, and the over-abundant joyfulness of my daughters, Nadira and Aradhya.

Introduction

THE PRIMARY CONCEPTUAL BUILDING blocks for this monograph are the process of musical creativity, the new spaces brought about by globalization, and creative mission as ICMs participate in the *missioDei*. I briefly introduce each of these in chapter 1. I also introduce some of the nuances that problematize the intersection of musical creativity, new spaces, and efforts in creative mission. This prepares us for the statement of the problem, research questions, and rationale for this study. I then proceed to explain the process of data collection, introduce key informants, and discuss issues pertaining to the method concerning this research. The nature of the discourse arising from interviews and the nature of the subject of musical creativity lend itself to interpretation in the context of a postcolonial research paradigm.

In chapter 2, I distinguish and develop separately the concepts of music and creativity. Ethnomusicology helps to outline some of the pertinent characteristics of music as a "lived experience." I also discuss aspects of the spirituality of music as it pertains to this research. As part of a cultural system, theological creativity is to be distinguished from popular concepts of creativity. I clarify the concepts of musical creativity, cosmopolitanism, and indigenous cosmopolitanism for this research. Now, we are in a better place to understand the role of ICMs in mission in the context of global new spaces.

In chapter 3 we explore the intersection between musical creativity, globalization, and mission. We begin to encounter some of the dynamics of the new spaces that ICMs construct for the negotiation of creative being in the context of mission. Interstitial identity emerges in response to the neoliberal hegemonies that govern the movement of music in this era of globalization. A central concern therefore is the authentic translation of Christianity *with* the other.

In chapter 4, we begin to develop a theology of creativity (*creatio Dei*), which offers a theological spectrum for exploring musical creativity amongst ICMs for mission. The *creatio Dei* may be understood as a five-fold Missiological Framework for Theological Creativity (MFTC): creative being, which serves as the hub for creative construction, creative community, creative beauty, and creative performance, of which we develop only three.

In chapter 5 we begin critical interaction with data from interviews with ICMs in mission. We discover that for some, "fusion" music is a "way out" of essentializing hegemonies. Authentic mission is a "byproduct" of creative being. We further apprehend issues concerning the legitimacy of indigenous creative agency in the context of neoliberal market capitalism through music, the tension between "Christian music" and "worship music," and how ICMs negotiate "authentic" creative being amid the challenge of overcoming fear, insecurity, and prejudice in the context of the mission of God.

In chapter 6, we come alongside ICMs in mission as they negotiate their identities through the creative construction of new sites for the generation of knowledge, the participation of others, and for exploring the relation between concepts of indigenization and contextualization. We encounter the role of the conscience in contextualization, the nuances of indigenization as a reciprocal process amid postcolonial logics, and musical creativity as a process of unification and ongoing contestation of notions of authenticity. The active translation of Christianity through music is the work of a hermeneutical community, a place for the articulation of difference, and invites the intentional overlap of "poetic palettes" with the other.

Chapter 7 explores the performative discourse of ICMs in mission. Creative performance refers to sites for prophetic dialogue in the context of a "diasporic consciousness" for the development of new relational networks and the emergence of public liturgies with others. It involves a spatial/temporal, conceptual, and "performative" extension of the presence of the church. This allows for ecclesial renewal. However, the social relocation of ecclesial identity is also a threat to existing structures. Creative performance calls for clear articulation of the uniqueness of Christianity especially where it appears that "there are no boundary lines." Creative performance spaces are sites for the generation of knowledge along with the other, mutual enactment of creative identity, and the serving of God's justice.

In chapter 8, by way of concluding thoughts, we revisit our thesis and the primary research questions in the light of interaction between theory and data. We summarize issues pertaining to creative method for a contextual theology of creativity. We revisit the issue of creativity within the context of Christianity. We also summarize issues of creative theological orientation through revisiting our original research questions. We discuss some missiological implications for "the creative church." The question is: "Where is church?" in the context of global migration and the dynamics of global complexity. We also take the opportunity to briefly address some gaps in the context of the creative mission of ICMs. We suggest some ways through which ICM agency allows for fresh incarnations of the church in this era of globalization—creativity in the context of diversity for community in Christ.

1

Introduction

> In the beginning, God created the heavens and the earth.
>
> —Genesis 1:1

> The God of the Jews was living, personal and creative; he was supreme Being and transcendent Act. And his claims were inescapable and paramount.
>
> —E. L. Mascall

THE GREATEST FREEDOM KNOWN to humanity is found in the first few words recorded in The Holy Bible. At the same time, however, the words "In the beginning..." also represent the greatest limitation imposed upon humankind. Authentic creativity is never without form or boundary.[1] In the tradition of the "God of the Jews," the first creative act is ascribed to a "living, personal and creative" God who reveals himself in history in Jesus Christ and is present in God's people by the power of the Holy Spirit.[2] Subsequently, we assume that all human creativity (being and activity) is derived from the creative being and activity of the Triune God of Christianity who is fully embodied

---

1. Vanhoozer, *Is There a Meaning in this Text?*, 435; also, 9; 433–36. Vanhoozer makes the case that the context for all "true" human creativity, the use of words and meanings, and modes of representation all have their "freedom" in the covenant relationship with the Trinitarian God.

2. Mascall, *He Who Is*, 1–7.

2   Creativity and Captivity

in the church and wholly given for the world.[3] The implication therefore is that creativity is primarily relational. It emerges and is sustained primarily in relationship with the Creator and his mission.

In this dissertation, however, it is not creativity in general that we are concerned with, but musical creativity. Here we explore the process of musical creativity amongst Christian musicians in this era of globalization as they understand and practice their creativity in the context of the mission of God.

The themes of musical creativity, the new spaces created as a result of globalizing processes, and creative mission are three main strands that together weave the process of exploration for this dissertation. The arena for exploring the process of musical creativity is the new "interstitial" spaces that emerge as a result of globalizing processes in a postcolonial environment. These new spaces form the arena for the emergence and sustenance of indigenous cosmopolitan musician (ICM) identity. The mediation of Christianity through the process of musical creativity in these new spaces for the full participation of others in the mission of God is what we refer to as creative mission. In the next section I offer a brief overview of musical creativity, new spaces, and creative mission. Before that, however, I would like to draw our attention to some initial concerns regarding music, space, and mission that we need to bear in mind as we set forth.

PROBLEMATIZING MUSIC, SPACE, AND MISSION

The "opacity" of the process of musical creativity is problematic.[4] While there seems to be a general acknowledgment of the power of musical creativity, "how" it serves to shape and to serve the mission of the church is "anything but clear."[5]

Further, the perceived "amorphous"[6] nature of the concept of creativity affects perceptions of the process of musical creativity as a system of

---

3. Dickerson, *Mind and the Machine*, 126–43. Interestingly enough, however, the general use of the term, "creativity," does not necessarily entail attribution to the Creator God of the Bible.

4. Begbie, *Theology, Music and Time*, 4. Begbie does not use the term "creativity." He uses the phrase "musical communication." In the light of the thrust of this study, however, I feel it is more appropriate to use the phrase, "musical creativity." Further, Begbie offers a systematic theology "through" music. Here, I focus on musical creativity in the context of the missiological agenda.

5. Cf. Begbie, *Theology, Music and Time*, 4.

6. Conversation with a member of the Society of Ethnomusicology and co-participant at the International Council of Traditional Music 42nd annual conference, Shanghai, July 17, 2013.

knowledge. As a result, the ambiguity that is typically associated with the concept of musical creativity negatively impacts the full embrace of the process of musical creativity for the mission of the church. The mediation of Christianity through musical creativity is further problematized in a globalized and media-saturated culture.[7]

In a postcolonial context it is imperative to realize that perceptions of "opacity" and "amorphous" are not blanket terms for the ways in which musical creativity as a system of knowledge is perceived and embraced in the world. Rather, these are terms that have been used to typify certain hegemonic ways of knowing over and against "other" ways of knowing. In a postcolonial world, the processes of typification often represent systems of knowledge that are "indigenous" to the West and the structures of Euro-Western thought. These methodologies of knowledge production result in the exclusion and peripherialization of the knowledge systems of the formerly colonized, marginalized, and oppressed peoples who represent the "other."[8]

The dilemma is intensified in that people operating in "peripheral" knowledge systems in turn are "suspicious" of the West.[9] The implication is that the new spaces created as a result of globalizing processes are sites of continual construction, contestation, and conflict.[10] In terms of a postcolonial paradigm, new spaces are places for a struggle to legitimize, reclaim, and create alternate ways of knowing.[11]

The implications of the above for mission are summarized below. Here, by mission I refer to the Christian missionary enterprise located in the mission of the Triune God in redeeming, reconciling, and restoring the world to God through the Gospel. The church is called to participate in the redemptive, reconciliatory, and restorative mission of God through Jesus Christ and by the power of the Holy Spirit and thus, mission is central to the identity of the church.

First, the failure to recognize the process of musical creativity as a legitimate or authentic vehicle for carrying the weight of Christian truth undermines the effectiveness of the church when it comes to embracing the fullness of its creative and missional being. A root issue that needs to

---

7. See Romanowski, *Eyes Wide Open*, 13–23. The idea is not so much whether or not music might be used in the creative purposes of God, but in what sense does faith inform understanding and practice in the employment of the creative arts in bringing about the purposes of God. See also, Detweiler and Taylor, *Matrix of Meanings*.

8. Chilisa, *Indigenous Research Methodologies*, 1–43; 75–92.

9. Chilisa, *Indigenous Research Methodologies*, 4.

10. Rynkiewich, "New Heaven and a New Earth?," 33–46.

11. Chilisa, *Indigenous Research Methodologies*, 4.

be addressed therefore is the legitimacy of musical creativity as a system of knowledge.[12]

Relatedly, given the relational intimacy between creative being and creative activity, it follows that a devaluation of creative expression amounts to a devaluation of the creator. The separation between being and activity results in a spiritual alienation, both within the conscience of musicians—the struggle to reconcile creative expression and human identity—and in terms of their ecclesial calling. Such separation is detrimental for mission and in particular for the self-understanding and practice of musicians who see themselves as participating in the creative mission of God.

A portion of this study therefore attempts to articulate the beginnings of a theology of creativity for mission (*creatio Dei*) as a response to "captive" notions of authenticity derived from systems of knowledge with palpable roots in modern foundationalism.[13] We explore the concept of the "epistemological captivity" as it pertains to the process of musical creativity for mission in chapter 2.

Second, the term "musical creativity" is popularly conceived as a metric for individual prowess, innovation, and capital gain. In the context of mission, however, musical creativity is first of all a relationship with a personal God. The strategy to align the process of creativity (ontologically speaking) with a relationship with the Creator God of the Bible is contested in postmodernity's rejection of any metanarrative for humanity. At the same time, however, "decentering" due to poststructural impulses generates multiple and interconnected "nodes"[14] for the invitation of others to participate in God's mission. Musical creativity, therefore, is not a mere instrument to an end[15] but a formational process, a "performativity"[16] to be enacted in mutual

---

12. Myers, *Eerdmans Bible Dictionary*, 632. In the Old Testament, knowledge is not so much about gathering more information "about" something. Neither is knowledge made up of intellectual perception or objectivity. Rather, knowledge implies a deep personal relationship between worshiper and deity (Ps 135:5; Isa 1:2–3, a social relationship (Gen 29:5, and more intimately, a sexual relationship between a husband and wife (Gen 4:1; 1 Sam 1:19). Knowledge was borne in experience; true knowledge was in a relationship with Yahweh (Ps 111:10). In the Hellenistic understanding, knowledge was perceived as static and something that depended upon intellectual comprehension. In the New Testament, however, in continuity with the Old Testament, knowledge is that which is revealed. Further, ultimate knowledge comes through sharing in an active relationship with Jesus Christ and in the "mystery" revealed for all generations (Rom 16:25; John 1:18; 1 Cor 4:1).

13. Bosch, *Transforming Mission*, 262–345. Wood, *Theology as History and Hermeneutics*, 225–42. See also, Abraham, *Canon and Criterion in Christian Theology*.

14. Castells, *Rise of the Network Society*.

15. Begbie, *Resounding Truth*.

16. Austin, *How to Do Things with Words*.

collaboration with others.[17] Here, therefore, we pay attention to the discourse of musicians as they attempt to articulate the uniqueness of Christianity for the participation of others through their music.

Third, musical creativity construed primarily in terms of a given "aesthetic" as the container for the "right" sound or music is burdensome. According to Plato music is inferior. It is a mimetic form, a copy of the original and therefore an illusionary representation of reality. Musical forms, therefore, cannot embody true knowledge. The cumulative impact of Plato's influence through the Enlightenment and modernity cannot be brushed off lightly. We will explore this further in chapter 2.

Nowhere, however, is the hegemony of the Western aesthetic more apparent than in the colonial era where knowledge was bound in certain (Westernized) forms of music rather than in the indigenous knowledge systems associated with local music traditions. The impact of global hegemonies is ongoing through neoliberal processes in the new spaces (chapter 3). The point, however, is that ethnocentric formulations of musical creativity forfeit and exclude diversity rather than embrace it. If the final scenario is an innumerable multitude gathered from every nation, all tribes, peoples, and languages together singing a "new song" before the throne of God (Rev 7:9), then learning how to sing along with the "other" is a necessary step to that eventual reality. The creativity of the Godhead is reciprocated amid the diversity of the gathered community. The ways in which musicians serve to bring about "a new heaven and earth" with others in the new spaces brought about by global diversity is a key focus of this study.

The issues of the opacity of music, the amorphousness of creativity, and the challenge of creative mission in new spaces brought about by globalization all call for further clarification. The mediation of Christianity in these new spaces presents challenges for mission as well as opportunities for "prophetic dialogue."[18] What follows immediately is a brief overview of musical creativity, new spaces, and creative mission. The concept of indigenous cosmopolitanism serves to describe and to explore the identities and mission of Christian musicians operating in these new spaces.

MUSICAL CREATIVITY

The process of musical creativity refers to the ways in which people relate to themselves, to others, and to happenings in their worlds through music. The story of humanity abounds with illustrations of the power of music to shape lives, to transform people's imaginations, and to affect emotion. Music has

17. Charland, "Constitutive Rhetoric," 133–50.
18. Bevans and Schroeder, *Prophetic Dialogue*.

been known to inspire hope, to dispel fear, and as a weapon of war. Music is a tool for justice, healing, and shaping the collective consciousness of a nation. Music reveals peoples' values and beliefs; it plays a vital part in all the major religions of the world, Christianity included.[19] Interestingly however, discourse pertaining to the formative potential of music, until very recently, has for most part been lacking in missiology.[20]

Additionally, area ethnographic studies concerning the role of music amongst people groups across the world have yielded deep insight into the ways in which people order their lives in their respective social contexts. However, the creation of new spaces for the interchange of identities problematizes notions of "area" that are based upon the construction of identities primarily associated with geographical, national, and racial boundaries.[21]

NEW SPACES

The reconfiguration of cultural and social boundaries brought about by globalizing processes issues fresh spatial and temporal challenges for the understanding and practice of the process of creativity amongst musicians for mission.[22] New spaces are "places" for the enmeshment of multiple ideologies, the emergence of diverse hybrid identities, and the development of relational networks brought about by the migration of peoples and the movement of global capitalism.[23]

---

19. Beck, *Sacred Sound*; Foley, *Foundations of Christian Music*.

20. Please see *Appendix A*, "Musical Creativity and Missiology."

21. Levitt, "God Needs No Passport." In the context of the migration of religious impulses amongst transnational migrants, Levitt writes that "religion is the archetypical spatial and temporal boundary crosser" (55). See also, Cannell, *Anthropology of Christianity*.

22. For example, the significance of diaspora communities in the Global North to "reach the nations" everywhere, including in the Global North, and the realization that the bridge from the North to the South is at least a "two-way" street need addressing. In addition, the spread of the church in and from the Global South to the rest of the world and the struggle for power associated with this movement for the production of a truly globalized hymnody is significant. The proliferation of new technologies and abilities to duplicate and to innovate—products, contextual theologies, and resources for theological education denote a paradigmatic shift for missional praxis. From a postcolonial standpoint the significance of indigenous knowledge systems, postcolonial discourses, and oral as well as literate research methodologies that draw from indigenous knowledge systems call for a rethinking of existing strategies for mission. See also, Tennent, *Invitation to World Missions*, 18–50. Concerning postcolonialism and approaches to research in a postcolonial research paradigm please see Chilisa, *Indigenous Research Methodologies*. Also, Lipsitz, *Dangerous Crossroads*.

23. See Dufoix, *Diasporas*, 35–105.

The challenges of postsecularism[24] and postmodernity[25] for the mediation of music are palpable. From a poststructural standpoint the shift in legitimizing authority from the "traditional" church (center) to the more "contemporary" (peripheral/indigenous) venues and identities is problematic. Multiple centers for the generation of knowledge imply the extension and distribution of power. The negotiation of power involves compromise, rules for ordering, and a new discourse[26] for the legitimization of "authenticity."

Further, in the context of a postcolonial era we cannot ignore the peripherialization of the "other" through music.[27] Take for instance the emphasis on certain forms of music (lyrics/Western) as more authentic than others (instrumental/other).[28] Or consider, instances where "worship" is conceived "primarily by the mind as opposed to the body" (Stringer 2005, 16).[29]

Interstitial spaces are characterized by intensified interactivity, disjuncture, and diversity. These interstitial spaces are places for the articulation of differences, conflicts of identities, and contestations for authenticity.[30] In these new spaces, music offers a "creative space of articulation and demand, revolt and resistance, innovation and negotiation" (Young 2003, Kindle location 1389).[31]

Diverse, asynchronous, and asymmetrical contexts create opportunities for the urgent and "radically contextual" (Bevans and Schroeder 2004, 31) translation of Christianity with others. The spatial and temporal

---

24. Taylor, *Entertainment Theology*, 33–35. Barry Taylor proposes the "imploding" of modernity in four areas: time, space, bodies, and governance. In the light of a spirituality constructed in a "digital democracy," the idea of the "postsecular" suggests a deep "restructuring" of "temporality, spatiality, corporeality, and authority." See also, Siapera, *Cultural Diversity and Global Media*.

25. Lewis, *Diffusion of Black Gospel Music in Postmodern Denmark*, The Asbury Theological Seminary Series in World Christian Revitalization Movements in Intercultural Studies, No. 3.

26. Foucault, "Excerpt from *The Archaeology of Knowledge*," 1436–60.

27. Young, *Postcolonialism*, 69–92. See the discussion on the "hybridity" of Rai music.

28. Born and Hesmondhalgh, *Western Music and its Others*.

29. Stringer, *Sociological History of Christian Worship*. Stringer's source reveals the nature of embodiment of ritual in the perspective related to post Vatican II as differentiated from the practice of ritual pre Vatican II. Further, in tracing a "sociological history of Christian worship" Martin Stringer reminds us that a part of the issue has also to do with how dominant discourses are maintained by "establishing a legitimacy for the discourse" and a "consensus" whereby it becomes hard to conceive of an alternate discourse and even "to challenge the dominant form" (90). See also, John 4:23–24.

30. Bhabha, *Location of Culture*.

31. Young, *Postcolonialism*, loc. 1392–93.

dislocation in these new spaces creates an atmosphere for the formation of hybrid identities. Cultural hybridity emerges in the "interstitial" passages between "fixed identifications" (nation, race, ethnicity, class) (Bhabha 2004, Kindle location 519). Hybridity challenges dominant hierarchies. Hybrid constructions represent the desire to thrive in the interstices of tradition and modernity and other colonial binaries and their logics of power.[32] One such construct is the concept of indigenous cosmopolitanism.

Indigenous Cosmopolitanism

The concept of indigenous cosmopolitanism represents the tension experienced by those who do not to abandon their "roots" (indigenous)—cultural, national, ethnic, or geographical fixity. Indigenous cosmopolitan identity emerges as a result of a desire to retain aspects of indigeneity and simultaneously search for newer ways of self-representation (cosmopolitanism) in alternate cultures and knowledge systems.[33]

Indigenous cosmopolitanism, therefore, may be interpreted as a desire to create a place for the articulation of difference arising in the context of reconciling hybrid identities within one's own self-understanding and in terms of relational networks with others and context.

The concept of indigenous cosmopolitanism is characterized by the reality of the lived experience of those occupying sites of ongoing resistance in the context of postcolonial pathways.[34] In a "culture of survival" indigenous ways of perceiving reality and the value and knowledge systems that accompany such ways are constantly under threat of compromise.[35] Indigenous cosmopolitanism, therefore, is a strategy for resistance and a posture for learning between multiple intersecting ideologies in order to thrive in these new spaces.[36]

32. Ashcroft et al., *Postcolonial Studies*. The ambivalence of hybridity resists the stereotyping of imperialist discourse; it changes the terms of engagement from "one way" to a "two way" discourse that shapes both the identity of the colonizer and the colonized (28).

33. Forte, *Indigenous Cosmopolitans*.

34. Forte, *Indigenous Cosmopolitans*, 1–2. See also, Chilisa, *Indigenous Research Methodologies*, 11. The spaces that ICMs in mission occupy are sites of resistance, contestation, and change in relation to "Euro-Western thought and the further appropriation of their knowledge."

35. Bhabha, *Location of Culture*, loc. 144. See also, Chilisa, *Indigenous Research Methodologies*, 13.

36. Chilisa, *Indigenous Research Methodologies*, 14. In a postcolonial context, ICM identity may be interpreted as a strategy for living in order to liberate the captive mind from the oppression of voices that tend to marginalize and silence the "subordinated, colonized, and non-Western societies that encountered European colonization."

Indigenous Cosmopolitan Musicians (ICMs)

Indigenous cosmopolitanism is a way of being that is pertinent for a vast majority of musicians whose music and audience is not limited to a local geographical area. The ways in which the music of ICMs is conceptualized, produced, and received is extended and distributed along transnational and transcultural pathways. Their hybrid identity is often captured in the fusion of sounds that they generate.[37]

There are several agents who operate in the capacity of the definition of indigenous cosmopolitanism that we adopt here. However, in this dissertation we are particularly interested in the creativity of Christian indigenous cosmopolitan musicians for mission. The concept of indigenous cosmopolitanism offers a pathway to theorize the identity of musicians for mission (and potentially as well for the ministry of the church and the academy).

CREATIVITY AND MISSION

Stephen B. Bevans and Roger P. Schroeder emphatically write, mission "is prior to the church, and constitutive of its very essence" (2004, 13); and agreeably so—the church is "missionary by its very nature." By the same logic,[38] it may also be possible to say that creativity is prior to the church and constitutive of its very essence. Here we begin to clarify that the church is creative by its very nature.

From an ontological perspective, we maintain that in the creative economy of God[39] there exists no dichotomy between the imaging[40] of God

---

37. Hybrid identities are often expressed through fusion music. But this may not always be the case. See also, Chaudhari, "Into the mix," 38–39. More than what is heard audibly, however, the concept of indigenous cosmopolitanism represents the inner tensions associated with creative identity and outer obstacles to creative expression in the context of postcolonialism and neoliberal capitalism. See also, Proulx, "Aboriginal Hip Hoppers," 39–62.

38. See, Bevans and Schroeder, *Constants in Context*, 10–31. Stephen Bevans and Roger Schroeder build their argument concerning the outward movement of the church on the Acts of the Apostles. Regarding the "priority of mission" please see Shenk, *Changing Frontiers of Mission*; "New Wineskins for New Wine," 73–79.

39. Jüngel et al., "Translator's Introduction," xv. In the light of Barth's doctrine of God, Webster reiterates that the perichoretic interpenetration of the members of the Trinity cannot be separated from the differentiated unity as Father, Son, and Spirit.

40. I use the word, "imaging" as a verb to refer to the intentional activity that at once locates the image of God in the revelation of the person and mission of Jesus Christ. Jesus Christ is not only the full and final image of the Living God. He is also the ultimate pinnacle of the common humanity of all peoples. The word, "imaging" therefore refers to the intentional activity of God that is also ongoing in the light of the formation of the new humanity in Christ and in which all are invited to participate. Grenz, *Social*

(*imago Dei*), the creativity of God (*creatio Dei*), and the mission of God (*missio Dei*). And therefore, the creative being of the church reaches full blossom in creative engagement with the cultures of the world, inviting all to participate in the celebration of the becoming of the Body of Christ.

The concept of creativity—theological creativity (*creatio Dei*), as we develop here— lends itself toward the development of a missiological hermeneutic for the translation of Christianity for mission (Missiological Framework for Theological Creativity, MFTC).[41] The MFTC offers a spectrum for the exploration of the creative practice of ICMs in mission. It provides a way for a renewed ecclesial posturing through the creative agency of ICMs for mission as they negotiate their creative identities in Christ (Creative Being) through the construction of new places (Creative Construction) for participation with others (Creative Performance) in the mission of God.

ICMS, EXPANDING THE TRIBE OF BEZALEL

What is the place of the creativity of artists in the mission of God? In Scripture, artists or craftspersons/artisans have a specific place when it comes to embodying, enacting, and performing the creativity of God. As pointed out to me by one of my key informants, the job description of the "four craftsmen" in Zech 1:20, 21 is a prime example of the task of bringing about social justice in the context of the economy of God's justice for all, the full implications of which we do not go into here.[42]

We observe that the first person anointed with the Holy Spirit in the biblical narrative, Exodus, is Bezalel, a craftsperson. Furthermore, we note that the context of the Exodus is the movement of God's people from slavery to freedom, a people who are able to worship the Lord God of Israel and to invite participation from others to do the same. This is actually a community task. God instructs Moses to appoint Bezalel, Oholiab and others with the "spirit of skill" to build the instruments to be used for worship in the Temple.[43] When it comes to the process of crafting a "meeting place" for

---

God and the Relational Self, 223–64. See also, Walls, *Cross-Cultural Process in Christian History*, 72–81.

41. This is not a comprehensive framework for creative mission. But it serves to begin to ask questions pertaining to the construction of a theology of creativity. It is also intended to serve as a base to further extend the discussion pertaining to the discourse of creativity and mission.

42. Further, see the reference to Jesus of Nazareth as artisan/craftsperson (Mark 6:3).

43. See Exod 31:1–11; 35:10–36:2, 8a. Guthrie, *Creator Spirit*, 117, distinguishes between the giving of the Spirit as a gift versus Plato's appropriation of Spirit-possession in

people to encounter the living presence of a Holy God, we find a parallel in the New Testament, Eph 4:11ff.[44]

We notice that the inspiration of Bezalel results in the gifts of ability (skill), intelligence (understanding), knowledge (obedience, the opposite of which is rebellion—1 Sam 2:12; Isa 1:3; Jer 31:34; Isa 41:23, and the rejection of false gods), and "all craftsmanship" (work) (Exod 31:3). If Bezalel, Oholiab, and other craftsmen were called of God by name to create works of art through which the real presence and beauty of God was to be mediated, then artists in Christ are called and are meant to mediate such reality.[45] Therefore, like Bezalel, ICMs are to equip the saints, to build the Body of Christ, to be knowledge bearers, to be mediators of truth whereby people are able to not only experience the amazing glory of God but through works of art to mature and grow in Christ, and be accountable in their roles as leaders in the context of the creative mission of church.[46]

NEGOTIATING IDENTITY

It is crucial to understand that for ICMs in mission, the struggle for authenticity may be understood as being carried out in two distinct yet interweaving planes. The first has to do with the negotiation of identity from within, in terms of their own self-understanding as musicians called by God to bring about God's purposes with others through their creativity. There is scope for theological clarity concerning the linkage of creativity as a gift from God and its missional potential through the agency of ICMs for mission. We begin to explore the theoretical and theological framework for creative mission in chapters 2–4. The role of Bezalel, master craftsmen who was called, anointed, appointed, and commissioned for building a meeting place for the authentic encounter with the Living God of Israel serves as penultimate prototype[47] for the embodiment of creative agency. The ultimate creative posturing for mission is Jesus Christ. We return to this in chapter 8.

Ion, where the person is not enriched, but a passive recipient; whereas Bezalel becomes a person of skill.

44. "And he gave the apostles, the prophets, the evangelists, the shepherds and teachers, to equip the saints for the work of ministry, for building up the body of Christ until we all attain to the unity of the faith and of the knowledge of the Son of God, to mature manhood, to the measure of the stature of the fullness of Christ, so that we may no longer be children, tossed to and fro by the waves and carried about by every wind of doctrine, by human cunning, by craftiness in deceitful schemes" (Eph 4:11–14 ESV).

45. Brink, "Significance of Beauty and Excellence in Biblical Worship," 9–12.

46. Exod 35:11b; 36:1.

47. See Exod 31:1–11; 35:10—36:2, 8a.

The second arena for the negotiation of identity lies without, in terms of practice. A question is raised as to the ways that ICMs enact and perform their creativity in the midst of the "regimes of representation" that plague the new spaces for mission.[48] We turn to the narratives concerning the embodiment, enactment, and performance of ICM mission practice in chapters 5, 6, and 7 respectively.

THESIS

Christian indigenous cosmopolitan musicians for mission (ICMs) understand themselves as participating in the creativity of God and, by implication, become channels of the creative activity of God through their musical creativity as they renew the church and its form with others in the context of the mission of the creative God.

STATEMENT OF THE PROBLEM

To speak of the creativity of God expressed through music in the service of God's mission through the church invites more questions than answers. As a field of academic inquiry, in general, creativity is approached as a psychological aspect of human potential. Furthermore, the perspective that favors verbalized rational cognitive processes as preferred pathways of truth as opposed to musical processes has curbed the extent to which Western-influenced Christian communities have perceived and encouraged the formative potential of the processes of musical creativity. A significant part of the problem therefore has to do with the lack of a clear missiological (and ministerial) discourse concerning the ways in which we define and practice music as a creative process that has its source and expression in the creativity of God. This research explores ways in which ICMs understand

---

48. Siapera, *Cultural Diversity and Global Media*, 131–48. What "constitutive tensions" are apparent as ICMs mediate cultural difference? How do ICMs control, dominate, and condition cultural difference? What instances are there of "subversion, questioning, and rejection of representations"? What "regimes of representation" are inherent in the rhetoric and representations of ICMs? Eugenia Siapera considers three regimes—racist, domestication of difference, and commodification of difference. These provide a helpful framework to identify patterns of "captivity" and possibly to address these in our conclusion. The Racist Regime views people with static biological and cultural properties. Here, difference is typified as "irrational," "brutal," or as victim and in need of being rescued, which justifies hegemonic practices against such. The Domesticated Regime views difference superficially, treats it as unthreatening and safe. This view ultimately "breeds intolerance" toward meaningful and "substantive diversity." The Regime of Commodification appreciates difference to the extent that it can generate "profit." Here the emphasis is on appearance and branding for consumption. This view "levels all identities" and reorders them in order to capitalize on difference.

and practice the creativity of God as they negotiate their identity in the task of building the church for mission with others.

The emergence of new spaces as a result of globalizing processes brings to light the disparities and range of diversities in understandings and practices of musical creativity in the world of the "indigenous cosmopolitan musician" (ICM). In the context of transnational landscapes and the liminality of borderland places as the arena for the Christlike creative posturing of ICMs, the question of which form/s are appropriate to use needs to be held in balance with the question of whose meaning is legitimate. Authenticity concerning form of musical creativity is continually contested in the context of postcolonial binary oppositions. The problem in the form of a question might be stated as such: In what ways do indigenous cosmopolitan musicians (ICMs) understand and practice the creativity of God as they go about their task of building the church for mission in Christ?

RESEARCH QUESTIONS

Three broad areas emerge for our exploration—creative being, creative construction, and creative performance. From these areas emerge the major research questions for this dissertation. Concerning creative being, music is a distinct way of being in relationship with God and the world. It is knowledge embodied, enacted, and performed by ICMs in mission. Our first question, therefore, explores the ways in which such knowledge is apparent in the understanding and practice of ICMs in mission: How do ICMs understand and describe their music? As far as can be understood from their verbal self-descriptions, what affects ICMs' thinking and creative processes?

Regarding creative construction, music is a process of creating a place for participation with others in the mission of God. Our second question, therefore, explores how ICMs enact their knowledge in the places of transition that they occupy: What do ICMs actually do (what are their practices?) as they negotiate their Christianity through the process of musical creativity in their respective contexts/global spaces?

As ICMs embody and enact musical creativity in mission, they also perform it in unique ways that correlate theological understanding with missional practice. In terms of creative performance therefore a third question arises: What kinds of theological interpretations do ICMs make that links their practices with their beliefs through the process of musical creativity?

RATIONALE FOR THIS STUDY

Psychometric evaluations of human potential form the basis for most "secular" theories of creativity. The concept of theological creativity that we develop here rests upon the understanding that human creativity is derived from participation in the creativity of God.[49] Enlightenment-tainted perspectives tend to assign things labeled as "art" to the realm of non-cognition, symbolic, and non-discursive, rendering these things, by definition, as difficult to interpret, define, and understand. This research offers a corrective by emphasizing a theological perspective (*creatio Dei*) that enriches general Westernized theological assumptions concerning the creativity of God. In terms of theological creativity, we make an argument for music as transformative discourse that is at least equally as valid as verbal or other forms of discourse.

Why do we need a creative hermeneutic as signified through the musical creativity of ICMs for mission? A simple answer is because it offers a minority perspective—a postcolonial and subaltern perspective, if you will—when it comes to ways in which we choose to interpret Scripture. For example, a biblical scholar comments on the description and detail of God's design for the priestly garments in Exodus 28 and refers to such detailed description as "redundant."[50] A hermeneutic of creativity might attempt to further interpret the nature of such redundancy in the context of the passage. For example, a question may be raised as to the nature of such redundancy, to what extent might it have served a purpose for God and for the people who are given a "spirit of skill."[51] A creative hermeneutic is not necessarily the only way to interpret the Bible but it does draw attention to the "performative" dimension as a way of interpreting Scripture that is often overlooked in a regular exegetical application of the "text."

It has been pointed out that over 80% of the world's population, "5.7 billion people in the world are oral communicators because either they are illiterate or their reading comprehension is inadequate" (Lovejoy 2012, 29). A *creatio Dei* hermeneutic clarifies that people are "oral" not merely "because" of illiteracy or reading inadequacy, but that both oral and literate

---

49. Moran, "Role of Creativity in Society," 74–92; Bellini, *Participation*, 69–94. Zizioulas, *Being as Communion*, 101. The Greek patristic synthesis identified "truth with communion," where truth is not something that is additional to communion but truthful *being* is essentially constituted *as communion*. Viladesau, *Theology and the Arts*, 113. Here we approach music as a language that not only expresses the purpose and identity of the creator who is merely "preexistent" to the expressed form, but whose very "selfhood" or personhood is the product of such language.

50. Durham, *Exodus*, 384.

51. See, Exod 28:3; also, cf. Exod 35:31; 1 Sam 16:16.

forms are preferences subject to creative interpretation in Christ. Further, theological creativity invites us to consider alternate approaches to what may or may not be considered "text" and further ways such text may be embodied, enacted, and performed.

The dissertation offers a postcolonial perspective that recognizes that the "canonical Scriptures are not the sole conveyors of truth" (Sugirtharajah 2007, 456).[52] In keeping with a postcolonial hermeneutic that recognizes the "whole spectrum" of "different and rival schools of thought," a creative hermeneutic offers an alternate way of interacting with the Scriptures by taking into account artists as collaborators in the creation of knowledge by their active participation in such knowledge.[53] It opens the door to asking are we seeking to understand Christian artistry in the light of the Bible or to understand the Bible in the light of God's artistry. The question takes seriously the role of music in the translation of Christianity, not merely through the words of the Bible but in translating the experience of God in alternate creative forms.

The research explores ways in which musical creativity creates "space" for "prophetic dialogue" across religious and cultural borders.[54] The language of musical creativity assumes creativity as prior to religious identity. This assumption offers the possibility of a new discourse for evangelism. The way we see the other need no longer be purely in terms of categories of "reached" or "unreached," but to join with and create with others a new reality in Christ.

---

52. Sugirtharajah, "Postcolonial and Biblical Interpretation," 455–61. From a postcolonial perspective, "All sources—canonical as well as non-canonical, and oral as well as written—have played a decisive role in the historical formation of the early church and enlarge our understanding of it" (456). According to Sugirtharajah, "Bible and its Asian Readers," 61, the "closed Christian canon" represents a particular hermeneutic that does not necessarily capture the approach of Asian readers immersed in a religious culture and who bring a different interpretive lens in their reading of Scripture, one that is influenced by diverse and alternate religious-cultural histories. See also, Lee, "Reading the Bible in the Non-Western Church," 152–55.

53. Wood, *Theology as History and Hermeneutics*. Lawrence Wood articulates "a relational ontology" and amongst others, uses John Macmurray's argument concerning the deconstruction of modernity by adopting a fresh approach (62). The fact that one is able to think indicates the prior existence of knowledge and not the other way around—"knowing is not the result of thinking, but thinking already presupposes knowledge" (64). Artistic productions, similarly, do not occur in a vacuum. In keeping with Wood's argument, knowledge that is produced as "a result of our action and participation in the world" in return helps us to rethink and re-imagine our own roles in the world.

54. Rock and Mealy, *Performer As Priest and Prophet*; See also, Bevans and Schroeder, *Constants in Context*.

There has never been a greater need for Christian artists to respond to the "gospel" of the culture. Musicians like Jay-Z coax this generation "if you feel low ain't got no place to go head into the party life."[55] This reinforces the fact that music (in this case "hip-hop") is not a genre but a "lifestyle" that invites the listener to embrace in order to transcend earthly situations.

DATA COLLECTION

The bulk of the data presented here consists of ethnographic interviews with key informants, web-based resources, and literature and music produced by key informants.[56] Library research on the topic of music, meaning, and identity began in 2007. Ethnographic field research related to the dissertation began in 2010, although some interviews were conducted in 2009 with key informants. I also draw from my own semi and professional experience as a musician/composer in the context of the "secular" music world over the last approximately 25 years and within the scope of Christianity, serving the church, in India (beginning 1994) and the United States (beginning 2000).

As such I bring a little more than a ringside view to the issues broached in the dissertation due to my own immersion and participation in the field. In this sense, maintaining an objective perspective, or at least revealing my biases, has been a key focus. For this, I thank my mentor. Further, I worked hard to let concepts emerge from the actual data generated from interviews. Thus, the concepts and my own experiences merge to address the issues raised above.

It may be worthwhile saying a little more on the journey of research methodology *via* library research. The core aspect of my research interest lay in the arena of globalization, particularly the negotiation of identity in the context of the process of musical creativity. From a methodological perspective, it included a "waiting period." The exploration of Indigenous Cosmopolitan identity did not begin until 2010, which is when I first came across the term that seemed to capture my own envisioning.

The exportation of theology and music into the domain of creativity took the bulk of research time and space—appropriating theological criteria in terms of creativity. This was necessary in order to create a semantic field within existing academic domains (ethnomusicology, theology, missiology). The purpose was to retain a dynamic linkage to these domains as well as to create some amount of academic distance for an objective outlook, yet one that would serve the field of musical creativity with integrity.

---

55. "Rap Basement: Hip Hop Lifestyle Network."
56. Please see Appendix H for a list of sample questions.

The main criterion for selecting key informants is that these are directly engaged (and see themselves as such) in "building the church for mission." Here, we journey with the key informants as they negotiate their identities in transcultural contexts. The borderland and liminal spaces they occupy are generally characterized by mobility and complexity.[57] Further, such mediation is a critical component of their Christian witness. The data generated help explore how they integrate their creative being, creative construction, and creative performance for Kingdom purposes, as well as their ability to join with others in creating fresh opportunities for creative witness.

In the course of research, I interacted with several artists and musicians from diverse backgrounds and nationalities and who work in more than a single country/context (United States, Canada, China, Korea, Caribbean nations, Thailand, and India). Even so, as I discovered, mobility is not necessarily a qualification for cosmopolitan identity. Here, we are interested in how ICMs orient to the creativity of God in the context of diversity in their respective contexts.

I have included as many direct quotes as possible, particularly as it pertains to the subject matter of our discussion here. I will include data from other key informants as well as knowledge from other sources (literary and other persons in the creative arts) as we discuss and analyze themes and issues arising from interaction with data.

INTRODUCING KEY INFORMANTS

As recommended by my mentor, I am using initials to identify informants in order to protect their identity. ML, a son of North American missionary parents, was raised in South Asia since the age of 1 for the better part of the first 17 years of his life. He gained fluency in the indigenous languages of both countries. He developed a love for Indian classical music and the Hindu devotional genre of bhajan. ML's interest in the sitar as the instrument of choice was inspired by the appropriation of the sound of the sitar by a North American rock band called Yes. After listening to the sound of the sitar on Yes's album "90125" he decided to take up sitar in the Indian music department in his school that he attended in India. He had virtually ignored the Indian music department until that point in time preferring

---

57. Sanger and Giddings, "Teaching Note," 369–76. Sanger and Giddings' sources reveal that: even though "there is no commonly accepted definition of complexity," there is a general agreement among scholars of complexity, "that a complex system consists of numerous subsystems interacting with each other through multiple, nonlinear, recursive feedback loops" (371).

instead to take up jazz band, choir, and trumpet in the Western music department of his school.

ML returned to America for further study but returned to India as an adult for approximately another 10 years. In 1991 he formed a band that toured all over India for six years. Later, he teamed up with another musician, a British citizen who was born in India, to form a band that recorded several albums using a mixture of Indian classical music, bhajan, and popular music from the West (guitar and drums). They performed extensively in India, North America, and the South Asian Diaspora in South Africa, Guyana and Suriname. The band's goal is "to produce a prodigious body of work and build lasting bridges between disparate communities throughout the world" (source withheld for privacy). ML currently is a solo artist working primarily amongst the South Asian Diaspora. He is based in North America.

I had the opportunity to meet and interview ML over a course of about four years in various contexts, visited performances, and served alongside him in his home church in New York where his parents play a significant role especially amongst the Bhutanese Refugee community. ML's wife is an artist and violinist. She serves alongside ML.

JB is an Indian immigrant living in New York. He was born and raised in Nagaland, North East India, part of what he refers to as the "Seven Sister states."[58] JB and I first met at a Christmas Outreach initiative organized by the Capital Region Indian Fellowship in Albany, New York. JB was performing along with his music team using a fusion of Western and Indian folk sounds. JB fuses *bhangra*, 'Punjabi folk music,' with guitar and other instruments associated with Western music. The next time I met JB was on location in Jackson Heights, Queens, New York. We met outside a Tibetan restaurant in a central area in Jackson Heights. Next-door is a community center where he now teaches English to immigrants in the area. I met with JB over two days and invited others who work with him into the discussions that served the purpose of focus groups. I also had follow up sessions with JB via Skype and email.

Interestingly, according to JB, Jackson Heights is the most diverse borough in the United States. We decide to eat lunch at an Indian-Chinese restaurant in Jackson Heights, one of the several options for desi (homeland) food. We joked about our own ethnic diversity amidst the diversity of Jackson Heights—he, part UP'ite (from Uttar Pradesh) and Naga (from Nagaland),

---

58. Indira Gandhi National Centre for the Arts, "Art & Crafts of North-East: North-East India, An Introduction." North East India comprises of seven states commonly known as the "Seven Sisters." They are Arunachal Pradesh, Assam, Manipur, Meghalaya, Mizoram, Nagaland, and Tripura.

and I, part Tamil, Andhra, and Rajasthani (from Rajasthan), meeting for lunch outside a Tibetan restaurant but finally eating at an Indian-Chinese restaurant where we ordered American Chopsuey!

JB is of mixed racial heritage—part Indian, his father being from Uttar Pradesh, and mother, from Nagaland, which is now considered a part of India. According to one source, Nagaland is "the only state in India where over 90% of its population is Christian."[59] Interestingly, however, the history of conflict and discrimination of the peoples in the North East region of India, the oldest of which involved the Nagas, began at the time of Indian independence in 1947.[60] The creation of a separate state, Nagaland, in 1963 is not entirely resolved.[61] What implications might such a backdrop have on the negotiation of JB's identity in his context?

JK was born in Korea and moved to Texas with his family at the age of sixteen years. He considers himself a Korean-Texan. He and his wife, Joy, are "missionaries" with a mission organization that is based in Nashville, TN.

JK seeks to integrate worship, arts, and mission. He travels extensively leading and teaching missional and multicultural worship in the US and in Korea. He is part of a core group that facilitates the multicultural worship leaders' network in the US. He also leads the King's Region, a worship-arts group in Dallas and serves as a Lausanne ARTS catalyst. JK currently lives in Dallas, TX with his wife and two children.[62]

I had the opportunity to meet JK in Dallas at a gathering of twenty-five people for the North American World Evangelical Alliance (WEA)/ Lausanne Conference). The second time I met with him was at Lausanne 2013 in Bangalore, India. All quotes are takes from my interaction with JK unless otherwise noted.

I had the privilege of meeting JR at a gathering of 25 North American Leaders in Arts and Mission hosted by the WEA and Lausanne Consultation in Dallas during May 2013. In addition, we were a part of the Arts and Mission focus group at the Lausanne 2013 Global Leadership conference in Bangalore, India. JR introduces herself to the world on her website as per the following:

> Driven by her passion for God's mission, holistic worship and culturally relevant liturgy, Jo-Ann Richards– Jamaican teacher, ethnomusicologist, singer/songwriter, worship leader, missionary and author—is commissioned to "tell the whole world to

59. Von Reidemann, "Nagaland," comment posted on May 2, 2010.
60. Das, *Conflict and Peace in India's Northeast*, 5; 22–35.
61. Talukdar, "Who Failed the Nagas?"
62. Glocal Worship, http://glocalworship.net.

sing a new song unto the Lord!" (Isa 42:10, CEV) She has ministered on almost every continent in fulfilling her mission.[63]

According to her website:

> Jo-Ann, author of Godincidences! Adventuring with an awesomely Sovereign, sovereignly Awesome God, is a lecturer in the Music & Media Department of the Jamaica Theological Seminary. She holds a MA in Ethnomusicology from Bethel University in Minnesota and a BA in Theology from the Jamaica Theological Seminary. She is also a facilitator with the Haggai Institute, a member of the International Council of Ethnodoxologists (ICE) and the Society of Ethnomusicology (SEM) and has been appointed Arts Catalyst for the Caribbean on behalf of the Lausanne Movement. As Arts Catalyst she is committed to promoting and facilitating the appropriate use of the arts in worship, evangelism and missions through prayer, networking and training.
>
> Jo-Ann currently resides in Kingston, Jamaica and receives the support of her home church First Missionary Church on East Street, Kingston, where she has attended all her life and has been a member since 1979.[64]

FP is popularly known as "the singing priest" or *padum pathiri* in his native language, Malayalam. An online publication describes him as such:

> A priest with a Music Mission. His music is for world peace and religious harmony. [FP], popularly known as *'Paadum Paathiri'*, disciple of Padmabhushan Dr. K. J. Yesudas and Chandramana Narayanan Namboothiri, is an ordained priest in the congregation of Carmalites of Mary Immaculate, a religious order founded by blessed Cyriac Elias Chavara. He is the first Christian Priest who has completed Ph.D. in Karnatic music in India.[65]

Concerning his journey to priesthood in the Roman Catholic Church, FP provides some background in an interview I had with him:

> I was born and brought up in a Catholic family in Kerala, Trichur district. And when I was in the 6th standard, I was assisting in a Carmelite monastery nearby. From plus two level . . . I got a golden opportunity to have close contact with the clergy and priests especially in the Carmelite monastery. There was a great

---

63. Website of Jo-Ann Richards, http://JRrichards.com/about-me/.
64. Website of Jo-Ann Richards, http://JRrichards.com/about-me/.
65. The Singing Priest, http://www.youtube.com/watch?v=PIJbQFnWtuM.

priest, Father Canecius. He was called "the living saint." His life style influenced me greatly to become a priest. Of course, Jesus Christ was the prime model, but through this priest I could get a little closer to Jesus' values. He really touched me through his simple committed life. Then when I was in the 12the standard I decided to become a priest.

FP began singing in the church choir when he was in school. He began to learn classical music after he joined seminary when he was 17 years of age. He pursued further education in music along with philosophy and theology.

METHODOLOGY

The methodology for this research is best understood as a convergence of the assumptions about the nature of reality, theory, and values as they pertain to the topic under consideration.[66] For us this implies a convergence of a theology of creativity, theories of ethnomusicology and creativity, and a postcolonial lens through which to observe the process of musical creativity amongst ICMs for mission in the context of globalization. A postcolonial indigenous research paradigm (PIRP) challenges hegemonic modes of thinking and reconstructs a given body of knowledge in order to usher hope, healing, and social transformation for a given context. Further, a PIRP is informed by indigenous knowledge systems, the relational nature of socially constructed ontologies, epistemologies, and axiologies.[67]

For the purposes of this research, the assumption is that the process of musical creativity is itself an "indigenous" way of knowing, being, and doing for ICMs in mission. It is the primary dynamic and hermeneutic through which we enter into the world of the ICM. The PIRP is a process of "researching back." The methodology explores how ICMs as subjects are theorized, the ways in which they create relationships with others through their music, and how this process brings hope through prophetic dialogue with others. Second, the methodology uses a "mixed method" approach in that it proposes a theology of creativity as a response to and interrogation of the experiences of ICMs in mission.

Third, according to a PIRP the process of researching back is to "produce knowledge that has a liberatory and transformative intention" (Chilisa 2012, 51). The research values the verbal propositions of ICMs, their "lived experiences" and discursive practices, emotions, and cultural sensibilities

---

66. Chilisa, *Indigenous Research Methodologies*, 162.
67. Chilisa, *Indigenous Research Methodologies*, 40–41.

with the intent of exploring how these elements can contribute to the ongoing work of Christ in the building of the church for mission.[68]

Here, we apply ethnographic method in the context of developing the concept of "theological creativity"[69] that rests upon the understanding of creativity and music in the context of cultural systems.[70] Traditional ethnographic methodologies relying mainly upon race, ethnicity, nation, and culture as bounded sets alone seem inadequate to capture the dynamics of musical creativity in global complexity.[71]

Ethnographic method today is useful not just with "ethnicities," but as a way of observing, describing, analyzing, and documenting any type of cultural scenario, for example, the cultural patterns of dancers, firefighters, pastors, and midwives.[72] More pertinently, ethnography is a well-attested methodology in the context of the arts and creativity for Christian mission.[73]

With respect to creativity as a cultural system, Kaufmann and Sternberg write:

> The evolving systems approach focuses less on understanding the particulars of a specific creative act than on how those particulars fit into the context of an individual creator's goals, knowledge, and reasoning, as well as larger social forces and creative paradigms. The evolving-systems approach is primarily an account of what creators do . . . . Its emphasis is on dynamic,

---

68. Chilisa, *Indigenous Research Paradigms*, 50–51. See also, Moustakas, *Heuristic Research*, 9. In keeping with a PIRP this research adopts a heuristic approach. The term heuristic derives from the Greek word *heuriskein*, which means to find or discover. It is used by Clark Moustakas to describe the process of an inner search whereby knowledge is generated by reflecting on the quality of one's own experiences. Further, based upon the inner search in the context of life experiences, a heuristic approach develops methods and procedures for further investigation and analysis.

69. Bromiley, "Evangelicals and Theological Creativity," 4–8.

70. Geertz, "Art as a Cultural System," 1473–99; Neuman, "Indian Music as a Cultural System," 98–113; Csikszentmihalyi, "Creativity," 313–35.

71. Levitt, "God Needs No Passport," 47. According to Levitt: "Religion, like capitalism, is no longer embedded in a particular territory or legal regime; nor is it encumbered by external political, cultural, or moral principles. Cultural referents, once bounded by ethnicity, language, and nation-state borders, are being disconnected or lifted out of national territories, rendering discussions of national religious practice off the mark." See also Biddle and Knights, *Music, National Identity and the Politics of Location*.

72. McCurdy et al., *Cultural Experience: Ethnography in Complex Society*, 112ff.

73. Schrag, *Creating Local Arts Together*; Schrag and Neeley, *All the World Will Worship*.

developmental processes that play out in complex ways and contexts, over very different timescales (2010, 39).[74]

To bring it all together, we propose a Missiological Framework for Theological Creativity. This consists of Creative Being, Creative Construction, and Creative Performance (chapter 4). This framework serves to fulfill the purpose of exploring data in the light of a theology of creativity (*creatio Dei*) as well as a way for envisioning and extending the agency of musicians and, in general, the arts and mission. Here I develop three of the main aspects of the MFTC that are most pertinent to this research: Creative Being, Creative Construction, and Creative Performance.

The insights and observations concerning an arts-based methodology are helpful. I do not incorporate musical sound as part of the dissertation thesis. I pay attention to the discourse of the artists and interact with data generated from such discourse. I focus on the exploration of ICM identity and the negotiation of musical being based upon observation and interviews.

An "arts-inspired inquiry" is a subaltern hermeneutic.[75] As such, it is suitable for research in a postcolonial context. The method of inquiry requires a paradigm shift from one way of knowing to another way of knowing. In accordance with an indigenous research paradigm, the methodology emerges in part from interacting with the context and experiences of subjects.[76] For example, the formulation of a Missiological Framework for Theological Creativity in the first place was in response to a need to experience Scripture through the lens of the arts and/or musical creativity.

A theology of creativity seems to offer a fresh paradigm for visiting and evaluating missiological perspectives as it pertains to music and mission. In keeping with an indigenous research approach, an arts-based research methodology is characterized by "openness to ambiguity and tolerance for ambiguity" (Knowles and Promislow 2008, 519). In some ways, this approach is an uphill battle in the academy. Arts research scholars indicate that the biggest obstacle to arts-based research is the "persistence of the dominance of conventional views of empirical research" (2008, 522).[77] As per a postco-

---

74. Kaufman and Sternberg, *Cambridge Handbook of Creativity*.

75. "Inspired by the arts, especially, with regard to process and representation" is to be engaged "in the process of this work" so as "to act as a visual artist, poet, painter, photographer, dancer, dramatist, performer, and so on. Process is informed not only by bringing to bear one's creativity given that art form but also by knowing how it is that artists in that sphere or genre may work. It is about incorporating both the inspiration of an art and the processes that an artist might use." Knowles and Promislow, "Using An Arts Methodology To Create A Thesis Or Dissertation," 519.

76. Chilisa, *Indigenous Research Paradigms*.

77. Arts-related inquiry "seems somewhat . . . subversive . . . . Research needs to be

lonial indigenous research paradigm (PIRP), the juxtaposition of multiple overlapping narratives and the necessary ambivalence that results from the process forms an essential part of the research "montage."[78]

DEFINITION OF KEY TERMS

I have attempted to define most terms in the context of writing. But here are some basic definitions to help get started.

Artist—I use the term in general to refer to those who express creativity through the arts along with terms such as, craftsperson and artisan (one who conceives and produces works of skill through music, visual art, or other expressions).

Indigenous—for the purpose of this study we define indigenous as referring to a group's perception of reality, ways of knowing, and values. We also use the word in tandem with the term, "cosmopolitan." In this sense, indigenous refers to those with roots in a given culture or geographical area. Some indigenous peoples are defined as "non-state" and typically represent a lifestyle that leaves them "vulnerable" in the context of the mediation of identity amid the logics of neocolonialism.[79]

Postcolonialism—in this dissertation refers to the nature of power exchanges that affect cultural, social, political, and ethical pathways in the mediation of music and the negotiation of musical identity. It offers a subaltern perspective.[80]

DELIMITATIONS

For most part, in academia, the discussion of Christianity and music has focused on music in the context of Christian liturgical worship. As significant

---

systematic.... There must be a sense of rigor, a clearly defined purpose and problem, a certain structure—an introduction, a literature review, a methodology and tangible results and conclusions, and all of those components linked through various substructures in the thesis ... I mean, how can you hand in a thesis that's merely a series of stories?" Gouzouasis and Lee, "Sticky Knot Danish," 16.

78. See, Young, *Postcolonialism*. Also, according to Chilisa indigenous research emphasizes the local phenomena instead of beginning with "extant theory from the West to identify and define a research issue" (*Indigenous Research Methodologies*, 13). Further, it is sensitive to the context and devises methods and theories derived from local experiences and indigenous (in this case, music) knowledge. Indigenous research also involves borrowing from other/Western models to the extent it is needed. Importantly, what counts as "what counts as reality, knowledge, and values in research are informed by an indigenous research paradigm."

79. Eriksen, *Ethnicity and Nationalism*, 125–26.

80. See, Young, *Postcolonialism*; also, Chilisa, *Indigenous Research Methodologies*.

as this is, here we focus on the agency of ICMs and their discourse as they go about their task of building the church for mission in Christ. This research focuses on the discourse of ICMs as they transpose liturgies in the context of the liminal and borderland spaces that they occupy, creating new spaces for the becoming of the Body of Christ.

It would be interesting to see how Christian musicians in general perceive themselves as creative and how they might enhance the worship of the church. But here we focus on a particular breed of Christian musicians—Indigenous Cosmopolitan Musicians. We observe their discourse from the vantage point of their otherness in relation to the church and the contexts in which they serve.

In addition, we need to bear in mind that this is not a traditional ethnomusicological study although we borrow principles from the field to explore music as more than sound.

Here we cast the exploration of music in the context of creativity. Creativity is envisioned through a theological lens—theological creativity—that is rooted in the person and mission of God. There exists much scope to apply insights from Creativity Theory in general (for example, Torrance Tests for Creative Thinking, TTCT; Kirton Adaption-Innovation Inventory, KAI; and the Myers-Briggs Type Indicator, MBTI) for congregations or the ways in which people might adapt to mission. However, here we propose a missiological framework for creativity by emphasizing a different set of assumptions (missiological) than most creativity scholars. The idea is not to come up with a model that is applicable to study creativity in general, but to offer a pathway to begin to explore musical creativity in the context of mission.

As I attempted to articulate a missiology for theological creativity, the concept of *creatio Dei* as distinct from and in contiguity with *missio Dei* and *imago Dei* proved revelatory. Some may argue that one cannot separate the being of God into such arenas. This is true. However, the process of making the distinction has been helpful to distinguish in my own mind how not only creativity but also *musical* creativity might relate to the mission of God. The idea of creativity being prior to mission as a theoretical construct has served to pay closer attention to the discourse of creativity, simply by virtue of validating it as a distinct realm. This in turn turned out to be a liberating process for me—"the artist within"—and like-energized others.

The development of an argument to validate musical creativity as a legitimate system of knowledge is in and of itself a process of decolonization. According to Poka Laenui (2000), the process of decolonization consists of rediscovery and recovery of one's own voice and identity. Second, it is a process of lamenting—identifying with the stories of the other. I have had the opportunity to hear the stories of rejection of musicians and their creativities in the context of ecclesiological praxis with roots in modern foundationalism. A third factor of the decolonizing process is dreaming—imagining alternate ways of doing research, invoking indigenous knowledge systems; in this case, musical creativity.[81]

I am not a systematic theologian. The missiological framework suggested here will benefit further from deep theological reflection. Significant scope exists for the further development of a theology of creativity as it might apply to missiology. Here I have only begun to piece together such a theology. For example, it would be interesting to further the development of the ontology of musical form (sound and instrument) in the light of a biblical framework. Further, much of the theological discussion takes place within the context of my exposure to Western systematic theologies. Significant scope exists to test inherent claims in the light of alternate theologies and philosophies.

The missiological framework that we propose explores the creative process rather than focusing on purely on sonic or lyrical dimensions. In the past, methodologies have focused upon the rich theology in lyrics. This is extremely helpful. In contrast, here we focus on certain broader dynamics of pathways for the construction of the process of musical creativity—the verbal reflections of ICMs. Further, as a postcolonial study there is an effort to move beyond logocentrism when it comes to evaluating musical discourse as knowledge.

As we will observe the pathway of each ICM is unique. It is presumptuous to think that we could delve deeply into every major issue that ICMs deal with in the course of their ministry. Therefore, based upon ethnographic interviews and library research, and the space and time allowed herein, I have had to pick certain aspects to focus on with reference to a given key informant, rather than explore a single issue (for example, language) through the discourse of every ICM.

In chapters 2, 3, and 4, we move to the conceptual and theoretical development of musical creativity, new spaces, and creative mission respectively as it pertains to the study of ICMs in mission in this era of globalization. The following chapter addresses some of the gaps in understanding how musical creativity may function as a knowledge system in the context of mission following which we hope to be in a better place to explore the new spaces for the enactment of musical creativity with others.

---

81. Laenui, "Processes of Decolonization," 150–60. See also, Chilisa, *Indigenous Research Methodologies*.

2

Musical Creativity

MUSICAL CREATIVITY, NEW SPACES, and creative mission—these three form the core theoretical and conceptual frameworks for our exploration of how Indigenous Cosmopolitan Musicians (ICMs) understand and practice their mission. In this chapter we explore the concepts of music and creativity. Musical creative identity is continually mediated and reciprocated in the spaces in-between artist, domain, and field through ICMs in mission. Others are invited to participate in the process of musical creativity and, thereby, the formation of creative identity in the trajectories of transition in between artist, domain, and field. The epistemological captivity of creativity raises the question of whether or not musical creativity is an authentic means for the mediation of truth and knowledge and therefore adequate for the translation of Christianity. After familiarization with some of the dynamics of the process of musical creativity, we are in a better place to explore the process of musical creativity in the new interstitial spaces inhabited by ICMs for mission in chapter 3.

MUSIC, CULTURE, AND IDENTITY

In discussing the future of missiological anthropology, Michael A. Rynkiewich defines culture as "knowledge, values, and feelings that are learned, shared, and employed to define reality, interpret experience, and generate appropriate strategies for living."[1] Furthermore, culture is constructed (consciously put together on a regular basis), contingent (based on interpretations of already existing stories, myths, histories, and texts), and contested (every agent has a different idea of which parts to use, how to put them together,

---

1. Rynkiewich, "New Heaven and a New Earth?," 36.

and what that means for action).² Rynkiewich's understanding of the concept of culture is adapted here as a way for exploring the link between music and culture: music as a construct of culture, music as contingent upon the local and global historical and cultural particularities and processes of a given context, and music as a way of contesting the ways in which a given music is conceptualized in various contexts to embody reality.

A definition of music might have general attributes, such as the claim that music has

> ... roots in sound and movement, heterogeneity of meaning, a grounding in social interaction, and a personalized significance, together with an apparent inefficacy. Music embodies, entrains, and transposably intentionalizes time in sound and action.³

From ethnomusicology we learn that music is not a universal language, but it is a universal phenomenon.⁴ It is patterned sound, but the patterns depend on the creator and the listener.⁵ Music is expressive culture.⁶ It does not merely reflect people but produces people, creates them, and invites participation by others.⁷ The generative capacity of music makes it an invaluable instrument for the creation and recreation of identities.⁸ In broad terms, music includes the complex performative activi-

---

2. Rynkiewich, "New Heaven and a New Earth?," 33–46.

3. Cross, "Music and Biocultural Evolution," 24.

4. Nettl, *Study of Ethnomusicology*, 57.

5. Seeger, *Why Suyá Sing*, xiv. The issue is, who is doing the patterning. Further, according to Alan Merriam, music is "a complex of activities, ideas, and objects that are patterned into culturally meaningful sounds recognized to exist on a level different from secular communication." Merriam, *Anthropology of Music*, 27. The boundary between "music" and "noise" is challenged by innovations in sound composition, Cox and Warner, *Audio Culture*, xiv. "How do musical practices within the new 'audio culture' complicate the definition of 'music' and its distinction from 'silence,' 'noise,' and 'sound'? In what ways do they challenge traditional conceptions of authorship, minimalism, free improvisation . . . and electronic experimentation employed by artists from different backgrounds?"

6. As "expressive culture" music embodies the beliefs, values, and attitudes of the culture. In expressive behavior, the experience itself is a central part of the meaning. Hiebert et al., *Understanding Folk Religion*, 237.

7. "It is in deciding—playing and hearing what sounds right—that we both express ourselves, our own sense of rightness . . . and lose ourselves, in an act of participation." Frith, *Performing Rites*, 110.

8. For example, the repetition (of musical phrases) is not merely an affirmation of mental categories of thought, but the process of repetition allows one to go further into the experience of the reality being performed. The steady beats of Ojibway songs or that of hip-hop and trance would be "boring" if merely analyzed in terms of text alone. Similarly improvisation patterns of chordal harmonies or melodic movements in jazz

ties that comprise "musicking"—fundamental aspects of what "normally endowed" people do.[9]

In the light of ethnomusicology, the first major factor that we need to bear in mind for this study is that music is a process. From a sociocultural perspective, musical identity/being refers to identity that is consummate with music as a way of life including conceptualization, behavior or production, and the ways in which people respond to and participate in such identity.[10]

Second, the process of music signifies a dynamic correspondence between the person/musician and what is produced/music, and invites others to participate in the same. When it comes to discerning how music brings about personal and social transformation Marshall McLuhan and Quentin Fiore's thesis cannot be overlooked. In their quasi-ontological perspective, mediums of communication are not totally divorced from the personhood of their human actors.[11] They make the point that from a socio-cultural perspective all forms of media are "extensions" of some aspect of what constitutes humanness.[12] In the light of their thesis we might infer that music is both a medium and an environment for ushering social and cultural change.[13] We begin to explore some implications of McLuhan and Fiore's thesis for ICMs in mission by investigating music as knowledge, the phenomenon of music as "more than words," the non-representational nature of music, and a methodological approach to music as symbol in the mediation of Christianity.

MUSIC AS KNOWLEDGE

Daniel J. Levitin, a neuroscientist, demonstrates that music is a core component of human identity; it is "an activity that paved the way for more complex behaviors such as language."[14] He suggests that music actually

---

by themselves do not constitute musical behavior in its entirety. Lewellen, *Anthropology of Globalization*.

9. Small, *Musicking*, 8.

10. See, Merriam, *Anthropology of Music*; Blacking, *How Musical Is Man?*; Seeger, *Suyá*; and Nettl, *Study of Ethnomusicology*.

11. McLuhan et al., *Medium Is the Massage*.

12. McLuhan et al., *Medium Is the Massage*, 26; Frith, *Performance Rites*, 249–78.

13. Goldwater, *Artists on Art*, 1976. The artist Henry Matisse wrote concerning the relationship between the artist and the artwork as that which "cannot be conceived as separate from his pictorial means." Further, according to Matisse, "I am unable to distinguish between the feeling I have for life and my way of expressing it." See also, Geertz, "Art as a Cultural System," 1475.

14. Levitin, *World in Six Songs*, 3.

enhances cognitive development and understanding. Levitin's research in neuroscience and music reveals that the affective (feelings) and the evaluative (judgment) are as important in creating meaning and shaping theology as is the cognitive. Neurological research on the relation between music and the functioning of the brain suggests, "music evolved because it promoted cognitive development."[15]

Conceptually, from a relational ontological perspective, we learn that knowing does not proceed from thinking, but thinking signifies the pre-existence of knowledge.[16] Similarly, music as a way of "knowing" signifies the pre-existence of knowledge. It is not a knowledge based on "synthetic propositions whose truth value can be determined."[17] Rather, the concept of music as knowledge is based upon the role that music plays in informing the sensory dimension of human experience.[18] Conceived in this way, music as knowledge-generative process opposes the logic of Cartesian dualism. In fact, the very activity of making music is knowledge creation.

As far as the construction of human identity goes, the creation of music is a conceptual reversal of Cartesian claims to reality. In other words, musical identity is not to be conceptualized as resulting from rational thought ("I think therefore I am").[19] Rather, music is itself a legitimate way of defining reality.[20] It is not merely information. As knowledge, music is a direct result of human "action and participation in the world."[21]

---

15. Levitin, *World in Six Songs*, 260. See also, Patel, *Music, Language, and the Brain*, 3–4. Modern cognitive science continues to explore the reality that together with language, music is central to what constitutes humanness. But such research has a long history. Plato perceived certain musical modes as better than others for the wellbeing of humans. Patel bases his study on how Charles Darwin considered a combination of music and language might have played a crucial role in determining faculties of human communication. A similar line of thought may be followed through Vincenzo Galiliei (father of Galileo), Jean-Jacque Rousseau, Ludwig Wittgenstein, and more recently, Leonard Bernstein (3, 4).

16. Wood, *Theology as History and Hermeneutics*, 61–76, especially 64.

17. Eisner, "Art and Knowledge," 3.

18. Eisner, "Art and Knowledge," 4.

19. Newbigin, *Gospel in a Pluralist Society*, 29. Interestingly, in response to Descartes's approach to defining the locus of being, "I think therefore I am," Leslie Newbigin writes, "We may take mathematics as our ideal of a kind of thinking which is not open to doubt, but mathematics is itself a construct of the human mind, and we should heed the words of Einstein: 'As far as the propositions of mathematics refer to reality, they are not certain; and as far as they are certain, they do not refer to reality.'" Newbigin owes this reference to T. F. Torrance.

20. Hiebert et al., *Understanding Folk Religion*, 237. The act of music making is itself part of the experience. See also, Sapir-Whorf hypothesis, Sapir, *Language*.

21. Wood, *Theology as History and Hermeneutics*, 64. In addition, it seems clear that

In addition, music is also a place for the articulation of "knowledge of other people, places, times and things, and ourselves in relation to them."[22] The formative power of musical expression lies in its ability to create with the other a new reality. The rhetorical power of music is more than mere persuasion; it is the creation of a new identity, individual and collective.[23] The aesthetics of music therefore is not simply "to reflect a reality which stands behind it but to ritualize a reality that is within it."[24] In other words, music itself is a form of "text"; it serves as a primary form of documentation for perceptions of reality.[25]

---

rationality alone is not enough to lead one to decision-making. People who had brain damage that separated the rational and emotional parts of their brains could figure out all the options, but could not make a decision . . . because they did not care about the decision. So, the extreme of following logic alone does not actually work in the real brain. "For example, work from my laboratory has shown that emotion is integral to the processes of reasoning and decision making, for worse and for better." "These findings suggest that selective reduction of emotion is at least as prejudicial for rationality as excessive emotion." Damasio, *Feeling of What Happens*, 41.

22. Stokes, "Introduction," 3.

23. Constitutive rhetoric serves to construct a collective identity for an addressed audience. It constructs the audience as a subject in history and demands that subjects act in accordance with their identity as enacted in history. Charland, "Constitutive Rhetoric," 133–50. See also, Meyer, *Emotion and Meaning in Music*. Concerning the significance of Charland's theory, see Lewis, *Diffusion of Black Gospel Music in Postmodern Denmark*.

24. Frith, *Performing Rites*, 1996. Alexander G. Baumgarten coined the term "aesthetics" in 1735 to "describe what he called the new 'science of sensory cognition.'" García-Rivera, *Community of the Beautiful*, 9. However, the meaning today includes questions about art, "its nature, conditions, and consequences." For García-Rivera, this definition "makes aesthetics equivalent to the philosophy and psychology of art." Burch Brown, *Aesthetics*, 103. Burch Brown suggests three "artistic clusters" for interpreting art in the context of Christian tradition: (1) Art that is "made in such a way" that is perceived as beautiful; (2) art that is made with skill, knowledge, and creativity; (3) art that uses "forms that express, fictively represent, and imaginatively transform 'worlds' in a revelatory or prophetic way." Brown's suggestions are helpful for constructing a framework to examine aesthetics in the light of Christianity: beauty, knowledge, and transformation. When we speak of aesthetics, however, we are referring to particular ways of perceiving, constructing, and experiencing beauty and truth. The scope of this dissertation does not allow a full study of music and aesthetics. The term that we focus on is, creativity—not so much as an aesthetic criterion but more purposefully as an embodiment, enactment, and performance of creative being as pathway for participation in God's creativity as exemplified through the mission of Jesus Christ.

25. Geertz, "Art as a Cultural System," 1478; see also, Seeger, *Why Súya Sing?*

Music as More Than Words

A further consideration for this study is that the experience of music encompasses "more than words."[26] Music captures and reveals experiences that cannot ever be put into words or syllogisms. We do not dispute the place of lyric in the construction of meaning in music.[27] Yet, words need not necessarily be the primary yardstick for the effectiveness of music as a system of knowledge. For Jacques Derrida, "logocentrism" emphasizes the privileged place of words in the context of Westernization.[28] Music, however, is not "monolithic" in form, "but a composite of aspects consisting of text, tone, and context."[29]

The issue of "whether music is merely a vehicle for theology or whether it can be, in itself, theology,"[30] depends upon how each context or "symbolic universe" chooses to create meaning with respect to the "composite" (text, tone, and context) dimension of music. For instance, while sacred music in the West is to a large extent dependent on textual form, for Indian classical music sound itself is the ultimate reality.[31] Even apart from words music signifies intention and realization.[32]

Even in its sonic dimension, music creates the environment for the intersubjective association between persons. And therefore, according to John Blacking, "music can never be a thing in itself . . . it cannot be transmitted or have meaning without associations between people" (1973, x). What this means is that music forms the pathway by which identities are negotiated, meaning is communicated, and reality is transformed.

In addition, music is more than sound; it is movement. In the dominant classical and musical traditions as well as folk and tribal music within

---

26. The significance of music lies beyond an understanding of the text. Rather, "it crosses over into what is not heard." Saliers, *Music and Theology*, 2–9. The concept of *synaesthesis* conveys this crossing over, "the awakening of the deeper dimensions of reality and of the soul." The term "synaesthetic" refers to a multisensory response to "what is real," an "interanimation" of the senses. More than "ordered sound," music includes kinesthetic patterns—body movements or gestures. "The body remembers shared music-making long after the mind may be dimmed."

27. Parsons, "Text, Tone, and Context"; Woods and Walrath, *Message in the Music*; Kimbrough, *Lyrical Theology of Charles Wesley*.

28. Derrida, *Margins of Philosophy*. The meaning of words however was deferred to a metaphysics of presence rather than something that is negotiated via philosophy. Reynolds, "Metaphysics of Presence/Logocentrism."

29. Parsons, "Text, Tone, and Context," 54.

30. Sirota, "Exploration of Music As Theology," 24.

31. Wulff, "On Practicing Religiously," 164.

32. Seeger, *Why Suyá Sing*, 14.

Indian culture, music (the sonic phenomena) can never truly be separated from bodily enactment.[33] For some, to "hear" music is literally, to embody it.[34]

Music as Nonrepresentational

The embodied nature of music includes action and a multiplicity of reference and meaning that is not always explicit.[35] The polysemic nature of music makes it an ideal form for communicating religious truth since the nature of religious experience is multidimensional.[36] The ambiguity associated with music may be problematic where perceptions tend to validate certain forms of music over others as more authentic transponders of meaning in some contexts. We will address the issue of preferential claims to authenticity later in the context of the epistemological captivity of creativity. For now, however, we make the case that for music to have inherent value it does not always need to have "meaning" that can be unpacked in terms of dominant rational cognitive categories, such as, words. Perceived in this sense, music is non-representational. That is, music does not always need to represent or be represented by logical proposition.

Consider the following statement on video by Alissa Wilkinson concerning the release of world-famous Christian artist, Makoto Fujimura's illumined, "the Four Holy Gospels":

> [H]aving Mako's art, which is non-representational, next to the words of scripture invites the reader to take the words of scripture and sort of see what they see in the art and how that connects with the words that they're reading, because the words

---

33. The *Natya Shastra*, an ancient (fourth century AD) treatise on the arts, emphasizes the unity of all "true art." Kumar, *Essays on Indian Music*, 85. The prevalent Hindu perception is that the essence of all sound has roots in movement, specifically, the cosmic rhythm of the dance of Shiva. In the ritual context, music is revelatory of God's action, it is relational activity, includes body movement, multidimensional and multi-channeled performance, and evokes and expresses relatedness beyond the community. McGann, *Exploring Music as Worship and Theology*, 38.

34. Glennie, "How to Truly Listen." Evelyn Glennie, a percussionist who is deaf testifies to how she learned to hear subtle differences in tone through reverberations in different areas of her body. Glennie's embodiment of music is an indication of the potential of all persons, irrespective of "intellectual" capacity, to embody and thereby wholly participate in the physicality of music.

35. Cross, "Music and Biocultural Evolution," 23. See also Merriam, *Anthropology of Music*, 27.

36. Sylvan, *Traces of the Spirit*, 6. Beck, *Sacred Sound*. The multivalency of music is evident in that it functions simultaneously in differing degrees (physiological, psychological, sociocultural, seiological, as well as virtual, ritual, and spiritual contexts).

are transcendent. And the art, in a lot of ways, reflects that transcendence."[37]

Music often appears "beyond the reach of discourse," "hard to talk about," and even "seems unnecessary to do so" (Geertz 1976, 1473). This may be a problem not because of music, *per se*, but because of the conditions for discourse in any given context. As we will see, in the context of the postcolonial strain within "world music" discourse and neoliberal "assimilation" strategy, musical identity articulates the difference between perceptions of authentic and inauthentic experiences of/through music.[38]

Music and Symbol

Neither category of "western" music or "non-western" music refers to a "homogenous whole."[39] A full study of the role of music as symbol is not possible here. However, Mark Parsons's suggestion for the analysis of musical form according to its composite nature—text, tone, and context—is a helpful method to understand the role of music in mediating reality.[40]

According to Parsons, cultures might emphasize a "logocentric-conformist model" that prefers a "conformance of tone to text, the basic decision being that music is subservient to words" (2005, 56). In this approach, communication is primarily through discursive language. Here the text is the primary form of communication.

The "symbolic-assimilative model," on the other hand, develops a theology "based on the phenomenology of sound" (ibid., 58). In the "symbolic-assimilative model," music communicates information at a more "subterranean" way than other forms of communication.[41] The amount of information conveyed might be little as compared to the logocentric model, but communication in this context is not dependent upon the meanings of words. Rather, the focus is on shaping the spiritual identity of people.[42] Music, as "acoustical symbols," goes beyond words in pointing toward what is real, while "participating in the meaning and the very being of those realities."[43]

---

37. Fujimura, "Four Holy Gospels."

38. Middleton, "Musical Belongings," 59–62. See also, Frith, *Performing Rites*, 307; and Haynes, "World Music and the Search for Difference," 365–85.

39. Nketia, "Aesthetic Dimension in Ethnomusicological Studies," 20.

40. Parsons, "Text, Tone, and Context," 54ff.

41. Hunter, "Crash Course in Communication and Culture."

42. Parsons, "Text, Tone, and Context," 60.

43. Saliers, *Music and Theology*, 75.

Another way in which music creates meaning might be understood through the "performative-convergent" model, which does not see words or tonal aspects of music as conforming to each other. Rather, words and tone "converge on a common function in a specific performative context" (Parsons 2005, 61). Here, the text remains primary, while tone plays an integral role by fostering participation. The theological significance of music lies in its ability as mediator of spiritual reality (ibid., 64). This is best observed in the context of ritual. The fact that musical symbols reveal "something more" in the context of ritual, calls for a study of musical symbols in the public liturgical spaces created and occupied by ICMs. This is subject for further study.[44]

Music is a conceptual language "capable of expressing coherent thought on existence and on the World" in an interactive and "intersubjective" environment "shared by others."[45] Music, as "acoustical symbols," goes beyond words in pointing toward what is real, while "participating in the meaning and the very being of those realities" (Saliers 2007, 75). Recollecting Suzanne Langer's proposition concerning music as symbolic meaning:

> The limits of language are not the last limits of experience, and things inaccessible to language may have their own forms of conception . . . Such non-discursive forms, charged with logical possibilities of meaning, underlie the significance of music.[46]

To sum up thus far, music is a process. Music signifies a dynamic correspondence between personhood, process, and product. Music is a palpable form of knowledge. Its non-representational nature does not diminish its capacity for embodying knowledge. Music is often "more than words." It includes movement. In terms of a "pre-systematic ontology" of music that we adopt here, music is a way of being in relationship with God, oneself, others, and the world. We turn to identify some ways in which music mediates spirituality as it might apply to ICMs for mission.

MUSIC AND SPIRITUALITY

As part of the discourse in Western systematic theology, according to Oskar Sohngen, the act of music composition is an act of devotion since it has to

---

44. Please see, Deflem, "Ritual, Anti-Structure, and Religion," 1–25; Turner, *Ritual Process*; Boje, "Victor Turner's Postmodern Theory of Social Drama."

45. Eliade, *Symbolism, the Sacred, and the Arts,* 3; Berger and Luckmann, *Social Construction of Reality,* 23; King, "Negotiating the Gospel Cross-Culturally," 69.

46. Langer, *Philosophy in a New Key,* 265.

do with orienting oneself in accord with the ways in which God creates.[47] The idea of music as sacred or divine, however, is not limited to western systematic theology.[48] First, in many traditions, sound is sacred.[49] It carries the potential to draw people into the "joy and the glory of being human in a God-given created order" (Begbie 2007, 148). Music mediates the spiritual by reinforcing identities and distinguishing boundaries between secular and sacred in worship/religious ritual "as if by some mysterious thread" in all the major religions of the world (Beck 2006, 1).

Second, spiritual dimensions of music are not necessarily limited to traditional religious environments (for example, church, temple etc.) or concepts of worship of deity.[50] Increasingly, pop music venues are sites for cultural struggle, the formation of "individual identities into communal solidarities" and active configuration of self, others and modes of interaction at individual, communal, national, and transnational levels.[51] Popular music contexts are venues for spiritual formation. Music is able to tap into a "deep longing for the sacred in contemporary life, touching people at a level beyond and beneath emotion, will, and intellect."[52]

---

47. Sohngen, "Music and Theology," 4.

48. As simplistic as it may sound, to state that the experience of God may be found in the musical spiritual traditions of others as in Christianity is inherently problematic, for some.

49. The issues of music and morality are linked in Plato, but must lead to a further question: "To what extent is music grounded in or obliged to be faithful to a world we did not make, a world that we did not fashion but that is in some sense given to us" (Begbie, *Resounding Truth*). S. F. Nadel refers to Greek, Egyptian, Chinese, and Hindoo ways of signifying music as "something withdrawn from the conditions of ordinary existence, something at variance with the natural order of things." Nadel, "Origins of Music," 283. See also Beck, *Sonic Theology*. More than a few authors cite sitar maestro, Ravi Shankar's perspective with regard to the religious significance of sound; according to him, the Hindustani music tradition teaches that "Sound is God . . . Nada Brahma . . . . [Music is] a kind of spiritual discipline that raises one's inner being to divine peacefulness and bliss . . . a knowledge of the true meaning of the universe . . . to reveal the essence of the universe it reflects . . . through music, one can reach God." Wulff, "On Practicing Religiously," 153.

50. The "decline of religion" in many parts of the Western world is not so much a decline as it is a migration of the "religious impulse" from one part of culture to another where "religious sensibilities" flourish and impact many people. Sylvan, *Traces of the Spirit*, 3.

51. Matsue, "Stars to the State and Beyond," 72. Popular musical subcultures provide almost everything for its participants that a traditional religion would, emphasizing "liminal" and "communitas" experiences. Sylvan, *Traces of the Spirit*, 8–9; 35–38.

52. Begbie, *Theology, Music, and Time*, 129, uses these terms to describe John Tavener's views of Tavener's own music.

Third, according to Jeremy Begbie, Plato integrated the Greek concept of "ethos" by which music influenced the soul and the formation of good character, especially through certain musical modes. Plato linked music and morality.[53] Such dualism in the spirituality of music can be traced through the Enlightenment[54] into modernity.

Fourth, Adrian Nocent points out that in the Old Testament although instruments were used, they were suspect.[55] The idea of music being relevant for Christian practice so long as it serves the text is not without problems.[56] Albert Blackwell agrees that music can convey "mystical experiences" that "ordinary verbal language is inadequate to convey" (1999, 211). For Blackwell, the concept of "Musizieren" captures the essence of what it means to "commune" through the medium of music with others,

---

53. Begbie, *Resounding Truth*, traces Platonic influence through the "Great Tradition"—the thought of musical sound as coinciding with or giving expression to cosmic order. See Begbie and Guthrie, *Resonant Witness*; and Irwin, "'So Faith Comes from What is Heard,'" 65–82. Irwin addresses tensions between "verbal" and "musical" forms in the West. In addition, we note Pythagorean influence on Plato's philosophy. For Pythagoras (580 BC–500 BC), God's grace was revealed through contemplation on the mathematics of music, an intellectual pursuit. The relationships of one part of creation to another, of soul to body, people to others, were all "held together by, and subject to, a single cosmic mathematics." Blackwell, *Sacred in Music*, 47, 80.

54. Begbie, *Resounding Truth*, 86. For Augustine (AD 354–430), the purpose of music was mainly to draw people to God. Blackwell, *Sacred in Music*, 128. He saw music as a source of temptation and potential addiction because of its capacity to penetrate deep into the soul and influence people. Augustine represents the most influential adaptation of the ancient Platonic tradition with Christian ideas that ever occurred in the Latin Christian world. "Saint Augustine," http://www.britannica.com/EBchecked/topic/42902/Saint-Augustine. In addition, this might be true even for his views on music.

55. Nocent, "Words and Music in the Liturgy," in *Music and the Experience of God*, 128–29. For Isaiah certain instruments were obstacles to prayer (Isa 5:12, 16:11, 23:15). Ezekiel considered music a symbol of luxury and the evil life (Ezek 26:13). Job associates music with evil (Job 21:12, 30:31). All instruments were excluded except for the Shophar. For Christians in the New Testament, the apostle Paul recommends song, "but with what music?" For Clement of Alexandria, man is the only true instrument; worship is spiritual and so instruments are secondary.

56. What about cultures that might view instrumental music as fully capable connecting people with God, without need for it to be associated with any kind of text, leave alone Scripture? Foley, *Foundations of Christian Music*, 14–19. Emphasis on the "word" in early Christianity does not necessarily amount to focus on the "written" word. In the early church, the "non-clerical, lay-led, word-centered worship—with a spiritualized sacrifice of praise at its heart—provided an important model to the followers of Jesus." Foley draws attention to the larger "auditory environment" as the context for investigation of the role of music in oral cultures. The significance of writing lies in its "concealed oralism": the dominance of auditory over visual imagery in divine manifestation, the importance of the organs for hearing and seeing, and the dynamic nature of the Hebrew language and thought (for example, understanding is not a faculty but "is action").

music itself, and with the "transcendent source of music's deep structures and complex manifold" (ibid., 23).[57]

Fifth, there is the significance of liturgical and ritual contexts. Public liturgies as ritual contexts are a significant "domain" for transformational modes of listening[58] and participation. Ritual contexts assign special significance to instruments and body movements as well.[59]

MUSICAL CREATIVITY AND EPISTEMOLOGICAL CAPTIVITY

Thus far in this chapter we have observed the nature of music as that which is capable of mediating knowledge and spirituality in palpable ways. Yet, the dichotomy between perceptions of what constitutes rational cognitive forms and those that are deemed less intellectual (musical) forms have inhibited the church from a wholesome employment of the processes of musical creativity for mission. The detrimental impact of the Enlightenment emphases on rational processes for mission is already demonstrated elsewhere.[60] The captivity of the church to Enlightenment notions of

---

57. For Blackwell, *Sacred in Music*, 38–46, the "universal aesthetic" of music is provided by a Christian worldview that views music as "panentheistic" ("everything in God") in nature. It embodies God. How does one get a sense of the divine through music? Blackwell suggests two traditions–Incarnational and Pythagorean—that make up "sacramental consciousness." The Incarnational tradition refers to the audibly perceptible music as a means of God's grace. The Pythagorean tradition refers to the conceptual or that which is perceived in our minds, the "logic of music," as potentially sacramental, "an intellectual joy." According to Blackwell, together, these two traditions provide for a well-rounded grasp of the significance of music and its "sacramental potential."

58. Saliers, *Music and Theology*, 76. Further, we are not referring to music as it pertains to worship in the context of the gathering of Christian believers. However, the *leitourgia* in terms of the public service on behalf of the people takes place not merely in the context of "worship" within the walls of the church. But liturgy is enacted when God's people respond to His Spirit to serve God wherever they may be. In fact, "liturgy may break out anywhere." Hawn, *One Bread, One Body*, 5.

59. "Musical interaction takes place in a ritual event when a group of performers engaged in music-making respond to one another or behave in a manner intended to respond to or influence the disposition, attitude or behavior of a deity, an ancestor, a person or a group of person." Music affirms communal values and renews bonds and sentiments that bind a community. Nketia, "Musical Interaction in Ritual Events," 112. If body movements are a principal feature of ritual action, then it is these that must be used rather than words, to communicate (Begbie, *Resounding Truth*, 217). In addition, in certain contexts movement is regarded as a "process of becoming" or the transformation of individual or group from one state of being to another. Burnimm, "Performance of Black Gospel Music as Transformation," 52–61.

60. Bosch, *Transforming Mission*, 262–67. Mission is negatively impacted due to the Age of Reason and its effects: The undue emphasis on rationality as that which defines

"mind over matter" and the undue emphasis on reason (rational cognition) as that which defines what it means to be human, over and against other forms of cognition, and the application of this understanding toward the role of musical creativity for mission, is what we refer to here as the epistemological captivity of creativity.[61]

While the negative effects of the Enlightenment on mission are in general well attested and affirmed by those in the church and academy, a critical knowledge of the homogenizing impact of the Enlightenment for processes of musical creativity for mission is less common. David Bosch's evaluation of "mission in the wake of the Enlightenment,"[62] helps to see some ways through which the crystallizing effect of the Enlightenment continues to plague the church. For now we recognize the epistemological captivity of creativity in the following ways.

First, when it comes to musical creativity for mission the epistemological captivity of creativity is evident in the persistent preference extended to rational cognitive forms as prime containers for the Gospel over

---

what it means to be human marked an epistemological shift with an ontological dimension. This chain of thought resulted in the treatment of Westerners as prime representatives of rationalized processes over others. Second, the subject-object dichotomy meant that everything could be objectified due to the capacity of the human mind to reason; the concept of creation, was reduced to that of nature that could, and needed to be, studied and understood if it was to be used for the benefit of humankind. Third, the scientific cause-effect rationale trumped belief in God's purpose. Fourth, the capacity of the human mind to conquer all things resulted in humanity itself being evaluated in terms of progress and development that could be verified via scientific procedure. Fifth, this meant that science was the ultimate measuring rod and therefore was equated with "fact" and "value-free"; "values" became a matter of individual choice or preference. A sixth impact of the Enlightenment was the heralding of the individual as one who is ultimately free to choose. Freedom itself was defined by the capacity to make individual choices over and against being repressed by, for instance, doctrinal formulations of the church. In fact, according to this perspective, there was no need for humans to be defined in so-called spiritual terms when the spirituality was rationality itself.

61. Abraham, *Canon and Criterion in Christian Theology*. William J. Abraham argues that Scripture, as a canon of the church, is not a criterion for truth; it is a means of grace. The argument is made in the light of the modern emphasis on scientific rationalism and its criterion as that which determined what was true and authentic versus what was deemed false and inauthentic. Abraham argues that Scripture is a means of grace and therefore cannot afford to be in competition with rational criteria. Wood, *Theology as History and Hermeneutics*, 226. With respect to Abraham's argument, the shift of Scripture, in the context of Western Christianity, into "the arena of becoming a criterion of truth" resulted in the Church "being held in '*epistemological captivity*' with disastrous consequences" (italic mine). The Scriptures are authoritative not because they function as rational criteria to justify truth, but because of their "soteriological intent." See also, Johnson, "Canon and Criterion," 1–12.

62. Bosch, *Transforming Mission*, 262–345; see n134.

and against musical forms (the dichotomization of knowledge as information and formation).

Second, the emphasis on scientific "fact" versus the ambiguity of musical "value" negatively affects perceptions of the identity of artists and musicians as carriers of knowledge and disseminators of truth.[63]

A third area where the epistemological captivity is evident is in the negation, and in extreme cases, "demonization," of other musical-rich indigenous cultures and histories as compared to the rich theology evident in lyrics and Westernized approaches to music (the compartmentalization of culture).[64]

In the context of the mediation of music, the symptoms of the epistemological captivity have been traced elsewhere, from the "radical dualism" of Socrates (Wood 2005b, 11) through Plato, neo-platonic influences, the Enlightenment, and "Cartesian rationalism" (ibid., 57–69) along with its progeny in modern foundationalism.[65]

---

63. The term, "orphan," was used by more than one artist I interviewed to describe the experience of alienation with relation to the ecclesial structure. According to RF, a dancer, it was not that he was unappreciated for what he brought in terms of his dance; people seemed to enjoy the performance. However, his identity as a dancer, as someone who could mediate spiritual truth and knowledge through his craft as tantamount to truth mediated through other more commonly perceived "intellectual" forms, was neither recognized nor affirmed. "Discipleship cannot happen if the fundamental anger of many artists toward the church goes unresolved." Castleman, "Response to Redeeming the Arts," 36–37. In a Lausanne Occasional Paper that explored the "engagement of the arts within the life and mission of the church": "Apart from a small number of important voices, the church as a whole has been virtually silent on the topic [art and mission] for generations." Harbison, "Redeeming the Arts," 1. With regard to art, church, and the evangelical tradition, there is a lack of a "comprehensive, systematic, integrating, and grounding vision." Taylor, *For the Beauty of the Church*, 21. "Art is not simply a tool or a piece of technology to be used for a predetermined purpose. The integrity of both art and artist require something more." Harbison, "Redeeming the Arts," 7.

64. The insistence upon a certain form of music as "essentially" being more authentic over other forms has in the past had disastrous effects in the context of Christian worship and mission. For example, the "worship wars." See Chapell, *Christ-Centered Worship*. In the colonial context, see Irving, *Colonial Counterpoint*; also, Harris, "Great Misconception," 82–89.

65. See Wood, *God and History*; Faulkner, *Wiser Than Despair*. Chua, "Music as the Mouthpiece of Theology," 138. The problem of modernity was not its emphasis on processes of reason, but its "marginalization of God" in the process. Much of Western thought on the matter has been shaped by Platonic dualism. Begbie, *Resounding Truth* and Blackwell, *Sacred in Music* recount portions of this history, summarized here. Plato (428 BC–348 BC) integrated the Greek conception of *ethos*, by which music influenced the soul and thereby the formation of good character. For Plato, music and morality become closely linked; music was an "imitative art" that did not accurately portray the ultimate reality. Furthermore, the potential of music to disrupt the harmony of the soul made the intellectual understanding of the science of music more important than

It is worth stating that the "effectiveness" of music is not a simple case

the practice of music. Music did not exist for pleasure but to seek truth. In addition, we note Pythagorean influence on Plato's philosophy. For Pythagoras (580 BC–500 BC), God's grace was revealed through contemplation on the mathematics of music, an intellectual pursuit. The relationships of one part of creation to another, of soul to body, people to others, were knitted together and accountable to a unifying cosmic mathematical process. According to Boethius (c. 480–c. 525), music is something to be understood rather than done or experienced in action. It is formative and affects characters. It still is a mathematical process. For Artistoxenus (fourth century BC), music is not grounded in numbers and ratios, but in the way the elements of music actually sound in practice—"music is 'sound in our ears' before it is 'ratios in our minds'" (Begbie, *Resounding Truth*, 93). For Augustine (AD 354—430), the purpose of music was mainly to draw people to God (86). He saw music as a source of temptation and potential addiction because of its capacity to penetrate deep into the soul and influence people (Blackwell, *Sacred in Music*, 128). Augustine represents the most influential adaptation of the ancient Platonic tradition with Christian ideas that ever occurred in the Latin Christian world. See, "Saint Augustine," http://www.britannica.com/EBchecked/topic/42902/Saint-Augustine. In addition, this might be true even for his views on music. Augustine, and Knight, *St. Augustine's De Musica*.

Luther departed from Platonism concerning his views on music. For Luther, music was a gift from God, a vehicle for praising God. Unlike Plato, he did not see any aspect of music as inherently destructive. It fulfilled its preaching role when linked directly to the Word (Begbie, *Resounding Truth*, 102). For Calvin, music was more of a human practice; it needs to be "tempered by words"; He was apprehensive about linking music to experiences of God (110). For Zwingli, worship was primarily an inward matter and did not concern outward actions. For him Scripture did not make it clear that singing was "instituted by God; it is to be seen there as a human initiative, not a divine one" (115). For Schleiermacher, music was not a referential or a representational art and therefore lends itself better to articulating the nature of deep religious experiences by being able to "articulate the wordless stirrings of immediate self-consciousness" (150).

More recently, according to Best, *Music Through the Eyes of Faith*, 17, music is representational, somewhat like abstract art. Music operates at different levels and it depends largely upon what people bring to it in terms of historical background, social context, and personal preferences. For Best, music is always rooted in human work and creativity. Concerning the flow of thought on the role of music and how it relates to the rational and affective spheres of human consciousness, we might ask: Are theological values that govern the use of music and intellectual (cognitive?) experiences related to music, mutually exclusive categories (Begbie, *Resounding Truth*, 151).

Collins, "Editorial," 5. We discover a tendency among Western approaches, in general, to consider words as being more significant to music than the music itself. This view, once again, finds roots in Platonic dualism that deems music, by itself, "incomplete." In the past, the Catholic Church in the *Sacrosanctum Concilium* distinguished between music as "true art" and "sacred music" as that which is "intimately linked with liturgical action." Hoffman, "Musical Traditions and Tensions in the American Synagogue," 31, observes the influence of the German pietistic tradition, Hasidei Ashkenaz (c. twelfth century), on later American synagogue worship practices that viewed music as serving text and not the other way around ("liturgical logocentrism"). According to Saliers, *Music and Theology*, 26, the focus of "liturgical theology," is to discuss the various ways music interprets key notions as time, transcendence, and eternity from a theological perspective—how music is theological.

of either "good" or "bad" music but rather a measure of rhetorically appropriate music for any given context. The formation of identity is a rhetorical process rather than something that exists without capacity for transformation "prior to persuasion and upon which persuasion depends."[66] Further, rather than divide music into categories such as "acceptable" or "unacceptable," Jeremy Begbie urges us to ask, "How music might connect with the gospel and its widest implications?" (2007, 24).

In the context of a new "ecumenical paradigm," David Bosch refers to contextual theologies as an "epistemological break" from traditional theologies. Bosch's concept is helpful in articulating a response to the commodification of knowledge in the light of the epistemological captivity and an "emerging epistemology" associated with "Third-World theologies" and various manifestations of the same as a "pivotal" phenomenon in the history of the "emerging ecumenical missionary paradigm."[67] Bosch outlines the features of the "new epistemology" whereby knowledge is no longer to be understood as the ability of the human mind to grasp a given reality. Rather, knowledge is generated by active participation in the "human and physical" world; it is not a static phenomenon, but a process of transformation to be brought about along with others.[68]

We conclude therefore that intuitive understanding via music needs to go hand in hand with cognitive reasoning especially when it comes to establishing a framework to evaluate the potential of music to communicate and define reality. The problem has been addressed in "secular" academia to some extent. The Sensory Formations Series by BERG publishers is a case in point.[69]

---

66. Charland, "Constitutive Rhetoric," theory demonstrates that identity is rhetorically produced collectively, people are constructed as a subject in history, and people act in accordance with their constructed identity. See "Constitutive Rhetoric," 617–18.

67. Bosch, *Transforming Mission*, 423–25.

68. Bosch, *Transforming Mission*, 424.

69. Howes, "Sensory Formations," opening comments. The series editor by way of introduction poses these questions among others: What is the world like to cultures that privilege touch or smell over sight or hearing?" Other questions include: What lies beyond aesthetic gaze? How has the proliferation of 'taste cultures' resulted in new forms of social discrimination? Who says money has no smell? How is the sixth sense to be defined? What is the future of the senses in cyberspace? He goes on to write:

> From the Ancient Greeks to medieval mystics and eighteenth-century empiricists, Karl Marx to Marshall McLuhan, the senses have been the subject of dramatic proclamations. Senses are . . . . [s]ites of intense personal experience, they are also fields of extensive cultural elaboration. Yet surprisingly, it is only recently that scholars . . . have turned their full attention to sensory experience and expression as a subject for enquiry . . . .

SECTION SUMMARY

The larger context for this study is the exploration of the ways in which indigenous cosmopolitan musicians (ICMs) understand and practice their musical creativity for mission in the transcultural musical spaces in this era of globalization. The purpose of the immediately preceding section has been to develop the concept of music as it pertains to this study. From ethnomusicology we understand that music is a sociocultural process. In terms of identity, music signifies a dynamic correspondence between personhood and expression (music). Music is not merely a tool for transmission of truth. The process of music is itself knowledge-generative. While words form an important component of music, the formative scope of music goes beyond words alone. Music includes the movement of the body. Music is non-representational in the sense that it does not always need to be substantiated by rationalized cognitive processes such as logical propositions. The multivalent nature of music as symbol allows for wide application in religious and spiritual contexts. The potential of music for mission is hampered by onto-epistemic criteria that relegate music as less effective when it comes to mediating truth over and against other more "intellectual" forms. This in turn negatively affects the agency and identity of ICMs for mission.

WHY CREATIVITY?

In the last section we saw how music plays a crucial role in the formation of identity. In this section we begin to lay a conceptual and theoretical foundation for a theology of creativity for mission to be developed further in chapter 4 (Missiological Framework for Theological Creativity). Different eras have defined creativity as per their contexts.[70] For our purpose we use the phrase "theological creativity" to signify a distinct onto-epistemic orientation. Here are a few reasons: First, popular notions locate the source of creativity in the

---

[The series'] objective is to enhance our understanding of the role of the senses in history, culture and aesthetics, by redressing an imbalance: the hegemony of vision and privileging of discourse in contemporary theory and cultural studies must be overthrown in order to reveal the role all sense play in mediating cultural experience.

70. According to Mazzola et al., *Musical Creativity*, 139, creativity is that which is considered "appropriate" in a given context. See also, Sternberg and Lubart, "Concept of Creativity." For others, creativity is what is considered "good, novel, and relevant." Kaufman and Sternberg, *Cambridge Handbook of Creativity*, xiii. Creativity as the interactivity between aptitude, process, and environment for a "perceptible product" that is considered "novel and useful." Plucker et al., "Why isn't Creativity More Important to Educational Psychologists?" 90. Creativity implies originality, quality, and acceptance. Kim et al., "Relationship between Creativity and Intelligence," 400.

individual person, while theological creativity roots creativity in God and links human creativity to the image of God found in all humans and uniquely in the relationship of followers of Christ to the living God.[71] From the ontological priority of creativity assumed here we discern that rather than innovation or the psychometric evaluation of human potential, creativity is an essential core of what it means to be human.[72]

Second, in terms of a relational axiology,[73] the concept of theological creativity is helpful to articulate a postcolonial counter-response to the hegemony of creativity as individual propriety as emphasized in Enlightenment ideological discourses.

Third, it follows that theological creativity reveals the inherent moral fabric of the creative process primarily by the dynamic linkage of the creative process with creative personality.[74] This reinforces the dynamic correspondence between musician and music as discussed earlier.

Fourth, the shift from asking, "What is creativity?" to asking "Where is creativity?" is significant in terms of an expanding "network topography" as a way of articulating a relational onto-epistemic framework for creativity[75] for mission in the new spaces in this era of globalization.

---

71. In an article announcing the release of their book on creativity, authors Tim and David Kelley, "Reclaim Your Creative Confidence," write: "*Most* people are born creative." It is significant that the Kelly's use the word "Most" as opposed to "All." A part of the problem with the Kelley's approach is that creativity is defined as something that is "essential to success in any discipline or industry." The direct linkage of creativity as *essential* to success is understandable for good reason, given the Kelly's context of business innovation and industry design. However, all people are essentially creative in the image of the Creator.

72. Bellini, *Participation*, 10. The theological understanding that creativity is *essential* to what it means to be human is antithetical to the more popular view adopted by prominent thinkers such as Howard Gardner, for whom creativity is intrinsic to a particular personage and breakthrough). Gardner, *Creating Minds*. For Ken Robinson (*Out of Our Minds*), creativity is the capacity to innovate. Creativity includes the process of natural selection. Gabora and Kaufman, "Evolutionary Approaches to Creativity," 291. Creativity is amoral, but does not relieve from social responsibility. Moran, "Role of Creativity in Society."

73. Chilisa, *Indigenous Research Methodologies*, 21–23. Ontology and epistemology refer to the nature of reality and knowledge respectively. Axiology refers to the place and role of values in a given context. It emphasizes the esthetic relatedness and connectedness between participants.

74. The fact of music being a human creation accounts for the "character of the musical works that are made," Davies, *Musical Understandings*, 174.

75. Csikszentmihalyi, *Creativity*; Gardner, *Creating Minds*, 37. "Psychologists tend to see creativity exclusively as a mental process, [but] creativity is as much a cultural and social as it is a psychological event. Therefore what we call creativity is not the product of single individuals, but of social systems making judgments about individual's products. Any definition of creativity that aspires to objectivity, and therefore

CREATIVITY AND INTELLIGENCE: ENCOUNTERING POPULAR PERSPECTIVES

The linkage of uncommon creative potential or intelligence to particular kinds of peoples or dispositions is a common notion. Further, that all people possess some degree of creativity is also a popular conception. We recollect that for Plato music was merely a mimetic faculty and therefore could never truly communicate truth. The problem is further accentuated however when creative intelligence is located in particular constructs of identity such as race, ethnicity, caste, or class as in the case of the relationship between music and caste in Indian classical music traditions.[76]

The problem of associating authenticity in music to a particular lineage, race, group, or language is not unique to the Indian classical music traditions.[77] In other instances of the problem, creative intelligence is linked with the notion of being intellectually "engaged." We note that for Ken Robinson, a creativity consultant, "creativity is possible in any activity in which human intelligence is actively engaged."[78] Robinson's approach calls upon persons to draw upon their distinct unique creative potential for greater effectiveness: "Real creativity comes from finding your medium, from being in your element" (ibid., 10). However, the question is, how do you find "your medium"? What is the essence of one's "element"? These fundamental questions are left unanswered, which further contributes to perceptions of the "amorphous" nature of creativity. The reader is meant to provide those answers based upon personal predilections.

In addition, for Robinson, the arts are "powerful ways of unlocking creative capacities and of engaging the whole person" (ibid., 11). There seems to be a general understanding of the "power" of the arts to bring about change. However, Robinson makes some inherent assumptions that need to be challenged in the context of theological creativity. For instance,

---

requires an intersubjective dimension, will have to recognise the fact that the audience is as important to its constitution as the individual to whom it is credited." Csikszentmihalyi, "Creativity." See *Appendix* B.

76. The following autobiographical narrative serves to illustrate. Once while working with a traditional Indian drummer (*mridangam* player) in the process of composing music for an event, he commended me on my accomplishment in composing some rhythms that were complex and appealing to him and commented, "You must be Brahmin." When I asked him why he thought I was Brahmin, his reply implied that only Brahmins were capable of composing such (good) music. He saw an intrinsic link between musical proficiency and caste (identity) that was not a reality to me with my hybrid "Christian" upbringing. Did he really believe that a higher caste somehow privileged a person to produce "better" music than others of a lower caste?

77. Please see, Hoffman, "Musical Traditions and Tensions."

78. Robinson, *Out of Our Minds*, 111.

while there seems to be an implicit notion of the power of the arts in ushering transformation, about what sort of power are we talking? How is it accessible? Where is it located—in the work of art or in people's perceptions of reality that somehow attribute power to a work of art? Second, there appears to be a general acknowledgment of an inherent "creative capacity" of persons that somehow needs to be unlocked. Third, for Robinson, there is an implicit assumption that there indeed is something more to the "person" that warrants intellectual engagement of some kind in order for that person to live a better life, the limits of which may not be central to harnessing creative potential. Some people manage to unlock this creative potential and therefore are apparently successful.

There appears to be some truth to the assumptions inherent in Robinson's statement. The literature on creativity in the last decade or so would affirm Robinson's approach.[79] The root of the problem, however, is theological, which we explore in terms of a Missiological Framework for Theological Creativity in chapter 4. In the following section, we quickly survey the background to some of the approaches to creativity as they pertain to this study.

BACKGROUND TO THEORIES OF CREATIVITY

In *Musical Creativity: Strategies and Tools in Composition and Improvisation* (2012), Guerino Mazzola, Joomi Park, and Florian Thalmann have summarized approaches to creativity in the West. For them, "The urge to be creative has been central to human life and culture for tens of thousands of years, and it can be traced back to the early days of human civilization" (132).[80] In the pre-Christian era, the Greeks associated creativity with genius and the emphasis on a person's "guardian spirit." For Aristotle, creativity took on social significance. The Romans associated creativity with being male (giving birth being the exception) and thought it was hereditary.[81] For the Greeks, "nothing new was possible in art." Creativity was meant to reflect the perfection of nature.[82] With Roman culture, the

---

79. Steve Guthrie mentions several works in the past decade that discuss the notion of creativity and spirituality and highlights Cameron's *Artist's Way*, that sold over a million copies (*Creator Spirit*, xiii). More recently, see Catmull with Wallace, *Creativity, Inc.*

80. Concerning musical creativity from an evolutionary perspective, "the progenitors of man . . . before acquiring the power of expressing mutual love in articulate language, endeavored to charm each other with musical notes and rhythm." Darwin, *Descent of Man,* loc. 10141–42. This approach, however, unwittingly prefers articulation in terms of language to music. See also, Gabora and Kaufman, *Evolutionary Approaches*, 291.

81. Runco and Albert, "Creativity Research," 5.

82. Mazzola et al., *Musical Creativity*, 133.

notions of imagination and inspiration became significant with relation to creative expression in art. These notions returned to prominence in the West with the value placed on the individual (ibid.).

It is helpful to observe an early Western conception of creativity based upon the biblical account of Creation. I do not want to confuse what I mean by "creativity" with "Creation." However, the account of Creation in the Bible is a primary encounter with the creativity of God. According to Daniel Boorstin,

> For man's awareness of his capacity to create, the Covenant was a landmark. It declared that a people become a community through their belief in a Creator and His Creation. They confirmed their creative powers through their kinship, their sharing qualities of God, their intimate and voluntary relationship to a Creator-God. Christianity [by] turning our eyes to the future, played a leading role in the discovery of our power to create.[83]

According to Stephen Prickett, during the eighteenth century, the Bible "underwent a shift in interpretation" where it was viewed as a cultural artifact and a "literary and aesthetic model."[84] The rise of individualism as a reaction to divine authority coincided with scientific thinking as the preeminent instrument for discovery and models for thinking about the physical world (ibid.). Creativity was not so much about idealism but about cause and effect within the world of space and time. In the era of scientific naturalism, history came to be understood more in terms of "before and after" rather than the story of God as that which is being enacted in this world.[85]

In the Renaissance, the general belief was that the creativity of God was the source of divine inspiration for the creativity of artists.[86] However, larger social changes[87] in the light of colonialism and its impact formed

---

83. Boorstin, *Creators*, 42, 55. Italic mine.

84. Prickett, *Origins of Narrative*, ii.

85. From a cause and effect perspective of the Scientific Revolution there came about a change "from a world of things ordered according to their ideal nature to a world of events running in a steady mechanism of before and after." Bronowski, *Common Sense of Science*. We need to remember, however, it is not that the dynamic of cause and effect is unique to the Scientific Revolution. In a basic sense, everything depends upon some sort of ordering or patterning. What shifted in the Scientific Revolution is that the "hierarchy," or the *natural* order of things, of the Middle Ages, was overthrown in favor of a mechanistic ordering of world *events* in the Scientific Revolution.

86. Brand and Chaplin, *Art and Soul*, 16–24.

87. Runco and Albert, "Creativity Research," 6. Social transformations included the spread of the English language, religious diversity, reduction of serfdom, and growth in medical and judicial professions.

the context for the shift from "ideal natures" to the event-oriented perspective of the Scientific Revolution.[88] The intellectual philosophy of the Enlightenment was expressed through the "intellectual attacks on what was believed to be *unwarranted* authority emanating from a variety of (dogmatic) *nonscientific* sources" (Runco and Albert 2010, 6, italic mine). Interestingly, artists and poets were at the helm of the movement as it unfolded in continental Europe (ibid.).

The Romantic period again saw an "artistic counterthrust to scientific rationalism" (ibid., 10). In response to the Industrialization of Europe, artists emphasized "inner feelings as natural and therefore democratic sources of wisdom and artistic inspiration" (ibid.). This grew into a conflict between science and feeling, which was personified as the contrast between scientist and "genius," or commonly, as the deviance of artists.

The idea of creativity as innovation finds a root in Darwin's idea of adaptation through the process of natural selection.[89] A problem that evolution theory brought was that the process of evolution was believed to happen at random and so adaptations are seen as "fortuitous" and unable to be controlled, except of course by the process of natural selection itself.[90] Assigning divine or mystic origins to creativity was viewed as unscientific. This began to change after F. Galton, who departed from locating creativity with genius, but in the general population and who asserted that creativity was measurable.[91]

According to Mazzola, Park, and Thalmann, in the Middle Ages, Christianity's influence was to relegate "*creatio*" to God's act of "creation from nothing" (2012, 133). They argue, "neither art nor poetry nor any other human creation was perceived as a product of a creative act" (ibid.). Further, Christianity's effect[92] was to revert notions of creativity to those of "Greek

88. Bronowski, *Common Sense*, 1951.

89. Dennett, *Darwin's Dangerous Idea*, 42–43.

90. Dennett, *Darwin's Dangerous Idea*, 248. For details on problem with the Darwinian view, please see Kozbelt et al., "Theories of Creativity," 36–37. The problem with the Darwinian view is that (1) due to the complexity of the creative process, there is little control and therefore difficult to predict; (2) creators are not critical in the judgment process since works are ultimately judged by society; (Csikszentmihalyi, "Society, Culture, and Person"; Sawyer, *Explaining Creativity*); mass production demonstrates optimal productivity (Simonton 1977, 1984, 1988, 1997 in Kozbelt et al., "Theories of Creativity," 36).

91. Runco and Albert, "Creativity Research," 12–13. See also Galton, *English Men of Science*; *Inquiries Into Human Faculty*.

92. Leah Easley speaks to the influence of Platonic philosophy via Augustinian emphases on the concrete and abstract, rather than the tangible and sensible on Christianity, "St. Augustine: Theologian of the Arts."

antiquity," wherein artistic creativity "should imitate nature" in accordance with strict rules that honor God, and where the contribution of the artist was negligible or virtually non-existent. Talent was the result of influence "originating from an outside spirit" (Mazzola *et al*, 134).

It is not enough to demonstrate that creativity is "not primarily unconsciously driven."[93] Here, we affirm that human creativity is derived from participation in God's creativity. There is a history with ontological dimensions. Further, there are significant differences in the ways humans create and the ways in which God creates. In the light of God's creativity, the agency of ICMs for mission takes on immense significance not least because the artist is a mediator of God's creativity. Artists are also the locus for the generative and life-giving spirit of God's creativity to change the world. They extend God's invitation to others in order for them to participate in the bringing about of a heavenly Kingdom on earth (Eph 4:11).

SUMMARIZING SYSTEMS THEORY OF CREATIVITY

Several theories of creativity exist, each emphasizing various aspects.[94] According to Mikhail Csikszentmihalyi's,[95] creativity emerges via the interaction of the domain (the body of knowledge in a given discipline), the individual (who improvises on this existing knowledge), and the field of other experts in the discipline. The approach emphasizes the collaborative process of creativity. It establishes a relational framework for creativity. While it acknowledges sociocultural factors, the qualitative nature makes it more difficult to test hypothesis unambiguously, which is a "necessary risk" (Kozbelt *et al* 2010, 40).[96]

Systems Theory of Creativity takes into account multiple factors operating in a given system and with multiple and interactive variables.[97] Key

---

93. Cox, *Genetic Studies of Genius*, 21. Cox argued that creativity is not primarily unconsciously driven. Cox linked creativity amongst eminent individuals with "ego psychology's growing interest in mastery, confidence, persistence—the basic ego drives." See also Runco and Albert, *Creativity Research*, 15.

94. Kozbelt et al., "Theories of Creativity," 24, have summarized ten key theories of creativity—Developmental, Psychometric, Economic, Stage & Componential Process, Cognitive, Problem Solving and Expertise-Based, Problem Finding, Evolutionary (Darwinian), Typological, and Systems Theories.

95. Csikszentmihalyi, "Society, Culture, and Person."

96. "Most creativity research does not include an explicit definition, which often is due to the conflicting research on the same topic." Plucker and Makel, "Assessment of Creativity," 48.

97. Although psychologists may define creativity exclusively as a mental process, creativity is "as much a cultural and social as it is a psychological event." Csikszentmihalyi, "Creativity." It is not just individuals but social systems making judgments

concepts include Evolving Systems,[98] Network of enterprises,[99] Domain and Field, Gatekeepers, Collaborative Creativity, and Chaos and Creativity.[100] According to Kozbelt et al:

> The evolving systems approach focuses less on understanding the particulars of a specific creative act than on how those particulars fit into the context of an individual creator's goals, knowledge, and reasoning, as well as larger social forces and creative paradigms.

The evolving-systems approach is primarily an account of what creators do . . . .

> Its emphasis is on dynamic, developmental processes that play out in complex ways and contexts, over very different timescales (2010, 39).

The evolving systems approach to creativity lends itself to study the process of musical creativity amongst ICMs in the context of this era of globalization. The context for creativity of ICMs in mission is the new interstitial spaces that they occupy. These spaces are characterized by ontological, epistemological, and axiological diversity. The biggest challenge facing ICMs is the "translatability of the gospel"[101] in the context of the dynamics of transnational, transcultural, and interstitial spaces in this era of globalization.

---

about individual products. Cziksentmihalyi writes that "Any definition of creativity that aspires to objectivity, and therefore requires an intersubjective dimension, will have to recognise the fact that the audience is as important to its constitution as the individual to whom it is credited."

98. According to Kozbelt et al., Gruber (1978) pioneered the evolving systems approach to creativity that focused on the attributes of the creative person, such as ensemble of metaphors, network of enterprises (a system of goals describing concurrent and consecutive working of disparate goals)—but the level of detail involved makes using this theory difficult (1999). Gruber, "Darwin's 'Tree of Nature' and Other Images of Wide Scope."

99. Another concept is "a network of enterprises"—"a system of goals that describes how . . . [the musician] may work on seemingly disparate topics and projects, consecutively or concurrently, and continually evolve a sense of the relations between the topics." Kaufman and Sternberg, *Cambridge Handbook of Creativity*, 39.

100. Csikszentmihalyi, "Creativity," defines a systems theory of creativity by emphasizing the creativity of individuals to domain and field. He discusses the nature of interaction between gatekeepers in the field, knowledge about a domain, and the activity of creative individuals.

101. Hiebert, *Missiological Implications of Epistemological Shifts*, 110.

Thus far we have observed the nature of music as a sociocultural process, a way of being, and a process for the embodiment of knowledge. The concept of theological creativity has helped to further channel our study in terms of a distinct ontological and epistemological framework. Together the concepts of music and creativity as discussed above form one of the building blocks for this study—musical creativity. We recollect that the other two major components for this study are new spaces and creative mission. We are now ready to explore the negotiation of ICM identity through the process of musical creativity in the context of new spaces for creative mission.

The social and cultural dislocation brought about by the reorganization of sociocultural boundaries due to globalization process has created opportunities as well as challenges for mission. A postcolonial context calls for greater agility on the part of ICMs for mission in the wake of neoliberal agendas. As we prepare to explore the new terrain for ICMs in mission, we recollect a biblical scenario. In this scenario, God's people find themselves in a "new space" between indigenous roots and the demands of the other. The crisis that they face in translating their identity in the context of this new space is captured in the Psalmist's phrase: "How shall we sing the Lord's song in a foreign land?" (Ps 137:4). The lament of the Israelites in that day serves to carry us forward in order to explore the spaces of disjuncture and difference amongst ICMs for mission in the present day.

CREATIVITY AND CAPTIVITY: A BIBLICAL SCENARIO

The formation of transcultural creative identities in the course of migration is not new. Psalm 137 voices a lament of the exiled community in Babylon.[102] For the Jews, being "by the rivers of Babylon" signified a loss of identity, a thwarting of God's intended purpose, and a period of emotional upheaval and moral confusion. From this site of transition a fervent and fearful appeal is made to God to wreak destruction on the enemies, the "daughter of Babylon" (Ps 137:7–9).

Three themes emerge from the language of the song from Psalm 137. First, it signals the dilemma of a displaced people. The Israelites are no longer in the "place" of their origin and choosing. Second, they are a dispossessed generation; no longer surrounded by the land, objects, and networks that inform their identity as a people/ nation. Third, the Jewish people in Psalm 137 are a disembedded populace. They are out of their "comfort zone" and cultural context, in a "foreign land." In many ways, they have lost their story. As we shall see, their experience in the context

---

102. Holladay, *Psalms through Three Thousand Years*, 307.

of captivity was to teach them significant lessons in order to fulfill God's creative mission as the people of God.

First, for the Exiled Jews in the Sixth Century BCE, "By the rivers of Babylon" is a place of captivity. The onto-epistemic captivity[103] is evident beneath the rhetoric of lament. "How" indeed were they to sing "the Lord's song" when the locus of their identity as God's people, Zion, was in ruins?[104] Could it be that they had to learn the hard lesson that their identity as a people did not lie in a place, but rather as a people who live by the mercy of God and in obedience to God?[105] In order to be creative in the place of their captivity, the Jews had to transcend spatial and temporal notions that they had previously embraced that defined them as the people of God. Further, we learn that the onto-epistemic captivity as a collective experience for the people of the God of Israel was not a mere accident. We recall the journey of the captives of Judah, from Palestine to Babylon in other parts of Scripture (2 Kgs 24–25; Dan 1). The fact of the matter is that God sent the Babylonians (Hab 1:5–11) for a purpose—that they might know Him.

Second, who is the "we"? For the Israelites in exile, the idea that "non-Israelites may well be a part of the future plans of God in constructing a people again after the exilic crisis"[106] was a lesson that they seemed to have forgotten and which they had to re-learn and re-imagine in a very specific sense. For the Jews, in Psalm 137, learning to "sing" with the other was a foreign idea, let alone doing so on foreign terms and turf; the Babylonian is the "other." We notice that the rhetoric of the psalmist's query in Ps 137:4, "How shall we sing the Lord's song in a foreign land?" exposes a dichotomy in the Israelites' self-understanding in the context of their missional identity as God's witnesses. God's people had to learn that creativity was to emerge in the process of identification along with the other in the

---

103. The problem from a theological perspective: "To what degree and how can finite human language convey knowledge of the transcendent Creator?" Reno, "Theology's Continental Captivity." And for this reason we might refer to it as "epistemological captivity" (Abraham, *Canon and Criterion*). Singing "songs of Zion" had direct implications for their identity as people of Zion, which was in ruins! It was not so much a problem of a lack of human creativity, but a "retreating renunciation of human dignity" and therefore it was an epistemological captivity with ontological dimensions.

104. The symbolic and rhetorical use of the terms, "Zion" and "Babylon," in Ps 137 has served to polarize perceptions of empire or colonial hegemonic influence (Babylon) on one hand and the ultimate hope and destiny of God's people (Zion) on the other hand. Jerusalem and Zion had a deep religious meaning with tangible teleological bearings. Zion referred to the stronghold of Jerusalem, the city of David, the place for the ark of the covenant, the place, forms, and the assemblies of Israel's worship, the name applied to the city of Jerusalem, and the "city of God." Swanson and Nave, *Zion*.

105. See, Hos 1:9,10b; John 4:21–4; 1 Pet 2:10.

106. Smith-Christopher, *Biblical Theology of Exile*, 134.

course of a shared task—not only "How shall we *sing* the Lord's song?" but also "How shall *we* sing the Lord's song?"

Third, for God's people, creativity in the context of captivity meant transcending ideological, circumstantial, and existential boundaries concerned with perceptions of ethnicity and purity. In the context of Psalm 137, creativity with the other meant confronting the inner dilemma of what does [our] "Lord's song" have to do with "them"? In a postsecular context we recollect Barry Taylor's insight of the need for a deep "restructuring" of "temporality, spatiality, corporeality, and authority."[107] Creativity as an activity with the other implied overcoming inherent dichotomies. This meant the willingness to enter into a process of change, which often comes through a blurring of boundaries, a destructuring of sensibilities in order for a restructuring of possibilities with the other.

Fourth, the question of "how shall we sing" *with* the other is a necessary question where often truth is subsumed under logics contrary to the Gospel. If so, what is it going to take as we re-imagine how to sing the Lord's song, along with others who mysteriously may be fellow heirs and partakers of the Gospel in Christ (Eph 3:6)? The construction of unique Yahweh songs that clearly differentiated the identity of the Jews in Psalm 137 from the identity of the other, the Babylonians, was a challenge—learning to "sing" without compromising the truth. After all, were they not the chosen people and did not God tell them to separate themselves? In the light of the "anti-dogmatic prejudice" in current postmodern thought, ICMs are to learn to mediate Christianity with coherence, a sense of justice, and sustainability through their ongoing witness.[108]

Thus far we learn that for the Israelites in Psalm 137 the location of creativity is a place of captivity with the Babylonian other. In this interstitial passage they were to relearn how to mediate their creativity in the context of the unique covenant relationship with the personal God ("the Lord's song") and in alignment with this God's vision and purpose for the nations. The process of creativity invites transcending ethnocentric formulations of identity and reality. Transcending boundaries however needs to take place without compromise on truth. There is a creative tension involved in the process of identification with the other in sociocultural terms. However, the creative tension is also theological.

The problem in Psalm 137 may not be in the details of the song that the Jews are required to sing, which appears somewhat apparent at least for this group of aliens—it is "the Lord's song." However, embodying a distinct

107. Taylor, *Entertainment Theology*, 33–35.
108. Reno, "Theology's Continental Captivity."

liturgy in a hostile context is a challenge. From a missiological perspective, the idea of liturgy enacted "publicly" along with the "other" can be problematic. This is especially so in contexts where liturgies have grown to be dynamically linked to certain behaviors and power structures associated with dominant discourses within Christianity. For example, the thought that "liturgy is essentially captured in movement rather than intellectual ideas"[109] can threaten entrenched approaches to worship for a community with a practice of embodying worship ritual differently or primarily through more "proper" intellectual means.[110] Hostility may be overt, as for instance in the context of discourses antithetical to that of Christianity. Within Christianity, however, hostility is far more subtle and difficult to detect.[111] In either case, however, the following concern arises: the church in a sense has forgotten how to "sing the Lord's song" in the current geophysical (cf. implications of unprecedented global transmigration) and geo-spiritual terrain. Put in the form of a question, does the Western church only know how to "sing the Lord's song" from a posture of the victors?

The following table may be used as a framework for remembering the nature of the challenge faced by the Jews in Psalm 137 as compared with the Missiological Framework for Theological Creativity that we develop later (chapter 4) in order to address parallel issues faced by ICMs in mission:

Broad themes from Psalm 137:4	Missiological Framework for Theological Creativity (MFTC)
Creativity and Epistemology/ Ontology ("How" and "Why")	Creative Being (*creatio Dei*) ("In the beginning God created . . . ") (Gen 1:1)
Creativity and Collaboration ("we")	Creative Community ("let us") (Gen 1:26)
Creativity and Construction ("sing")	Creative Construction ("God created the heavens and the earth") (Gen 1:2)
Creativity and Particularity ("the Lord's song")	Creative Performance (Gen 1:5–7; 2:7; "new song"; Ezek 4, 5)
Creativity and Context ("in a foreign land")	Creative Beauty (doubly "good") (Gen 1:31)

109. Stringer, *Sociological History of Christian Worship*, 16.

110. Stringer, *Sociological History of Christian Worship*, 16. Martin Stringer explores the difference between discourse and worship and draws from Toreville, for whom embodiment of ritual in the perspective related to post Vatican II differs from the practice of ritual pre Vatican II where worship is conceived "primarily by the mind as opposed to the body."

111. Stringer, *Sociological History of Christian Worship*, 16.

SUMMARY

An unstated purpose in this chapter has been to clarify some of the major conceptual perceptions that seem to have qualified music and creativity as "amorphous" and "opaque" and thereby inadequate transponders for the mediation of Christianity. Certainly there is scope for further clarity. In a postcolonial context, however, more than inadequacy or good or bad musical creativity, the overarching concern is one of authenticity. The question of authenticity arises quite naturally with regard to the mediation of truth, the authenticity of the Gospel.

However, the situation is compounded when it comes to the translation of Christianity through the process of musical creativity. In the first part of this chapter we explored the concept of music as a sociocultural process, music and identity, and music as knowledge. In the second part, we developed the concept of "theological creativity" to be further addressed in chapter 4. Creativity is more than innovation or a psychometric evaluation of human potential. The process of musical creativity is a mode of being in relationship with God and others. It is through the embodiment, enactment, and performance of musical creativity in new spaces that ICMs invite others to participate in the mission of God.

As we prepare for the next chapter, we remember that although musical creativity is a way of knowledge, the ways in which the Gospel is translated through musical creativity may or may not always be explicit. The process of musical creativity with others is further problematized in the light of globalizing processes where multiplex meanings are to be realized along with the other. In these spaces, confrontation with foreignness is often the norm rather than the exception. The resultant diversity in these new spaces allows for the irruption of creativity for the "emergence of possibilities."

The ways in which ICMs negotiate their creativity in the context of cultural and religious diversity is a key endeavor as they go about their task of building the church for mission. Like the Israelites in Psalm 137, the negotiation of authenticity in the context of sociocultural dislocation and postcolonial difference is something with which ICMs constantly struggle. In the next chapter we take a closer look at some of the dynamics of the new spaces that form the arena for the enactment of ICM musical creativity for mission.

3

New Spaces

IN THE LAST CHAPTER we saw how, in the context of the biblical narrative, the place "by the waters of Babylon" was a site of encounter between the Jews and the Babylonians. Now, approximately 2500 years later, the 1978 hit song entitled "By the Rivers of Babylon" includes not just the Jews and Babylonians in Psalm 137, but also Rastafarians, West Indian immigrants in Germany, and consumers of popular music across the world.[1] The song "By the Rivers of Babylon," signifies the emergence of new spaces at the intersection of transnational flows of music (musicians and technologies), the neoliberal impulse of transnational musical corporations, and the narrative of Scripture.[2]

---

1. The British Recorded Music Industry, "Certified Awards Search." See Cummings, "Rivers of Babylon." For the ways the Rastafarian religious order have appropriated materials from the Old Testament and in particular, Ps 137, to inform their collective identity, please see Murrell, "Tuning Hebrew Psalms To Reggae Rhythms: Rastas' Revolutionary Lamentations For Social Change." The song "By the Rivers of Babylon" was recorded by a European-based music label that brought together singers of West Indian origin to create a product for the world market. In the late seventies, a European band, Boney M's hit single "By the Rivers of Babylon" was at the top of the charts in the UK. The song was originally composed and recorded by a Jamaican band, The Melodians, in 1970. It almost instantly became an anthem of the Rastafarian movement. In the later release in 1978, the singers were recruited by a European agent from the commercial music industry based in Germany to record and sing a "Disco" song with Zionistic overtones of the Rasta movement. The song hit the top of the charts in the UK (one of its largest selling singles) and subsequently became popular in the US and other parts of the world.

2. According to Hays, "How Shall We Sing?," 52, Psalm 137 is linked to the "actual events of the exile" and not generalized. For the Jews in Ps 137, the place, "By the rivers of Babylon," is a place of captivity. In general, the symbolic and rhetorical use of the terms, "Zion" and "Babylon," in Ps 137 has served to polarize perceptions of empire

In this chapter, therefore, we explore the new spaces at the juncture of transnational music flows, neoliberal capitalistic impulses through the category of World Music, and the creativity of ICMs for mission. Ethnomusicology has shown us that musical identity is formed in culture. In particular, indigenous cosmopolitan musician (ICM) identity emerges in the space "in-between" structures that inform and sustain indigeneity and cosmopolitanism. If this is so, then ICM identity itself is not something that exists prior to the process of musical creativity.[3] Rather, ICM identity as a form of postcolonial discourse is rhetorically "enunciated"[4] and sustained amid the dynamics of these new spaces.[5]

TRANSNATIONAL MUSICAL SPACE

In this section we offer a brief overview of transnational musical space for the emergence of ICM musical creativity in the current era of globalization.

Transnationalism refers to the ways in which migrants in varying "degrees" sustain "active, ongoing interconnections in both the home and host countries and perhaps with communities in other countries as well."[6] The phenomenon of transnational musical identities is pertinent today for a vast majority of musicians whose music and audience are not limited to a local geographical area. The creation of music, as well as the ways in which people listen to or participate in music, is so much more complex due to processes of globalization. According to the "Research Centre for Transnational Art. Identity. Nation" (TrAIN, all punctuation intentional), the reorganization of cultural boundaries has created,

> ... new identities outside and beyond those of the nation state. It is no longer easy to define the nature of the local and the international, and many cultural interactions now operate on the level of the transnational.[7]

---

or colonial hegemonic influence (Babylon) on one hand and the ultimate hope and destiny of God's people (Zion) on the other hand. This is especially true in the case of the Rastafarian movement. See Murrell, "Turning Hebrew Psalms to Reggae Rhythms."

3. Charland, "Constitutive Rhetoric," 213–34. Constitutive rhetorical theory predicts the construction of a collective identity for an addressed audience, the construction of the audience as a subject in history, and demands that subjects act in accordance with their identity as enacted in history.

4. Bhabha, *Location of Culture*.

5. Jameson, *Postmodernism*.

6. Lewellen, *Anthropology of Globalization*, 151.

7. "Transnational Art," Research Centre for Transnational Art. Identity. Nation, http://www.transnational.org.uk/about.

The torrent of popular culture, new age Spiritualties, technological development, and diverse social networks has resulted in a condensation of space and time resulting in an "intensification of interdependencies"[8] paving the way for global interconnectedness at an unprecedented level. Transnationalism, diaspora, pilgrimage routes, mobility, and the multiplicity and multi-directionality (of encounters) provide new spaces for "musical fission and fusion."[9]

Linda Basch et al use the term, "transmigrants," to refer to those who "develop and maintain multiple relationships—familial, economic, social, organizational, religious, and political—that span borders."[10] "Deterritorialization" in this context does not refer to being landless. Rather the concept refers to the process of migration that continues to take place across boundaries of the nation-state, which are "deterritorialized" (ibid., 9). Diasporic relational networks form the conceptual base for the emergence and sustenance of new spaces, rather than geo-political boundaries.[11] Basch et al go on to explain:

> In contrast to the past, when nation-states were defined in terms of a people sharing a common culture within a bounded territory, this new conception of nation-state includes as citizens those who live physically dispersed within the boundaries of many other states, but who remain socially, politically, culturally, and often economically part of the nation-state of their ancestors.[12]

Transmigrant musical spaces are ripe for the emergence of hybrid identities that thrive in the interstices between nation, religion, ethnicity, and class. The processes of musical creativity in these spaces reflect the nature of global complexity—diverse, multiple, polycentric, asymmetrical (transecting existing power structures), and asynchronous (multiple and diverse spatial/temporal experiences) relationships between processes of production, representation, and consumption. Transmigrant identity is often characterized by disrupture, transitoriness, "networks, activities, patterns of living, and ideologies that span"[13] places of origin and settlement. One such identity is indigenous cosmopolitanism. As we will learn through the experience of ICMs, the process of musical creativity is "the very terrain on which globalization

---

8. See Siapera, *Cultural Diversity and Global Media*, 25.

9. Stokes, "On Musical Cosmopolitanism," 4.

10. Basch et al., *Nations Unbound*, 3–4.

11. Lewellen, *Anthropology of Globalization*, 151. See also Levitt, "God Needs No Passport."

12. Basch et al., *Nation Unbound*, 3–4.

13. Basch et al., *Nation Unbound*, 3–4.

is articulated."[14] Before we discuss the making of indigenous cosmopolitan musical identity we take a look at some of the dynamics of cosmopolitanism in the larger phenomenon of globalization as it pertains to the negotiation of musical creativity amongst ICMs for mission.

COSMOPOLITAN CONSCIOUSNESS

The concept of globalization refers to the overarching condensation of space and time accompanied by escalated interdependencies and marked by a deepening "consciousness of the world as a whole."[15] Globalization signifies openness to cultures other than one's own, the world market, and neoliberal impulses in transnational space.[16] Within the larger context of globalizing processes, cosmopolitanism refers to social agency that is marked by awareness of and response to global consciousness.[17] Cosmopolitanism envisions a moral obligation of humans to others who are "beyond their immediate communal spheres."[18] Cosmopolitanism imagines an ethic of analysis of the various forms of interdependence between participants in relational networks.[19]

Cosmopolitanism is further characterized by multidimensional modes of being, multiple loyalties, and transnational lifestyles.[20] It is a cumulative

---

14. White, *Music and Globalization*, 1.

15. Robertson, "Globalisation as a Problem," 87.

16. Robertson, "Globalisation as a Problem," 88. Also Beck, "Cosmopolitical Realism," 132–35.

17. Brown and Held, *Cosmopolitan Reader*, 4. According to Brown and Held, Diogenes of Sinope (400–323 BC) claimed that he was a "citizen of the world" in response to questions regarding his place of origin. Diogenes was referring to the moral interconnectedness amongst all universal citizens ("*kosmopolites*") "and that as a member of the *cosmos* he could not be defined merely by his city-state affiliation.

18. Brown and Held, *Cosmopolitan* Reader, 6. An awareness of accountability to the larger community as moral instinct is evident from early monotheistic thinking from the Egyptian Anhnaton (1526 BC) to Cicero in *De Republica*, the Stoics, the Judeo-Christian thought of Augustine (354–430), Aquinas (1225–74), and Luther (1483–1546), and even among other Neo-thomistic thinkers, Las Casas (1484–1566). Further, in Acts 28:1–10 we observe "strong support for cosmopolitans (Paul, Luke, the Maltans themselves who spoke Punic but were ruled by Rome) offering hospitality (Greek: philanthropy) for those beyond their immediate communal spheres (residents and ship-wrecked sailors) and receiving in exchange healing and encouragement." In this case there is no account of Paul "preaching the gospel" in the conventional sense (Rynkiewich, email correspondence February 2014).

19. Beck, "Cosmopolitical Realism," 132–35.

20. Beck, "Cosmopolitical Realism," 136.

process of social transformation,[21] marked by mobility,[22] new learning competencies, and new geographies.

Cosmopolitanism is engendered by and further contributes to the polycentric emergence of new modernities,[23] multiple and intersected relational networks, and "interconnected nodes."[24] According to Manuel Castells, a network is a series of interconnected nodes, points in a network, whose topology is defined in terms of the "distance"—frequency and intensity of interaction—between nodes. Such nodes are able to expand without limit if they are able to maintain communication (share network communication codes). The "nodes" signify the experiences that contribute to the emergence of identity in the context of relational networks. Existence amid "interconnected nodes" is characterized by decentralization, flexibility, deconstruction, reconstruction, and "multiplicity of interconnected tasks."[25] Therefore, cosmopolitanism has served as a way for some to distance or separate from a "nationally defined discourse."[26] In the cosmopolitan nodal network, identity evolves amidst "spaces of flows" (interchanges between nodes) and "timeless time" ("continuous, always on, undifferentiated time"), which are the new organizing principles.[27]

Cosmopolitanism offers a way in which to theorize musical creative agency of ICMs for mission amid the complexity of globalization. Below, Fredric Jameson's (1991) development of the concept of postmodernity in the context of late capitalism helps to clarify some dynamics of global and cosmopolitan consciousness for the emergence of new musical identities. Further, Homi K. Bhabha's (1994) postcolonial rhetoric serves to extend the cosmopolitan "ethic of analysis" for a deeper understanding of the forces that shape transnational music space in the context of the creative mission of ICMs.

---

21. Hopper, *Understanding Cultural Globalization*, 178; Papastergiadis, *Cosmopolitanism and Culture*, 137.

22. Rantanen, "Transnational Cosmopolitan," *Global Media and Communication*, 25. See also Hopper, *Cultural Globalization*, 172 ("connected cosmopolitans").

23. Burkhalter, *Local Music Scenes and Globalization*, 13.

24. Castells, *Rise of the Network Society*, 184; 501–2.

25. Castells, *Rise of the Network Society*, 501–2.

26. Weber, "Cosmopolitan, National, And Regional Identities in Eighteenth-Century European Musical Life," 210.

27. Castells, *Communication Power*, 33–36. A question therefore is raised as to who/or what is contributing to the nature of such "organizing *principles*."

"Postmodern Hyperspace"

Modernity is characterized by a search for authenticity, "fixity,"[28] and a Westernized historiography in terms of past, present, and future.[29] In contrast, "postmodern hyperspace" is differentiated by pastiche, fragmentation, and waning of historical consciousness defined primarily in terms of sequential markers.

Postmodernity is further qualified by immediacy, rootlessness, and decentering of objectivity (values). The sense of disorientation is sustained in a "perpetual present" (Jameson 1991, 79) that seems unencumbered by the past or future. The concept of postmodernism offers a new "cognitive map" for human existence; it engenders new forms of resistance to the essentializing tendencies of modernity.[30] In postmodern hyperspace, transnational musical identities therefore represent not merely global interconnectedness but also a new more complex consciousness than that which characterized previous eras of globalization. The new consciousness, for some, embraces the "intensification of interdependencies" for the proliferation of diverse and multiple hybrid identities and self-fashioned ethics.[31] The cognitive remapping of Jameson's postmodernism is further elaborated upon by Homi K. Bhabha's articulation of the postcolonial atmosphere that characterizes the new spaces that ICMs occupy for mission.

Postcolonial Hybridity

The new spaces that ICMs occupy are spaces for the emergence of hybrid identities. These hybrid identities challenge and displace the binaries of West/non-West that are a legacy of colonialism. Hybrid identities emerge "in-between" the "interstitial passage between fixed identifications . . . that entertains difference without an assumed or imposed hierarchy."[32] To illustrate, indigenous cosmopolitan identity as a hybrid construct emerges as a conscious choice to construct difference in response to fixed notions/concepts of identity such as indigeneity, national, caste, ethnic, and class specifications. In these interstitial spaces, experiences of "nationness," community, and "cultural value" are constantly "negotiated."[33]

28. The term reflects the overlap between discourses of postmodernism and postcolonialism. "Fixity" refers to the crystallization of colonial structures that cause a "fixity and fetishism of identities." Bhabha, *Location of Culture*, loc. 647.
29. Jameson, *Postmodernism*.
30. Jameson, *Postmodernism*, 51, 309.
31. Nealon, *Post-Postmodernism*, 23.
32. Bhabha, *Location of Culture*, loc. 517.
33. Bhabha, *Location of Culture*, 464.

Jacques Derrida's concepts of iterability, performativity, the decentering of patterns of construction, and *différance*, are unmistakable in Bhabha's thought.[34] However, Bhabha's rhetoric amplifies the reality of the present in sites of hybrid emergence by taking account of injustices brought on by that which is "unhomely": a recognition of the invasive factors that force the emergence of boundaries that "presence" new realities (binaries) that must constantly be negotiated. The unhomely therefore represents ongoing disjuncture, boundary-crossing patterns of thought and behavior, and negotiation of identities.[35]

Bhabha uses the term "beyond" to signify that the "post" in postmodernity and postcolonial do not refer to markers of time in terms of sequentiality (before or after). Rather, "beyond" refers to the "restless and revisionary energy" that characterizes efforts of transformation of the "present into an expanded and ex-centric site of experience and empowerment."[36] For ICMs in mission, the sense of "beyond" is especially relevant in the message of hope and the "new song" that signals a site of experience and empowerment in the context of the Gospel and its emphasis on liberty from captivity.

The concept of hybridity and the ethic of "beyond" characterize the new spaces with an "ambivalence" that resists "holistic forms of social explanation."[37] Ambivalence creates opportunities for entering into the experience of the other and for the emergence of new histories, which often emerge through conflict. Ambivalence locates the power to change in the very making of hybrid identity. As we will see, the creation of fusion music is never an unconditional reaction to colonialism, but a conditioned response. Further, ambivalence promotes the negotiation of cultural difference. It threatens forms of knowledge that are universally applicable or self-evident and do not create space for rhetoric and dialectic.[38] The ambivalence of ICM musical creativity therefore creates space for "subversion, questioning, and rejection of representations."[39]

Ambivalence, however, does not mean the lack of structure or meaningful histories. Amid postcolonial flows in new spaces, the emergence of

---

34. Derrida, "Signature Event Context," 1475–90. See also Derrida, *Margins of Philosophy*.

35. Bhabha, *Location of Culture*, 643.

36. Bhabha, *Location of Culture*, 538. Bhabha draws from Martin Heidegger, according to whom, a boundary does not so much stop a thing but is the place from which "something begins its presencing." Heidegger, "Building, Dwelling, Thinking," 1523.

37. Bhabha, *Location of Culture*, loc. 4402.

38. Bhabha, *Location of Culture*, loc. 4400.

39. Siapera, *Cultural Diversity and Global Media*, 127.

ICM identity is never a random irruption. In postcolonial interstitial passages ambivalence, beyond-ness, and hybridity are all liberalizing strategies. The ethos of hope conveyed through these postcolonial postures may be understood in terms of a "cosmopolitan imaginary."

The Cosmopolitan Imaginary

On the subject of art and cosmopolitanism, Nikos Papastergiadis writes that in the current era artists aspire to "stage an open conversation between the local and the global."[40] Such "openness" is evident in the "range of locally grounded and globally oriented artistic tendencies—denationalization, reflexive hospitality, cultural translation, discursivity and the global public sphere" (ibid.). These are a result of a "cosmopolitan imaginary" that arises from encounter with the other resulting in a "shared consciousness" on matters of a global scale and fostering fresh approaches to cultural engagement and knowledge creation.[41]

The cosmopolitan musical imaginary is shaped by the neoliberal impulses of transnational musical corporations. The concept of musical cosmopolitanism refers to the mobility of sounds, performers, technology, capital, and knowledge between local and global locales.[42] However, these movements could "reinscribe" versions of modernity and neoliberal hegemony.[43] ICMs hold potential to alter processes of neoliberal hegemony through their musical creativity. Some possible postures ICMs may adopt for negotiating spatial flows in the world of music are summarized below.

Imaginaries, Public Spaces, and Intimacies

According to Byron Dueck (2011), a social imaginary emerges when people who may not know each other begin to affiliate with one another through a shared task or sensibility.[44] In the process, such persons begin to "engage"

   40. Papastergiadis, *Cosmopolitanism and Culture*, 9, italic mine. Although Papastergiadis does not refer to Umberto Eco in this particular reference, the word "open" to me signifies a poststructural stance evident in Eco's emphasis on multiplicity, plurality, and polysemy in art, and the emphasis on the role of the reader, on literary interpretation and response as an "interactive process between reader and text." Robey, "Introduction," viii.

   41. Robey, "Introduction," 9–11.

   42. According to Martin Stokes, popular consensus refers to the general mobility, global soundscapes, and hybridities; critical consensus refers to the processes of exploitation by large multinationals of regional musicians/music and the growth of the metropolitan market. Stokes, "On Musical Cosmopolitanism."

   43. Stokes, "Music and the Global Order," 57.

   44. Dueck, "Part 1 Introduction," 21–27.

with performances and publications and assume certain "roles in relation to these 'texts'" and thereby begin to participate in varying degrees in the process of musical creativity and invite others to share in the same[45]

One form is the "boundary-crossing imaginaries" that includes those who embody and express their music in such a way that the music they produce appears to identify more closely with cultures and identities of others rather than their own national identity and culture.[46]

"Public spaces" are venues that are open to all to participate, but these spaces do not really mean that those who gather in these spaces are totally unrelated. Rather, public spaces are often venues for the gathering of those who identify with certain histories. These spaces provide an opportunity to collectively respond to certain issues in society. More than audiences affected by broadcast technology, participants in public spaces are distinguished by the reality of "reciprocal, real-time interaction," "strategic and inventive repurposing," and could be subject to experiences of an immediate and "confrontational character."[47]

In addition to boundary-crossing imaginaries and public spaces, Toynbee and Dueck (2011) refer to another form of musical agency in the context of global migration—intimacies. Musical creativity in transnational musical space is characterized by encounter with otherness. While acknowledging encounter with otherness, the concept of "intimacies" refers to social interactions between "intimates—kin, friends and fellow musicians and dancers"; these "emotional proximities" play a significant role in the intersubjective formation of participants in a variety of venues.[48]

Musical cosmopolitanism could take a variety of forms of which we have noted three. It follows that musical cosmopolitanism may be characterized as a "cumulative process" of becoming and a "gathering of cultural influences, allegiances and experiences" rather than static "either/or condition."[49] The challenge: what happens when the non-negotiability of cosmopolitanism—the iterability, mobility, and cumulative histories in the construction of identity with others—confronts the singular truth of the Gospel and the need for its radical translation amid increasing diversity and postcolonial flows in the new spaces ICMs occupy for mission? The result is the emergence of a hybridity that is at once boundary crossing (even boundary dependent), radically public, and conspicuously intimate

---

45. Dueck, "Part 1 Introduction," 22.
46. Dueck, "Part 1 Introduction," 23.
47. Dueck, "Part 1 Introduction," 24.
48. Dueck, "Part 1 Introduction," 24–25.
49. Hopper, *Understanding Cultural Globalization*, 178.

with the ways of the other. We shift focus to the emergence of indigenous cosmopolitan identity.

INDIGENOUS COSMOPOLITANISM

According to Maximilian C. Forte, an indigenous cosmopolitan is someone who has not rejected indigeneity. Instead, he or she is "reengaged with wider fields, finding newer ways of being established and projected and acquiring new representational facets."[50] Forte raises four questions that address the dichotomy between the "rooted indigene" versus the "transcendent globetrotting cosmopolitan":

> What happens to indigenous culture and identity when being in the "original place" is no longer possible or even necessary? Does displacement, moving beyond one's original place, mean that indigeneity (being indigenous) vanishes or is diminished? How is being and becoming indigenous, experienced and practiced along translocal pathways? How are new philosophies and politics of indigenous identification (indigenism) constructed in new, translocal settings?[51]

The concept of indigenous cosmopolitan is characterized by an "ethical framework" (Hopper 2007, 170) that locates persons in relation with others "beyond" traditional markers of cultural identity, such as national identity. Indigenous cosmopolitan identity is shaped in the interstitial passages that signify the "beyond," a place of hope, for "historical and cultural re-visioning" (Bhabha 1994, 269). In this sense, indigenous cosmopolitans operate as ambassadors of an ethos that interrogates the boundaries created or held in place by traditional identity markers.

In a transnational economy national identity as a primary source of identification may no longer be sustainable.[52] We maintain that national identity offers a point of departure (and return) for the theoretical construct of indigenous cosmopolitan identity. The multiplicity of networks and interconnectedness of cosmopolitans makes possible simultaneous anchoring of identity in both indigenous as well as cosmopolitan networks. The concept of "rhizomic becoming" offers a way to envision the phenomenon of ICM identity.

---

50. Forte, *Indigenous Cosmopolitans*, 2–3.
51. Forte, *Indigenous Cosmopolitans*, 2.
52. Forte, *Indigenous Cosmopolitans*, 1–3.

INDIGENOUS COSMOPOLITANISM AND RHIZOMIC BEING

The rhizomic metaphor conceptualizes reproductive growth and spread as lateral, sideways, unfolding rather than downward movement.[53] The lack of single root from which all expressions have their source offers a rich visual for the conceptualizing of the rhizomic spread of indigenous cosmopolitan identity. The notion of roots as downward movement that signifies depth and quality of being may be lost in a metaphor that emphasizes lateral rather than downward growth. Lita Crociani-Winland, however, uses the phrase rhizomic "becoming" to signify "deep transformations that affect the very nature of things by reaching to its virtual roots."[54] The rhizomic nature of becoming is helpful to understand the formation of ICM identity for which mobility and fluidity do not necessarily entail rootlessness or the lack of meaningful relationships and experiences in specific geographical locales.

Craig Proulx employs the concept of "rooted cosmopolitans" to signify multiple allegiances amongst aboriginal Hip Hoppers in a North American First Nations context. He discovers that being cosmopolitan does not necessarily signify a detachment from locality or roots.[55] Cosmopolitanism is not restricted to transnationals who "experience separation between homeland and the place where they live"; "roots change" (ibid., 42). The transformative process of rhizomic "roots" is evident in the range of fusion or hybrid music. Dick Hebdige studies the interaction of culture, identity, and Caribbean music, rather than trace the "roots" of popular Caribbean music to their so-called source. He attempts to demonstrate that

> ... the roots themselves are in a state of constant flux and change. The roots don't stay in one place. They change shape. They change color. And they grow. There is no such thing as a pure point of origin, least of all in something as slippery as music, but that does not mean that there isn't a history.[56]

Indigenous Cosmopolitanism, therefore, refers to the creative reconfiguration of "roots and routes."[57] It is creating new histories. For instance,

---

53. A rhizome is defined as: "A horizontal underground stem which can send out both shoots and roots." "A horizontal plant stem with shoots above and roots below serving as a reproductive structure. A type of storage organ in plants which situates itself in a horizontal fashion underground," *Biology Online*, http://www.biology-online.org/dictionary/Rhizome.

54. Crociani-Windland, *Festivals, Affect, and Identity*, 84–85.

55. Proulx, "Aboriginal Hip Hoppers," 41.

56. Hebdige, *Cut 'n' Mix*, xi. Also in Proulx, "Aboriginal Hip Hoppers," 42.

57. Diaspora relational networks foster "community consciousness and solidarity that maintain identity outside the national time and space in order to live inside, with a

Dick Hebdige refers to the process of "versioning," where several hundred versions of a single song may exist.[58]

We conclude that indigenism is not a homogeneous phenomenon. In fact, it has been proven that indigenous peoples were never "isolates."[59] Indigenous peoples crossed borders and lived capaciously amongst other indigenous peoples as demonstrated by Proulx in his work with Aboriginal Hip Hoppers in a First Nations group.[60] Proulx discovered that Aboriginal Hip Hoppers refused to be essentialized in terms of an identity that was restricted to the reserve, but sought to be identified with the international community and globalizing processes.

"Rooted cosmopolitanism theory," therefore, enables exploration of the creativity of ICMs without subscribing wholly to homogenizing and non-indigenous "judgments based on cultural appropriation, invention of tradition, and authenticity discourses" (Proulx 2010, 43). At the same time, rooted cosmopolitan theory allows for ICM identity to be formed in process, between indigeneity and cosmopolitanism, where every individual narrative/history is significant and that contributes to the emergence of a new shared metanarrative.

MUSICAL CREATIVITY, NEOLIBERALISM, AND MISSION

The mission of ICMs in new spaces is affected in no small way by the neoliberal impulses of transnational musical corporations.[61] In this section we will explore the nature of the neoliberal impulse through World Music.

In the West, World Music was a marketing category created by industry professionals in 1987 to commodify ethnic sounds of the "rest" in relation to the West.[62] John Connell and Chris Gibson recollect the words of Ian Anderson of Rogue Records who was present at the meeting when such a genre was decided upon:

> The logic set out . . . was that an established, unified generic name would give retailers a place where they could confidently

---

difference." Clifford, *Routes*, 251.

58. Hebdige, *Cut 'n' Mix*, xiii. "Versioning" is the foundation for all Reggae and Afro-American and Caribbean music.

59. Headland and Reid, "Hunter-Gatherers and Their Neighbors," 43–66.

60. Proulx, "Aboriginal Hip Hoppers," 43.

61. Romanow, "But . . . Can the Subaltern Sing?" demonstrates how neoliberal processes of musical imperialism from the West silences the voice of the non-Western world in the area of Rock music.

62. See Bohlmann, *World Music*; Connell and Gibson, *Sound Tracks*, 349. Also, Born and Hesmondhalgh, *Western Music and Its Others*.

rack otherwise unstockable releases, and where customers might both search out items they'd heard on the radio (not knowing how to spell a mis-pronounced or mis-remembered name or title) and browse through a wider catalogue. Various titles were discussed including 'Worldbeat' (left out anything without drums), 'Tropical' (bye bye Bulgarians), 'Ethnic' (boring and academic), 'International Pop' . . . and 'roots' . . . . 'World Music' seemed to include the most and omit the least . . . Nobody thought of defining it or pretending there was such a beast: it was just to be a box, like jazz, or classical or rock.[63]

As a construct of modernity, the "logic" of World Music signified a particular interpretation of the world that grew out of the Age of Discovery, the Enlightenment, colonialism, and the emergence of the nation-state.[64] It was an interpretation with a distinct neoliberal impulse: encounter with the other as opportunity to commodify for consumption and profit.[65] The reconceptualization of "cultural imperialism" by the West and its power differentials through the genre of World Music cannot be ignored.[66]

To illustrate, Nitin Sawhney, musician and performer brought up in the UK and with family roots in India, questions "allegiances to prior ethnic nationalisms and new identities."[67] Sawhney recently received an award in the "culture crossing" category of Radio 3 World Music awards. Yet, he dislikes the term. According to him, "'World Music' is a crazy term; it's another way to marginalise and generalise music from other cultures that people don't want to give an equal platform to . . . . If it's a fair term, why isn't all music called 'world music'"?[68] The resistance to being labeled in terms that signify dominant and hegemonic culture is evident in Sawhney's rhetoric.

Sawhney also dislikes the term "fusion"—it "'presupposes that music exists in separate, independent strands, whereas I think music is part of

63. Connell and Gibson, *Sound Tracks*, 350.

64. Bohlman, *World Music*, Preface.

65. Bohlman goes so far as to suggest, "asserting that there is music everywhere in the world is . . . a concept that results from Western encounters with the world" (*World Music*, Preface). Further, Bohlman cites the significance of "encounter" as a site for transformation, revolution, and "conditions for exchange." He reasons that "Cultural encounter itself is by no means Western; nonetheless, the growing sense in the past 500 years that encounter is not isolated but rather has ramifications for world history is" (Bohlman, *World Music*, Preface).

66. Bayazitova, "Cultural Integration," 102–12. Bayazitova uses Drane *et al* (2001) to assert the "Americanization" of "cultural globalization" (106).

67. Connell and Gibson, *Sound Tracks*, 356.

68. Jaggi, "No Barriers" (italic mine).

something bigger" (ibid.). Sawhney's musical releases, *Beyond Skin* (2005), *Human* (2003) and *Migration* (1995) are linked to his experience of being persecuted growing up as a South Asian in his school years. But such experiences made Sawhney "more aware of holding on to my identity and not allowing others to swamp me with their preconceptions" (ibid.). Sawhney resists his identity being essentialized in terms of the rhetoric of the dominant ideology of World Music. The ideology is evident in the term World Music itself as that which is coined in the West, by the West, and is meant to serve as an overarching category that houses the existence of all other forms of music.

The hegemony of World Music, however, is evident in the reality that the other is to meet the need of the Western market if they are to benefit from the market of transnational music conglomerates. In other words, the creative relevance of the other is derived from the extent to which they are authentically "indigenous" in the eyes of the gatekeepers in the West—transnational music corporations. The category of World Music for many represents systemic and colonial hegemony of the West, the sustenance of "orientalism" in terms of the "fantasy of western imagination."[69]

A question is raised as to how ICMs negotiate their identity in the context of the dynamics of neoliberal ideology and hegemony. According to Michael A. Rynkiewich (2011) a postcolonial hermeneutic involves more than simply evaluating the exploitation of land and resources, the body and its commodification; it has to do with "the colonization of the mind."[70] The enactment of ICM musical creativity for mission therefore has to do with the liberation of the "captive mind."[71]

---

69. Stokes, "On Musical Cosmopolitanism." On the other hand it is recognized that World Music does provide artists from the non-Western world to market and advertise their products for commercial gain.

70. Rynkiewich, *Soul, Self, and Society*, 191. See also, Ngungi wa Thiong'o, *Decolonizing the Mind*. Also, for the distinguishing between ideology and hegemony in a postcolonial context, see Comaroff and Comaroff, *Of Revelation and Revolution*, vols. 1 and 2.

71. Alatas, "Captive Mind," 83–98. A "captive mind" could have various connotations depending on the context. For us it is enough to cite the need for further research in the meaning of this phrase in various postcolonial contexts. Alatas expands upon what "captive mind" could refer to in the Asian context, which overlaps with the approach for this study. According to him a captive mind is "the product of higher institutions of learning, either at home or abroad, whose way of thinking is dominated by Western thought in an imitative and uncritical manner." Further a captive mind is "uncreative." It is judged as "incapable" of making original analytical diagnoses of issues, of adapting "the universally valid corpus of scientific knowledge to the particular local situation." The captive mind is "fragmented in outlook," "alienated" from the crucial issues that concern a given social context. It is "alienated" from "its own national

MUSICAL CREATIVITY AND NEW ANTHROPOLOGY

Thus far we have observed that the new spaces for the enactment of ICM creativity is characterized by global interconnectedness, interdependency, multidimensional identities, polycentricities, multitextualities, and multiple networks. These dynamics form the complex framework for the emergence of a "new anthropology" that is sustained in the context of diasporic and transnational relational networks.[72]

In Migrating Music (2011) Jason Toynbee and Byron Dueck highlight the "interlinked objects" in the context of the global flow of music—first, migrant musicians, second, traveling instruments and characteristics that often precede the travel of the musicians themselves, and third, the mediation processes of circulation and distribution.[73] Citing a case of "African elements" being "preserved" in African-American practices, the authors posit that all this makes it possible for musicians to identify and connect with musicians in distant contexts.[74] But a collective reconstruction of a "shared history"[75] is seldom without conflict. Questions of authenticity emerge concerning which "elements" are to be considered "African," by whom, and under what circumstances.

DIVERSITY AND DIFFERENCE IN MUSICAL COSMOPOLITANISM

In "(Re) thinking Cultural Diversity and the Media," Eugenia Siapera (2010) defines cultural diversity as "the existence of groups with their own unique, culturally (as opposed to biologically) derived characteristics" that "share some commonalities of origins, histories, and traditions, and systems of beliefs and practices."[76] However, cultural diversity is to be distinguished from cultural difference. The concept of cultural diversity too often serves as merely a broad recognition of variances in culture from

---

tradition, if it exists, in the field of its intellectual pursuit," "unconscious of its own captivity" and the factors influencing such conditioning. Further, it is "not amenable to an adequate quantitative analysis but it can be studied by empirical observation," and last, but not least, "It is a result of the Western dominance over the rest of the world" (83).

72. Mintz, "Localization of Anthropological Practice," 117.

73. Toynbee and Dueck, *Migrating Musics*, 1–2.

74. Toynbee and Dueck, *Migrating Musics*, 3.

75. Toynbee and Dueck, *Migrating Musics*, 3. A new anthropology refers to the "interconnected social experience" and processes by which "immigrants forge and sustain multi-stranded social relations that link together societies or origin and settlement" (Basch et al., *Nations Unbound*, 8).

76. Siapera, *Cultural Diversity and Global Media*, 12.

the vantage point of a predetermined or preexistent knowledge. Therefore, cultural difference plays an extremely significant dimension within popular notions of cultural diversity.[77]

Cultural difference occurs in the meeting place of one or more cultures. In such a place, difference is articulated *via* discursive disclosure. It is often accompanied by conflict and contestation. From a postcolonial perspective, therefore, cultural difference is a necessary step in the larger process of reconciliation through mutual identification with cultures of the other in a given context. Homi Bhabha puts it appropriately when he writes of cultural diversity as an "epistemological object" wherein culture is an "object of empirical knowledge" (1994, Kindle location 1222). Cultural difference, however, is "the process of the enunciation of culture as 'knowledgable,' authorative" and appropriate for the "construction of systems of cultural identification" (ibid.).

In the new spaces for mission, it is not enough to study musical diversity in the current era as simply (or directly) a result of Western colonial encounter or neoliberal expansion through genres such as World Music. ICMs need to constantly learn to differentiate themselves especially in the context of the flattening impulse of World Music. The following episode by Ruth Finnegan illustrates the nature of the issue at hand.

In "What migrates and who does it?" (2011), Finnegan surveys the musical history of Fiji. She finds that Western paradigms of modernity and globalization are limited in understanding the nuances of musical histories elsewhere. According to Finnegan, contact existed between Fiji and the West, but also with several other neighboring nations and cultures. She goes on to explain:

> Fiji's changing and continuing musics [cannot] be shoveled into universal global epochs, whether in terms of British colonial experience, of economic structures, or of technological waves pushing all before them. The media did indeed have their importance, but their interactions played out in more complex

---

77. Appingnanesi, "Introduction: 'Whose Culture,'" writes: "The notion of cultural diversity in its current administrative form does not rightly acknowledge that culture within itself is already an assemblage of differences, diverse tendencies and unresolved tensions, but is instead focused primarily on the strains of separation between cultures. I should emphasise that in this view of cultural diversity the strains of disquieting difference come from the 'ethnic minority' cultures, those unsettled and problematic guests in the midst of the host mainstream culture. Mainstream, of course, meaning Western, European and pre- dominantly white; and mainstream also implicitly presuming itself wholly unified and homogeneous. Diversity from this viewpoint is disruptive, an upset of status quo normality, which must somehow be governed so that the mainstream culture can function undisturbed by any threat of 'difference' from the inside."

ways than allowed in the *West-oriented vision of a foreordained upward curve of oral to literate to electronic or*—in alternative but overlapping metaphor—*of tradition to modernity* (italic mine).[78]

The places ICMs occupy in the global arena are places for the emergence of new identities (and the revitalization of old ones) by forging new alliances within and amongst specific cultures/histories. The ways in which ICMs mediate cultural difference that is unique to the Gospel across varieties of cultural diversity is the subject of our exploration in chapters 5–7.

Who Is the "We"? Reconfiguring Cultural Space

A primary problem with conceptualizing difference in the past has been defining otherness in terms of the "we." The "other" need not be far away to be "other." We are not dealing merely with people who are different but actually different societies, different cultures and the relation between "here" and "there."[79]

Recalling our problem from Ps 137:4 of "How shall we sing the Lord's song in a foreign land?" the question is who is this "we"? Whether we answer the question from the perspective of the Jews or the Babylonians, the fact of the matter is that one's own identity is brought into question in the course of discerning the identity of the other and the collective identity of the group in question. This may be a first step in the conceptualization of difference along with the other. The willingness to identify with the other—to see oneself as part of the other—is an important step in the context of the creative mission of ICMs in the new spaces that they occupy.

In order to illustrate, Akhil Gupta and James Ferguson recognize that the problem for "displaced Third World scholars" is indeed that the "identity of 'one's own society' is an open question" (1992, 14). Further, it is not the stark or seemingly obvious difference that is the problem; it is the recognition of the "uncanny" "sameness"[80] of the other that is the deeper issue.

---

78. Finnegan, "What Migrates and Who Does It?," 146, italic mine.

79. Gupta and Ferguson, "Beyond 'Culture,'" 14. Place may be construed as a measure between spaces; we can occupy a certain space, but how we negotiate our place either invites or excludes.

80. According to Bhabha, "Cultural difference becomes a problem not when you can point to the Hottentot Venus, or to the punk whose hair is six feet up in the air; it does not have that kind of fixable visibility. It is as the strangeness of the familiar that it becomes more problematic, both politically and conceptually . . . when the problem of cultural difference is ourselves-as-others, others-as-ourselves, that borderline" (Bhabha, *Location of Culture*, 72 in Gupta and Ferguson, "Beyond 'Culture,'" 19, underline mine; see also Bhabha, *Location of Culture*, loc. 1658, for whom the uncanny is the space and time differential between "incommensurable differences").

The epistemological nature of the question of "how shall we sing the Lord's song?" may be seen as a first step to the deeper issue, which may be perceived as being more ontological in nature—the reconciliation of peoples in the scope of the mission of God.

A second step in the conceptualization of difference along with the other may lie in the recognition of the reality that "power is never only a symbolic relation" (Toynbee 2011, 73). It is not something that one can walk away from; one may, but only to return to the same persistent parabolic dilemma each day. Such was the dilemma of the Jews in Psalm 137. It is a lived experience. In other words, the articulation of difference begins with the discernment of collective identity. The question of who is the "we" creates a "third space" for the articulation of cultural difference in terms of collective identity.

A third factor in the articulation of cultural difference is that it is a process of abstraction and appropriation. What this means is that participants need to acknowledge the reality that material and structural dimensions exist prior to "musical mimesis." As an illustration, rappers in Iran identified with the "imaginary space of the 'ghetto'" as signified in "archetypal US rap" (Toynbee 2011, 74). Here is a case of reconceptualization *via* abstraction and appropriation. In other words, the original space is abstracted and then translated into a culturally relevant form. ICMs by virtue of their mobility and multiple "roots" hold potential to continually abstract and reappropriate spatial venues. In the process of abstraction-reappropriation, ICMs invite others to participate in creative mission.

Musical Authenticity and Cosmopolitan Indigeneity

A problem with regard to global processes is that there are aspects of culture that appear as "something unique and worthy of preservation" (Hopper 2007, 182). Further, the cultural enmeshment of varieties of personal histories, musical styles, and genres across glocal networks renders descriptions of "authentic" in such a context difficult to define.[81] World Music genres were affirmed as producers of authentic and local music.[82] In other words, despite its ideological expression, World Music afforded others an avenue to showcase talent and distribute their creativity for economic benefit. In the process, locality is constructed, enacted, and rhetorically defended with an eye and ear on [specific] others near and far.[83]

---

81. Connell and Gibson, "World Music," 356.
82. Stokes, "Music and the Global Order," 59.
83. Stokes, "Music and the Global Order," 50.

However, authenticity as exemplified in the genre of World Music may not be the same as authenticity in the light of indigenous or aboriginal creativity. Marcia Langton draws attention to two fields of Aboriginal knowledge that are

> [E]xemplified in the historical process of making Aboriginal designs available to non-Aboriginal people: the inner and the outer, the inside and the outside, the secret-sacred and the non-secret-sacred, although these are not entirely absolute and distinct.[84]

Langton demonstrates that in Warlpiri aboriginal art, originality in terms of authorship is not emphasized. In such a scenario or tradition, plagiarism is not the major issue. Rather, what is feared is "thievery"—the "unauthorized appropriation of a design" and the potential of such to transfer rights and authority to the thief (2003, 47). Here, authenticity takes the form of authority. It is authenticity that is derived, at least partially, from the bestowal of authority by another or others in a given community.

Gerardo Mosquera addresses the concern that "globalization will impose homogenised cosmopolitan cultural patterns built on Eurocentric foundations" that eventually will "flatten, reify, and manipulate" cultural differences.[85] The fear is legitimate. On one hand multiculturalism and plurality are acknowledged. On the other, however, as a global phenomenon World Music "has responded less to a new consciousness than to a tolerance based on paternalism, quotas, and political correctness" (ibid., 20). Mosquera further reiterates:

> The case of 'international language' in art reveals a hegemonic construct of globalism more than a true globalisation, understood as a generalised participation....
>
> The rhetoric regarding globalisation has abounded in the illusionary triumph of a trans-territorial world, decentralised, omniparticipatory, engaged in multicultural dialogues, with currents flowing in all directions. In reality, globalisation is not as global as it appears.... It is far more global for some than for others—the majority (ibid., 21).

What is evident in the above quotation is that cultural diversity alone without cultural differentiation is merely sustenance of colonial patterns of dependency. For World Music as a category, authenticity was conferred *via* a language of functionality, political opposition, and by analogy with

---

84. Langton, "Dreaming Art," 47.
85. Mosquera, "Alien-Own/ Own Alien," 18.

Black American music.[86] According to Connell and Gibson, authenticity in World Music was signified by distanciation of nonwestern artists from Western artists. They argue that global neoliberal marketing "criteria" included a need for the music of the other to meet a kind of "emotionality" or "feeling" that was perceived as missing in Western music (2000, 344). Connell and Gibson go on to write that:

> What is of concern to listeners is that world music has some discernible connection to the timeless, the ancient, the primal, the pure, the chthonic; that is what they want to buy, since their own world is often conceived as ephemeral, new, artificial and corrupt (ibid.).

On another front, for some the distinctiveness of Jamaican reggae was "lost" due to the "persistent reformulation, amendment and commercialization of [Bob Marley's] music" (ibid., 347). According to a West Indian source, this "suggests that we have been listening to an alien, inauthentic representation. Paradoxically, since it is the only one to which we have access, it automatically assumes a level of 'authenticity'" (ibid.).

"Strategic Inauthenticity"

Hybridity challenges notions of authenticity that are based upon dominant hegemonic paradigms.[87] The demands of commercialism are real. The issue is raised as to how ICMs for mission maintain a balance between structures that affect creative impulse and the structures that interpret the "needs" of the market in order to be commercially viable or "authentic" in the eyes of the neoliberal market. Cosmopolitan artists are often asked to "remain 'musically and otherwise premodern ... culturally 'natural'—because of racism and western demands for authenticity."[88] The Western demand for authenticity tends to make non-Western pre-modern.[89]

However, musicians such as Youssou N'Dour, a Senegalese by birth, resist being an object of modernity. He does this by incorporating indigenous traditional music and the local Wolof language along with more global sounds from the West. Hybridity, for N'Dour, is an intentional choice to resist modernization and "move in the other direction."[90] Rather, resistance for N'Dour entails "leaving the city for the country, not the other way

---

86. Stokes, "Music and the Global Order," 50.
87. Frith, "Discourse of World Music," 309.
88. Connell and Gibson, "World Music," 351.
89. Lalsangkima Pachuau, Email correspondence, March 2014.
90. Taylor, "Strategic Inauthenticity," 153.

around."[91] N'Dour's "strategic inauthenticity" is indicative of the fact that indigenous musical creativity is not a value-free zone. Indigenous artists are not available to manufacture according to the demands of the West without critical discernment in the light of indigenous conceptualizations of authenticity. Rather, music making in the global arena is an activity that defines the ethos of the space for the enactment of creative identity for the participation of all. By defying the Western insistence on authenticity, artists such as N'Dour model an alternate form of "authenticity" for ICMs.

Connell and Gibson cite the remark of a Brazilian performer who outright rejected the notion of performing "unplugged":

> We've been unplugged for a hundred years, my friend... There's ethnic, there's 'world music' but that's so limiting. They want to see a toothless face, so that when you hear the song you imagine rotten teeth and hunger. That's what I refuse to do. We need to get away from that (2004, 351).

"International success required artistic compromise" (ibid., 353). New spaces ensure that authenticity *via* processes of musical creativity always be worked out in the context of cultural borrowing.[92] Hybridity as a way of being creative is the new authenticity.[93] Locality is conferred in a language of place, roots, and opposition to the global.[94] However, the notion of authenticity being restricted in terms of prevailing concepts of locality is problematic.

Connell and Gibson cite Ry Cooder's "unearthing" of Cuban music that "capitalized on the apparent 'purity' of Latin sounds hitherto hidden within a socialist state, and 'kept alive' by a distinguished older generation of forgotten musicians" (2004, 353). Further, according to Connell and Gibson's research, for a broadcaster of an American radio show, "People want to connect with something that sounds like it's from somewhere. So many of us feel rootless.... Music like this gives people an opportunity to connect with something that transports them home" (ibid.). ICMs therefore are critically positioned to articulate cultural difference through their musical creativity in ways that invites participation in the enactment of the new space on Earth as it is in Heaven.

---

91. Taylor, "Strategic Inauthenticity," 154.
92. Frith, "Discourse of World Music," 314.
93. Frith, "Discourse of World Music," 314.
94. Stokes, "Music and the Global Order," 2004.

Mimesis, Authenticity, and Difference

In this section we explore a theoretical dimension of mediating cultural difference in the context of cultural diversity through the lens of Michael Taussig's (1993) concept of mimesis. Mimesis or copying (imitation or mime) refers to the process by which the copy draws on the "character and power of the original, to the point whereby the representation may even assume that character and that power."[95] Mimesis necessarily is an act of translation. Writing itself is a mimetic response to being in the world in the sense of it involving one's "capacity to imagine, if not become, Other" (ibid., ix-xi). It is the faculty of nature that "culture uses to create the second nature" (ibid., xiii). For Taussig, mimesis is "necessary to the very process of knowing as it is to the construction and subsequent naturalization of identities" (1993, xiii). Further, mimesis is a "two-way street" involving the cultural construction of reality between two "others" (cf. Ibid., ix-xvi); it is a way to negotiate difference.

Particularly where there are histories of colonialism, the mimetic exchange process does not as much reconcile difference but "affirms and reinstantiate[s]" it (Toynbee and Dueck 2011, 8). According to Toynbee and Dueck, copying might be a way to accommodate strangeness and foreign ways into prevailing "indigenous cultural categories and practices" (ibid.). For Taussig, mimesis is a postcolonial and culturally sensitive anthropology of signification that involves coming to terms with the "dialectic of civilization-and-savagery installed in contemporary signifying practices themselves" (1993, x). In other words, it is an ongoing pattern for dealing with the tensions of postcolonial new spaces.

Copying as Postcolonial Advantage

In the urban context, Bruno Nettl observes that some cultures tend to select features of a particular music that are generally regarded as characteristic of that particular style. The particular choices made through efforts to contextualize music are a way to respond to difference.[96]

However, copying does not necessarily bring about homogeneity. For instance, in the context of "popular music and Islamic identity in Turkey," Ayhan Erol (2011) observes that contextualization of pop music in the Islamic context does not necessarily link present localities in such a way as to bring about a homogenization of culture through the appropriation of imported images and metaphors. Rather, the encounter between local

---

95. Taussig, *Mimesis and Alterity*, xiii.
96. Nettl, *Eight Urban Musical Cultures*, 3–15.

Islamic pop music and globalization results in a glocalization that is "a deliberate reinforcer of heterogeneity through the reproduction of local traits as a means of taking advantage of global patterns."[97]

A postcolonial imagination is evident in Erol's rhetoric that signifies deliberate intentionality and a posture of taking back what rightfully is owed. The new spaces created by Islamic pop musicians are a means by which "rural urban migrants can transform themselves from a peripheralized Islamic identity to a modern or urban identity."[98] Contextualizing processes of Islamic pop musicians involve alignment with tradition (by the use of acapella singing) as well as with contemporary popular music styles (ibid.). The question that needs to be raised is to what extent does the process of contextualization through mimesis make participants in Islamic pop music more or less Islamic and in whose eyes.

The process of musical translation *via* mimesis is a knowledge producing activity—"something being displaced by a 'relating to'" (Taussig 1993, 26). Thomas Burkhalter (2013) provides an insightful perspective on the production of knowledge in the context of Lebanese musicians and the choices they make in translating music in Beirut. The idea is not to judge the approach of local musicians over and against that of the West. He observes that:

> Musicians do not necessarily need to have experience and knowledge of the material they use to transform it into great music. Such results would, however, help to minimize false labeling. A musician is not necessarily close to "tradition" when singing in Arabic, and a rock musician is not necessarily ignorant of his local surroundings. This analysis would help to break the strong link between "locality" and "traditional music," it would reveal alternative and hidden "local" knowledge. The often-heard claim that musicians are "Westernized" would stand out as absurd (Burkhalter 2013, 253).

In addition, according to Burkhalter, some Lebanese musicians describe "their transnational networks as 'taste' communities, but not always as 'knowledge' communities" (ibid.). They do not necessarily have the "same knowledge of the specific material with which they are working" (ibid.).[99]

97. Erol, "Understanding the Diversity of Islamic Identity in Turkey," 199.
98. Erol, "Understanding the Diversity of Islamic Identity in Turkey," 199.
99. Further, Burkhalter discovered that musicians offer "critical depth" in the context of conveying the reality of the conditions of war they experienced. However, in reality, many local musicians did not truly experience the war scenarios. They may have done so only in passing (*Local Music Scenes and Globalization*, 253). The episode has implications for reexamining situations through which ICMs establish themselves as

The process of musical mimesis therefore does not mean that the copy actually takes on the depth of meaning embodied in the original. However, this does not necessarily imply a lack of "power."

We recollect that for Taussig the copy takes on the power of the original. In a postcolonial context, such as the Lebanese musicians, power is negotiated. It is not power as represented in the original. Copying therefore involves a move toward becoming the original at the cost of the original. New spaces therefore are places for the mediation of authenticity that is copied and where authenticity is resignified, given new meaning to a certain extent, as per the terms of the copier. In this sense, therefore, the process of mimesis facilitates a subtle transfer of power that may slip under the radar of Westernized formulations of authenticity. Musical mimesis therefore could be a process for generating advantage, knowledge, and power and therefore serve as a pathway for the decolonization of the mind. In the next section we take a look at a way in which this may happen.

MUSICAL CREATIVITY AND THE REMAKING OF HISTORIES

To ask what music signifies for ICMs is to some extent to investigate particular colonial histories and unearth links to contemporary processes of musical creativity. Despite multiple modernities, history sets the tone for social and political organization, which must be confronted on a daily basis.[100] Bruno Nettl distinguishes between Westernization and modernization. He suggests that if Westernization refers to the process whereby a music becomes Western through the accretion of Western elements, modernization is the process whereby a music retains its traditional essence but becomes modern—that is, part of the contemporary world and its set of values. The motivation is counter to that mentioned above for Westernization: The traditional music is changed in order *to remain intact* in the modern world, *not in order to become a part* of Western civilization.[101] Westernization may be understood as a particular attitude. According to Nettl, in the context of urban musical cultures, it is "the interpretation that a culture gives to a set of changes taking place in its musical structure, as much as the nature of the changes themselves, [that] would determine whether such changes actually constitute Westernization" (ibid.).

Take the case of Paul Simon's use of Andean panpipes in the song, *El Condor Pasa*, translated as "If I Could" (1970). To the average listener the

---

contributors to knowledge in their respective domains.

100. Erol, "Understanding the Diversity of Islamic Identity in Turkey," 198.
101. Nettl, *Eight Urban Cultures*, 10, italic mine.

lyrics convey an aspiration to be something more than what one is, to break out of circumstances that somehow limit one's potential, for example, "I'd rather be a sparrow than a snail," "I'd rather be a hammer than a nail."[102] The lyrics together with the melody, conveyed in no small measure by the use of traditional Andean panpipes, appear to communicate the perspective of the vanquished—unreached dreams.

The idea is not to arrive at a consensus at what the song meant; a range of interpretations needs to be acknowledged. The linkage of Andean panpipes to specific colonial histories and the experience of particular peoples should not be ignored. To the informed or discerning listener, given the history of colonialism, the panpipe may signify the power and will to survive even when all is lost. The panpipe as an instrument in and of itself is indicative of a response to colonialism,[103] a statement about the value of retaining a sense of self, or what is considered indigenous, and thereby synonymous with freedom. Interestingly, the song itself was composed by a Peruvian ethnomusicologist and composer, Alomia Robles as part of a *zarzuela* (Spanish operetta), *El Condor Pasa*,[104] which was "of strong social content about Peruvian miners in Cerro de Pasco and their relations with the foreign mining company."[105] Paul Simon heard the song played by the musical group, Los Incas and appropriated the song but gave it different lyrics. The song appeared on the album, *Bridge over Troubled Water* (1970). The link between the background to *El Condor Pasa* and its compilation on Simon's record whose title encapsulates or refers to crossing over some kind of turbulence is call for further exploration.[106]

102. Paul Simon, "El Condor Pasa," http://www.paulsimon.com/us/music/paul-simon-concert-live-rhymin/el-condor-pasa-if-i-could.

103. Balasundaram, "Bartholomew de las Casas."

104. McGee, "El Condor Pasa."

105. Daniel Alomia Robles, http://en.wikipedia.org/wiki/Daniel_Alom%C3%ADa_Robles, accessed March 27, 2013). On Paul Simon's website, credit for the song is attributed to Jorge Milchberg.

106. According to a review of the record, quoted here:

> *Bridge Over Troubled Water* was issued Feb. 14, 1970 and was as close to pop perfection as any album ever released. It would spend ten weeks on top of the national charts and sell 13 million copies. It would go on to win six Grammy Awards.
>
> The 1960s had ended with the alienation of American youth. The Vietnam War, which was killing hundreds of young people each week, being chronicled on television. The draft lottery, the Manson family, the violence at Altamont, and the election of Richard Nixon all combined to move society far from the ideals of peace and love. It was against this background that the beauty of *Bridge Over Troubled Water* burst upon the music scene

As per context, here is a clear case of musical creativity in response to colonialism. Paul Simon in his capacity as a cultural intermediary served to unearth the link between specific colonial histories and the imaginations of participants (i.e., all of us today) in the process of his musical creativity. The song is also a clear example of the generation of knowledge-makers where all people are free to explore, to investigate, and to do something about in order to make the world a better place.

In the case of the Afro-Celt System, a London-based dance fusion group that uses samples of African and Celtic music, "The complex histories of mediation, exchange, and interaction of which they are, in fact, a product are discursively erased" (Stokes 2004, 60). However, while Stokes and others are genuinely concerned about such covering up of histories, could such concern be viewed as condescending by others? Connell and Gibson cite references that speak to the way Black musicians who worked on Paul Simon's Graceland "rejected the notion of cultural imperialism as a denial of their own agency, and supported its validation of urban African musical styles" (2004, 348). This would lead us to imagine that the adaptation of Western musical components within a given postcolonial indigenous tradition may not really be a compromise of authenticity. Rather, authenticity is mediated as the power to change, the freedom to express oneself in the culture of the "other," even using the terms of the other.

On the other hand, according to Richard Middleton, Paul Simon's *Graceland* (1986) album incorporates music and peoples from a diverse background. Yet, "Simon clearly dominates, both musically and commercially" by swallowing up the "lion's share of the royalties" and by "cleaning up and interpreting his ethnic sources [making it sound "reassuringly primitive"] so that they support the visions of a white, middle-class American singer-songwriter."[107]

The reality however may be articulated in such a way that "While music can never belong to us (as myths of authenticity would wish), belonging to a music (making ourselves at home within its territory) is distinctly possible" (Middleton 2000, 78). Middleton speaks to the idea of "Western Music" and its "alienating meaning systems" as the dominant hermeneutic

---

and in some way provided hope or at least a means of escape . . . .
Bridge Over Troubled Water is legitimately recognized as a landmark album. It is a series of songs that provide comfort and ultimately restore faith. It is not often you can receive this type of experience from a music album" (David Bowling, "Music Review: Simon & Garfunkel—Bridge Over Troubled Water," http://blogcritics.org/music/article/music-review-simon-garfunkel-bridge-over/ (accessed March 27, 2013). [/EXT]

107. Middleton, "Musical Belongings," 75.

by which to understand and come to terms with the difference of the other. For him, a clear acknowledgment of the multiplicities of meanings and histories are basic to meaningful dialogue.[108] Musical creativity is potential invitation to partake in the authentic histories at the core of such creativity. Martin Stokes refers to the "multidimensionality of musical globalization" whereby samples (the recording of sounds/tones/rhythms that are used to electronically generate further versions) or "copies" of sounds, invite further appropriations and reinventions in various formats "in dialogue with the 'originals'" (2004, 57). In this sense, therefore, the mediation of authenticity is at the same time the construction of difference.

In chapters 5–7, we observe how ICMs mediate such authenticity via their musical creativities, identifying with the "other" while constructing and maintaining difference. They "preserve, abolish, and innovate" from within their respective contexts (Nettl 1978, 12), while negotiating creative identity in the context of languages of hybridity, roots, authenticity, and locality.

SUMMARY

Our focus has been on the new spaces that emerge as a result of the interactivity between transnational music flows, neoliberal impulses that shape the construction and mediation of authenticity through music within these spatial flows, and the negotiation of ICM identity for mission. The reconfiguration of cultural boundaries brought about by globalizing processes has led to the irruption of multiple and diverse new spaces for the enactment of indigenous cosmopolitan musician (ICM) identity for mission. ICM identity is "enunciated" amid the interstitial passages "in-between" structures of indigeneity and cosmopolitanism. As such, ICM identity, by virtue of its rhizomic being, transcends and interrogates the structures that inform its identity. It is sustained by postcolonial hybrid impulses with claims to authenticity.

ICMs, therefore, constantly negotiate multiple claims to authenticity. These terms of negotiation are affected by experiences across multiple and intersecting histories in the "spaces of flows" and that occur in "undifferentiated time." The notion of difference plays a significant factor as ICMs embody and enact the Gospel in the context of a cosmopolitan ethos. The articulation of ICM authenticity in the context of cultural diversity—learning how to sing with the other without compromise on the Gospel—is central to the effective mission of ICMs in the new spaces they occupy. In many ways, hybridity is strategic authenticity.

108. Middleton, "Musical Belongings," 59–60.

Thus far we have explored the first two major components of this project: musical creativity (chapter 2) and new spaces (chapter 3). In the next chapter we begin to unfold the third major building block for this study—creative mission. Particularly, we begin to develop a theological heuristic framework (MFTC) for the ways in which ICMs for mission embody, enact, and perform a theology of creativity (*creatio Dei*).

4

Creative Mission

WE BEGAN CHAPTER 1 with the theological proposition that all human creativity is derived from the creativity of God. In chapter 2 (Musical Creativity), the concept of "theological creativity" served to locate the understanding and practice of musical creativity of ICMs for mission within the creativity of God. In chapter 3 (New Spaces), we saw that the site for the enactment of musical creativity is not a value-free zone. It is in the new spaces in-between indigeneity and cosmopolitanism that indigenous cosmopolitan musician (ICM) identity is constructed and sustained amid the crisscrossing of postcolonial currents. The question, however, concerning how ICMs in mission "sing the Lord's song" in their respective borderland spaces is an issue of ontological proportions.

In chapter 4, therefore, we begin to weave together the concepts of musical creativity and new spaces for a theology of creativity (*creatio Dei*), which is presented here in terms of a Missiological Framework for Theological Creativity (MFTC). With regards to ontology, the question is raised as to what it means to mediate creative difference through the process of musical creativity in the diverse cultural contexts that ICMs inhabit. From an epistemological perspective, if knowledge is relational,[1] then we ask in what sense knowledge as mediated through the musical creativity of ICMs is authentic in the context of the mission of God.

RATIONALE FOR A THEOLOGY OF CREATIVITY

Before we begin to develop *creatio Dei* a few broad reasons for why a theology of creativity is pertinent for this research will help to guide our dissertation.

---

1. Chilisa, *Indigenous Research Methodologies*, 1–2; 20–21.

First, a theological foundation serves not only to differentiate the creative mission of ICMs from their creative counterparts in the "secular" world, but as a field of pre-systematic ontological inquiry it holds potential as an apologetic and evangelistic tool.

Second, in the postcolonial environment of new spaces the intertextual enmeshment between concepts of indigeneity and modes of cosmopolitanism make the creation of music a process of ongoing conflict.[2] For example, exploring the role of "music in sacred India," Donna Marie Wulff observed that, while sacred music in the West is "largely or wholly dependent on its text," in India "religious music is not, by and large, regarded as merely a setting for a text.... Sound itself is viewed as powerful and revelatory."[3] A theology of creativity as we envision here opens the door to the construction of a fresh systematic sonic theology for mission amid cultures that place a high value on sonic dimensions for the mediation of spirituality.

Additionally, in Hinduism (and other indigenous traditions), the sacred nature of sound is reified through relationships, hierarchies, and the construction of musical instruments.[4] In comparison, contemporary missiological discourse is lacking as far as the articulation of a distinct sonic theology that is comparable to the all-encompassing sonic theology of Vedic Hinduism.[5] However, a theology of creativity—*creatio Dei*—is an attempt to begin the process of addressing this gap.

Geoffrey W. Bromiley's (1979) article, "Theological Creativity" initially motivated me to think in terms of a theology of creativity. Bromiley's appropriation of the term, theological creativity, bears some semblance to how

---

2. Bradshaw, *Bridging the Gap*, 58. "The greatest contrast between the relational emphasis of primal world views and the cause-and-effect emphasis of modern theistic world views is how each accommodates spiritual intervention."

3. Wulff, "On Practicing Religiously," 164, 149–72. Beck, "Magic of Hindu Music," 20. Classical forms of Indian music, both instrumental and vocal, are considered to be of divine origin and are closely identified with the Hindu deities; the instruments of the gods symbolize *Nada Brahman*—"the sacred, primeval, eternal sound, represented by the syllable Om, which generates the universe ... [and] symbolizes Brahman, the Supreme Absolute."

4. The caste system in India continues to be validated and sustained by the fact of its origin in the period of the emergence of the Rig Veda. Although, for some the hymn that is often referred to as a validation of the caste system is actually a late addition and is quoted by traditionalists in support of the caste system. "The hymn of the sacrifice of *Purusha*, the first man: Rig-Veda, Book X, 90.11–12" in Griffith, *Hymns of the Rig-Veda*, 2:519, 576.

5. Whether or not Christianity has a sonic theology is not the main point. The lack of a clearly articulated sonic theology however indicates a gap in contemporary Christian systematic theology. See Begbie, *Theology, Music and Time*, 3. Also, Begbie, "Future of Theology Amid the Arts," 152–82.

we use it for this study. However, his application of the phrase "theological creativity" also serves as a point of departure in order to clarify the term as envisioned for the creative mission of ICMs.

THEOLOGICAL CREATIVITY

In his article, "Evangelicals and theological creativity" (1979) Geoffrey W. Bromiley proposes that evangelical theology is at an "inherent disadvantage" when it comes to being creative—it blocks the paths of those in "creative aberration" and devises ingenuous means to maintain the status quo.[6] He uses the terms creativity and originality interchangeably. Bromiley goes on to argue that "the true creativity of God" should inform and direct human creativity, although the idea of creativity is not to be taken lightly and without critical discernment.[7]

Bromiley warns the reader to distinguish between true creativity and false creativity. For him, true creativity leads to a more accurate knowledge of God and divine revelation as mediated through Scripture. Bromiley associates false creativity with artistic process as opposed to scientific approach. Bromiley uses the analogy of the sciences and the arts to differentiate between true and false creativity respectively. According to him, the arts are equated with originality and inventiveness yet lack in capacity to convey deep theological insight. To this extent, what appears to be "authentic" creativity is not what it is purported to be. In fact, for Bromiley, "It is not theology at all" (1979, 5).[8]

---

6. Bromiley, "Evangelicals and Theological Creativity," 4–8.

7. Bromiley, "Evangelicals and Theological Creativity," 4–5.

8. Bromiley, "Evangelicals and Theological Creativity," 5. According to Geoffrey W. Bromiley: "Even when authentic creativity appears in theology, it may just as well be a false creativity as a true one. Indeed, there is perhaps greater scope for a false creativity. This is why creativity poses more of a problem for Evangelical theologians. False creativity arises when theology is treated as one of the arts instead of the sciences, or as one of the humane sciences instead of the divine science. In the arts especially freer rein is given to the imagination. Only the flimsiest of contact need be maintained with the original data. Face to face with a tree or a star, the artist or poet can obviously be far more creative than the botanist of astronomer. He can view and interpret as his fancy pleases whereas the scientist must engage in more precise observation, analysis, and description. Creative theology will often turn out to be merely a form of subjective impressionism in relation to its object. It may even part company with the true object altogether when it makes religious man its object instead of God. If, however, theology has the scientific task of studying God and the things of God according to God's own self-revelation, this imaginative creativity is false. It may be authentically creative at the human level, but it is not authentically creative theology. It presents or even creates another object—its own idea or general human ideas of God instead of God. It is not theology at all."

I affirm and appreciate Bromiley's effort to distinguish between true and false creativity. However, the relegation of the arts as a realm for originality and inventiveness as opposed to the sciences is reminiscent of the epistemological captivity of creativity that we have discussed earlier.[9] *Creatio Dei* extends Bromiley's use of the term "theological creativity." *Creatio Dei* implies more than originality or inventiveness. *Creatio Dei* may be regarded as a step toward a conceptual reorientation of the arts in the context of Westernized systematic theology; it legitimizes the arts as a way of theologizing. *Creatio Dei* is an attempt to clarify the dimensions in which the arts, specifically musical creativity in this study, might be a way of interpreting Scripture and in the process contribute to an authentic knowledge of the revelation of God. Earlier, in chapter 2 we asked, "Why Creativity?" Here, we build upon our earlier argument for *creatio Dei* in order to develop a missiological hermeneutic for the understanding and practice of the creative mission of ICMs.

CREATIO DEI

Creatio Dei refers to a theology of the "creativity of God." In this study particularly we use *creatio Dei* to facilitate the articulation of a theology of creativity as it pertains to the creative mission of ICMs as they understand and practice their musical creativity for mission. I initially conceptualized *creatio Dei* in terms of a 5-fold Missiological Framework for Theological Creativity (MFTC)—Creative Being, Creative Construction, Creative Community, Creative Beauty, and Creative Performance. The concepts of creativity identified here are not mutually exclusive. In this dissertation, however, I develop Creative Being as the central hub. Creative Construction and Creative performance are the other two major concepts that have shaped my interaction with data from research with key informants. Here, therefore, of the five concepts identified above, I have focused on developing Creative Being, Creative Construction, and Creative Performance.

MISSIOLOGICAL FRAMEWORK FOR THEOLOGICAL CREATIVITY

Theologically speaking, if the locus of the creative impulse is generated within and is inseparable from Trinitarian expressions of being, then a question is raised as to what are some ways in which ICMs for mission locate themselves

---

9. To recollect, the epistemological captivity of creativity amounts to an emphasis on rationalized intellectual forms as representations of true knowledge over and against other/art forms that are perceived to offer only proximate (mimetic) versions of truth.

within such an environment.[10] A missiological framework for theological creativity (MFTC) is a response to the need to situate the understanding and practice of ICMs for mission within a theological framework.

CREATIVE BEING

First, *creatio Dei* establishes creativity as activity (*actio*) of the Living God who creates in accord with his personhood. Creative being affirms the personhood and agency of the Creator in contiguity with the creative process and creation (product). Jürgen Moltmann suggests that the "first act" of creative expression is a step "inwards" rather than a step "outward."[11] The idea of creativity being first a step inwards runs counter to popular conceptions of creativity being primarily about outward expression. Further, a step inwards is a crucial dynamic especially in a postcolonial context where the inward of the other is most often the imagined interests of those who represent the dominant hegemony. The creative consciousness brought about by a resurgence of attention to the inward act of creativity from which the outward act is borne is thus a significant step to reverse the colonial unconscious.[12]

---

10. In what sense do ICMs in Christian mission exemplify the creativity of God? To put it in theological terms, in what sense do Christian musicians see their own selves and are regarded by others "as a *hypostasis* of the substance [of God], as a concrete and unique identity"? Zizioulas, *Being as Communion*, 46. For insights on creative participation in the community of the Trinity please see Seamands, *Ministry in the Image of God*.

11. Moltmann, *Trinity and the Kingdom*, 109–10. That creation, the material world we live in, is not separate and divorced from the being of God is illustrated by Jürgen Moltmann's (1993) appropriation of Isaac Luria's doctrine of *zimzum* or "contraction." According to this doctrine the existence of the world is made possible by the "contraction" or "concentration" of God. It refers to "shrinkage" within God's being since God is "all in all" and nothing can exist apart from Him. In response to the question of "how can God create from 'nothing' when nothing else exists apart from Him?" Moltmann summarizes Luria's response:

> The very first act of the infinite Being was therefore not a step 'outwards' but a step 'inwards', a 'self-withdrawal of God from himself into himself' . . . it was a *passio Dei*, not an *actio*. The very first act is therefore an act that veils, not one that reveals; a limitation on God's part, not a de-limitation. It is only in Act II that God issues from himself as creator into that primal space which he had previously released in Act I.

See also Moltmann, *God in Creation*, 86–87.

12. By colonial unconscious I mean those parts of memory-making mechanisms that shape imagined histories and are considered irrelevant or subject to the "permission" of the (neo) colonizer in order to be legitimate. Cf. "captive mind" Alatas, "Captive Mind and Creative Development," 83–98.

Second, the integral relation between creative being and creative expression implies that a departure from the will and purpose of God in the process of musical creativity amounts to a creativity that has lost its bearings. It is disharmonious with God's mission. It is in response to pagan art that the apostle Paul engages the "men of Athens" to reconsider the basis for their creative expression. For them it was an "unknown god" but according to Paul it is "In him—'The God who made the world and everything in it, being the Lord of heaven and earth'—that we live and move and have our being" (Acts 17:22–28). The problem for the Athenians was not necessarily "good" or "bad" art but an insufficient onto-epistemic framework that Paul seeks to redirect.[13] In the light of Paul's rationale, we may argue that music is not amoral.[14] It is not merely an addendum to faith.[15] It is a dimension of human personhood in the image of the Creator.

13. Mascall, *He Who Is*, 6, 9. The problem of creativity is not first of form and beauty; this line of questioning can be traced from the "attitude of Greek philosophy" with its tendency to conceive of God primarily as a "principle of form and beauty rather than as a creative living being." Second, another problem was that even if the Greek god was personal, it was not because of a personal interest he took in the world but because he exercised influence by virtue of "the attraction of his perfection" rather than deliberate action. Third, for the Greeks, God and the prime matter of which the world was composed were "probably co-eternal," which is antithetical to a biblical theology of *creatio ex nihilo*. Humans (and creation) derive their being from the being of God. The fact is that there is no "intrinsic value" of the created order of things, including humanity, apart from the fact of its Creator. Wright, *Mission of God*, 399. The approach to this research might be compared to the method adopted by Begbie, "Created Beauty" 84. With regard to establishing theological bearings pertaining to a "Christian account for beauty":

> Our primary orientation . . . will not be to an experience of the beautiful, nor to an aesthetics, but to the quite specific God attested in Scripture. . . . If an account of beauty is to be *theo-logical* in Christian terms, its *logos* or rationale will take its shape primarily from the being and acts of this *theos*.

14. Scruton, "Music and Morality." For Plato, music "was not a neutral amusement. It could express and encourage virtue—nobility, dignity, temperance, and chastity. But it could also express and encourage vice—sensuality, belligerence, indiscipline." In general, I concur with Plato on the morality of music. But it is important to recognize that we arrive at the understanding from two different directions—for Plato, the notion of the "ideal state" or absolute; for me, personification of the Absolute in the particular personhood of Jesus Christ—and so with different implications. One might arrive at a similar conclusion based upon what music "means." However, this perspective indicates the preferences of a particular person, group, or worldview. The differentiation between "secular" and "sacred" music is most often based on an unhealthy dualism with roots in Neoplatonism.

15. We observe that it is not the work of art that is being evaluated but the source of its inspiration. Does creativity lie primarily within the confines of the "art and imagination of man" or in a relationship with God? The "unknown God" is a product of the "ignorance" (Acts 17:30) of the artist (and community) of a personal God who is Judge

Third, Gen 1:1 might be translated as such: when God began to create, the Creator created the heavens and the earth—an all-encompassing reality.[16] The dichotomy between sacred heavens and secular earth is a corruption of the Judeo-Christian perspective. God created the context. God also created the experience—tangible ways in which to participate in His expressive nature. The division of the process of God's creativity (prior to Creation) into Act I and Act II as distinct spatial/temporal markers to explain something that happened before or outside of chronological space and time is difficult to explain.[17] However, Moltmann's appropriation of Luria's re-plotting of space and time from a conceptual perspective offers an argument for why *creatio Dei* is suitable especially in terms of a postcolonial paradigmatic approach for ICMs in the new spaces for mission.[18] Carlos F. Cardoza-Orlandi's (2013) articulation of Christian historical method as that which bends time helps to clarify.

The notion of history as past, present, and future is contested from the perspective of some theologians. For example, according to Carlos F. Cardoza-Orlandi, representing the voice of Latin American and other Third World theologians, history is in the "now." In other words, "the prophetic implies the eschatological" by way of an "eschatological conversation in the time and space continuum."[19] Cardoza-Orlandi suggests the triad of hope, memory, and expectations as a way to challenge Western historiography. The gateways of hope, memory, and expectation extend evaluation of the process of musical creativity based upon lyrics or feelings generated, while not diminishing the significance of these metrics.[20]

---

of all things. In the NT, ἐνθύμησις at Matt 9:4; 12:25 and Heb 4:12, is the unexpressed and hidden thing in man which God's omniscience sees and judges. It can also imply what is foolish or wicked. It is not so much the piece of art or music that will be the subject of scrutiny on the Day of Judgment, but the imagination, which God sees. See Kittel et al., *Theological Dictionary of the New Testament*, vol. 7.

16. Hamilton, *Book of Genesis: Chapters 1–17*.

17. Moltmann, *Trinity and the Kingdom*, 110.

18. Moltmann, *Trinity and the Kingdom*, 110. Moltmann's appropriation of the doctrine of *zimzum* gives us a chance to think of all things being in God without falling prey to *pantheism*. This is helpful in addressing our initial question—the purpose of the form can be no other than to fulfill God's purpose in accord with His being. Also comparable is the doctrine of *panentheism* that helps us to think of all things being in God. Also, see n308.

19. "An eschatological conversation in the time and space *continuum* . . . means that in our Christian historical methodology we *bend* time!" Cardoza-Orlandi, "Prophetic Dialogue," 24.

20. Cardoza-Orlandi, "Prophetic Dialogue," 24.

Fourth, creative being draws attention to the cosmic moral consciousness that pervades the link between music, meaning, and identity. It is not merely that the Creator creates but the way in which he creates: "by understanding made the heavens, for his steadfast love endures forever."[21] Words like "understanding," "power," "knowledge," and "love" demonstrate the essential morality that is linked with God's personhood especially in God's creativity. To participate in creative being is in essence to participate in the character of God, his knowledge embodied in the way God creates.

To reiterate, for God, creativity is an act of "self-humiliation," (*passio*) which is endorsed by Moltmann's perspective that "God acts on himself when he acts creatively" (1993, 110). The creative consciousness evidenced in the context of the missionary activity of God radically expands the theological dimension of the cosmopolitan ethical consciousness referred to earlier (chapter 2). Without attempting to go into a detailed Christology for creativity, we discern that the activity of creative mission is mirrored in and anticipates the kenotic emptying and offering of Christ on the Cross. We will return to Christ-like creative posturing for mission in chapter 8.

Fifth, following from the above, creative being eschatologically relocates the process of creativity not merely in the first act of creation[22] but simultaneously in the recreation of humanity through Christ[23] (Heb 1:2) and by the power of the Spirit.[24] A theology of creativity, therefore, needs to consider in spatial terms the extended and distributed process of creativity that begins with the kenotic act of the Father "expropriating

---

21. Ps 136:5; also cf. Prov 3:19; Jer 10:12a.

22. Interestingly, Wolfhart Pannenberg's *Systematic Theology,* Vol.1, contains no direct reference to Gen 1. Pannenberg would agree that God's grace is not subsequent to the saving activity of Christ in the NT. But what is interesting is that the grace of God through the process of creativity, Gen 1, does not hold a central place in the development of his system. David Brown argues for "continuing revelation" post Incarnation, for "the conclusion was drawn that God, in sketching or defining himself through the human, had in effect endorsed all that was best in human creativity . . ." Brown, *Tradition and Imagination,* 326. A theology of creativity, therefore, extends the Incarnation in emphasizing Christ's role in creation as well as the Father's role in making space for the holy "other" (Moltmann, *God in Creation*).

23. "Creation is the temporal analogue, taking place outside God, of that event in God himself by which God is the Father of the Son . . . what God does as the creator can, in the Christian sense, only be seen and understood as a reflection, as a shadowing forth, of this inner divine relationship between God the Father and the Son." Barth, *Dogmatics in Outline,* 52.

24. Guthrie, *Creator Spirit,* xvi. "Art-making is a paradigmatically human activity" and the Spirit restores our humanity, voices, bodies, community, freedom, and vocation.

himself by 'generating' the consubstantial Son."[25] Furthermore according to Hans urs Von Balthasar:

> The first 'self-limitation' of the triune God arises through endowing his creatures with freedom. The second, deeper, 'limitation' of the same triune God occurs as a result of the covenant . . . . The third kenosis . . . arises through the Incarnation of the Son alone (ibid.).

The creation of a "third space" within the Space of the Godhead is a result of an "inner-Trinitarian covenant"—God created the world out of His love for the Son by the operative power of the Holy Spirit.[26] The concept of primordial "third space" is a theological antecedent for the creative reconfiguration of ICM identity in the context of Homi K. Bhabha's "third space." The creative being of God anticipates the spaces "in-between" indigeneity and cosmopolitanism for the emergence of ICM identity, which serve as theological environments where the postcolonial encounters and narratives of ICMs in mission find a point of "origin" and a place of rest.

From Moltmann we gather that God anticipated every possible response in making place for the Other within Himself. In the context of *creatio Dei*, diversity represents mutual self-differentiation and love for "otherness." Von Balthasar writes that the "Son is infinitely Other, but he is also the infinitely Other of the Father. Thus he both grounds and surpasses all we mean by separation, pain, and alienation in the world . . . ."[27] The perfect and complete reciprocity of the Son's love to the Father by the Spirit is now the context for human creativity, if it is to serve God's

---

25. Von Balthasar, "Excerpt from *Theo-Drama: Theological Dramatic Theory, Vol. III, The Dramatis Personae: The Person in Christ*, trans. Graham Harrison," 72.

26. Moltmann, *Trinity and the Kingdom*, 110–11.

27. Von Balthasar, "Excerpt from *Theo-Drama: Theological Dramatic Theory, Vol. IV, The Action,* trans. Graham Harrison," 69; Ford et al., *Modern Theologians Reader*, 68; Moltmann, "Excerpt from *The Crucified God: The Cross of Christ as the Foundation and Criticism of Christian Theology*," 91. According to Ford et al., Balthasar disagrees with Moltmann's "perceived 'process' theology" that Balthasar interprets as "God *requiring* the world in order to be God." In *The Crucified God*, Moltmann suggests that God is affected by the suffering of Jesus based on the reasoning that "there can be no love without openness to the possibility of suffering." However, I do not agree with Balthasar in his critique since I think it may actually misrepresent what Moltmann is saying in the light of the creativity of God in *The Trinity and the Kingdom* (1993). On this issue, I tend to agree with John Haught that "A vulnerable God, as the Trinitarian nature of Christian theism requires, could not fail to feel intimately and to 'remember' everlastingly all of the sufferings, struggles, and achievements in the *entire story* of cosmic and biological evolution." Haught, *God After Darwin*, 224.

purpose. In Christ, the artist participates in the "inner life of the Trinity" (Moltmann 1993, 113).

Summarizing, in terms of creative being, *creatio Dei* emphasizes creativity as dynamic correspondence between inward and outward acts of creativity. As such, creativity being rooted in the moral personage of God makes participation in the *creatio Dei*, through Christ-like posturing, a process of decolonization of the colonial unconscious. The primordial and immediately eschatological location of Trinitarian shared space antedates the "third spaces" of ICMs as places for the fulfillment of the creative mission of God through participation in Christ.

CREATIVE CONSTRUCTION

From Gen 1:1, we know that in the beginning, God created the heavens and the earth.[28] We also observe that God gives form to what is called "formless" and infuses meaning to what is considered "void" (Gen 1:2).[29] In other words, God creates form and he imbues the form with meaning. In Creation, God "saw," "said," "separated," "blessed," "gave," "made" "and "it was so." The active engagement of God through speaking, seeing, making, bringing about order in creation, including inviting Adam to share in the creative process through naming creatures, the charge to Adam and Eve to be fruitful and multiply, and Sabbath rest, has implications for missiological *methexis* ("sharing" or "participation") in the very creativity of God. Let us explore this further.

28. God did not create from existing matter as if to suggest that matter somehow was co-existing or is co-eternal with God. Mccomiskey, "278 בָּרָא," 127. The root bārāʾ is used of end time Restoration (Isa 41:20), the creation of a new heavens and earth (Isa 65:17, 18), change in the natural order of things (Jer 31:22), and the inner working of the Spirit (Ps 51:10), and is limited to the divine activity of God. The root bārāʾ has the basic meaning, "to create." It differs from yāṣar "to fashion" in that the latter primarily emphasizes the shaping of an object while bārāʾ emphasizes the initiation of the object.

29. Here we affirm three realities: 1) things exist; (2) things exist for a purpose; (3) humans assign meanings to things (construction). A theology of creativity links these three realities in a dynamic way for mission. However, if form/matter is God-created, then what does this mean for the construction patterns of ICMs for mission? For Plato, forms are "exemplars." Brickhouse and Smith, "Plato (427–347 BCE)." The concept of forms as "exemplars" allows a basis for evaluating forms, which I agree with. However, what this basis or "perfect" form is, from which forms derive their nature or meaning is the question. When it comes to music the situation is amplified because the "form" of music, at least in its sonic dimension, is unseen. A theology of creativity invites further reflection upon the dynamic linkage of expressive forms, instruments included, to the purest of all forms—the person of Jesus Christ. In terms of a relational ontology, to what extent does the process of craftsmanship embody the personhood of the Craftsperson (cf. Matt 13:55; Mark 6:3 and the prophetic agency of craftsmen in Zech 1:20)?

First, as a process of construction, *creatio Dei* embraces a relational ontology and epistemology that is broader than typical Euro-Western theological paradigms.[30] It acknowledges relational realities and forms of knowledge prevalent amongst indigenous cultures. Indigenous cultures tend to pay attention to spiritual interconnectedness between persons, environment/nature, and "the living and the nonliving" more than Euro-Western traditions.[31]

Second, the dynamic correspondence between creator and expression, the medium and the message, is already affirmed in sociocultural theory.[32] In the context of a theology of creativity, the relational ontology of creative construction must consider a deeper relation between creator and created.[33] As adhered to earlier, the ritual enactment and affirmation of the deep-level connection between material forms (instrument and bodily) of creativity is less heeded, generally speaking, in Western Christian theology than in primal cultures or religions with a "sonic theology" as in the Indian classical music tradition.[34] The point is not to assign to material substances a spirituality that amounts to pantheism, but perhaps to revisit the metaphysics of substance

---

30. Chilisa, *Indigenous Research Methodologies*, 3. Chilisa reflects on how Euro-Western research processes do not account for the "multiple relations" with community, "the living and the nonliving." She asserts: "I belong to the Bantu people of Africa, who live a communal life based on a connectedness that stretches from birth to death, continues beyond death, and extends to the living and the nonliving. I am known and communicate in relational terms that connect me to all my relations, living and the nonliving. It is common for people to refer to each other using totems as well as relational terms such as uncle, aunt, brother, and so on."

31. Bediako, *Christianity in Africa*, 106. The crisis of modern theology in the West in general is that it has failed to sufficiently respond to the deep spiritual issues that are "essentially religious: questions of human identity, community, ecological equilibrium and justice." See also, Paul Hiebert's "excluded middle." Hiebert, "Flaw of the Excluded Middle," 35–47.

32. McLuhan and Fiore, *Medium Is the Massage*.

33. Seamands, *Ministry in the Image of God*, 122. A theology of creativity with its valuation of the material "causes us to value the particulars of the material world—cabbages and mountains, insects and rocks, songs and statues in all their concrete uniqueness."

34. See Beck, *Sonic Theology*. Further, in Hinduism, there is a day that is set apart in the year for musicians to honor or "consecrate" their musical instruments for their "spiritual" purpose. The idea of materials being used or set apart for God's purposes may be compared to King David's construction of musical instruments that were to be used only for worship (*zamar*, in 2 Chr 7:6). The idea of setting apart instruments as being somewhat "holy" is frowned upon in contexts where spirituality is associated, for most part, with the ethereal and non-material.

with a view to explore the construction of sonic patterns and instruments as these relate to participation in the creative mission of God.[35]

The material significance of the human body[36] amplified in the resurrected body of Christ in no uncertain terms, and through Him the promise of the Resurrection for human body forms, reinforces the "primordial goodness of embodied human existence."[37] In terms of the individual and collective nature of the body of Christ and the roles of ICMs therein, we might argue that creative construction invites a re-imagination of what it means to believe, for *"intelligent bodies,"* permeated by Christian commitment, *"believe in a different way than rational minds"* (Miles 2012, 52).[38] For further discussion of the relation between matter, form, and meaning as well as initial thoughts concerning the ontology of form as it pertains to the construction of a sonic theology, please read Appendix C.

Third, the locus for creativity is the diversity of the community of the Trinity. The collaborative impact of the process of creativity of Father, Son, and Holy Spirit serves as a theological precedent for the creative collaboration of ICMs in creative mission. In a postcolonial context, creative construction in spaces "beyond" (Bhabha 1994) serves to subvert existing constructs of power sustained in existing hierarchies, unities, binaries, and centers. As an extension of Trinitarian "third space," creative construction in Christ invites a re-signification of the "location of culture" not merely as space for encounter and engagement in terms of otherness and difference but as psychosomatic relocation for collaborative engagement with others. It creates a place for the embodiment, enactment, and expression of creativity with others and their "dis-relations" (Walls 2002).

---

35. We cannot afford to provide a detailed theology of form here but the purpose is to revisit some of the issues underlying a theology of form and meaning that will help explore processes of creativity amongst ICMs in this era of globalization. Music is "a matter of both nature and nurture, and in gaining a Christian perspective on music, much depends on holding both of these perspectives together." Begbie, *Resounding Truth*, 49. Some questions that may be raised in the process of creative construction: In what sense does Christian artistry pattern God's freedom in creation? What are some of the issues and challenges in the processes of Christian artistry; and, for example, in the construction of music—text, tone, contexts, instruments, and experiences? How do artists choose to infuse their particular cultural constructions—music, art, and instruments—with meaning? What sorts of influences (epistemologies) shape the ways in which they construct their music? In what way is it continuous or discontinuous with the surrounding culture? What contingencies are involved?

36. Micah 6:7; Rom 12:1; Luke 22:19:1; Cor 9:27.

37. Smith, *Fall of Interpretation*, 154.

38. "To seek, *in the present*, to live out into the resurrection body, seems both a more realistic and a more demanding definition of belief than that of the rational mind's assent." Miles, "Resurrection of Body," 52.

Fourth, as creative construction, *creatio Dei* serves to conceptually reorient the ways in which ICMs understand and practice the creativity of God for mission through the "enunciation" of a subaltern hermeneutic—the "arts" as opposed to the "sciences"—for theologizing.

Indigenous or so-called "primitive" music is often interpreted in the context of Western aesthetic formalism, which Clifford Geertz (1976) reminds us is a relatively recent (mid-eighteenth century) phenomenon.[39] The conceptual qualifiers of aesthetic containers developed in one context are irrelevant for application in another. As such, creative construction could be viewed as a postcolonial response to dominant paradigms of theologizing (content and dissemination) that emerge in the West and then are exported to other parts of the world through colonial and neocolonial currents. Creative construction offers a theoretical subversion of Westernized aesthetic formalistic traditions that tend to dominate theories concerned with theological aesthetics in this era of global artistry.[40] *Creatio Dei* as a theological paradigm is an initial step in the process of decolonizing dogma

---

39. García-Rivera, *Community of the Beautiful*, 9. Alexander G. Baumgarten coined the term "aesthetics" in 1735 to "describe what he called the new 'science of sensory cognition.'" However, the meaning today includes questions about art, "its nature, conditions, and consequences." This definition "makes aesthetics equivalent to the philosophy and psychology of art." Brown, *Aesthetics*, 103. Frank Burch Brown suggests three "artistic clusters" for interpreting art in the context of Christian tradition: (1) Art that is "made in such a way" that is perceived as beautiful; (2) art that is made with skill, knowledge, and creativity; (3) art that uses "forms that express, fictively represent, and imaginatively transform 'worlds' in a revelatory or prophetic way" (103). Brown's suggestions are helpful for constructing a framework to examine aesthetics in the light of Christianity: beauty, knowledge, and transformation. When we speak of aesthetics, however, we are referring to particular ways of perceiving, constructing, and experiencing beauty and truth. The scope of this dissertation does not allow a study of aesthetics. The term that I focus on is creativity—not so much as an aesthetic criterion but more purposefully as a mode of being for participation in God's creativity as exemplified through the mission of Jesus Christ. Therefore, while Burch Brown introduces "creativity" as an aspect of his second artistic cluster—creativity as pertinent to knowledge creation, I prefer to use it first as a right orientation of the artist to the Creative Being and mission of the Creator through Jesus Christ. Geertz, "Art as a Cultural System," 1477. Theological aesthetics as a hermeneutical category invariably facilitates "externalized conceptions of the phenomenon supposedly under intense inspection but actually not even in our line of sight."

40. In doing so it operates as a liberation theology. Hassan Mahmadalli in "Breaking the Code" recalls Rashid Araeen's observation that: "The presence of artists in Britain originating from Africa, Asia and the Carib-bean is totally absent from the official narratives of art history.... Although some Afro-Asian artists have been received benevolently and with admira-tion, there is little institutional recognition that the absence of non-white artists from mainstream art history has falsified the history of modernism."

as predominantly enunciated by Western language ideologies especially as it pertains to the process of musical creativity.[41]

Summarizing, creative construction embraces a relational ontology that values material and embodied dimensions of creation. In invites further exploration of the ontology of form as it pertains to developing a theology of form (for example, sonic theology) for the mission contexts of ICMs. Creative construction is a collaborative process. It relocates the creative environment of the Trinity in the new spaces with others through the creative agency of ICMs in mission. Creative construction is a subaltern hermeneutic amounting to redefining notions of Westernized aesthetics. As a form of postcolonial discourse the concept of creative construction interrogates structural paradigms that reinforce Euro-Western hegemonic processes of creative construction. Creative construction operates as a theology of liberation in the context of the creative mission of ICMs amid the diversity of global new spaces.

CREATIVE PERFORMANCE[42]

The concept of creative performance refers to the ways in which ICMs understand and practice of a "theology of dialogue" through their music with others in the new spaces that they occupy for mission. Creative performance may be understood in two ways. First, as prophetic dialogue creative performance is something that is more a spirituality than a strategy for mission.[43] Second, as prophetic performance the creativity of ICMs for mission in the new spaces they occupy are places for the embodiment and enactment of public liturgy—liturgical spaces for the collective performance of identity through musical creativity.[44] The prophet Ezekiel's prophetic performance act in Ezekiel chapter 4 serves to demonstrate the embodiment of Scripture as public liturgy.

41. Cf. Begbie, "Future of Theology Amid the Arts."

42. When we speak of performance, we need to ask as *per* which, or whose, *form*? The assumption is that the resurrected body of Jesus Christ is the ultimate Form of all forms. In His relationship with the Father all persons, by the Spirit, "live, move, and have our being."

43. Bevans and Schroeder, *Prophetic Dialogue*, 22.

44. The *leitourgia* in terms of the public service on behalf of the people takes place not merely in the context of "worship" within the walls of the church. However, liturgy is enacted when God's people respond to His Spirit to serve God wherever they may be. "Liturgy may break out anywhere." Hawn, *Gather Into One*, 5. Constitutive rhetoric, serves to construct a collective identity for an addressed audience, constructs the audience as a subject in history, and demands that subjects act in accordance with their identity as enacted in history. Charland, "Constitutive Rhetoric," 213–34. See also, Mark Lewis's *Diffusion of Black Gospel Music in Postmodern Denmark*.

In a biblical context, performance is not so much the act of presenting something with a focus of what is being presented. Rather, the general use of the word in both testaments appears to emphasize the radical and dynamic congruity between personhood and what is being performed in the context of a relationship with the Living God.[45] In the context of borderland "liturgical

45. For example, in Ps 56:12—"I must perform my vows to you"—the word translated, "perform" is a preposition. This implies a pre-positioning of "performance" in accord with "vows to you." The relationship of preposition to noun (vows) suggests that the act of performance is not separate from what is being offered to God. In Gen 38:8—Then Judah said to Onan, "Go in to your brother's wife and perform the duty of a brother-in-law to her, and raise up offspring for your brother"—there is no single word that might be translated as perform. But the phrase "perform the duty of a brother-in-law" is used to indicate the compliance of *acting in accord with* one's perceived or commonly understood role in that context. In Lev 8:35 the role of the priests is "performing what the Lord has charged, so that you do not die, for so I have been commanded." Here the word translated "performing" is the same root word, "to keep, watch, preserve." Further, in this instance, performance is far from an act divorced from God's purpose. A failure to "keep watch or preserve" one's being in accord with what the LORD "has charged" ends in drastic consequences.

In Lev 25:18—" . . . keep my rules and perform them, then you will dwell in the land securely"—the word for "perform" is "asah," "do, make, accomplish." Here performance is *collective* (plural) acts to be accomplished in accord with the statutes and rules established with *consequences* for the fruitfulness of the land. In Neh 9:10, the word perform is used in reference to the Lord's performance of signs and wonders in response to the affliction of the Israelites in Egypt. Here performance is *directed against* Pharoah, his household, and people of the land (scope). Further *it stems from the Lord's knowledge* of the arrogance (*zid*) of the people. In addition, through such performance, the Lord announces and proclaims his identity that lasts for generations—"you made a name for yourself, as it is to this day." In the next few verses Nehemiah recollects the wondrous ways in which God performed and revealed himself to the people (dividing the waters, leading by a pillar of cloud, descending upon Mount Sinai, giving of "right rules and true laws," the provision of bread from heaven, and the command to possess the land"—vv. 10–15; also, cf. v. 17. In Ps 78:43, the word, "sum" or "sim" in Hebrew is translated "perform" (ESV)—"when he performed his signs in Egypt."

In Ezek 12:28 the Lord GOD proclaims an impending performance in immediate response to the laxity of Israel, the people who do not take the Lord at his word (Ezek 12:27). The root word here "asah" is used in the sense of *accomplishing God's purpose*. But here performance is integrated with the prophetic *nature of God* (cf. v. 27, "prophesies," niphal participle absolute) and "the word that I speak," the speech-act (*dabar*) of God by which prophetic performance is an extension of "the divine personality, invested with divine authority, and is to be heeded by angels and men"; it stands forever and cannot return unfulfilled. Taylor, "Word." In the NT, in Matt 5:33, Jesus uses performance in the sense of "to give or do something which one should in fulfillment of an obligation or expectation." *Theological Dictionary of the New Testament*. It also is interpreted "to cause to happen what has been promised, often in relation to vows or oaths" (Louw and Nida, "Psychological Faculties"). Here again, the act of performance indicates action in accord with *fulfilling what is expected* from the performer. Jesus performs in the sense of bringing to completion in accord with his overall life purpose and mission (Luke 13:32); his performance of miracles is *never an isolated act*. In John

spaces" occupied by ICMs, creative performance explores the ways in which ICMs are called to sing a "new song" along with the other.[46]

CREATIVE PERFORMANCE AND PROPHETIC DIALOGUE

In this section we summarize the concept of prophetic dialogue as it pertains to the creative performance of ICMs for mission. "Christian theology is a theology of dialogue."[47] In outlining a theology of mission, Stephen B. Bevans and Roger P. Schroeder propose prophetic dialogue as a synthesis of: (1) mission as participation in the life and mission of the Trinity, (2) mission as continuation of Jesus's ongoing mission in preaching, teaching, and witness in the "already, not yet" fact of the kingdom of God, and (3) mission as proclamation of the uniqueness of Christ as Lord and Savior.[48] Participation, radical continuity in Christ, and authentic witness are foundational for prophetic performances of ICMs in mission.

As Christ-like posturing, prophetic dialogue is characterized by "bold humility."[49] "Bold humility" entails a deep humility for the ill effects of past missionary endeavors in the name of God as well as a genuine recognition and respect for other cultures. Prophetic dialogue is therefore a process of healing. It is to begin with the understanding that God is already at work in other cultures prior to the missionary.[50] Prophetic dialogue is prophetic

---

6:30 Jesus is asked for a sign—"what work do you perform?" Here there is no separate word for "perform," but the stem is derived from "ergon," to work, and is used as a verb. It denotes, "action or active zeal in contrast to useless busy-ness" (Kittel, *Theological Dictionary of the New Testament*). In this context, the query suggests that performance in order for it to be effective needs to be *authentic*. Prophetic performance, therefore, does not have its authority in the perception of people merely, but in the identity of Jesus Christ performing in accord with the will of the heavenly Father.

46. Beale and Carson, *Commentary on the New Testament Use of The Old Testament*, 1102. In the Old Testament, the "new song" was used to express praise to God for victory over the enemy and in some cases included thanksgiving for creation (Ps 33:3; 144:9); there is a tangible link between the playing of a harp and singing a new song (also, see Ps 40:3, 96:1; 98:1; 149:1; Isa. 42:10) (Beale and Carson, *Commentary on the New Testament Use of The Old Testament*, 1102). In the New Testament its use is more analogical or typological, given the complete victory in Jesus Christ over sin and death; what is to be noted is the eschatological significance of the "new song" in Judaism and hence its direct linkage to its use in the New Testament (Rev 5:9; 14:3) (cf. ibid.).

47. Bosch, *Transforming Mission*, 483.

48. Bevans and Schroeder, *Constants in Context*, 348.

49. Saayman and Kritzinger, *Mission in Bold Humility*. See also Bosch, *Transforming Mission*, 484–85.

50. Bevans and Schroeder, *Prophetic Dialogue*, 3. It presupposes commitment to the gospel. For Bosch, the goal of mission is not merely to make the Christian a better Christian and to make the Buddhist a better Buddhist—this is dialogue, but not

due to the kerygmatic nature of the Gospel and interrogates ecclesial, political, and patriarchal structures. It is dialogue because of the "imperative" of particular contexts that require a "letting go" before one "speaks out" and values human experience and reason.[51]

In terms of the scope of prophetic dialogue, Bevans and Schroeder recollect six "essential components of God's mission in which the church is called to share," which are summarized here: (1) authentic witness (individual, congregational, institutional, and communal) and proclamation (of and about Jesus, invitational, out of "weakness and vulnerability"). (2) A foundation of liturgy that in of itself is worship (inside and out), equips, challenges, nourishes, and empowers for mission (outside in), and performed with an "eye to the borders" (inside out); missional prayer and contemplation. (3) Commitment to justice (socio-economic-political and environmental), peace (inviting people to an intentional and "conscious choice," responding to prophetic witness, and shalom) and the integrity of creation (ecological responsibility and the re-centering of human integrity in the context of eschatology). (4) The practice of interreligious dialogue ("the discovery in the knowledge of the other new depths and possibilities in oneself" via inclusivism, exclusivism, and pluralism or mutuality models, helping people to ask the "right" questions). (5) Efforts of inculturation (translating what is "infinitely translatable"[52] while being wary of a "universalized" theological expression. (6) The ministry of reconciliation (personal, cultural, political, and within the church).[53]

The prophetic nature of dialogue is concerned with how the "prophets" (for us, ICMs in their prophetic capacity) discern and interpret current events in society and address these in the light of God's Word. This includes "speaking forth" (casting a vision of God's plan "without words" and "with words") and speaking "out" (calling people to repentance and living faith in Christ by addressing prevailing worldly powers with truth and countercultural witness), in love and awareness of own weaknesses.[54]

---

mission; Christ as paramount and unique distinguishes prophetic dialogue from simply dialogue (Knitter in Bosch, *Transforming Mission*, 487), expects God to be at work already, and is couched in humility, vulnerability.

51. Bevans and Schroeder, *Constants in Context*, 349–52.

52. Andrew Walls speaks of the indigenizing and pilgrim principles—making one feel at home but not so much that no one else can live there. Walls, *Missionary Movement in Christian History*, 7–9. See also Bevans and Schroeder, *Constants in Context*, 387.

53. Bevans and Schroeder, *Constants in Context*, 351–94. Also Bevans, "Letting Go and Speaking Out," 133–46.

54. Bevans and Schroeder, *Prophetic Dialogue*, 40–48.

PROPHETIC PERFORMANCE: METAPHOR AND EMBODIMENT

In the context of the mission of ICMs, prophetic performance as embodiment of the scriptural narrative is an activity that transforms the performer and in turn invites the participation of others to an act of collective transformation.[55] The following passage from the Book of the prophet Ezekiel, chapter 4:1–17, illustrates the power of prophetic performance:

> And you, son of man, take a brick and lay it before you, and engrave on it a city, even Jerusalem. 2 And put siegeworks against it, and build a siege wall against it, and cast up a mound against it. Set camps also against it, and plant battering rams against it all around. 3 And you, take an iron griddle, and place it as an iron wall between you and the city; and set your face toward it, and let it be in a state of siege, and press the siege against it. This is a sign for the house of Israel.
>
> 4 Then lie on your left side, and place the punishment of the house of Israel upon it. For the number of the days that you lie on it, you shall bear their punishment. 5 For I assign to you a number of days, 390 days, equal to the number of the years of their punishment. So long shall you bear the punishment of the house of Israel. 6 And when you have completed these, you shall lie down a second time, but on your right side, and bear the punishment of the house of Judah. Forty days I assign you, a day for each year. 7 And you shall set your face toward the siege of Jerusalem, with your arm bared, and you shall prophesy against the city. 8 And behold, I will place cords upon you, so that you cannot turn from one side to the other, till you have completed the days of your siege.
>
> 9 And you, take wheat and barley, beans and lentils, millet and emmer, and put them into a single vessel and make your bread from them. During the number of days that you lie on your side, 390 days, you shall eat it. 10 And your food that you eat shall be by weight, twenty shekels a day; from day to day you shall eat it. 11 And water you shall drink by measure, the sixth part of a hin; from day to day you shall drink. 12 And you shall eat it as a barley cake, baking it in their sight on human dung." 13 And the Lord said, "Thus shall the people of Israel eat their bread unclean, among the nations where I will drive them."
> 14 Then I said, "Ah, Lord God! Behold, I have never defiled myself. From my youth up till now I have never eaten what died of

---

55. "Once the story gets 'inside' the actor, the actor is able to get 'inside' the story." West, "Performance Criticism of the Narratives in the Hebrew Bible," 80.

itself or was torn by beasts, nor has tainted meat come into my mouth." 15 Then he said to me, "See, I assign to you cow's dung instead of human dung, on which you may prepare your bread." 16 Moreover, he said to me, "Son of man, behold, I will break the supply of bread in Jerusalem. They shall eat bread by weight and with anxiety, and they shall drink water by measure and in dismay. 17 I will do this that they may lack bread and water, and look at one another in dismay, and rot away because of their punishment (English Standard Version).

The language of participation is helpful to establish a paradigm for the ontological positioning of ICMs in the ongoing work of Christ.[56] In this section we attempt to bring together perspectives from the anthropology of performance and prophetic performance as per Ezekiel's act above to explore the creative performance of ICMs in mission.

Anthropology of Performance

In the past, performance studies included the broad areas of praxis ("ordinary practice"), enactment (public events), and oral poetics (performing for a given group of people).[57] The per-formative nature of musical creativity in this study refers to its varied and emergent nature—interactive, collaborative, collective (tradition- and habit-forming), multi-sensorial engagement between participants and cultural productions.[58]

In addition, within the scope of ethnomusicology, musical creativity includes bodily enactment. Theories in dance are helpful to explore this phenomenon. In "Global Breakdancing and the Intercultural Body," Halifu Osumare defines performance as a "series of bodily enactments that bring conscious intent and purpose to the physical execution of rhythmically patterned movement."[59] From Osumare we gather that experiences of the body far outweigh rational-intellectual processes in terms of being real ways for generating knowledge. Osumare reiterates in the context of dance performance what we have gathered from ethnomusicology thus far, that performance often consists of "codified, learned systems of movement practices" and patterns representing cultural values.[60] In the light of the scope of performance thus defined, Osumare prefers the term, "performativity" to

---

56. Bellini, *Participation*.

57. Korom, *Anthropology of Performance*, 2–3. Among others, he recollects the work of Limón and Young, "Frontiers, Settlements, and Development" 437–60.

58. Korom, *Anthropology of Performance*, 2–3.

59. Osumare, "Global Breakdancing and the Intercultural Body," 261.

60. Osumare, "Global Breakdancing and the Intercultural Body," 261.

refer to the "unconscious but meaningful series of bodily postures, gestures, and movements that implicitly signify and mark a sense of social identity" (2013, 261) in everyday life. According to him,

> The performativity of gestures and body language constitutes the manner in which we understand ourselves through our bodies, literally through the muscular and skeletal structure as well as semiotically and metaphorically (ibid.).

As far as the role of the human body, or shall we say, performativity, in facilitating cognition, we recollect David Kirsh's discussion on the concept of "enactive thought" whereby movement is "more than embodied cognition, it is extended and distributed."[61] In his presentation, Kirsh quotes Ludwig Wittgenstein (1953), according to whom, "When I think in language, there aren't 'meanings' going through my mind in addition to the verbal expressions: the language is itself the vehicle of thought" (ibid.). Furthermore, this applies to auditory mental images of words as well as external expressions of words.[62] Responding to Wittgenstein's thesis, David Kirsh makes the case that communication is sent in a vehicle of thought, in the head or the external representation. The point he makes is that performance in terms of the embodiment of thought *via* movement is not any less an intellectual cognitive act than other more formal or traditional modes of thought.[63] In the light of this emergent and "enactive" nature of cognition, we turn to explore the biblical scenario in Ezekiel 4 as embodied prophetic performance.

---

61. Kirsh, "How to Think with Bodies and Things."

62. Kirsh, "How to Think with Bodies and Things." See also Wittgenstein, *Philosophical Investigations*.

63. I am thinking of Rodin's (1840–1917) sculpture of Dante ("The Thinker") that captures "thought" in motionless beauty as opposed to the embodiment and enactment of knowledge in the image of the "Dancing Shiva" (Nataraj). "*The Thinker* was entitled *The Poet*, who represented Dante, author of the *Divine Comedy* which had inspired *The Gates*, leaning forward to observe the circles of Hell, while meditating on his work. *The Thinker* was therefore initially both a being with a tortured body, almost a damned soul, and a free-thinking man, determined to transcend his suffering through poetry." The museum website further describes, "This image of a man lost in thought, but whose powerful body suggests a great capacity for action, has became one of the most celebrated sculptures ever known. Musseé Rodin, Auguste Rodin, The Thinker, http://www.musee-rodin.fr/en/collections/sculptures/thinker. See also "Arts of South and Southeast Asia."

Ezekiel's Prophetic Performance

Prophetic performance for our purpose here refers not only to the enactment of musical thought but also to the radical embodiment of prophetic vision.[64] In the passage above from Ezekiel, the embodied nature of the prophetic performance is radicalized through the agency of the prophet Ezekiel. We notice the following directives from God to the prophet: "take," "lay," "engrave," "put," "build," "cast," "set camps," "plant," "place," and "press" (all in just the first three verses). Furthermore God says, "let it be in a state of siege." What might this mean, except that Ezekiel is supposed to engage his being by interacting with his environment of objects and onlookers (co-participants) in what might be perceived as a "state of siege"!

In interpreting this particular biblical scenario, Yvonne M. Sherwood chooses to go where biblical scholars seldom choose to go.[65] She notes that much of the genre of "'prophetic eschatology" is characterized by "linguistic inadequacy." In other words, for Sherwood, the discourse of biblical criticism has tended toward a manicured interpretation of the reality of embodied prophetic discourse. According to her:

> Rhetorical studies suggest the idea of the prophet as a disciplined gentleman; Romanticism—almost oppositely—suggests a kind of wildness of inspiration, but a wildness that expresses itself in beautiful, elevated, and gentlemanly style (2000, 189).

She further explains:

> Criticism is suffused with a sense of deflected worship—if not for the religious content of the texts, then for its high literary style. It is almost as if religious value is being converted to, or reinforced by, literary value, as if there is no other appropriate mode of talking about these texts than by bowing and crying "holy holy holy"—or alternatively "marvelous," "great," "jolly well-made," or "what a lovely example of copulatio" (Sherwood 1998, 189).

Sherwood might be accused of unwarranted tenacity. However, she seems to address what we here have termed the "captivity" of creativity. In "Prophetic Scatology," Sherwood goes on to explain the difference between the "gauzy protection of commentary" and the biblical reality:

---

64. "Prophetic vision penetrates everydayness to go deeper than conventional wisdom in order to reveal the story behind the story, the baseline behind the headline." Greg Mobley, "EthicsDaily Weblog."

65. "For fear of getting their shoes, and their critical personae dirty." Sherwood, "Prophetic Scatology," 183.

Unfortunately Jeremiah, Ezekiel, Isaiah, et al. had no sense of the white-covered, gold-cross embossed Bibles in which their prose was to be packaged, nor had they been briefed on the standards of Western literary decorum against which they would inevitably offend. They don't just use copulatio; they talk graphically about the body and sex—the Egyptians have penises the size of stallions' according to Ezek 23:20. And they don't just strip bare the naked beauty of the world, but, as feminist critics have painfully noted, they strip bare the woman-nation, and then starve her, imprison her, parade her naked, and afflict her "genitals" with "violence" (Jer 13:22)—all for her betrayal of the marriage-covenant. The prophet is not always "fair spoken" and is rude beyond the bounds of provocatio: the rhetorical medicine he administers is often repulsive, poisonous, vitriolic rather than sweetly cherry-flavoured . . . if prophecy is a discourse flowing with curds and honey and milk and streams of water, it is also awash in scum, blood, pus, entrails and—for want of a better word—shit (Sherwood 1998, 192).

Sherwood's interpretation above communicates the significantly countercultural thrust of prophetic performance for mission. A few points stand out in the context of Ezekiel's prophetic creative performance that are relevant to the metaphorical embodiment of the liturgy amongst ICMs for mission especially in the context of postcolonial borderlands. First, Ezekiel is the embodiment of the metaphor. His creative performance was a psychosomatic process.[66] Ezekiel had to imbibe and endure physically the emotional duress of the task over a sustained period of time.[67] Some scholars refer to the physical condition imposed upon Ezekiel as "catalepsy," a nervous system disorder characterized by muscular rigidity and fixity of posture, a form of psychoses.[68] In the biblical scenario, we note that God brings about such a condition upon Ezekiel, for mission. Concerning ICMs

---

66. Scientific evidence demonstrates the essential linkage between mind (psyche) and body (soma). According to an article addressing Psychosomatic Disorders from the Institute for Studies in Psychotherapy and Emotional Body-work (ISPEB), "'Psyche' refers to emotions or mind related aspects and 'somatic' refers to physical and symptoms and signs." Further, "A new perspective to treatment of psychosomatic disorders focuses on the fact that patients' minds should not be considered as separate from the body" (http://cirrie.buffalo.edu/encyclopedia/en/article/139/consumer/,.

67. Ezek 3:14, 15, bitter in his spirit and "overwhelmed."

68. Catalepsy is: "A condition characterized by waxy rigidity of the limbs, which may be placed in various positions that are maintained for a time, lack of response to stimuli, mutism, and inactivity; occurs with some psychoses, especially catatonic schizophrenia." Medilexicon, http://www.medilexicon.com/medicaldictionary.php?t=14932.

for mission, therefore, the course of suffering on behalf of others is a defining feature of prophetic performance.

Second, Ezekiel's role as prophet may be compared with Homi K. Bhabha's reference to the historical agency of the artist as "critic." For Bhabha, the artist has a "political responsibility."[69] For him, the "critic must attempt to fully realize, and take responsibility for the unspoken, unrepresented pasts that haunt the historical present" (ibid.). Bhabha's purpose is to demonstrate how "historical agency is transformed through the signifying process."[70] The implication for ICMs in mission is that they are the "critic" who must embody the scriptural narrative in ways that interrogate culture and thereby authentically represent the historical context whilst being transformed in one's own agency.[71]

Third, the location for the embodiment of the metaphor was a public setting, specifically, to "the exiles" (Ezek 3:11, 15). Ezekiel's public location signifies the space "beyond" the epistemological and ontological "limits" of the participants.[72] The space "beyond" signifies a call to participants "to live somehow beyond the border of our times"; it also "throws into relief the temporal, social differences that interrupt our collusive sense of cultural contemporaneity" (ibid.). In other words, prophetic performance calls ICMs to a radical relocation of their scriptural performativity with others thereby making the sites they occupy places for learning; the stretching of their own theological "limits" to include others in their respective contexts for mission. It is in the boundary places that knowledge is generated along with the other. Bevans and Schroeder observe that post *Ad Gentes 2*, mission is no longer a territorial concept "but a basic attitude of the church where it is."[73]

---

69. Bhabha, *Location of Culture*, loc. 725.

70. Bhabha, *Location of Culture*, loc. 735.

71. The reality of *lived metaphor* is an excruciatingly present ontological manifestation. We recollect from Kozbelt et al. that Gruber (1978) pioneered the evolving systems approach to creativity that focused on the attributes of the creative person, such as *ensemble of metaphors, network of enterprises* (a system of goals describing concurrent and consecutive working of disparate goals) (in Kozbelt et al., "Theories of Creativity"). Central to the creativity of "great creators" is the use of "an ensemble of metaphors rather than one dominant metaphor." Along with the use of metaphor comes the hermeneutic of ambiguity, as a valid, yet incomplete, interpretation of scriptural reality. Csikszentmihalyi's "Systems Model of Creativity" (discussed in ch. 2) provides an overarching framework for analyzing the "ensemble of metaphors" that arise in the context of creative processes.

72. Bhabha, *Location of Culture*, 532.

73. Bevans and Schroeder, *Prophetic Dialogue*, 140. Bevans and Schroeder base their concepts of prophetic dialogue on the approaches to interreligious dialogue from documents of the Catholic church such as *Ad Gentes, Evangelii Nuntiandi*, and *Redemptoris Missio* (Bevans and Schroeder, *Prophetic Dialogue*, 138–54). Knowledge is to be

Fourth, Ezekiel's creative performance lasts for over four hundred days (Ezek 4:5, 6) during which time Ezekiel "bears" the punishment of the house of Israel. The question may be raised as to what might such sustained "missionary" activity mean for the creative performance of ICMs in the spaces that they inhabit for mission. James S. Hanson's definition of performance is helpful. According to him performance is a "translucent instrument through which we encounter a living Presence."[74] In the context of the performance of scriptural themes, the idea is not so much to get a single correct interpretation of the "text," but to allow for the emergence of truth in the enactment and embodiment of one's own struggles along with and in the context of biblical characters and their experiences.[75] The prophetic task for the Jews by the waters of Babylon and for ICMs in the new spaces for mission involves extending an invitation to others to participate in the collective task of mediating a new reality on earth as it is in heaven.[76]

SUMMARY

A theology of *creatio Dei* helps to lay a hermeneutical framework (Missiological Framework for Theological Creativity, MFTC) for creative mission. We proceeded to develop the concepts of Creative Being, Creative Construction, and Creative Performance as a theology of creativity that will inform the understanding and practice of ICMs for mission in this era of globalization. Creative being emphasizes the correlative integrity between creative entity and process, the creative reconfiguration of historiography, the cosmic moral consciousness inherent to the creative process, and the primordial and simultaneous eschatological relocation of creative space as the context of the contestation of ICM identity for mission. Creative construction draws attention to an expanded relational ontology, creativity as a collaborative process with others, and creativity as a subaltern hermeneutic to articulate a theology "through the arts." Creative performance in the context of ICMs for mission is prophetic activity that is enactive in nature and is the embodiment of a unique knowledge in Christ. Creative prophetic

---

found in the boundaries between religion and culture, church and society, heteronomy and autonomy, and faith and doubt. Tillich, *Dynamics of Faith*, 16–22; also in Bevans and Schroeder, *Prophetic Dialogue*, 97.

74. Hanson, "Faith Comes From What Is Heard," 154.

75. Hanson, "Faith Comes From What Is Heard," 154–69.

76. The creative performance of ICMs as prophetic activity "is to mediate a relinquishment of a world that is gone and a reception of a world that is being given." Brueggemann, *Practice of Prophetic Imagination*, 145.

performance mediates the very presence of God in the public arena as an invitation for participation with others in the mission of God.

In chapters 5–7 we move to exploring the creativity of ICMs in the context of the concepts and dynamics of musical creativity, new spaces, and creative mission introduced and developed thus far.

5

Creative Being: Embodiment

THE FORMATION OF CREATIVE being in the context of the mission of God was to be an ongoing battle for the Jews "by the waters of Babylon." As captive migrants, for the Israelites, the idea of a "nation unbound" (cf. Basch *et al* 1994)—a de- and reconstruction of their experience as a nation of God's people—almost certainly did not figure in their imaginings of what it meant to be a people set free to worship the God of Israel. Yet in the economy of God's salvation, the "beyond" (Bhabha 1994) of freedom from captivity lay within their grasp in learning how to sing along with the other "in a foreign land." So it is with ICMs in the new spaces that they occupy for mission.

With respect to the anthropology of "space" in the twentieth century, Akhil Gupta and James Ferguson echo James Clifford: "What does it mean at the end of the twentieth century to speak . . . of a 'native land'? What processes rather than essences are involved in present experiences of cultural identity?"[1] In the twenty-first century, these questions are even more poignant. According to Gupta and Ferguson, space has functioned as a "central organizing principle" in the context of general notions of "culture areas," and "ethnographic maps."[2]

However, notions of space are not without problems. First, the concepts of borderlands, frequent border-crossings, and migrants challenge the "isomorphism of space, place, and culture" (ibid.). Second, "multiculturalism" often refers to the subsuming of cultural plurality and distinctiveness under the rubric of national identity. Third, what do we make of the hybridity arising from colonialism? Are both (neo) colonized and

---

1. Gupta and Ferguson, "Beyond 'Culture,'" 9. See also Clifford, *Predicament of Culture*, 275.

2. Gupta and Ferguson, "Beyond 'Culture,'" 7.

colonists changed?[3] Fourth, a question is raised as to how change and transformation occur in this context.[4]

AUTHENTICITY AND REPRESENTATION

We recollect ML was raised in Nepal and India with North American missionary parents for his first 17 years. His interest in the sitar was aroused while listening to a recording by a North American progressive rock band. In his expatriate school in India, he ignored the Indian music department in favor of Western jazz band, choir, and trumpet. From a missiological perspective, ML's choice to play sitar evinces a crucial shift in the deconstruction and reconstruction of his musical identity. ML's desire to play the sitar did not begin with a desire to "reach" others by the adoption of cultural relevant forms. The sound of the instrument moved him. Earlier, ML grew up immersed in the sonic phenomena of the folk and tribal environment of Nepal and India. The stirring in his heart to adopt sitar playing as a way of life is significant, given the fusion of sounds and textures that he currently employs.

The perception that "fusion" music is a "departure" from "canonical music traditions" contributes to its label as a hybrid genre.[5] Amit Chaudhari suggests that "fusion" is simultaneously located in class, history, and physical environment. Fusion transcends nationality as well as locality. Fusion signifies a search not merely for interracial encounter, but it is a language that articulates the complex dynamic between creative identity and surrounding context. Fusion occupies a "quasi-mystical" space, a "now globalised—plane where two unlikes constantly embrace, and where conflict is not openly admissible" (2007, 38–39). Creative being as embodied discourse in a space where "conflict is not openly admissible" problematizes the enactment of identity by ICMs in the spaces that they occupy. For, the truth is that conflict is inevitable.

The adoption of Western music may be seen as a local response to the global. It emphasizes what people "accomplish."[6] This is significant in terms of creating the space in-between for the engagement of mimetic faculties for the

---

3. Sartre, "Introduction," 8. Albert Memmi is one of those who appear privileged by the colonized masses, yet at the same time rejected by the colonizing group. On one hand, they (the colonized) must rediscover their unity in opposition to the project of the colonizer. On the other hand, however, it is in a reciprocal relationship with the other where own identity is forged.

4. Gupta and Ferguson, "Beyond 'Culture,'" 7, 8.

5. Chaudhari, "Into the Mix," 38.

6. Toynbee and Dueck, *Migrating Musics*, 7.

creation of new mutually transformative histories.[7] If what is accomplished is primarily Christianity in Western terms, then the effectiveness of such rhetoric is problematic, especially in a post and neocolonial context. Jacques Attali addresses the particular nature of such exchange in the light of the place of recording technologies in musical fission—how recording technologies reproduce social relations through a network of repetition.[8]

ML (a Caucasian in the South Asian context), however, redefines the nature of the exchange of power in musical fission through his fusion music. The decision to learn sitar draws him into a place for the negotiation of identities for the "transfusion" of the Gospel with the other. By adopting the sitar as his instrument of choice, ML embodies a place for the exchange of multiple identities—glocal and translocal—and the mediation of cultural distinctiveness. It is an act of "othering."[9] Through the sitar, ML enters into a process of deconstructing his own identity through the cultivation of a transnational (and transcultural) sphere "of global music discourses and practices" (Feld 2000, 264). In other words, ML opens himself to a process of ambiguity through his act of copying, a willingness to be interpreted by the other on their terms. This is especially significant since typically, as a Caucasian, ML is the one to be copied.

Therefore, ML's fusion approach offers a corrective to a norm of modernity.[10] It is significant to note that fusion is not about a simple meet and mix. Rather, from ML and his willingness to be represented in and through the form of the other, he has risked vulnerability to being rejected by the other. At the same time, it is through this portal of risk that ML invites open conversation. The reality of the still-to-be negotiated power relations has not disappeared, but the process of becoming through copying is at least

---

7. Taussig, *Mimesis and Alterity*, 71; Bhabha, *Location of Culture*.

8. Attali, *Noise*, 32. Steven Feld draws on Attali's approach to address the effect of World Music in colonial and postcolonial Africa (Pygmy Pop): such a "'repetitive machine has produced silence, the centralized political control of speech, and more generally, noise.'" "'Everywhere, power reduces the noise made by others and adds sound prevention to its arsenal.'" Feld, "Poetics and Politics of Pygmy Pop," 264.

9. Toynbee and Dueck, *Migrating Musics*, 7, 9. Through mimesis, both powerful and subordinate groups appropriate and transform aspects of one another's difference, and in doing so attain power over that otherness.

10. Feld, "Poetics and Politics of Pygmy Pop," 264. In modernity, representation is often interpreted in terms of reflection and revelation—"a direct appeal to the senses to imagine an interconnected world of objects." Interestingly, however, the mimetic process "elides the form of the split original, the split resemblance of a simultaneous unity and multiplicity." Such *rupture* evident in ML's "postmodern discourse" is where, as Feld strongly asserts, "The appropriation born of mimesis is both the official bastard of social hierarchy and the living mark that every relationship of copy to copied is an icon of unequal power relations" (underline mine).

a two-way street. To reiterate, rather than a replication of Westernized notions of inculturation, mediated through the creative being of ML—others copying the Caucasian in ML—the process of mimetic exchange is about a collective "crisis, about destabilizing ideas about authenticity and truth, about disrupting presumptions about primal reference or originality" (Feld 2000, 264). In modernity the relation between copy and copied may be one of "unequal power relations." With ML, the invitation is extended to challenge such a notion. Hope is harbored at the thought of overcoming hegemony for mutuality through fusion music.

On another level in the representation and negotiation of identity, ML's choice is not merely conceptual but a definite performative act setting the "scene" for the expression of symbol or (sonic) image. Michael Taussig interacts with James George Frazer's principles of mimesis, imitation and contact, in determining how "symbolic identities form an image of likeness" (1993, 56). Taussig discerns that the formation of symbolic identity is "not so much in the association of ideas as concepts, but in the association of images of sadness and anger"[11] (ibid.). It is real.[12] It is a place for overcoming the barriers endemic to a post and neocolonialist context.[13]

When ML picks up the sitar to perform, he is embodying and enacting an "image" by creating a "scene" that invites others to participate in a

---

11. The idea of emotional awareness and bodily enactment as an interpretation of decision-making lends itself to understanding the creation of music in a given space and time. Based upon Carl Jung's insight that "objects draw and invoke emotions," it has been scientifically ascertained that there is an inherent connection between emotions/feelings and body systems. Further, the process of enactment of such emotion/feeling by the body may be explained to consist of: awareness—being aware of the context that elicits a given emotion (fear etc.), body change—awareness triggers bodily change, heart rate, muscles etc., Interpretation—using all sensibilities for the preservation of identity (escape, stay and fight etc.), action—execution of decision. Authentic Systems: "Motivation Research and Development."

12. Pachuau, "Engaging the 'Other' in a Pluralistic World," 69. Identity is never static nor is it constructed in a vacuum. Symbolic manifestations of identity by themselves are not problematic; it is "the threat which accompanies the process of globalization to homogenize cultures" that catalyzes the "assertion of ethno-identity and cultural difference."

13. Taussig, *Mimesis and Alterity*, 57. The interpenetration of image (what is represented) and contact must have the (reciprocal) effect of "making us reconsider our very notion of what it means to be an image of something, most especially if we wish not only to express but to manipulate reality by means of its image."

performance.[14] Action is its own image (ibid.).[15] Therefore, we conclude that musical creativity is both, exegesis (interpretation out of the text) and eisegesis (what is read into the text). It is here where "senses cross over and translate into each other. You feel redness. You see music" (cf. Taussig 1993, 57). Mimesis or copying involves translation. It is bringing "another's music across into your own system of conceptual and aesthetic categories" in which it operates and signifies in ways quite distinct from the prior context.[16]

However, whose conceptual and aesthetic categories are we talking about? The idea of translating "another's music" is actually the creation of space for ambiguity and for the psyche to dwell. Ambiguity is a condition for the mediation of difference.[17] In this sense, the embodiment of creative being through the process of musical creativity for mission is a "wager on transcendence" through which "we encounter the other in its condition of freedom."[18]

Authentic Mission, a "byproduct" of Creative Being

There is more to musical creativity than meets the ear. ML's sense of mission is not borne primarily out of his desire to "reach" people with his music. According to him, "My primary motivation as a musician in general has been simply to fulfill what is clearly a gift that God has given me to use; in using

---

14. Taussig, *Mimesis and Alterity*, 53. Taussig reframes Frazer's focus on the symbols in the larger perspective of the "scene" that includes the "gestus" of the ritualist. The reality of the ontic—the motivational aspects determining the real place and role of human sensibility and response—makes embodiment and enactment (cf. gestus) a core factor in the signification of the image, thereby creating an atmosphere for the larger scene for the performance.

15. Taussig, *Mimesis and Alterity*, 57. We cannot allow for the "tyranny of the visual notion of image" to be the sole or primary determinant of meaning. When it comes to enacting creative being, it is not only the sound of music—"the visual imagery"—but the "nonvisual imagery" as well that needs to be considered. In the "medicinally triggered visions" amongst the Putumayo in the Upper Amazon where nonvisual imagery includes nausea, sound, smell, chanting, and the "less tangible qualities of presence, atmosphere, and movement."

16. Toynbee and Dueck, *Migrating Music*, 8. "Distinctions . . . arise out of a great central moltenness, where all is merged." Burke, "Excerpt from *A Grammar of Motives*," 1300. For Burke, in order for A to become non-A, it cannot make a direct leap; it must return to the "ground of its existence, the logical substance that is its causal ancestor, and on to a point where it is consubstantial with non-A" before it can emerge as non-A.

17. Born and Hesmondhalgh, *Western Music and Its Others*, 32. Derrida, *Margins of Philosophy*, 3–27. Difference is continually being deferred in the process of interactivity with the other.

18. Steiner, *Errata*, 4.

that gift the byproduct of that is mission." His creative being is intrinsic to his ability and desire to identify with others.

ML views his primary responsibility as being faithful to his calling in Christ through his musical identity, which includes others. In a manner of speaking, his mission is not so much to reach others but to create with them, to invite others to participate in his creative being with God and through Christ and Spirit, with the world. In his own words:

> In order to try to defend ourselves as artists in terms of this history of church attitudes towards artists, what have we done? We try to put the Gospel very overtly before anything we do. We try and explain what we are doing, why the song is communicating the Gospel. But what I am realizing now is that myself as a person even if I did not say a word communicates something, because I am a person, because I am an artist; I have decided that being an artist is something that I can be in God and with God and together with God!

ML is essentially endorsing the innate connectedness between his creative being and the quintessential nature of music itself as that which is embedded culturally, involves interactions with the "configurations of the physical world," is undoubtedly "bodily," and has real linkages to the emotional life.[19]

ML goes on to raise the question, "What does it mean to glorify God through my art?" and answers it: "It is the inner commitment to glorify God in mission with my life and my art." It is more than trying to justify oneself through words or other means. He says:

> I have experienced saying nothing but having people leave and say something about me such as, "we felt like we were in the presence of something really much more important than we realize; we feel inspired somehow." And I think about it and I realize all different kinds of people who don't say anything; but we leave and my life has changed in some way.

To speak of authenticity is to speak in relative terms to the perceived absolute. Theologically, as ML indicates, when it comes to exploring the process of musical creativity the issue of authenticity is foremost one of being true to one's inmost being. The intangible, yet palpable link between personhood and productivity—what is often termed "spiritual"—indeed seems to be what is (ultimately?) authentic. Creative integrity begins at this core—the maintenance and sustenance of ensuring that what provisionally

---

19. Begbie, *Theology, Music and Time*, 9–28.

becomes creative expression is intimately and substantially a part of the self. To recollect John Zizioulas's articulation of such dynamic:

> Love is not an emanation or 'property' of the substance of God ... but is constitutive of His substance, i.e., it is that which makes God what He is, the one God.... Love as God's mode of existence 'hypostasizes' God, constitutes His being (1985, 46).

It is at this core that others participate. Earlier we asked: In what sense do artists in Christian mission exemplify and share in the creative being of the Creator? What God creates, God inspires (Gen 2:7); and what God inspires, God inhabits (Ps 22:3). Authentic creative mission invites others to share in such creativity. We observe such rhetoric in the introduction from the website of a band with which ML is affiliated:

> Popular music is often made to settle into the nooks and crannies of our daily humdrum, like an elixir against the pain of human existence. We drink it in and feel a bit better but we don't expect it to change anything beyond our emotional state.... is a band with higher aspirations, making music that is centered around <u>spiritual enlightenment and transformation while keeping ethnic integrity intact</u> (emphasis added).[20]

Here, we have an example whereby the reconstitution of creative identity in others is engendered via an invitation to participate in the creativity of the artist.[21] But how is this played out in ML's life?

ML currently does not himself participate in the life of a typical "church." In other words, he is not a regular contributor to a Sunday church service with a specific group of people. He does however continue to fellowship with other believers. He cites Heb 10:25. But for him to actually be involved in the ongoing life of any given church would be a distraction from the main task that he feels called to do—develop authentic relationships with others (Christians and non-Christians alike) through his music. This he does by inviting others to his home for meals, playing at weddings, and giving classical music lessons among other things.

ML's home church in America (consisting of a White majority) continues to support his ministry financially and on occasion invites him to

---

20. The website offers justification for contextualization through the particular genre of music ML adopts: [The band] "is among the few who have created a new and enduring sound out of diverse musical traditions of North India and North America. Somehow, [the band] has been able to glide past the subterfuge of globalization and establish itself as a band that is genuinely interested in creating cross-cultural dialogue through the arts."

21. Charland, "Constitutive Rhetoric," 133–50.

minister in church. However, one wonders if ML is a good fit even in his own home church when it comes to the expression of his gifts in musical creativity.[22] The novelty that he embodies is attractive. The difference that he brings in terms of his music is not compatible with the dominant culture, where the music for worship is mostly CCM (Contemporary Christian Music) or music in the genre of the Western Classical music tradition (for example, Handel's Messiah).

Michael Hawn identifies some of the issues related to musical authenticity, which itself varies from one person and context to another, in a cross-cultural context. In the Euro-North American classical tradition, a high value is placed on written music—what the eye sees is as significant, if not more, to what the ear hears. Literate contexts tend to passive audience participation and lesser degree of improvisational flexibility, less use of the body (e.g., dancing) signifying less distance between "'congregation and choir'" as compared with oral contexts (2003, 247). Further, according to Hawn,

> To deny a congregation a fuller range of cross-cultural musical expression within liturgy limits the potential for liminality and increases the possibility of ethnocentrism. Liturgical ethnocentrism shapes God de facto into a provincial image that reflects the values of the normative culture (ibid., 249).

Captive institutions typically hesitate to invite minority input in the structuring and planning of majority-related development of liturgies. ML is strategically located on the margins of the church to create new spaces for cross-cultural liturgical environments with others. The ambivalence of location—borderlands, transnational crossings—emphasizes "processes rather than essences" when it comes to the mediation of authenticity.[23]

Lessons in Authentic Mission from N. V. Tilak

To further illuminate the dynamic of authenticity let us look at a prominent Christian artist, N. V. Tilak, who worked approximately a century before ML in the Indian context. ML has borrowed from Tilak's lyrical compositions for his own music. Narayan Vaman Tilak (1862–1919) was an Indian Christian poet who intentionally sought to reach the Hindus of his day. An incident is recalled here that radically affected Tilak's approach in reaching Hindus with his expressive art form. According to J. C. Winslow:

---

22. Sources close to ML in his home church disclosed to me that ML is not really a good fit to lead in worship; perhaps lead in a "special song" or two on occasion.

23. Gupta and Ferguson, "Beyond 'Culture,'" 7, echoing Clifford, *Predicament of Culture*, 275.

Tilak, on a walk with some Christian friends, met a procession of Hindu pilgrims on their way to Pandharpur, dancing and singing in praise of Vithoba, and ready to travel 150 miles on foot in the enthusiasm which their songs and praises inspired. Tilak saw at once how much inspiration Christians might receive from similar hymns, and composed on the spot the first, and one of the most popular of all, "Christ the Mother-guru," which the party sang there and then on the banks of the river Mula. From that time onwards the singing of bhajans began to take its place both in Christian worship and Christian preaching (1923, 37).

The above incident serves simply to open the door to the complex nature of the missional task encountered by Christian artists through the ages and in every context—contextualizing Christianity through their expressive art forms. What prompted Tilak's creativity? Tilak was able to see "at once" the potential of "their songs and praises" as a means of spiritual inspiration. Tilak's previous identity as a devout Brahmin and as a poet steeped in traditional Hindu literature provided a framework for translating the Gospel to Hindus in contextually relevant ways in his context—in his case, *bhajan*, *kirtan*,[24] even changing his clothes, appearance, and ultimately even his lifestyle (becoming a *sanyasi*).[25]

ML appears to mimic Tilak's stance in several ways including the distanciation of self from the institutionalized church, adaptation of Indian lifestyle/clothing, and music. Tilak attempted to de-Westernize the Indian church.[26] He envisioned a united Indian church that was free and operated autonomously without foreign domination. A united church and indigenous leadership does not necessarily result in more Hindus coming to Christ. However, Tilak saw the need for a new structure for Christianity, a release from organized religion as he experienced and understood it. Take for example, his conviction that, according to Richard, "the hope for reaching India lay in moving beyond the existing church rather than

---

24. Winslow, *Narayan Vaman Tilak*, 62–63. Tilak used *kirtan* as a means for preaching. It is a form that incorporates speaking as well as singing hymns of praise, and telling stories of God in his incarnate form. It is said to have been popularized by *Namdev* in the fourteenth century. For Tilak, a *kirtan* consisted of a "happy combination of music, poetry, eloquence, humour, all contributing to drive home religious truth." The word *bhajan* means "to share in/give/belong to/serve God in many ways and forms and to seek his blessings." It follows a simple call and response patterns of sung prayer between priest and devotees. Both forms *kirtan* and *bhajan* are widely used both among Hindus as well as indigenous movements of Christianity in India and amongst Indian diaspora. Norman, *Bhajan*, 35–38.

25. Winslow, *Narayan Vaman Tilak*, 123.

26. Richard, *Following Jesus in the Hindu Context*, 31.

within it" (ibid., 59–60). ML too realizes the need for a new structure for being the Body of Christ. However, his stance within the context of Western Christianity is different.

First, Tilak adapted the musical forms (for example, *bhajan* and *kirtan*) indigenous to the Hindu community because he saw how such forms efficaciously reinforced the identity of the Hindu community. Moreover, Tilak did not merely adopt the sonic forms of *bhajan* and *kirtan*.[27] For example, the fusion of the name of "Christ" with a phrase like "Mother-guru" evidences thoughtful and intentional (albeit spontaneous and creative!) contextualization of Christianity in terms that he thought were pertinent to the people of India, Christians as well as potential converts to Christ from amongst the general Hindu population. Such forms of music represented core aspects of Hindu identity.

Tilak also saw how such forms might help in re-embedding participants in the context of the larger story of Scripture without compromising on the message of the Gospel. The approach underlies a central thesis for this study: musical expression is a universal phenomenon; it is not a universal language. Musical anthropologist John Blacking asserts that "no musical style has 'its own terms': its terms are the terms of the society and culture, and of the bodies of the human beings who listen to it, and create and perform it" (1973, 6). ML realizes this and draws widely from the *bhajan* repertoire of Tilak and other contemporary Indian composers.

Second, the road to Pandharpur was a site of transition, for Tilak first, and thereafter for the history and tradition of Christian music especially amongst Marathi Hindus and Christians.[28] Tilak did not condemn the Hindus for dancing and singing music in forms that were intrinsically different compared to those adopted by the church of his day. His openness to learn and to receive from Hindus indicates his personal victory

---

27. Beck, *Sonic Theology*; Walls, *Cross-Cultural Process in Christian History*, 39. While the sonic forms in and of themselves are theologically significant especially in the Indian context and so for the identity of the Indian people, mere translation of the written language of Western hymns in Indian tunes does not necessarily amount to the "translation" of Christianity, which, at least for the sake of this study, is more about new ideas being apprehended in terms of ideas already there or more concerned with the processes and challenges encountered in order "to make Christian affirmations within the constraints of someone else's language" (Walls, *Cross-Cultural Process in Christian History*, 42). See also Norman, *Bhajan*; Sherinian, "Dalit Theology in Tamil Christian Folk Music," in Raj and Dempsey, *Popular Christianity in India*.

28. Tilak had a deep love for his Hindu brethren. But did he love them enough to do whatever it would take to reach them with the love of Christ? I liken Tilak's experience to Peter's "conversion" in Acts 10 that allowed him to first see himself and the "other" in the context of Christ's mission to reconcile all peoples. Kinds of food (or for us, styles of music) should not be obstacles in the way of Christ's mission to the world.

over fear of the other.[29] Tilak did not view religions in terms of their distance in relation to Christianity.[30] Here we are concerned with processes of musical creativity that prevail at the margins of liturgical innovation;[31] a creativity that proceeds from an encounter with those of an orientation other than that of Jesus Christ as Lord and Savior. Sites of transition are opportunities for mutuality in mission.

Concerning the role of music in the construction of "place," Martin Stokes writes,

> Music and dance . . . do not simply 'reflect'. Rather, they provide the means by which the hierarchies of place are negotiated and transformed . . . . Music does not then simply provide a marker in a prestructured social space, but the means by which this space can be transformed (1997, 4).

It is a sacred place in a palpable sense;[32] it is where we encounter the presence of God in the face of the other. Place created through musical encounters with others are a hermeneutical necessity for the "mediation of new meanings and the emergence of possibilities" (Papastergiadis 2012, 15), where Scripture engages culture and culture engages Scripture.[33] ML seeks out venues such as temples and yoga studios to enact his creativity with others.

Third, Tilak's musical creativity was not captive to the theological boundaries and institutional fences of the church of his day. In fact, he drew his inspiration, among others, from Tukaram, a famed Hindu poet, as well as from Hindu mythologies.[34] The problem was not so much the recogni-

---

29. Tilak's experience with the institutional church taught him that "'The light' is not to be identified with the religious life of humankind; religion is in fact too often the sphere of darkness, Christian religion not excluded." Newbigin, *Open Secret*, 175.

30. Concerning the potential to learn from other religions see Pope Paul VI, *Ecclesiam Suam* (http://www.vatican.va/holy_father/paul_vi/encyclicals/documents/hf_p-vi_enc_06081964_ecclesiam_en.html): "The aim of this encyclical will be to demonstrate with increasing clarity how vital it is for the world, and how greatly desired by the Catholic Church, that the two should meet together, and get to know and love one another." See also Bosch, *Transforming Mission*, 486.

31. We are *not* referring to music as it pertains to worship in the context of the gathering of Christian believers. However, we recollect, liturgy is enacted when God's people respond to His Spirit to serve God wherever they may be. In fact, when it comes to congregational song, "liturgy may break out anywhere." Hawn, *Gather Into One*, 5.

32. The conversion of "space" to "place" is a sacral and "mystical" process. Hale, *Sacred Space, Sacred Sound*; Beck's *Sacred Sound*; and Eliade, *Sacred and the Profane*.

33. Rynkiewich, "Mission, Hermeneutics, and the Local Church," 48.

34. Winslow, *Narayan Vaman Tilak*, 58–59. Tilak was able to appreciate the land from "whence mighty *rishis*, saints and sages spring!" and contrary to the stance of the church of his day, was able to appreciate, love, and learn from Indian poets and writers

tion of humanity's "epistemic alienation from God" (Begbie 2000, 275) that has generated much concern and discussion especially as it has evolved in the West. Rather, it was the "epistemological captivity" of the Westernized church that curtailed the contextualization of Christianity through indigenous expressions and therefore prevented the church from effectively reaching the people of India.[35]

Such captivity was evident through preferences of certain ratio-cognitive means of knowing over and above creative means as equally valid and proper channels for conveying truth.[36] If musical discourse was a way of defining reality and not a mere channel for communicating information, then the epistemological captivity of the church prevented it from recognizing God's truth through processes of musical creativity indigenous to the cultures prevalent. The traditionalism of modern foundationalism lay at the root of practices such as the "demonization" of music steeped in a "sonic theology" rooted in the Vedic hymns.[37] ML travels and performs widely in churches teaching and encouraging the Body of Christ to adopt friendly lifestyles towards Hindus and South Asians in their contexts.

Fourth, musical creativity for Tilak did not begin with the act of composition; it had roots in his experience of God through musical processes endemic to Hinduism. His radical reorientation in Christ—from staunch Brahmin to Cross-carrying disciple—served as a fulcrum for the bridge of contextualized processes of creative mediation. This process invited others to an active participation in experiencing Jesus Christ as Lord and Savior in culturally relevant ways.[38]

Tilak and ML alike serve as models to embrace and to draw from the diversity of local and global contexts. Their lifestyles may serve to liberate captive churches to respond creatively within their own diverse

---

like Jnaneshwara, Namdev, and Tukaram.

35. The message Tilak would convey to Western doctrine-first forms of contextualization would be to "Pack up all your doctrines" "and let us first find Christ" (Winslow, *Narayan Vaman Tilak,* 101). Notably, for Tilak the idea was not to get rid of Western missionaries but to change the dominating nature of "father-child" to that of "brothers" working together in Christ (Winslow, *Narayan Vaman Tilak,* 64).

36. It is worth noting that it is not merely the fact of such preference but the endemic nature of such that "reflects the values of the normative culture" (Hawn, *One Bread, One Body,* 249).

37. Beck, *Sacred Sound,* 114. The ancient Vedas and Upanishads are "believed to embody the eternal and primeval sacred sound that generated the universe . . . ." For this reason, music is considered sacred.

38. E.g., borrowings for Tilak's own lyric from the sayings of Hindu saints that served as a "first Old Testament" (Winslow, *Narayan Vaman Tilak,* 60) and the strategy of "God's Darbar," a place for dialogue with others.

cosmopolitan contexts. The intensity of the exchange of information is more acute in ML's experience than in Tilak's. Other commonalities include the non-hierarchical nature of (global) networks that foster relations that go beyond national identities and the multidimensionality of the flows[39] for the fostering of self-knowledge[40] as potential threats to established notions of the nature of truth and knowledge. Further, their musical agencies on the margins challenge established notions of "place" for the mediation of Christianity, i.e., the physical location of the church as a place to "come to" on a particular day of the week in the search for knowledge and truth as well as for experiencing God.

Both ML and Tilak embody dynamics of cosmopolitanism where the "sense of attachment" to a culture or group does not necessarily preclude authentic engagement with "other cultures, groups and societies" (Hopper 2007, 175). Depending upon the situation, this could be a hindrance or a vehicle for authentic witness.

In the context of cosmopolitan mobility and complexity, musical authenticity is evident in environments that allow persons to respond in the "now"—to be able to retain the flexibility and fluidity to flow in between multiple centers and peripheries. We recollect that the act of choosing to forge distinct identities from diverse cultural orientations[41] is indicative of the reflexive role of self-constitution in the making of cosmopolitan identity. Musical authenticity creates space for the "spontaneous combustion" of creativity in the context of diversity for the sake of authentic community. The creativity of ICMs is potentially a "mechanism" for articulating a "new collaborative ethos"[42] amid the complexity, heterogeneity, and plurality of globalization.

---

39. Castells, *Rise of the Network Society*.
40. Hopper, *Understanding Cultural Globalization*.
41. Hopper, *Understanding Cultural Globalization*, 166, 186.
42. Lamb, "Summary Analysis of 'Our Global Neighborhood.'" Among other things, the UN effort called for new structures that would: "Require the articulation of a collaborative ethos based on the principles of consultation, transparency, and accountability. It will foster global citizenship and work to include poorer, marginalized, and alienated segments of national and international society. It will seek peace and progress for all people, working to anticipate conflicts and improve the capacity for the peaceful resolution of disputes. Finally, it will strive to subject the rule of arbitrary power—economic, political, or military—to the rule of law within global society." Also in, Held and McGrew, *Globalization/Anti-Globalization*, 191.

"I never tried to be Indian"

Post- and neo-colonial contexts emphasize the "importance of attaching causes to places" (Gupta 1992, 13). Such "cause" may be evident in ML's desire to be a bridge builder, to identify with others through his musical creativity. ML's "passion in life is to build bridges between cultures." According to him, "A good bridge builder has a strong foundation on his own side and then builds a strong foundation on the other side, and then he crosses over."

At the same time, however, he asserts, "I never tried to be Indian." ML sees his "Indianness" helpful as he immerses himself in the South Asian diaspora so that "who I am as a person, which includes my faith, will be shown and illustrated in real living situations among them." ML recollects that after a performance an Indian lady came up and said to him, "'I accept you as a true son of India', even though the total evening was about Yeshu Bhakti; she was a Hindu woman." Here we are reminded of how cosmopolitan musical creativity may serve as "a human principle"—not merely that we are all connected in some "shallow political message"—that is evident through the reality and the lived ("how we live in it") experience of the "encounter" with another or others as a process with specific histories through time.[43]

Cultural immersion for ML amid the South Asian diaspora in North America is dynamically linked with ML's own historical narrative with palpable moorings in both India and North America. Such identity is further entrenched through performances amongst South Asian diaspora communities worldwide as well as amongst North Americans and Europeans. ML and his fellow band member, "never tried too hard to fit in"; "it was the music that touched us, we enjoyed it, we played it."

ML's "Indianness" as mediated through his musical identity is a central pathway to overcome polarizing distinctions between traditional binaries such as cultural outsider and insider perceptions. According to Bill Ashcroft et al: "The binary structure, with its various articulations of the underlying binary, accommodates such fundamental binary impulses within imperialism as the impulse to 'exploit' and the impulse to 'civilize.'"[44]

Upon analysis, the notion of "Indianness" as embodied in the identity of ML challenges the binary of national/foreign or Indian/Western. It draws the categorization of notions such as national identity into the arena of ambivalence.[45] Whether or not a person is Indian need not play out in terms of dominant markers that tend to "lock the project of resistance into the semiotic opposition set up by imperial discourse" (Ashcroft 2000, 26). So,

---

43. Robins, "Migrating Music and Good-enough Cosmopolitanism," 151–62.
44. Ashcroft et al., *Postcolonial Studies*, 25.
45. Cf., transnationalism, Levitt, "God Needs No Passport," 47.

while, according to M. M. Thomas, Tilak sought to "end the foreignness of Christianity" (1970, 283), ICMs like ML attempt to reiterate that Christianity is not "foreign" in the first place.

For ML, overt association with Christianity—its popular discourse and institutions—would be detrimental to the stance he and his wife have adopted in the cosmopolitan urban context of where they are located at present in North America. He prefers to go by a "pseudonym when it comes to actually teaching the church how to be out in the world." The purpose is "to get trust within the non-Christian community." He says: "I want some Yoga journal to like come up with my interview, so then they can say: 'he looks like he's legitimate; he is going to be fine.' That's why I prefer a pseudonym when it comes to actually teaching the church how to be out in the world."

In addition, ML is aware of the potential of being branded in terms of existing categories such as World Music. However, category notwithstanding, he draws upon his identity as a "world" musician in order to culturally assimilate to the South Asian diaspora as well as those (White North Americans) seeking spiritual affinity with his kind of music (a fusion of Eastern sounds with Western elements) and the spiritual expressions broadly and popularly representative of the Hindu community, for example, Yoga. According to ML:

> Indian music has definitely built numerous bridges between South Asians, and me but remarkably, just as many if not more bridges have been built between Caucasians, and me through Indian music. I have more bridges built between me and Caucasians who are relating to and loving my music than I've had with Indians.

"Fear, Insecurity, and Prejudice"

If there is an alternate view to "world music" as a "pernicious neoliberal myth-making" category (Stokes 2004, 51), it did facilitate dialogue. It allowed for inclusion and encouragement whereby people's conception of ethnicity or race was challenged. The conceptualization of difference underwent transformation. Jo Haynes observes that just as difference can be about race or ethnicity (or other traditional binaries), in the context of the category of World Music, the articulation of difference may also be caused by fear, insecurity, and prejudice of the Other.

Haynes's refers to a description of the role of World Music in mediating difference by a director of a world music organization:

> People are not, I think, threatened by difference, I think they are actually attracted by difference.... I think that in this inner city society that we're talking about ... white people are <u>afraid</u> of black people and that is why communication does not occur.... People I think are kept apart by <u>insecurity</u> and by an important word, <u>prejudice</u>.... It just doesn't matter if you are a black man, a white woman, a brown person or whatever. It is just that people are people and so yet I think that this idea that people are therefore somehow excited or inspired by differences I think is something radically different from what tends to happen in normal society.[46]

Interestingly, what is "normal" for the participant above is shaped by immersion in the World Music scenario. Negotiating identity involves risk—a risk of finding out that however hard you try, it may still be inadequate. Risk is accompanied by a degree of insecurity. For ML, concerning how he identifies with himself and how he comes across to others,

> The answer is evolving as I mature. Today, I have a much more <u>integrated</u> way; I find myself quite content being an American, quite content being someone who clearly relates to the host culture that I lived as a child, India. I don't need to be Indian, I am Indian in a sense; so, I feel at peace with the level of Indianness that is in me; and I enjoy accessing that. I don't feel a sense of, any longer, a sense of need to be more American or more Indian than I am; but in past years I would feel <u>insecure</u> about one or both those (emphasis mine).

Regarding the journey from insecurity to integration, he offers the following justification:

> When I lived in India as an adult, I sought to live a simple life in India and relate to Indians of lower class backgrounds (North India). I did not have a fridge, used clay pot for water, did not use a motorcycle, used a bicycle; I tried to relate to being Indian on a particular level. Ultimately, I learned a lot but was not able to succeed in that naturally. I still was looked upon by strangers as straight off the boat from America. They wouldn't have known that I had a "matka" [clay pot for storing water] at home. So, constantly I am faced with the reality of the situation of being Caucasian. And that caused in me a questioning of whether or not—who I was—or whether I was more American and embarked on more of a search out back toward the West. I came

---

46. Haynes, "World Music and the Search for Difference," 370.

back to America, in some part because of the need to identify myself here as an American.

In addition, according to ML, "The insecurity of being a musician is well-founded." He goes on to add: "Artists are constantly fighting insecurity in their music; and I have fought all my life and (am) still fighting insecurity in my music quite a lot . . . in the sense that I don't feel good enough . . . that's the sense in which I feel insecure, I don't feel good enough." He goes on to talk about how insecure he felt playing rock music. He eventually gave that up to learn sitar. He adds, "But as I listened to the classical sitar performances, I thought this is the most impossible thing in the world. I will never be able to do this! So, I was faced with insecurity upon insecurity in every style of music I was approaching."

In ML's story, we learn that insecurity may result in fear of two kinds: a fear that causes one to retreat into ethnocentrism, or a fear that results in vulnerability exposed in the context of relationship with the other. While ML's narrative illustrates difference that arises from insecurity, JB shares his story—a complex intertwining of the effects of colonialism, racialism, and prejudice.

"I Finally Found My Identity in New York City"

If ML needed to return to America in order to get in touch with his American identity, JB was able to discover his identity in the cosmopolitan urban scenario of one of North America's most diverse borough—Queens, NY. He describes his musical heritage:

> My dad is from the bhajans, my mom is from the chanting, and so I've always kind of struggled with my identity—where to set my foot more firmly. Back in days the Indian government and Naga government were having a lot of issues. So I was always struggling to find my identity.

He goes on: "I finally found my identity in New York city [laughs] of all the places." That identity is dis-covered amidst diversity, at least in part, is true in JB's case.

Let us recollect briefly, JB Joseph is an Indian immigrant living in New York. He was born and raised in Nagaland, North East India. His father is from Uttar Pradesh, and mother, from Nagaland. In the light of the backdrop of alienation and hostility between the "mainland," India, and Nagaland, the mediation of JB's identity takes on a prophetic dimension. JB traces the history of his musical creativity:

> In Nagaland music came early. Our history was marked by animism, tribal culture, and wars that happened between 16 major tribes in Nagaland. One of the practices that Nagaland is known for and emphasized too much is called headhunting—a fierce and violent place. It was a very fierce and violent place. In 1837 Miles Bronson came to Nagaland as a missionary. When the missionaries came they not only brought their Bibles but their music.[47]

JB learned to play on the "church guitar" as a child in Nagaland. According to JB, "just like the organ, in the West or Westernized churches, churches in Nagaland had guitars." JB moved to Pune because his family had moved there while he finished studies at a boarding school in Nagaland. He went to Pune, Ferguson College, received a BA in Arts (Literature and History). After college, he immigrated to the US to join his father, who had been appointed by the church/denomination that he served in India in order to plant a church amongst North Indian immigrants to the United States. The racial association with a group of "headhunters" was a way, among others, by which JB experienced being marginalized by others.

While the situation has changed in the present day, JB had yet to confront his own prejudices. JB spent the first 16 years of his life in Nagaland. In his words, "That's foundation right there." The backdrop of division between center (India) and periphery (Nagaland) is not popularized but has not gone unheeded.[48] The historical disjuncture between Nagaland and India are not central to this dissertation. However, it invites a fresh perspective on the role of JB's diasporic (and prophetic) identity, given that he unifies within his musical being the inherent tensions of being Naga and Indian.

JB moved to Pune, India for further study after school. However, growing up in Nagaland, he says, "I did not learn one single Hindi song. We did not speak Hindi; English is the common dialect; I did not know any Hindi

---

47. JB goes on to say, "Now Nagaland is said to be the most Baptist state in the world." See also Singh, "The Soul Hunters of Central Asia."

48. According to the General Secretary of *Dravida Peravai*, Nandhivarman, "Nagaland Struggle": The Nagaland struggle is based on few beliefs. "*The Nagas who inhibit the land of Nagaland are a different race who had been occupying their land from time immemorial. Beginning from 1832 until 1947 a small portion of Naga country was conquered by the British and was ruled by their administration. As far as its relationship with its neighbor India is concerned, prior to 1947, no Indian king or prince had ever set foot on Naga country. Also prior to 1947 Nagas had no affinity with India whether racially, historically, politically, culturally, religiously or any other wise. Therefore Nagaland is not par of Indian Territory neither Nagas are Indians*" writes Kaka D. Iralu in the book *Nagaland and India: the Blood and Tears*, distributed secretly to Indian Members of Parliament in 2000."

songs; only later on when Bollywood came in." The significance of popular music (for example, Bollywood) in reconstituting the collective identity of a people is implied elsewhere.[49] The role that popular music of so-called "mainland" India played in cementing the relationship between itself and the North East is subject for further study.

However, the political and cultural alienation that he experienced between his ethnic Naga identity and as an "Indian" was a major factor in his embrace of Western music. It was a way out. The political struggle between India and Nagaland had a significant impact upon JB in reconciling his own identity. He says,

> The political struggle between the Indian government and Nagaland government is huge. I grew up being told that the rest of India is our enemy. Bollywood is from the enemy. Hindi is the enemy's language; and I kind of grew up sort of being brainwashed in a way, in that way and my struggle then was that my dad was Indian.

He goes on to say:

> I struggled with my identity and so I embraced even much more the Western music because I wanted to get the approval of people that I'm a Naga. But you know, everyone knew that I was not and even my [skin] color kind of gave it away. In Nagaland everyone is fair, more Chinese, Korean. I don't pass that test.

Being in New York offered JB the chance to freely be both, Naga and Indian. JB experienced "otherness" while being in his own hometown. He goes on to explain:

> I've experienced some degree of racism in Nagaland myself. There is a term that you would use for someone from the plains, mainland India. That term is *khalami*. It's a word to identify [someone] but it's also not a very good word. It comes with a negative baggage; and so my friends in schools would call me a *khalami*. It could be a joke, but then to me, it affected me hugely, deep inside. Part of my journey in music was venting those grudges and emotions out.

For JB, music—singing and playing guitar—was a way to gain the approval and recognition of his peers; according to him, it was a solution to being "marginalized." Looking back, he says: "God would use all that need

---

49. Matsue, "Stars to the State and Beyond," 5–20; Morcom, *Hindi Film Songs and the Cinema*; Manuel, *Cassette Culture*.

and self-centeredness for his glory, as a tool to worship him. That our [need for] approval can only be satisfied when we recognize that God loves us in spite of all our shortcomings and failings."

"Now I began to see": Authenticity, Overcoming Prejudice

I asked JB to describe his music. He begins with the following narrative: "In the Hindustani Covenant Church [the church where his father was a pastor; it included people who were from a lower economic class with liturgy in the vernacular] I just sang along. When I came here in 2002, after the Lord had got hold of my heart . . . " He pauses and then reflectively says:

> I think being in New Life Fellowship [NLF] and having a more of an educated and upper class atmosphere, when I would go to the HCC, I would look down at them [and say something to the effect of] *dholak baja raha hai* [Hindi, for "they are playing the dholak"].[50] Usually it would not be very well coordinated, and I would sit in the back and [have] almost like a whole prejudice against it. But those were some songs that I was listening to. I was . . . at a place where in NLF it was better coordinated . . . [the music would] sound better, more "together," and reflected the churches here [in the US]. I would have that experience (emphasis mine).

In retrospect, JB admits being prejudiced against the HCC "type" of church. On another front, however, the church that he identified with, the NLF church, did not entirely embrace the part of him that identified with others who were not part of the Christian "bubble." Furthermore, we notice that the admixture of the NLF community proved not to be the context where he would come to terms with his prejudice against the HCC type of community. The shift in his perspective was to happen in an entirely different context—the diversity of New York. He continues to narrate his journey of transformation through his experience after coming to the US:

> So, I had that negative view of just looking down at Hindustani churches. I was only 21. Then, at 23 when I came here, and more fully committed myself to the Lord, [I] took up the guitar again to lead worship. The first year in my dad's church in Yonkers, I

---

50. The dholak is an Indian drum, typically used by folk or tribal groups; a very popular instrument in Punjabi folk music as well as commercial film musics. See "Dholak," http://chandrakantha.com/articles/indian_music/dholak.html). JB's reference to it in relation to a group of people is intended as a derogatory remark indicating how JB identified himself, as a Westernized English speaker in relation to people such as these who play the dholak.

began to lead worship, and sang songs like "Shout to the Lord." Nobody connected with me because almost all the people came from a Hindustani Church background. They would wait until I finished my songs so they would pick up their hymnbooks and Hindustani songs and start singing. But now even in my own life <u>I am not just interested in singing and performing</u>, <u>I am really interested in the church worshipping Jesus</u>. To see that they are not connecting with the Western songs.... *Tho maine kya kiya* [Hindi, a rough translation of which would be: "then this is what I did," typically used in order to emphasize what is to follow], I made a step, 7–8 years ago I made a step—"I will learn Hindi songs"—that was a huge step for me, a huge step!

However, the "step" came with an inevitable price. According to JB:

> That meant I would have to break my prejudice. The root for me not to get to my root was a prejudice that I had, a false idea that this subculture... was not good enough or... [There was a rootedness there]... I did not like it.... It was just this very unfortunate prejudice of just not liking. It might have been the college circuit, going to NLF (I really hope I am not butchering NLF, because I really liked it....) but the Hindustani church became a... you know aunties clapping, sitting on the floor... I don't know why the prejudice was there.... Once I made the decision [to learn Hindi songs] and this is Christ, Christ changed my heart; and I said, 'God changed me'... I recognized it... because now I began to see some of those words, those Hindi songs, they were so rich. As a Christian, now I am beginning to read it and say: what a wonderful song this is. That song: *jab say maine yeshu ko paya, mere jeevan badal gaya* [trans. Ever since I found Jesus, my life has changed]—that whole song of how Christ transformed our lives, just one example, where the Gospel was just so rich.

Apparently singing in church is not tantamount to worship (cf. Amos 5:23). If JB was truly interested in the church worshipping Jesus then he was to learn about justice (cf. Amos 5:21–24); Justice begins with overcoming prejudice. JB realizes, the struggle that he had to embrace a part of his culture was real—"The root for me not to get to my root was a prejudice that I had." JB's remark strikes me as an extremely pertinent and revealing statement. In other words, JB realizes that he did not really want to recognize himself as part of his own people. There was an essential dislike of his own kind that was rooted in his consciousness. JB's comment exposes a potential fallacy of hybridity as some kind of a value-free zone. In the case of ML, we noticed how "fusion" or hybridity, conceptually, merged disparate identities in a creative tension. This might be attributed to the fact of ML's strong sense of self in his relationship with Christ.

However, could JB's identity as a Westernized Christian who identified with a Westernized church (NLF) have served somehow to numb the extent to which he could truly experience the other in himself through the experience of the other at HCC? In both cases, the life-transforming moment was discovered in humble service to the other in ways that are meaningful to the other. Christ-like service overcomes prejudice.

JB goes on to explain:

> When that barrier was crossed and I started learning Hindi music and playing it even on the guitar, obviously I had to change the way I play the guitar too. I am still learning, that was a whole different area of learning and enjoyment. Before, I was out of it, I was being a critic and looking down on it. *Abhi*, now, I am playing and leading these songs, and singing these songs, I don't know how to describe it.

He pauses, and then goes on emphatically:

> It was in my soul *yaar*; this music is in me! As much as I enjoy English songs even now (I just led worship at a church last night) but when I sing Hindi songs, I feel like I am connected with my identity. Now I understand why Islam [a Muslim whom JB has befriended] enjoys that music so much.[51]

I asked: But why do you enjoy? His answer was revealing:

---

51. Space prohibits a full discussion on the subject of "heart music." "God is more profoundly comprehended when the music of "home" or "heart" is employed in worship." King, "Music," 585. Interestingly, here "heart" is interchangeable with "home"; would the same definition be applicable to those occupying borderland spaces? Further, is "heart music" merely another term that essentializes a people or a culture? Garcia-Riviera recasts the philosophical nature of theological aesthetics in terms of a "more profound question: *what moves the human heart?*" García-Rivera, *Community of the Beautiful*, 9; 170–75. In the light of the Judeo-Christian tradition and meaning of "heart" (*leb* or *kardia*), the act of music becomes a spiritual and knowledge generating process—a "third type of knowing." For our purpose, therefore, the theological context of the "beautiful" expands popular usage of the phrase "heart music" to refer to a process of musical creativity that invites participation and the creation of space for the enactment of new histories. According to Stokes, "Music and the Global Order," 50, locality is constructed, enacted, and rhetorically defended. So, heart music may not necessarily be about a genre or style alone, but also about a place of becoming along with the other.

> I just got to know two years ago that my grandfather was a Hindu before he converted to Christianity. That was a big thing. That shook me up. I share that with people; to share about God's grace, where we have come from. Part of that made me [feel] more deeper into the roots of the Indus valley civilization and people that come out of that. My roots go back to the people of India.

It is significant that although JB grew up being taught that the people of India are the "enemy," his creative being displays salvific significance in the fact that he now carries that tension—Naga identity *vis-`a-vis* Indian roots—within him in a way that witnesses to the saving work of Christ.

Authenticity Overcoming Fear

What prevented JB from reaching the Indian community for Christ whilst he was in India? Although this was, in his own words, "a very important question," he "never really got to see what would happen." The reason? He explains:

> I think I was kind of afraid—young. I was still in college and did not want to be this kid who was asking these questions. The church was already established; also . . . just wanting to be part of the crowd . . . we had our own gatherings, our own Christian bubble.

We infer from JB that fear is also paralyzing, preventing authentic mission. He says:

> In my opinion, everything we did catered mostly to Christians . . . . At times I would think "what are we doing?" But I did not dare obey [such prompting] and do something . . . I just had those questions and followed the crowd. Transformation—I think the step that I took from thinking to action, [actually] doing something happened in New York!

The diversity of diaspora in New York played a significant role in bringing to the foreground JB's boldness,[52] which demonstrates the place

---

52. According to Chhaya community development corporation based in Jackson Heights, New York, "Indians continue to be the largest ethnic group within the South Asian category, and following the Chinese community, the second largest Asian community in New York City with a population of 192,209. The Bangladeshi community tripled in size since 2000, seeing the second highest growth rate, surpassing Pakistanis as the second largest South Asian category with 53,174 members. Pakistanis are now the third largest ethnic group within the South Asian American population in New York City at 41,887; followed by Nepali at 5,681, Sri Lankans at 3,696 and Bhutanese at 345. The Indo-Caribbean population is potentially among the largest of these groups,

of diversity and the formation of diasporic identity as a "technological possibility of proximity" that "allows nonterritorialized links (networks) to emerge (cf. Dufoix 2003, 107).[53] However, the making of ICM being is a journey; a journey of "dislike" and "self-alienation" that needs to be worked out in the context of diasporic multiculturalism.

Self-Alienation

The paucity of literature on the history of the spread of Christianity through music in Nagaland in the colonial era warrants further research. However, in the light of research done in other parts of the region, some speculation may be possible. According to Joanna Heath, in Mizoram, either the new Christians feared the use of their pre-Christian music in their worship, or perhaps they considered the missionaries' appropriation of their cultural music to be insulting.[54]

Heath cites Lawmsanga according to whom the rejection of Mizo tunes was due to "self-alienation." The posture of self-alienation is endorsed in Lalsangkima Pachuau's reference to the role of "the traditional drum" in Mizoram. According to him, the early Mizo Christians shunned the use of the drum in the practice of the life of the church for the first couple of decades of its growth as a community of faith.[55] This was due to the association of the traditional drum with indigenous festivals and "drinking bouts."[56] Akin to the use of traditional Mizo songs, the drum was considered a "representation" of "'old'" and profane ways of life.[57]

According to Pachuau, however, the argument that the early converts willingly chose to reject "traditional tunes and poetical expressions is not convincing" (2002, 135). The role of the missionaries in the decision-making process cannot be ignored. Further study is necessary in order to discover the ways in which the rejection of indigenous expression may have contributed to

---

however the census data does not collect information for this community. Based on our knowledge of the community, these numbers actually do not fully reflect the population size of South Asians in the City." Chhaya CDC. http://www.nyc.gov/html/dc/downloads/pdf/chhaya_cdc_rasel_rahman.pdf.

53. Dufoix, *Diasporas*, 108. Dufoix provides a clue of how the term "diaspora" takes into account "the challenges of modernity and supermodernity," designating both, "root and rhizome," spatial and temporal persistence, the emergence as well as negation of fresh constructs of space and time, and various structures for the formation of identities.

54. Heath, "Lengkhawm Zai," 25.
55. Pachuau, *Ethnic Identity and Christianity*, 136.
56. Pachuau, *Ethnic Identity and Christianity*, 136.
57. Pachuau, *Ethnic Identity and Christianity*, 136–37.

the development of the identity of the early Mizo Christian community. The question may also be raised as to the extent the rejection of indigenous cultural forms might have impacted attitudes of the non-Christian indigenous community toward the early Mizo Christians.

It appears, however, that in the context of the Mizo Christianity, self-alienation is reversed through Christian revival. The resurgence of the Mizo church through the revival movement is enhanced through the incorporation of the traditional drum along with "new native hymns" and "revival dance" (ibid., 131–41). Pachuau also observes that the embrace of indigenous music pushed the church "beyond" the "bounds of Christianity" as the church had previously known it. This in turn contributed to the parting between denominationalists and the revivalists and thereby to the future development of the nature and character of the Mizo church (ibid.).

The cultural and historical contexts of Mizoram and Nagaland are vastly different. We do not intend to conflate the two contexts. However, we may draw some conclusions as to the role of indigenous music in the transformation of the church. First, indigenous musical forms play a crucial role in translating a people's "deepest feelings" (Pachuau 2002, 137). Second, the mixing of foreign hymn tunes with native melodies has a definite role in the reconstruction of the collective identity of a people (in this case, the Mizo's). Third, the radical engagement of indigenous music in the life of the church could push the church beyond the boundaries of its current missiological perimeter.

The combination of the appropriation of indigenous music within the life of the church, its effect in shaping the identity of the people, and its tendency to usher radical change for growth are significant factors for ICMs to consider as they build the church for mission. In the light of the above, we may speculate that the submergence of tribal or folk sounds in Nagaland may in part be due to a degree of "self-alienation"—the need to separate oneself from one's pre-Christian identity—on the part of Naga Christians. Again, the issue of whether the Naga-Christians chose this of their own accord and the possible influence of missionary and/or colonial influence needs to be considered. We cannot address this in depth here.[58]

Concerning the place of "indigenous" music in relation to perceptions of the same as being "demonized," the apostle Paul's admonishment to the

---

58. There is also a generational issue. The generation that converts often has to make a clear separation with the past. The next generation inherits the new identity without much question (they honor the first converts). However, the third generation begins to wonder what it has missed in giving up its own culture, its own music and art, for Western Christian music and art. Then begins the process of recovery of what was good. Dr. Michael Rynkiewich, email correspondence, February 28, 2014.

Corinthian church in 1 Cor 10:19–20 offers light.[59] Paul's rhetoric implies that neither food nor idols amount to "anything." In the light of the conversion of a person from paganism to Christianity (1 Cor 7:5–6; 8:1–2), Paul's rhetoric implies that the Christian is never in bondage to sin.[60] The "pagans" sacrificial offerings are made to demons and not to God because of the fact that they are indeed pagans who do not believe in God. The offering—food or music—has its worth in the context of a trust/faith relationship with the Lord.

According to a Carnatic violinist and one of the key informants based in Chennai, India, "I give life to that instrument. The instrument is not that important." He suggests that as opposed to the Hindu practice of praying over the instruments, churches should "pray for the instrumentalists. What is the instrument going to do on its own?" Similarly, based upon the Apostle Paul's evaluation, in and of itself there is no true worth in the music. If value is not borne in terms of a relationship with God through Christ, then the offering of music is of no value, i.e., not made to God.

The phenomenon of self-alienation is prevalent even amongst new Christian musicians in India and elsewhere in the world. The demonization of rock music in the West and even certain instruments due to their association with pagan practices (across the world) is common knowledge. Further, self-alienation, usually associated with feelings of guilt and condescending attitudes may not be unique to the colonized alone, but might also factor in amongst those who do the colonizing or inherit and share histories with those of the colonizer.

"Our 'Dislike' Journey

SJ is a Korean American, an ethnomusicologist, trained in Western classical music. She spent several months in India assisting victims of the Tsunami, is currently learning Tamil, and has been involved in researching the popular film music of India. She loves to learn any kind of music, but "the purpose is not the music." She and her husband, AJ, were part of a focus group along with JB to further discuss the complexities of negotiating identity and musical creativity in the context of Jackson Heights, NY. AJ was born in Frankfort, KY. His family moved to France until he was three years old. From the age of 4 until 18 he was brought up in Senegal, West Africa. SJ and AJ both share in JB's mission in Jackson Heights.

---

59. "What do I imply then? That food offered to idols is anything, or that an idol is anything? No, I imply that what pagans sacrifice they offer to demons and not to God. I do not want you to be participants with demons." 1 Cor 10:19–20 ESV.

60. Witherington, *New Testament Rhetoric*, 220.

SJ refers to a diasporic "consciousness"—a shared attraction of sorts, or even a shared history-in-the-making, among diaspora people regardless of their origin.[61] She asks:

> Why do people latch on to a music at a certain time? We moved from Ohio to Bowling Green State University. We went to a bilingual Hindi church. I came there after living in Chennai for 2 years. I was romanticizing culture. What's the attraction? It is very complex. What is it that draws me to them [people in Chennai]? Do I really think that I can be a part of them?

She adds, "When I returned to the United States, I did not like it." JB identifies with that statement and says, "We have both talked about our 'dislike journey.'"[62] SJ experienced being "subjectified" and "essentialized" in the United States. According to her, "it was prejudice against all Asians or anything Asian was seen as inferior or not good enough." JB and SJ appeared to share a similar "dislike"—SJ, of the homogenizing tendency portrayed through media in the United States, and JB, of the homogenizing tendency of the Westernized church. SJ also experienced a distanciation between herself and the Korean church in the United States.[63]

As an ethnomusicologist, SJ comments:

> Ethnomusicology was essentializing culture so much to the point that . . . [she pauses] . . . others have agency too . . . Why do

---

61. Baum, "Expanding Role of the Librarian in Oral History," 322. I am tempted to use the phrase "oral history" in place of "origin," although here there is no systematic and intentional process of documentation in terms of creating, curating, consuming, and counseling. See also Schwarzstein, "Oral History in Latin America," 422. Diasporic sharing does contribute to "historical discipline. It allows the recovery of experience in history. It allows history to gain in complexity and texture, to be inhabited by more actors, to include everyday life," and importantly, especially when it comes to the extension of the ministry of Christ beyond the ideologies of captive ecclesial environs.

62. SJ explains the effects of racism as she grew up in the United States. She says, "I felt subjectified." She realizes what it was: "I did not want my identity to be based on classical piano." Being "subjectified" is perhaps the dark side of being "valorized"— "Korean Americans associated with playing classical piano." SJ continues, in the context of multiculturalism in the United States, "you would never see an Asian in the media." According to her, Koreans in general did not possess language acquisition skills, which accentuated their being subjectified. According to SJ: "There are a lot of issues with multiculturalism in the US. Now you are essentializing people into certain kinds of categories. Subjected, essentialized, you might think of self and others as bounded entity. Of course, I have this White privilege—power, travel, English [language], money."

63. She says: "I think I really did resent the Korean church for taking American songs. I resented the fact that they couldn't think of new songs, tunes. I resented the whole influence of Nashville, Christian music industry. I was like, why don't they have new tunes and not just old tunes from the 80s."

I have to tell somebody, 'look at your roots.' Are you supposed to play Indian music just because you are Indian?" She goes on to illustrate: "In his [JB's] church . . . I was thinking Indian musicians should be playing Indian music to reach Indian people.

For SJ, popular and "fusion" music is "a way out" of an essentializing culture. This perspective appears to be a common factor amongst most ICMs that I interviewed.[64] For SJ, there needs to be a balance between indigenous music and Westernized/ pop music. According to her:

If you continually play Western music all the time, people are going to think that Christianity is a Western religion. People think that all the time. But things always change, especially with younger people too; More resources, technology, now; less baggage with young—Christian rap, YouTube, Internet.

CHRISTIAN MUSIC = WORSHIP MUSIC

A general notion exists that identifies Christian music primarily with worship or liturgical music. This is problematic given the understanding that there may actually be more to musical creativity than one's experience of Christianity. Another part of the problem relates to the structural paradigms and behavior patterns that reinforce the notion that equates Christianity to worship liturgy (in some cases, particularly, liturgies that originate in the global North).

As compared with the church in Nagaland, JB wonders why the Indian church [the church that he attended—NLF in Pune—as opposed to the Hindustani church, HCC, that incorporated local styles in its worship] became so westernized despite the "richness" of Indian music. Apparently, tradition (in this case at least) however rich, did little to stifle the diffusion tactics of Westernization.[65]

In an overview of "Christian Global Hymnody" Michael Hawn draws attention to the impact of Vatican II in promoting the liturgies and

---

64. The role of popular music and identity formation is subject for an entire dissertation. Earlier in this dissertation we referred to Sylvan's *Traces of the Spirit*; also cf. Lynch, "Role of Popular Music in the Construction of Alternative Spiritual Identities and Ideologies."

65. Observing the difference between the Nagaland church and the Indian church, JB comments: "This is my opinion, I think we could have reached India by now if we had recognized that Christ is not a European or American Christ; he was first of all from the Middle East . . . and that we don't have to change our culture into a Westernized culture [in order to be Christian]."

cultural patterns of various cultures.⁶⁶ In the wake of this document, according to Hawn, the Milwaukee Symposia report challenges allusions to the musical superiority and aesthetic criteria of the North. Further, cultural diversity is an invitation for alternate ways of thinking in terms of music and worship.⁶⁷

JB testifies to experiencing a disjuncture in the context of mixed worship involving the HCC (more indigenous) and NLF churches (less indigenous). Indigeneity is not to be contrasted with Westernization. Indigeneity is not a fixed and unchanging paradigm.⁶⁸ Rather, we might consider degrees of indigeneity in relation to Westernization that allows participation and creates disjuncture at the same time. The tendency toward essentialization that compels thought primarily in terms of binary opposites of either indigeneity or something other is an unnecessary dichotomization.

JB realizes that participation in a people's music is hindered when interpreted in terms of an experience of one's own music. Therefore, we conclude, apart from entering into an authentic relationship with the originators of a given expressive culture, without subjecting oneself critically to their experiences of histories, outside of imbibing the emotional content in compassionate ways and acting upon such (which could range from clapping, dancing, surrender to Christ, or even going on a mission trip), participation in terms of covenantal intersubjectivity is not what it is meant to be.⁶⁹ This may in fact be a reason why despite a well-defined theology of the presence of God, effectively there may be little or no perceptible change of heart or compassionate action toward another. Such a response is legitimized in captivity. At its core, therefore, contextualization is a heart issue.

In redefining the mission of the church, Tite Tienou offers insight: "Today race and ethnicity may represent a greater distance than geography. Unless the church crosses that 'distance' courageously, constructively and prophetically it will be difficult to be 'salt and light.'"⁷⁰ The acuteness of the captivity of the church is evident in JB's recollection of his participation in church in India:

---

66. Hawn, "Christian Global Hymnody: An Overview," 26. Cf. The *Constitution on the Sacred Liturgy*, 1963.

67. Hawn, "Christian Global Hymnody: An Overview," 30.

68. Chilisa, *Indigenous Research Methodologies*, 25.

69. McGann, *Exploring Music as Worship and Theology*, 38. In the ritual context, music is revelatory of God's action, it is relational activity, includes body movements, multidimensional and multi-channeled performance, and evokes and expresses relatedness beyond the community. Also cf. "methexis," Bellini, *Participation*, 12).

70. Tienou, "Dare to Make New Mistakes," 27.

> Now I am sure the motives of our pastors were good. <u>But as far as reaching our community, I think we terribly failed</u> . . . . I would be biking through that to get to my church, forgetting my immediate context. Also, [I knew] that <u>if these people came to New Life Fellowship they would not be able to connect</u> (emphasis added).

He further adds:

> I think in India we safely justified ourselves that this is the work of the devil, satanic work . . . It was almost like it was in a gas chamber, imprisoned, you could do so much with that music but you use it only for your own people [i.e., the church "bubble"].[71]

We cannot rule out the effects of colonialism (and ongoing neocolonialism) on creating and sustaining disjuncture between two "likes" within a given context—for example, the music of a more Westernized Indian church and the music of a more indigenized Indian church.

MUSICAL CREATIVITY, HISTORICAL GUILT, AND NEOCOLONIALISM

With regard to the ethos undergirding mission in the light of the centenary of the 1910 Edinburgh World Missionary Conference, Tienou asks a pertinent question: "Is it possible to do Christian mission today with full awareness of mistakes done in the past"? (2010, 19). There are notable literary efforts that address the issue of the subjection of indigenous music in colonialism and the encouragement of authentic indigenous music/arts.[72]

However, there is scope for probing the question of "historical guilt" associated with mission, theology of mission through the arts/music, and the question of whom indeed is "fit" for mission. In order to illustrate the

---

71. JB illustrates such "imprisonment" of the church he attended in India by offering the following example:

"During Christmas, what we did as a church was have carol singing; we would visit all these Christian homes, during Christmas time for one purpose—Christ was born! [But] we know that. If we had only looked at Scripture and looked at where the shepherds did go. The angels went to people. The shepherds went to people. I never reflected enough. But carol singing should [actually take place by going] to our friends and neighbors. They would love celebrating it, just like they come to our homes with sweets on their festivals. They love Christmas carols. I think they would appreciate it. Everybody knows Jingle Bells. What if we [visited our] unbelieving friends [rather than believers on Christmas]?"

72. Irving, *Colonial Counterpoint*; Krabill, *Hymnody of the Harrist Church Among the Dida of South-Central Ivory Coast (1913–1949)*; Krabill et al., *Worship and Mission for the Global Church*; Fortunato et al., *All the World is Singing*.

"historical guilt" associated with musical creativity and mission, here is an episode from my own experience:

> Kavi and Madhu[73] live in a suburb in Chicago. Kavi and my wife attended school together in Chennai, India. We planned a trip to visit Chicago and they graciously provided us with a place to stay. One evening, we started to talk about music, given my musical background and their musical passions. They were marveling at how fortunate they were now since Kavi could resume her lessons in Indian classical music (Carnatic); it was being offered at the local Hindu temple they frequented. I was not quite prepared intellectually to fathom the profundity of what was to follow; but it subsequently spurred my thoughts concerning the link between my musical identity, Christianity, and the task of mission. They inquired which instrument I played; but before I could answer, Madhu commented: "But since you are Christian, you must be playing guitar."

There is a broad recognition of the conflation between Christianity and Westernization as an obstacle to the rapid spread of Christianity amongst non-Christians in India.[74] The above episode is evidence of the historical guilt that is associated with any person who is Indian, yet professes Christianity. The root of such guilt lies in the "perceived historical link between mission and colonialism" (Tienou 2010, 20). In the context of this study, the issue is augmented given the underlying perception of Indianness as uniquely aligned with the Hindu classical music heritage of India. Given the proliferation of colonialism in more than just the Indian subcontinent—and the potential burden of "historical guilt" carried by some or most ICMs, a key task of ICMs is to themselves overcome the hurdle of guilt and to engage in creative mission whilst helping others do the same.

How Indigenous Is Indigenous?

For JB, "music is so much a part of life. It gives much meaning to life." Historically, for the Nagas, music and life are well integrated. JB recognizes the persuasive potential of music and attributes the Westernization of his culture in Nagaland to such potential:[75] "in Nagaland, the Westernization is so

---

73. Names have been changed.
74. Hedlund, *Quest for Identity*; Oddie, "Constructing 'Hinduism.'"
75. JB recollects a famous quote, in JB's words: "Give me the music of the nation and I will change the mind of that nation." The quote is attributed to a few sources including Napoleon who apparently said: "Give me control over he who shapes the music of a nation, and I care not who makes the laws" O'Donnell ("Music and the Brain," accessed

rich because of the music."[76] The degree of Westernization has proceeded so far that both he and his wife were "shocked" on a recent visit to Nagaland.[77] Concerning music, he reasons,

> Our music literally went from strings that you would use for chanting to guitars. Part of it was that when hymns came you <u>needed</u> Western music to accompany them; you could not use tribal music.

The so-called "need" for Western music is lamentable; it is a complex phenomenon with roots in colonialism. In the article, "Application of Memmi's Theory of the Colonizer and the Colonized to the Conflicts in Zimbabwe" (1986), Dickson A. Mungazi identifies three stages in the effects of education on "nationalistic consciousness" and the struggle for freedom that might be helpful to understand the dynamics here. One of these refers to the colonizer's belief of the <u>need</u> for training in order for colonization to be profitable.[78] Interestingly, JB's perceived need for learning Western music in order to sing the hymns aligns with the colonizer's belief (or agenda) concerning the need for training the colonized in the ways of the colonizer in order to benefit the interests of the colonizer. Such need, of course, coincided with the elimination of the need for indigenous music and, by implication, the need to sustain the livelihoods of traditional instrumentalists as well as the negation of specific histories associated with such practice.

---

online at http://www.cerebromente.org.br/n15/mente/musica.html) and popularly to Scottish political activist, Andrew Fletcher. See Ravi Zacharias's Twitter page, accessed May 13, 2020, https://twitter.com/RaviZachrias.

76. Heath, "Lengkhawm Zai," 27. In a study of Mizo music, Heath observes: "Aware of the widespread enthusiasm for hymn-singing described above, the missionaries adopted numerous means for western music education that began to shape Mizo musical life even before the mass conversions brought about by the revivals." Mizoram is not adjacent to Nagaland and has its own unique history in terms of the development of its music. I am comparing processes between the two states since they together form part of the Seven Sister states in India. This does not necessarily justify a comparative study, but some degree of speculation might be permitted.

77. He says, "When my wife went to Nagaland last year, she was shocked . . . shocked—no sarees, lungis [wrap around clothing at the waist], I mean, no curry, no nothing; its all shirt, pants, our newspapers are all in English. Part of it is that our languages did not have a script. We didn't really develop it because by the time the missionaries came they taught us so much. We had an oral language but nothing was written. Our language was never scripted; it is written even now in English. That itself is a huge example of Westernization."

78. Mungazi, "Application of Memmi's Theory of the Colonizer and the Colonized to the Conflicts in Zimbabwe," 519–20, emphasis added.

"They Think It Is Bad English"

If self-alienation in the Indian context took the form of reluctance to use Indian classical music, in Jamaica it was a hesitancy to use, and even to recognize, Jamaican as a local language of the people. According to Jamaican "born and bred" musician, JR: "Unfortunately, the majority of people still don't realize that it is a language ... They think it is bad English, because it is an English-based vocabulary."

The lack of the significance of Jamaican language in the current self-image of the people of Jamaica, presents a major hurdle in reimagining the identity of the Jamaican people. This is due to a postcolonial unconsciousness. According to JR:

> They [those who oppose Jamaican as a local language] have made up their mind to oppose it. They believe it will hold Jamaica back. They say no other nation uses this language. So why should we invest time and energy developing it? We should be able to communicate on an international level.

The perceived need to make a difference at an "international level" on the terms of the dominant culture—i.e., English—to a certain extent has roots in the unhealthy intersubjective experience of colonialism: perception of self, capabilities and potential, in terms of the oppressor. Introducing an account of Arabesk music, a Turkish popular music genre, Martin Stokes recounts Edward Said's "postcolonial critique"—"'the East's' participation in its own representation (2000, 213). He goes on to paint an avid picture:

> The issue evokes an unstable and potentially infinite regress. East looks at West looking at East; servant looks at master/ mistress looking at servant; distinctive shapes and patterns fade into the murky green darkness that one glimpses peering into the gap between mirrors facing one another (ibid).

JR emphasizes the significance of the Jamaican-Creole language: "They [Jamaicans, in general] don't understand the importance of it." She reasons: "And it is all because we were beat down so much that they really believe that it is bad, genuinely believe that it is bad."

However, given the powerful role of language in creating a people, might the refusal to speak a language be considered a subtle form of rebellion—e.g., "if we are not a people, then who are you colonizing"? Such theorizing is somewhat premature and certainly speculative, but not altogether irrelevant especially in a postcolonial and neocolonial context. According to JR: "It is not going away. Our language is going to remain." She goes on,

"We just completed a New Testament in December and now we really have to work hard to empower people to use it."

The translation of the New Testament in Creole is significant, especially for those who read. However, in the context of the profundity of the language of musical creativity, might the so-called translation in literary form of the Scriptures itself be a form of imposition? Moonjang Lee alludes to the degree of difference of the "hermeneutical environment of the non-Western world" in comparison to the West.[79] Lee suggests alternate methods of affirming biblical authority through re-enactment of the text and inferential as well as interactive reading,[80] which is where the embodiment and enactment of the ontology of participation through the language of musical creativity is crucial.

"I Grew Up With Ethnic Pride and Ethnocentrism"

The thin line between colonizer as colonizer and missionary as passive colonizer is clearly not an apparition in the case of JK, a Korean-American based in Dallas, TX who travels extensively for his ministry. JK traces the separation of Korean Christianity from indigenous culture. According to JK, the music of the "missionaries" was significantly different from Korean music: "Hymns used more than 5 tones." Further, "few missionaries encouraged Korean music and to write [indigenous] songs." JK emphasizes that Korean ethnicity was discouraged. He adds: "Koreans were not encouraged to be creative in church. How can we use the form of music that was offered to Shamanism, Confucianism, and Buddhism?"

In addition, according to JK: "Missionaries were not interested in redeeming the culture.[81] They were under pressure to work with the Japanese government." He recollects, "The Japanese said that they [missionaries] could do whatever they wanted as long as they did not talk politics or encourage ethnic forms of art. So, theologically and politically Korean churches drew away from [indigenous culture]."

Authenticity in JK's context is subdued not merely due to fear, injustice, and insecurity, but also, "ethnic pride." According to JK, the adoption and adaptation of Western cultural influences was easier due to the dynamic linkage of economic growth, political change (the shift to a democracy), and

---

79. Lee, "Reading the Bible in the Non-Western Church," 155.

80. Lee, "Reading the Bible in the Non-Western Church," 153–54.

81. This is a perception, but in fact, the missionaries were responsible for providing some of the only defense of the Koreans, including language and culture. Michael Rynkiewich, email comment, January 2014.

church growth. In his words, "the model [of church growth] was adapted from the West without being evaluated." He adds:

> The church began to grow in the 1970s. This coincided with Korea becoming a democracy and the spurt in economic growth. In this scenario Western forms were received uncritiqued. It gave permission to youth to use Western forms in church. Folk music never earned a platform. Few churches did it [used folk music], but they lack a theological perspective. It is more, ethnic pride.

The statement that a "platform" needed to be "earned" by folk music (and by implication, the specific histories related with such tradition) is indicative of a subaltern perspective, a voice that did not get a sufficient chance to be heard in the process of the adoption of Western forms as the primary mode of expression in Korean Christianity. In this case, indeed, "mission is colonialism."[82] According to Tienou, "God is the subject and the object of mission"; it is not a mere human endeavor.[83] Where this is not the case, it is indicative of the failure of the missionary endeavor to allow for the creation of space for deep reflection on the role of indigenous music in culture before or during the process of transmission/translation of the Gospel, in this case, in the soil of Korean hearts.

In addition, JK's "heart music" is Western pop music.[84] At the age of seventeen years, JK led worship in a Korean American church in Dallas. He says, "But that time, Asians in Korea were influenced by praise and worship music from the West—Western pop music with Korean lyrics." JK writes how as child he grew up "learning, being forced to think" that "we should have Korean pride since Koreans are smarter than other ethnic groups."[85] He confesses,

---

82. Tienou, "Locus of Historical Guilt," 19, draws from Jan H. Boer who speaks to the allegations of "missionary collusion with colonialism."

83. Tienou, "Locus of Historical Guilt," 24.

84. He was never exposed to traditional music and culture except on national holidays. His parents were "baby boomers" influenced by "hippie music" and The Beatles. His grandparents listened to Japanese music; "but even then they were not encouraged to use their music." On the role of "heart music," please see 131n28. Thinking further, if the concept of heart music properly signifies authenticity, in what sense is it possible to engage in "true" worship at other times? In the context of a cohabitation of diverse "heart" musics, it is helpful to bear in mind that an antidote to "ethnic pride" and ethnocentrism "based solely upon cultural accessibility and personal significance" is taking steps toward "liminality and an openness toward liturgical interpathy." Hawn, *Gather into One*, 251.

85. "A Multi-ethnic Worship Leader Has Conviction," blog post at http://multiculturalworship.org/a-multi-ethnic-worship-leader-has-conviction-by-jaewoo-kim/.

Yes, I grew up with ethnic pride and ethnocentrism. When Christian faith is mixed with ethnocentrism, it gives you a theological justification to think that one ethnic group is higher than others. And you believe that God wants a specific ethnic group to be the dominant group since His favor is on them. History shouts to us how that mentality created discrimination, racism and even genocide. At times, God chooses specific ethnic groups to serve His purpose by His sovereign grace, but that doesn't justify any ethnic group thinking they are better than another (ibid.).

Relatedly, in the light of the multicultural makeup of Jamaica, JR's concern is that "Jamaicanness" is founded upon the collective identity of peoples of all descent in Jamaica. However, according to JR, "Jamaican," in its popular use, is the common term for people of African descent. Could this indicate that the reluctance to affirm a single Jamaican language as the "official" language indicates a certain "freedom"? It preserves the freedom to be ambiguous about their collective identity, especially when it comes to musical expressivity. This could offer the chance for greater inclusion and tolerance. Rather than calling on the people to recognize a so-called national language, JR could focus on celebrating both English and Jamaican to signify what may qualify as authentically "Jamaican," depending upon the place/context for the enactment of musical creativity. Arriving at such a creative tension requires healing—deep level musical healing.

MUSICAL CREATIVITY AND PARTICIPATION

The ontological dilemma facing JR—employing musical creativity in ways that invite the Jamaicans to participate and collaborate in the recreation of Jamaican identity in the light of the Gospel—demonstrates and affirms some underlying principles of this research, such as, the "irreducible complexity" of musical representation (Born and Hesmondhalgh 2000, 37). The "multitextuality" of ways in which music generates and sustains meaning (sound, lyrics, and dramatic discourses) points to the fact of music as culture. Second, subjectivity is produced in discourse (cf. Foucault) (ibid., 38). Earlier we saw that musical discourse is not merely "referring" to something but is "more": it is a "set of practices that systematically form the objects of which they speak."[86]

---

86. Foucault, "Excerpt from *The Archaeology of Knowledge*," 1444, italic mine. However, we might ask, just what sort of system is implied here? We recollect that for Siapera, the "function of representation" is not simply reproduction, but a way of "condensed symbolic value of cultural *difference*" (*Cultural Diversity and Global Media,*

Third, ICMs in Christ negotiate theological difference and/or "sameness" (cf. Frith 2000, 305). Born and Hesmondhalgh identify a range of musical interpretations of identity that are helpful for analysis. The homology model reinforces "extant sociocultural identities" while repressing other alternatives.[87] The "macrohistorical, transformative dynamic" is revelatory of the "inevitable" subjugation of music to reinterpretation by historical processes and then reinserted into ongoing processes of sociocultural formation; a sort of "practical reflexivity" (2000, 35–6). The "structural articulation," is when music creates "a purely imaginary identification" (ibid., 35). This refers to an imaginary construction of sociocultural identity without intent to actualize such identity. However, this may be a "precondition for the emergence or negotiation of new identities" and "prefigure" emergent forms thereby renegotiating the boundaries that differentiate between self and other (ibid., 35).

ICM identity, however, may represent an anti-structural enunciation of musical identity. It is a "gap"—a place where people negotiate their place in the world—that is often left unheeded; untended may be a better word. Such space serves as a cushion for the diffusion of creations that could lead to a premature "semiotic implosion, the ultimate fate of all binary oppositions, and the subversion and eventual collapse of the forms of coercion and domination in which they participate" (Stokes 2000, 213). The "binary" in JR's case is the mirage of choice that the Jamaicans face: to retain English as their "front" in order to be relevant internationally or to learn and to express their "Jamaicanness" and risk so-called isolationism. Returning to Tienou's suggestion concerning the "confusion" surrounding mission in the face of historical guilt: the way ahead lies "in a renewal of commitment to mission and we will, indeed, dare to make new mistakes" (Tienou 2009, 29).

INDIGENOUS = AUTHENTIC?

We observe that what was previously the sustenance of "orientalism" in the past as per the "fantasy of western imagination" (cf. Stokes 2004) is in some sense reiterated through the processes of modern hymnody. Western

---

112). In "Discourse of World Music" Simon Frith cites Kofi Agawu who writes: "When was the last time an ethnomusicologist went out to discover sameness rather than difference? When did we last encourage our students to go and do fieldwork not in order to come back and paint the picture of a different Africa but of an Africa that, after all the necessary adjustments have been made, is the 'same' as the West?" (305).

87. This begs questions such as: who decides on which or what identities are "extant"? Who is included or excluded in the process of determining such factors? Similar questions might be applied toward the macrohistorical model.

hymnody, while theologically inspiring and hence validated by some, is also culturally divisive and alienating.[88]

What cannot be ignored is the transformative effect of not merely Western music but the fusion of various genres and styles that have affected Nagaland.[89] However, "fusion" does not necessarily imply the absence or negation of tradition. Stokes reminds us that in the context of cosmopolitanism, "spaces of musical encounter and exchange" cannot be explained purely in terms of colonialism (2007, 4).

In addition, it is important to demarcate the missionary exchange and value in terms of cultural renewal through Christianity versus the colonial enterprise as the thin line between Western missionary enterprise and colonial activity is cause for much confusion in the context of postcolonialism (for example, in India, Korea, and Jamaica). JB speaks for his people. He differentiates between "two kinds of White people"—Britishers who came with guns, and "Whitemen who came with books and with love." With regard to JB's "two kinds," interestingly, Dickson Mungazi, reflecting Memmi's theory of colonialism, argues that in the light of the colonizer's hegemony, two types of colonizers materialize:

> The colonizer who accepts is one who advocates perpetuation of the existing conditions of colonization without any changes or modifications. The colonizer who refuses is one

---

88. JR describes herself as a pioneer when it comes to writing worship songs in Jamaican that are received as that which can be used *in* Christian worship services *amongst* Jamaican communities in Jamaica and elsewhere. The prevailing trend was to use English for Christian worship. In her words: "As a Christian Jamaican missionary who has studied ethnomusicology and applied it on the 'mission field' in West Africa, the Americas and the Caribbean, I have observed cultures grappling with the task of answering the question: 'Who am I?' through their choices of musical expressions in corporate worship. There appears to be a struggle between wanting to establish their religious identity, and needing to connect with their cultural ethnic identity" (2011, source withheld). In addition, I recall my own experience: for some in India I came across as a foreigner, primarily due to my religious identity as Christian. In the context of diversity and exchanges between peoples due to mobility and technology within the musical world, what is considered authentic?

89. See Heneise's recent article "Bel Canto in India's Northeast: Young Naga Artists Fuse Opera, Rockabilly, and their Faith." Also, according to the observation of a journalist writing for the *Times of India*, a national Indian newspaper: "The hills, which once echoed the sound of bullets and bombs, now rocks to the sound of different genres of music. Be it folk, western or Hindi, Naga youths take music very seriously here. Inclined towards the land's own tribal music and western hard rock, Nagaland has produced over a hundred music bands in the last decade. Many bands from this part of India have also won national and international glories, forcing the Nagaland government to announce music as its next venture of tourism and revenue." Baruah, "Music replaces sounds of bullets, bombs in Nagaland."

who advocates changes because he believes that the only way to ensure his own long-term interests is to ensure those of the colonized (1986, 519–20).

It may not always be the case that some colonizers accept,[90] but what about in the context of the current global scenario. At a recent world conference on congregational music in the context of local and global perspectives in 2013, an announcement was made for the release of a new Hymnal produced in the United States to be distributed and sold in and outside the US. It incorporated songs written by people from various parts of the world including the United States. Such efforts call for applause. On the other hand, we need to ask to what extent might this meet with glocal efforts around the world to conceptualize, produce, and distribute works from the South to the North?[91] Could this be an effort to control both English hymnody and World Music hymnody?

At root is the issue of validation of the other by the West. Lalsangkima Pachuau records how the new hymnody developed by the Mizo church never really "acquired the status" to be approved for worship in the context of the liturgy of the church (2002, 136). Although a collection of hymns was published in 1930 it was only in 1985 that a few of these hymns were included in the "Major Hymnal Book" (ibid.). Further, it is worthwhile to note that the value of "these new hymns" was directly linked to the observation that these compositions were derived from hymns contained in the "old Hymn Book" (ibid.).

Rashid Arareen addressing the issue of "Ethnic Minorities, Multiculturalism and the Celebration of the Postcolonial Other," in the context of the art world offers deep insight into "the spectacle of multiculturalism" which sheds light on so-called solutions to the problem of diversity, i.e., the idea of leveraging diversity for the so-called common good. He writes:

90. Dr. Michael Rynkiewich cautions: "Be careful with Zimbabwe. There, British missionaries supported the colonizers, who were British; but American missionaries, particularly some Methodists that I know personally, resisted and undermined the British regime" (email, January 2014).

91. The reason for this line of reasoning is not without precedent. At the recent Lausanne gathering of the Arts and Mission focus group, a suggestion was for a shift in the center of production of music from the North to the South. However, this was opposed by some in preference for a subtle rewording—rather than "shift," the preference was to encourage a balance or redistribution (of power, although this was not explicitly mentioned) in such production. It was argued that the word "shift" implied a recognition that there indeed was a problem that needed to be rectified. But the majority felt that this (the shift) would further alienate the North from the South, something that was unnecessary at present (Discussion at Lausanne Global Leadership Forum, Bangalore, 2013).

> Nor is it any wonder that most artists today have succumbed to the pressures of globalised capital and the expansion of the art market and its constant appetite for exotic objects. My point is that most of the work of contemporary artists from the Third World, whether they live in the West or in their own countries, and particularly that work now being institutionally celebrated as part of the multiculturalism of the West, is not entirely what the artists might have produced had they been free to act historically by taking a radical position in art, or even as an expression of their imagination as free individuals. Those who pursue art as a profession and aspire to a successful career are subject to coercion by the power and benevolence of the West into producing something that does not pose any threat to the structures of Western institutions and their philosophical underpinning. The success of these artists can then also be used to create an illusion of change, to show that change does not mean abandoning old cultural forms, and that people can in fact benefit from staying within the boundaries of their own cultures.[92]

Further research is warranted in each context to determine the systems at play that seem to proliferate the use of such technologies, for example, to what extent is such process/technology reproducible using indigenous resources? That is, to reproduce the process, not just the product. David Ruiz addresses the "Global shift from North to South" in the context of Latin American Worship:

> Sadly, in more recent times, the emergence of megachurches and the use of mass media, iPods, and iTunes are popularizing imported music from famous singers and groups from the North, which are, again, shaping the worship expression of the church. Deep reflection is needed to affirm our identity and to continue expressing through worship the discovery of our relationship with God that is taking place in Latin America (2013, 45).

"SONGS THAT SELL BETTER": A NEW AESTHETIC

Continuing in the light of Mungazi's "two types of colonizers," how might we perceive the commodification of music in terms of "Christian music" given the overwhelming influence of CCM (Contemporary Christian Music)?[93]

---

92. Arareen, "Ethnic Minorities, Multiculturalism, and the Celebration of the Post-Colonial Other."

93. Chris Tomlin is "most likely the most often sung artist anywhere." CCM Magazine, http://www.ccmmagazine.com/article/chris-tomlin-tour-makes-history/.

Noticeably, the overwhelming majority of artists in the CCM genre are Caucasian. In the course of my research with a Nashville-based Christian label I discovered that music produced for consumption by the CCM industry needs to go through a certain "industry standard"—approval of a recording company (usually a producer), personal financial investment (several thousand dollars), design preferences, and related expenses based upon the commercial viability for the company's marketing preferences.[94]

JK explains what he experienced and understood as the "power of globalization":

> When I went to the Calvin Worship Symposium, there was an EMI/ BMG Christian music [publishing] group. They produce about 80 songs per year—most of the CCLI top twenty songs are produced by EMI. These guys say they try their best to produce songs that are theologically balanced. [But] They tend to produce <u>songs that sell better</u> (emphasis added).

Is this the new aesthetic? Does this reflect the extent to which evangelical Christians place a value on their "products" to "sell better"?[95] According to JK, and others may agree, secular labels such as EMI exert a powerful influence upon the CCM industry in terms of its (CCM's) marketing and distribution worldwide. Furthermore, this posture reflects an inherent self-deception wherein commercial viability is a primary hermeneutic in defining, at least outwardly, a "theologically balanced" approached.

Returning to JK's episode, the people from EMI compared the sale of worship-related music in the context of a Christian label or Christian demographic to the success of Hollywood movies. According to JK, their rationale was: "people like movies with [a] happy ending rather than sad

---

94. In a conversation with a Nashville based label with distribution rights around the world, the first question that was asked of an ICM from the global South was: "Do you have ten thousand dollars?" This money was to cover production costs as per the standard of this record company. Further, the ICM was informed that the cover should not have the artist's image—the fact of his international status would decrease chances of sales in the US as well as in other parts of the world. The artist discovered this to be true. To his surprise, when he returned to his home country the artist was told by the owner of a local record company with international affiliations in the West (I paraphrase): "Why did you come back? Why market your music, when we can get the original for the same price?"

95. The consumer-driven model of church is broadly acknowledged. Smith, *Desiring the Kingdom*. But the larger issue is brought into focus by asking: What is the relationship between sale-ability and being contextually relevant? Gormly, "Evangelizing through Appropriation," 254, observes that most CCM labels are owned by secular record companies and therefore feeding American Consumerism. See also Romanowski, *Eyes Wide Open*; Gersztyn, *Jesus Rocks the World*.

endings." So, for JK, Western capitalism influences the production of worship music, both content and style. Further, it is being exported to the rest of the world. In the case of Korean Christians in Korea this is happening without sufficient critical interaction. JK is a bridge in what he is doing through his organization, Art and Mission.

JK asked the representatives of EMI at the Calvin Worship Symposium for their rationale for selling worship songs based upon commercial sensibilities. They responded to him admitting that while "they produce [the final products for sale and distribution], the bottom line is that it is each local church's responsibility what to sing." According to JK,

> [That] is true but people are not that mature. Even the sincere brothers and sisters who lead worship here, they are sincere, but they are exposed to that most of the time—Hillsong, Passion. So, they end up singing that song. So, it's really celebrating a culture, and not a community-driven worship. I don't know how to solve this problem. Trying to be as non-offensive as possible.

However, is being "non-offensive" an effective response for Christian ICMs in this global moment?[96] A "non-offensive" response appears to be at odds with the performance of creative others who do not mind being "offensive." Secular artists adopting this approach would include Chinese artist and political activist Ai Weiwei who has been harassed and jailed for being outspoken through his art in his context in China.[97]

The driving force of market capitalism significantly influences what music Christians in the West and their Westernized constructs in the rest of world end up listening to and using as an expression of "local" Christianity. Eric Gormly draws from Alexander's study of televangelism (1998) where he argues that evangelical reaction to secular culture is based upon a perspective that views popular culture as an immoral influence with purposes that run

---

96. We will explore this phenomenon more fully in Creative Performance. For now, we might recall the image of God as a "man of war" (Exod 15:3). Further, God's desire to test Israel and teach those who had not experienced war: "it was only in order that the generations of the people of Israel might know war, to teach war to those who had not known it before" (Judg 3:2, emphasis added).

97. Alison Klayman a journalist in China made a film on Ai Weiwei that received international acclaim. According to a website promoting the film: "Ai Weiwei is China's most famous international artist, and its most outspoken domestic critic. Against a backdrop of strict censorship and an unresponsive legal system, Ai expresses himself and organizes people through art and social media. In response, Chinese authorities have shut down his blog, beat him up, bulldozed his newly built studio, and held him in secret detention" (*Never Sorry*).

counter to what might be considered Christian beliefs and moral sensibilities.[98] In what sense do ICMs like JK respond to such a scenario?

Gormly cites Alexander's observation of television programming as ritual performance that "takes the participant to a special, and often sacred, place" in three ways: first, "ritual legitimation" indicates enabling religious conservatives to be politically active in the battle to "morally regenerate American society." Second, "ritual adaptation," which refers to the way that conservatives are enabled to more efficiently "accommodate secular society and its demands into their lives." Third, "ritual community" points to how programming supports the community in their "'ongoing struggle for greater inclusion in mainstream American society'" (2003, 260).

Issuing from Alexander's observations, ICMs on mission might consider the following. First, create ritual spaces that legitimize music/artists from the South as well as the North. Second, foster spaces for intercultural understanding and partnership between artists and participants from both hemispheres. Third, encourage the emergence of community by not compromising on their musical identity as embodied, enacted, and expressed through their hybrid identities.

---

98. Gormly, "Evangelizing through Appropriation," 259. Concerning the paradoxical relationship between Christian evangelicals and the use of popular media and technology, Gormly explores the role and implications of CCM (Contemporary Christian Music) in evangelical subculture and in the broader secular culture in the United States. He argues that: "In addition to the strident rhetoric still found in the debate over the corrupting force perceived by Evangelicals in popular culture, Evangelicals' use of media has moved to a new level of sophistication to enable much more effective entry into the national discourse" (253).

6

Creative Construction: Enactment

IN THIS CHAPTER WE explore the discourse of ICMs in mission as they negotiate their identities through the creative construction of their music. In the process, ICMs create new sites for the generation of knowledge for the participation of others in the mission of God. Currently, lyrical theology and logocentric conformism play a key role in the conceptualization of music as knowledge in Christianity.[1] However, with intensified global interchanges in the mediation (conceptualization, production, and reciprocation) of music across the world, the palette for creative construction is greatly expanded. The shifts from previously peripheral formations to the polycentric emergence of "pluriform potentials"[2] present an unsurpassed opportunity for the emergence of fresh hybridities for the translation of Christianity. Martin Stokes's interrogation of the mobilities and global soundscapes in this era of musical cosmopolitanism helps paint a context for ICM creative construction:

---

1. Kimbrough, *Lyrical Theology of Charles Wesley*; Woods and Walrath, *Message in the Music*. For Jacque Derrida, "Logocentrism emphasizes the privileged role that *logos*, or speech, has been accorded in the Western tradition." Reynolds, "Metaphysics of Presence/ Logocentrism." We acknowledge the place of lyrical theology in translating Christianity through music. Here we seek to explore the making of ICM identity through processes of construction that may not place lyrics at the center of meaning making.

2. I owe the phrase to Brian Schrag, The Lausanne Movement Consultation on Arts in Mission, May 29–31, 2013, Dallas at Graduate Institute for Applied Linguistics (GAIL), hosted by GAIL, ICE (International Council of Ethndoxologists), and co-sponsored by WEA (World Evangelical Alliance) and Lausanne. For further information, go to: www.brianatplay.com.

> If hybridization and musical translation are the new creative principles, how are musical intelligibility and meaning to be maintained, by whom, and for whom? How is diversity and cultural in-between-ness to be celebrated, without eroding core identities? Who are to be the gatekeepers, the explainers, the interpreters, the go-betweens, the intellectuals? Who are to be the guardians of propriety and fairness as the recording industry and it[s] superstars sink their teeth into vulnerable local communities?[3]

Eugenia Siapera identifies several theories of representation including stereotyping, framing, critical discourse analysis, semiology, discursive formations, and performatives.[4] We recollect, however, that music is more than words. It is also more than sound. Further, the non-representational nature of music offers fresh ways to reconceptualize the correspondence between musical creativity and mission in a postcolonial context. The "epistemic primacy" of an artwork lies in the understanding that art (for us, musical creativity) challenges and reshapes our epistemological, metaphysical, and theological categories.[5] It is in the mediation of a specific hermeneutic of knowledge that ICMs create a pathway for others to participate in the process of bringing about a new reality on earth as it is in heaven. We begin to look at some of the dynamics of this process of construction through a musical presentation by FP.

MUSICAL CREATIVITY AND REPRESENTATION

A typical musical presentation for FP begins with a prayer and invocation for communal harmony and world peace. FP is a vocalist. He often uses the accompaniment of *mridangam, ghattam,* and violin—instruments accepted as tradition amongst Carnatic musicians. In a concert he begins with a Sanskrit phrase, which he then translates for the participants gathered as "let there be peace and harmony all over the world." He then invites people to pray for world peace and communal harmony and announces

---

3. Stokes, "On Musical Cosmopolitanism," 1.

4. See Siapera, *Cultural Diversity and Global Media,* 111–30. Stereotyping (Lippman, *Public Opinion*; Tajfel, *Human Groups and Social Categories*); framing (Goffman, *Frame Analysis*; Gamson, *Talking Politics*; Entman, "Framing"); CDA (Fairclough, *Critical Discourse Analysis*); discursive formulations (Barthes, *Mythologies*); performatives (Foucault, *Order of Things*; Austin, *How To Do Things With Words*; Butler, *Excitable Speech*).

5. Monti, *Natural Theology of Arts,* 8. Monti draws upon John Polkinghorn's understanding of the dynamic correspondence between the subjective nature of "how we know" and the very nature of the object itself that controls and is revealed through our knowledge of the object.

that "the world today is craving for this great, great prayer today." After the prayer, he leads in a vocal invocation in Sanskrit, using the phrase, "Om Shanti" an extremely popular phrase usually chanted as a mantra by Hindus.[6] He goes on to tell participants:

> We strongly believe that music is <u>beyond</u> all religions. *Ragas* and *thalas* [rhythm patterns] are universal. And also music, we consider, is a bridge <u>between</u> religions. Today we are living in a world where we hear now and then communal riots and clashes; lots of fundamentalism. So, here we have [an] interreligious team.

He then proceeds to introduce the members of his team. He introduces the violinist, a Muslim, the *mridangam* player, a Hindu, and then introduces himself, dressed in a white cassock that he wears as a visual symbol for all his performances, as "a Christian, a priest, a Catholic priest." FP then goes on to proclaim: "We would like to communicate this great message: We all belong to one family, whatever religion, we ultimately belong to one family." The audience demonstrates their acknowledgment by clapping at this point. He then proceeds to sing a song on national unity and integration: "*jai ho, jai ho, bharat ma ki, jai, jai, jai*" (translated: let there be victory . . . to Mother India, victory, victory, victory). On other occasions, he also includes a devotional song addressed to Ganesha, a Hindu deity, a praise song to Jesus Christ, and a praise song to Allah.

Responding to the opening scenario above, an immediate concern is, how does FP justify singing praise songs to Jesus Christ as well as Ganesha and Allah. Does such activity entail a compromise on his identity in Christ and the unique mission of God through Jesus Christ? Before we address that issue, however, we make a few observations.

FP endorses the place of musical enactment in shaping people's perceptions of reality. Just as language plays a key role in processes of conceptualization,[7] music too plays a key role in shaping people's concepts of reality. It engages people's imaginations and helps them to "discover truth."[8] This formative potential of music to create meaning and to shape identity (individual and community) is central to its role as symbol, "the

---

6. Beck, *Sonic Theology*, 205. Guy Beck speculates on "the primal syllable," Om and "its parsing into at least four or five degrees after the time of the principal Upanishads."

7. Nida, *Message and Mission*, 3.

8. Hunter, *Celtic Way of Evangelism*, 61. We see this occurring in the strategies employed in the Celtic Christian movement where creative embellishments around the text of Scripture were justified based upon the way in which it enhanced the reading of the text.

embodiment of that shared memory that is the foundation for social and religious community identity."[9]

By bringing together peoples from dominant religious traditions within the country, FP is challenging and crossing the existing social boundaries typically associated with symbolic representation of such musical tradition. FP's words, "beyond" and "between," bring a recollection of postcolonial discourse whereby sites of creative construction are thresholds for the launching of new epistemological foundations for the construction of identities "in-between" (Bhabha 1994) concepts of indigeneity and cosmopolitanism.

FP demonstrates that as part of a "symbolic universe," the process of musical creativity is essentially a social process with a history. If one is to understand its meaning one has to understand the history of its production.[10] In such "space," music is the transformative "means by which hierarchies of place are negotiated and transformed."[11]

In FP's context, Carnatic music along with its counterpart in the North, Hindustani music, is considered "classical" traditions. The dominant perception is that Hindustani and Carnatic classical music traditions are perceived as more authentic representations of what it means to be Indian as opposed to other hybrid forms. FP's adoption of a secular democratic approach—the linkage of his creative construction with notions of national identity—signifies an intentional inclusion of persons from major religious traditions in India performing together. The discourse of nationness embedded in FP's creative construction communicates unity, a popular notion and value given the backdrop of communal violence and history in the light of colonialism and the Partition (India and Pakistan).[12]

The conflation of Christianity with Westernization is conveyed through the prolific import and adaptation of Western musical forms of worship in many urban churches in India. In such a context, FP's approach is significant in terms of the construction of space for the engendering of

9. Apostolos-Cappadona, "Humanity in the Arts," 1171.
10. Berger and Luckmann, *Social Construction of Reality*, 97.
11. Stokes, "Introduction," 4.
12. The adoption of forms of construction that clearly relate to the cultural and national consciousness of the people of India is significant. Here, we do not explore the particular dynamic between music and Indian national identity. This is subject for an entire dissertation. We proceed based upon the correlation of such to investigate the construction of musical creativity as it pertains to the linkage between personhood and productivity of the artist as a process. Concerning FP and the method of construction he adopts, the Preamble to the Constitution of India is helpful to see some correlations. Please see, "The Constitution of India," http://lawmin.nic.in/olwing/coi/coi-english/Const.Pock%202Pg.Rom8Fsss(3).pdf.

156   Creativity and Captivity

knowledge that calls for reimagining Christianity in the light of popular notions of Indianness (for example, classical music heritage).

"TO BRING THE WORLD TOGETHER INTO INDIA"

There is a broad acknowledgment of the link between music and national consciousness.[13] When it comes to musicians who have earned an almost prophet-like status in India, other than *Pandit* Ravi Shankar, none can escape the personality of A. R. Rahman.[14] In the light of Rahman's influence amongst Indians worldwide, I asked ML regarding the impact his "Indianness" might have on achieving his purposes amongst his audience. He responded: "Being White, it definitely sets us away from the ability to act Indian-patriotic. We are not Indians. I think it is pretty powerful."[15]

The "ability to [en]act" a hyphenated patriotism is a "powerful" skill that ICMs in mission must learn. The conflation of Indian classical music with Indian national and religious identity is the context for ML's constructive enactment. However, ICMs with roots in the global South but operating in the

---

13. Mach, "National Anthems," 65, 67. Chopin was a composer, a national hero and a prophet, and contributed to the international recognition of Poland as a nation; in fact, the "collective soul" of the Polish people was, in the opinion of one of the Prime Ministers of Poland, reflected in him. Chopin imbibed the values of the people of his country in his music; it was not religious music. See also Stokes, "On Musical Cosmopolitanism," 7–8. "Nationalist ideologues" through musical cosmopolitanism are not bereft of westernization. In the case of Turkey, musical cosmopolitanism was identified with westernization that denigrated Islamic local traditions in Turkey. Therefore, musical cosmopolitanism was identified as a problem to be countered by the modern state.

14. Rahman identifies closely with India as a nation. When he got the Oscar for *Slumdog Millionaire* (Pathé Distribution, 2008), his comments at the ceremony testified to the fact that he won it for India. Rahman worked in collaboration with a government institution to rearrange the tune for the national anthem. He also worked on an arrangement of the National Song of India, *Vande Mataram*, which became a hit and was aimed at unifying the country. See "AR Rahman-CNN talk Asia-Part 2- 'Converting'" posted May 20, 2009, http://www.youtube.com/watch?v=gLOB9OCj4lU. Rahman's rendition of the song is not without criticism given the communal atmosphere between Hindus and Muslims in the dawn Indian independence. However, Rahman's appropriation of the song sparked an ongoing discourse with regard to Indian national identity and communal consciousness of the nation. In addition, he wrote the music for the 2012 Olympics in London, UK. For further information: http://www.arrahman.com/index1.html. In November 2013 a street was named after him in Toronto, Canada.

15. He adds: "In China if you listen to the Canaan hymns, its full of China this and China that; there is an incredible pride of being Chinese; and that is a pretty powerful statement—a Christian community in China being persecuted still being proud of their motherland. We have it even in America—'My country . . . ,' 'Battle Hymn of the Republic' and all these crazy hymns, from one perspective should definitely not be translated into Hindi and force the villagers of Uttar Pradesh [a State of India] to sing those songs. I hope nobody has done that."

context of North America as well must learn to differentiate "root" identity from "shoot" identity in order to control/adjust at will the perceived distance between such polarities. The process of creative construction through musical creativity is a vehicle to navigate this territory. The need for the skill of negotiation comes to the fore especially in contexts where the "flag" occupies a central space in the "sanctuary" of American religiosity.[16]

The negotiation of ML's Indianness, however, is problematic in the light of a perceived hesitancy of some churches in India to identify themselves in palpable terms with the national agenda or even aspects of Indian nationalism as such (not least in response to Hindu fundamentalist taunts that challenge Christians to leave India and to go back to the West), ML comments:

> A worship song that has patriotic leaning is only applicable to that country, if that country's name is mentioned or if the landscape is mentioned. I think it's beautiful and that Indian Christians should get involved in it, for India. Why not? I think it is great to be proud of your country. I am proud of America, even though I have hardly lived here, but very proud of being American. And I think it is worthy of being proud of being Indian, especially an Indian Christian should cultivate that pride. Now it is really hard to do that when the Hindu fundamentalists are saying get out of our country.

He goes on to admit with regard to the notion of "Indianness": "I don't think . . . I can relate to the question but we can identify and support." Mark narrates an incident in which he is affirmed as "a true son of India" demonstrating the fluid nature of national identity as a construct in terms of the linkage between immersion within a cultural music system and how it creates virtual roots apart from one's own national or cultural identity:

> Whenever a white person affirms or praises India or learns an Indian art form, they are in a sense even a greater patriotic symbol. Because, "Look the foreigners even love our country." I get the comment all the time: "you speak Hindi better than us; you play Indian classical music better than us"—these kind of statements, which are not true but they just like to say it to complement you

---

16. When a key informant in North America attempted to change the location of the American flag from the front of the sanctuary to the back of the sanctuary some church members staged a walk-out. The argument of whether or not to have to flag "in" or "outside" church is complex. The point however is that negotiating the volatile nature of the construction of musical space for the contextualization of Christianity in "Christianity" requires careful consideration.

and ascribe greatness to India—that you would put that much effort to learn our stuff even better than we know it.

In other instances, according to ML, "Indian Christians say to us, 'for the first time in our lives, our Indianness and our Christianity has been reconciled through your music.'" Mark concludes: "so that's what has been accomplished through our music in hundreds and hundreds of lives from South Africa, to Guyana, Surinam. That's an amazing statement and an amazing thing to have happened." It is a ministry of reconciliation.

Similarly, FP's blatant fusing within a single constructive context, a process whereby songs that are meant to be sung in quite specific and exclusive religious contexts, invites others into a process of re-historicizing tradition within a canon of hope. In terms of a rubric for symbolic "traditioning"[17] of the process of musical creativity, Cardoza-Orlandi's description of prophetic dialogue is significant especially concerning the "sites" or "places" occupied by ICMs in their creative dialogue with culture. In such contexts, a historical and theological framework

> breaks down the modern categories of past, present, and future when interpreting Christian history. Prophetic dialogue suggests an eschatological hermeneutic where past is replaced by memory, present by experience, and future by expectation. Hence, history, from a Christian perspective, is a continuum; history is connected (2013, 22).

According to FP, his "mixed religious background" was a major influence in his thinking and music. He faced little opposition to his music ministry despite his overt Christian presence (for example, attire of a Catholic priest). Hindus as well as Christians have been a source of encouragement. In FP's experience, Hindus and Muslims are not so much the "other" to be reached but rather, those who form the very fabric or foundation for FP's musical creativity. He goes on to say:

> In spite of all religious barriers, we all belong to one family that is humanity so whether my brother is Muslim or Hindu we should all be able to help each other, love each other, that kind of thinking really came to my mind and that context has helped me to think like that.

---

17. Brown, *Tradition and Imagination*, 6; 169–70. Contrary to the popular understanding of "tradition" as that which is "boring," Brown argues that tradition involves the process of human imaginative interaction with history in such a way that serves to maintain continuity between text of Christianity and its ongoing interpretation in context that justifies the coinage of the phrase, "the moving text."

According to Thomas F. Torrance, true knowledge (epistemological and theological) must operate with an openness to "our way of knowing to be clarified and modified" as we continue to journey along the pathway of inquiry.[18] Pursuant to Torrance's "open epistemology" (ibid.), FP's creative conceptualization includes the other in the process of clarification and knowledge creation.

Musical Creativity as Indigenizing Process

For FP, religion is a barrier. Musical creativity, however, appears to be a portal into a relationship with the other that overcomes such barriers. In terms of an "indigenizing" process, it encapsulates the conditions of the culture along with its "disrelations" that shape one's indigeneity. "Disrelations" refer to the ethnocentrisms or prejudices inherent in the social context to which we belong.[19] The process of FP's musical creative construction reciprocates the context in which he lives and serves.

Singing songs to Ganesha and Allah to him do not compromise his Christian identity in any sense. For FP, such songs are mere cultural expressions to be re-signified through his personhood, his personal beliefs translated into behavior. He demonstrates the capacity for risk involved in translatability as a theological principle. It is, in the words of Kwame Bediako, the "capacity of the essential impulses of the Christian religion to be transmitted and assimilated in a different culture so that these impulses create dynamically equivalent responses in the course of such transmission."[20] What is worth emphasizing is the fact that while FP does not "compromise" on his personal/religious/spiritual identity, his culture is yet being constructed, i.e., knowledge is being generated, by the process he adopts in the process of overlapping his beliefs with that of the other.

For some, however, FP may be going too far in the effort to translate Christianity. We recollect, musical indigenous-cosmopolitanism is predicated on modes of translatability via existing and ongoing "dialogical relations between idioms, genres, the speech of characters, and always, the social location of language."[21] In other words, re-emphasizing Mikhail Bhaktin's thesis,

18. Torrance, *Knowledge of God*, 102.

19. Walls, *Cross-Cultural Process in Christian History*, 6–9. According to Andrew Walls, the "indigenizing" principle is the tendency to accept the other along with the culture and "group relations" that come with the other. The "opposing" tendency is the "pilgrim" principle, the process of transformation that ushers people into an inheritance in Christ, a new family of faith (along with its disrelations).

20. Bediako, *Christianity in Africa*, 119.

21. Toynbee and Dueck, *Migrating Musics*, 76. Toynbee draws from Mikhail Bhaktin's *The Dialogical Imagination: Four Essays* (1981).

Toynbee writes concerning the nature of "Migrating Music": "Language encapsulates social relations, and the dialogue between diverse voices in literature is a kind of transfiguration of these relations" (ibid.).[22] FP's audience is perceptibly open to his music, creating a path for the transfiguration of relations by the creation of knowledge along with the other.

Conscience and Contextualization

I asked ML about the apparent contradiction in FP's appropriation of praise songs to Ganesha, Allah, and to Jesus. ML offered some degree of justification, yet clearly differentiated his own stance with respect to such practice. Here is an excerpt from the interview:

> **ML:** Allah is the Arabic name in the KJV for Yahweh; so in the Arabic KJV, Allah in substituted for the word Jehovah; he was singing to Jehovah in that song unless there were compromising statements made in the lyrics to that song which were not in agreement with Christian beliefs as God, Creator of the Universe. So, I don't know what it would have been in the lyrics to the songs. I have no problem with him singing a song to Allah at all. I would have questioned him if he had sung songs to Krishna for example, in a devotional way.
>
> **Uday:** [What about the song] he sang to Ganpati?
>
> **ML:** I question that. I have a problem with that from my own perspective. My own conscience does not allow me to do that at the moment in my life. My conscience is ever-evolving. It is ever-changing because my conscience itself is not the truth; my conscience is clear but it does not make me innocent; God is the judge. So, my conscience is ever-changing. Twenty-thirty years ago I was singing Rock music lyrics in India, which I

---

22. Bizzell and Herzberg, *Rhetorical Tradition*, 1208. In Bizzell et al.'s analysis, Bhaktin's approach aligns with the structural linguistic (Saussure) semiotic assumption that meaning is patterned in culture. However, Bhaktin differs in the assumption that the sole purpose of linguistics is to analyze how signs make sense in given system. He prefers to recognize the primacy of the "utterance-in-context." Bhaktin disagrees that signs are primary psychological in nature; rather, they are a part of "material reality" "imbued with ideological meaning in a social context. He writes, "the study of ideologies does not depend on psychology to any extent and need not be grounded in it." Bhaktin, *Marxism and the Philosophy of Language*, 1213. Signs are not merely "mental phenomena," just as language, for Bhaktin, is not a mere expression of an individual's thought. He argues that consciousness emerges in the context of social relations; it "takes shape and being in the material of signs created by an organized group in the process of its social intercourse." Bhaktin's thesis establishes a foundation for the reconceptualization of musical creativity as knowledge generation overlapping postmodern approaches.

would never sing now. My conscience is no longer clear to sing those. Now there are things that I might not sing now but sing ten years from now. So, I'm on a journey with God, God is on a journey with me; so, likewise that Christian Indian singer is on a journey with God, and God is on a journey with him; if his conscience is clear that does not make him innocent, but it certainly does not give me any place to condemn him. Because it is very likely that he having being immersed in Indian classical music and thought has a very typical Indian musician's attitude toward these things, which is simply: there is only one god, so why are you all worried.

ML: (continuing) "However, I have a conscience and my conscience is drawn to worshipping Jesus Christ alone."

Conscience appears to play a significant role in the process of musical creativity especially in terms of the representation of knowledge. We discover a range of meanings for "conscience" in a secular Greek sense. It is through the faculty of the conscience that knowledge is shared, commonality is created, perception altered, and morality engendered in the context of connectedness with others. Further, it does not necessarily have to anything to do with deity.[23]

Apparently, the idea of a "good conscience" was relatively unknown in the Greek world. From a biblical standpoint, the conscience refers to self-understanding that originates in God who makes possible responsible action.[24] The voice of God and one's own is in agreement, a harmony and not a "rational autonomy" (Maurer 1964, 910). In the NT, it has been defined as "the psychological faculty, which can distinguish between right or wrong."[25]

In terms of conscience, representation by way of musical creativity may be conceived as place, kind, and way of knowing. As place, musical knowledge emerges in the context of cultural diversity. From a critical realist approach, the "deep structures" in art and music, as in linguistic categories, create and embody a reality, of not only divisions and differences in culture, but also varied perceptions in the nature of reality itself.[26] As place, the "epistemic primacy" of the artwork is evident. It brings into the

---

23. Maurer, "Sunoida, Suneidesis," 7:900. From a Socratic perspective, "knowledge of a contradiction opens the way to victory over it'" συνείδησις means a "percipient and active self-awareness" which is threatened at its heart by the disjunction of acknowledgment and perception, willing and knowing, judgment and action.

24. See Ps 139; Deut 30:14; also, on the link between conscience and action, for example, Paul's claim that his conscience is clear in Acts 23:1; 24:16.

25. Louw and Nida, "Psychological Faculties," 13. See Rom 2:15.

26. Hiebert, *Missiological Implications of Epistemological Shifts*, 73.

foreground the continuities, conflicts, and constructive habits of local histories—the gathering of multicultural perspectives expressed through music. Further, it shows us that the representation of difference is characterized by the spaces of interplay between participants in a cultural system, which reinforces the concept of creativity as part of an interactive cultural system and not primarily an individualistic enterprise.

As kind of knowing musical representation "enacts and explores" knowledge of a spiritual nature that invites participation in a very specific sense as "co-knowledge with God."[27] Further, the spiritual context is apparent not only in the religious nature of the songs presented, but by verbal cues offered by FP. As "way," "copying" what is being produced in the original and passed on for use produces knowledge.[28] In terms of copying, we recollect that representation of difference *via* musical creativity does not primarily emphasize knowledge in terms of information, but participative experiential knowledge. It does not require a universal acknowledgment on the rationale for what is being represented. Ambiguity is central to the process of meaning-making.[29]

Take the case of ML who has adopted the instrument and appearance of a traditional North Indian classical music exponent. The very fact that he has adopted such an instrument as a Christian is odd, not merely, because he is a foreigner, but because the instrument and way of life associated with learning such an instrument intrinsically represents a specific religious affiliation (North Indian, Brahmin) within Hinduism. In the light of Taussig's (1993) tautology—what the copy is representing takes on the power of the original—in what sense does ML's process of musical creativity assume the character and power of the "original"? What is the "original" anymore?

Taking on the role of a Christian musician in India, ML goes on to say:

> I am a professional musician; I am living in India where the majority community is Hindu; and I need to support my family, and I don't think there is anything wrong with this. I don't

---

27. Steiner, *Errata*, 4. Also, the first commentary on the passage in 1 Pet 2:19, with its strange διὰ συνείδησιν θεοῦ, "for the sake of co-knowledge with God," "for the sake of consciousness of God," bears the same meaning (Kittel et al., *Theological Dictionary of the New Testament*, 7:16).

28. Taussig, *Mimesis and Alterity*, xiii. The "mimetic faculty" is "the nature that culture uses to create second nature, the faculty to copy, imitate, make models, explore difference, yield into and become Other."

29. Born and Hesmondhalgh, *Western Music and Its Others*, 32. Cf. the "*hyperconnotative* character," of music that refers to "its intense cognitive, cultural, and emotional associations, and its abstraction" as compared with more denotative meanings in the literary and visual arts.

personally believe in these deities myself, but I am getting a paycheck for it myself and that's my job.

According to ML: "I really believe in celebrating people's consciences where they are at and giving them the benefit of the doubt, because I want people to give me the benefit of the doubt. That's the only way you'll get anybody's trust."

He further goes on to reason that:

> Classically in India, it is culturally appropriate to begin with Ganapati because Ganapati is the remover of obstacles. So, from a cultural perspective, if you despiritualize that, which some people's consciences are clear to actually despiritualize the actual specifics of Ganapati as a god, and just say: "you know, it's like sweeping the stage, we're going to remove the obstacles here . . . so we're going to pray to God and say to God, 'remove the obstacles' and in that sense we are seeing God in the form of an elephant [ref. Ganesha being the god with an elephant's head] because the elephant is a remover of obstacles in nature, constantly picking up trunks of trees with their trunks." And so, you know, I can see how your Indian Christian argues it in his own mind and therefore does not see any problem opening with Ganapati.

Responding to FP's praise song to Allah and to Jesus, ML says that he can envision seeing FP "singing the Allah song without any problem and then I can see him singing his Yeshu [Jesus] song, basically saying to his audience: 'this is my guru, I would like to sing a song for <u>my</u> guru. I would like to sing a song for my <u>guru</u>. I would like to sing a song for my God.'" For ML, "at that point the audience has been introduced to a fact that this specific song is the song that touches this man's heart the most, it is the song that drives this man's life; the other songs this man sang were formalities." ML justifies his rationale with Scripture (1 Kings 17). He explains:

> The Ganpati song was a formality, kind of like Naaman asking Elisha, with your permission I may have to bow down to that god because I am still going to be the servant of my master. Elisha says, "Go in peace" (Mark laughs). Because he knows the guy is basically only going to worship the God of Israel from now on. He's been healed of his leprosy. There is no devotion in his heart to that god whatsoever.

ML identifies with FP in the capacity of music to hold in creative tension polarizing differences. Conscience permitting, playing a form of devotional music does not necessarily indicate compromise of one's true spiritual devotion. In the light of Naaman the Syrian's experience of the God of Elisha, for ML, a godly witnessing lifestyle is a more relevant criterion to authentic creative enactment with the other than the "letter of the law":

> I would rather see that Indian Christian man's life and rather visit his home and see how he interacts with his wife and children and neighbors—whether he has shared in Christ in his life, and vocally as well as through his life, living for Christ—that's what I would like to see, rather than whether or not he is singing Ganpati or not. That is, for me, not the compromise breaker or non-breaker for me personally in terms of a journey with Christ.

So then, is singing praise songs to deities other than Christ permissible? ML quickly adds: "That said, I don't think I am going to do that myself! I don't think I need to do that." ML feels that he has "already stepped over the line as far as many Indian Christian's are concerned" by using Sanskrit names for representing God that are not conventionally accepted by the Indian Church. He adds: "I'm already in that camp with a clear conscience." Further, regarding FP, he says, "this Indian man perhaps is in that camp with a clear conscience; we differ regarding are own specifics as far as what we find acceptable and what we don't find acceptable." For ML, "Its all about a journey with the Holy Spirit—to maintain a clear conscience before God at all costs."

From ML and FP's discourse, we infer that the conscience plays a major role in determining the effectiveness of contextualization through musical creativity. We gather that it is also a collective conscience. It is not a black and white process of secular and sacred based upon one's own interpretation of Scripture. We also discern that ambiguity is not tantamount to vagueness. In fact, ambiguity is crucial to the knowledge-generating process. The representation of difference *via* musical creativity does not primarily emphasize knowledge in terms of information, but participative experiential knowledge. The creative conscience, in a theological sense, is the "spur" used by God to induce conversion, it leads to self-knowledge, and confession of sin.[30] Paul resignifies the term's usage;[31] it is "man himself

---

30. Maurer, "σύνοιδα," 910ff.

31. Maurer, "σύνοιδα," 910ff. Paul takes συνείδησις with a comprehensive breadth and variety not found in any of his predecessors. For him it is no longer just the popular bad conscience or the Hellenistic-Jewish ἔλεγχος. It has now become the central self-consciousness of knowing and acting man. With few exceptions it had never been anything like this before in literature, combining the Greek view of man as especially a thinking being with the Hebrew tradition, which stresses the primacy of the Word. Paul raises the whole problem of act, being, and knowledge in anthropology—a step of momentous significance for the centuries, which followed. Yet Paul did not present any uniform doctrine of συνείδησις. The concept is simply one of various attempts to

aware of himself in perception and acknowledgment, in willing and acting" (Maurer 1964, 914).[32] The conscience signifies a unity between act and the awareness of it (ibid., 916).

For this reason, ML is uncompromising when it comes to his own witness—he would not go where FP seems comfortable going. In this sense, the idea of musical creativity as a journey with the Holy Spirit is central to understanding the arena for contextualization *via* musical creativity. For ML, an effective critique of musical creativity considers a person's total way of life in relation to God, others, and environment. Adelin Jonas Jørgensen explores the historical relationship between anthropology and missiology in order to understand the "anthropology of Christianity as a new innovation."[33] Jørgensen makes the argument that Christian practice and theology should be based upon Christianity as not merely continuity but that of discontinuity as well. As significant as the terms "relativism," "etic and emic," "positioning," "dynamic translations," and "cultural universals" are for missiology, without a discourse of "radical discontinuity" missiology like anthropology is concerned only with continuity.[34]

The musical creative conscience as a palette for the mixing of perceptions can be a place for the enactment and embodiment of such "radical discontinuity." According to Jørgensen, postcolonial and postmodern anthropology are characterized by an appreciation of syncretism that "might not only represent decay but can also present a reintegration of elements and symbols in culture" (2011, 190). Jørgensen refers to Stewart and Shaw (1994) on syncretism as an analytical concept that is worth recollecting here:

> In Western religious discourses and scholarship in particular, the implicit belief remains that assertions of purity speak out naturally and transcendentally as assertions of authenticity. Yet 'authenticity' or 'originality' does not necessarily depend on

---

understand man, cf. Paul's use of καρδία, πνεῦμα, and ψυχή. Furthermore different streams of tradition flow together in it without intermingling. The whole complex is encircled and held together, however, by the new thing, which Paul connects with the idea of conscience. He declares that man is acknowledged by the one true but gracious God in Jesus Christ. This enables him not merely to see more sharply the conflicts of inwardly divided man but also to set them under the promise of healing. Further, the conscience, though weak need not be impure (1 Cor 8:7); it is "not to be defined as a power of religious and moral evaluation or the like which can be detached from man" (Maurer, "σύνοιδα," 910ff).

32. The attitude to one's συνείδησις is the attitude to oneself, and the attitude to the neighbour's συνείδησις is the attitude to the neighbor himself (Kittel et al., *Theological Dictionary of the New Testament*, 7:914).

33. Jørgensen, "Anthropology of Christianity and Missiology," 187–90.

34. Jørgensen, "Anthropology of Christianity and Missiology," 187–90.

> purity. They are claimable as 'uniqueness', and both pure and mixed traditions can be unique. What makes them 'authentic' and valuable is a separate issue, a discursive matter involving power, rhetoric, and persuasion. Thus both putatively pure and putatively syncretic traditions can be 'authentic' if people claim these traditions as unique, and uniquely their (historical) possession. It could be argued, in fact, that syncretic blends are more unique because [they are] historically unrepeatable. An apt example of 'syncretism/mixing = authenticity' is that of Sri Lankan Buddhist nationalism . . . a culture characterized by creative borrowing.[35]

The reference highlights the significance of the discourse of ICMs as that which evolves as a mix of cultures in the contexts of new spaces for mission in contrast/comparison to old anthropological approaches.

FPs "multitextual" approach—using representatives of three different religious/ spiritual traditions at a concert before the President of India—is a construction designed to invite people to rethink and reinterpret such texts within the given social conscience of the nation/ people (given the venue of such performance). His discourse illustrates a cosmopolitanism that focuses on the situatedness of musicians in the new geography of socio-economic networks, how they reinvent or revive traditions, create opportunities to "stir national political consciousness," shape transnational political movements, and shape the local culture in terms of recasting of western business and consumer values[36]

Concerning creative construction and differentiation, what Laikwan Pang writes in the context of creativity as capitalism in China fuels further thought: "Creativity, like writing, is an open structure based on differences."[37] Discerning a language of authenticity especially amid neoliberal and postcolonial currents is clearly not simple especially when it comes to defining criteria that help to distinguish between the truly authentic and the not so authentic.

Does Indigenous Mean Contextualized?

ML comments on how his music affects others. He refers to the fusion/hybrid nature of his music: "It is still in their world enough of rock music to connect with them." The implication for contextualized music, therefore, is

---

35. Jørgensen, "Anthropology of Christianity and Missiology," 189, Stewart and Shaw, *Syncretism/Anti-Syncretism*, 7.

36. Connell and Gibson, "World Music," 343.

37. Pang, *Creativity and Its Discontents*, 7.

that music has to "connect" with others. It is the nature of such connection that interests us. Differentiating his music from other forms, ML says, "It is not like a Mongolian Christian singing with their one little *ektara* [a single (*ek*) string (*tar*) instrument]." "Although," he goes on, "we are a transition for them into more like that kind of stuff."

In the course of such "transition," ML creates space for others to consider embracing their own indigeneity in a different light; to water the roots of their identity or perhaps to discern roots where they thought none existed. We recollect that hybridity in musical creativities emerging from imaginary interactions are not meaningless reactions to "World Music hybridity." It is a place for change. ML's reference to "their world" indicates the creation of a shared world in which both performer and audience participate in creating and sustaining.[38] Indigenization, therefore, is better understood as a process of becoming rather than as a static expression of identity.

In terms of Crociani-Windland's Deleuzian conceptualization, "becoming" indigenous includes "deep transformations that affect the very nature of things by reaching to its virtual roots."[39] As a process of mutual transformation in shared space, indigenizing is essentially a traditioning process of "profound receptivity and openness, based on fluidity" (ibid.). Indigenization, therefore, is a communicative event that transpires in shared space for the mutual transformation of participants.

However, indigenization is a collective process that involves the active participation of others as well. This could be problematic in the face of established notions of indigeneity as fixed categories. The discourse of ICMs like FP and ML suggests that indigeneity is an iterable process: that is, a repeated process of becoming in relation with the other, where innovation does not necessarily entail the negation of tradition.

When it comes to music, the definition of "indigenous" need not be explained purely or primarily in terms of categories contiguous with established notions of "tradition." In the context of Mizo Christianity, Lalsangkima Pachuau comments on the efficacy of "indigenous" tunes to convey more than established traditional musical forms. According to him, "indigenous" refers to the nature of the tune that "emerged from the community's heart and

---

38. Stokes, "Migrant/Migrating Music and the Mediterranean," 30. The "hybridity" of fusion music is evidence of the "rhizomic axes"—"layered, repetitive and circular movements between, and around . . . cities that have come somewhat adrift from national hinterlands and the teleologies of modernization and modernity."

39. Crociani-Windland, *Festivals, Affect, and Identity*, 84, italic mine. According to Crociani-Windland, we recall, the process of "becoming" "is an emergent, involuntary passive dynamic, where one is acted upon, affected, much as in the arising of reminiscence."

expressed its deepest feelings."[40] The process of indigenization involved both songwriter and people who sang the songs (ibid.).

In addition, in the course of research, Pachuau records the words of an interviewee stating that the newly composed songs were "not precisely the Mizo [traditional] tunes and the words neither poetical" nor in the colloquial language (ibid). Nevertheless, in the words of a Mizo songwriter, according to Pachuau, the tunes were "Mizo in that they are comfortable and touching in their flow" (ibid.).

We observe the comment that although the songs were "not precisely" "Mizo," they were nevertheless "comfortable and touching." A question may be raised as to whether the perception that the songs were "not precisely" "Mizo" refers to the authenticity or inauthenticity of such songs. A further question may be raised with regard to the process of contextualization if what is perceived as "indigenous" is still "not precisely" Mizo. The perception of indigeneity as being related to, but in a sense, extant, to a given "tradition" is problematized if we were to assume a "precise" definition of indigeneity. Could such an assumption be implied in the observation that the new songs were "not precisely Mizo"?

The songwriter's description of the songs as being "not precisely Mizo" is revelatory of a system of values that appears to guide the process of indigenization. The overlap between processes of contextualization and indigenization creates room for an imagined space that is characterized by what is described as imprecision ("not precise"). The ambiguity of imprecision invites us to reexamine the process of indigenization-contextualization through the lens of a postcolonial relational axiology that values imprecision.[41] Imprecision, so to speak, does not need any justification in the light of a postcolonial relational axiology since the perspective of being "not precise" creates space for the mutual becoming of sensibilities along with the other. Therefore, the declaration that the tunes were not "precisely" Mizo in the opinion of the songwriter does not necessarily undermine their indigeneity that in the context of postcolonialism is characterized by ambiguity.

Reflecting on the above, the following conclusions may be drawn for shaping our understanding of the relationship between indigenization and contextualization. First, in order for indigenization to move toward contextualization it must be a reciprocal process. The conferring of authenticity upon the new songs was based upon how the individual participant related to the song. Second, indigenization is a process of unification. The conferring of authenticity also implied the ways in which such songs

---

40. Pachuau, *Ethnic Identity and Christianity*, 133.
41. As per the approach of Chilisa, *Indigenous Research Methodologies*, 21–22.

were perceived to unify the Mizo community. Pachuau informs us that the "new tune type emerged out of the process of interaction between the western form of spiritual expression and the indigenous spirituality" (2002, 134). The scope of unification, therefore, was not merely amongst the Mizo but extended beyond Mizo identity as a construct of "traditional musical form" (ibid., 133).

Third, the process of indigenization for contextualization (or *vice versa*) involves the creation of shared space. This space is characterized by a strategic imprecision. The ambiguity of such an environment creates room for inclusion of the other. The nature of inclusion is characterized by a participation in the shared task of reconstructing a collective history. The conferring of authenticity implicitly included the recognition of the role of other in the construction of Mizo histories. In this sense, therefore, the act of conferring authenticity through the experience of the songs is a crucial part of the process of contextualization of indigenous expression.

In the context of the hybridity of fusion music, the deeper issue concerning indigeneity for ICMs may be the equating of mixed or "unoriginal" forms with perceptions of inauthenticity. This is clearly the case when it comes to situations where authenticity is dynamically linked to traditional music. In other words, authenticity is perceived in terms of existing categories of indigeneity.

According to a key informant who plays Carnatic classical music, when asked to speak to challenges to his music he replied:

> People say, why don't you try to cater to the needs of the younger congregation—they can't sit for long etc. By God's grace, I minister to a mixed congregation. I do not choose my congregation—old, young etc. I do my job. My question: it is only us Christians who say this—"O young people they want something different." What about our Muslim friends who are doing the same old traditional worship that their forefathers did in the same mosque, [the] same old way? They are also living in the present generation, working in the IT companies and engineers. Why [is it that] for our Christian boys this is old time religion, we want modern music; this [referring to classical music traditions] is conservative. Why? But if they can stick to their traditions, why can't we? The word "tradition" has become a bad word.

Kwame Bediako reflects on the transmission of Christianity to Africans and suggests that to seek the "indigenization" of Christianity is to erroneously assume that Christianity is "essentially" a Western and foreign religion. It puts the emphasis on foreign modes of Christianity that need to be internalized on Western terms rather than African religious perspectives.[42]

Jason Toynbee addresses the role of musical translation in connecting seemingly disjointed cultural and political occurrences. On the one hand Toynbee cites the case of the translation of African-American rap in Iran, wherein the "concrete nature of its 'original' specification has been abstracted and then translated into a new concrete form" (2011, 74). ICMs moderate an area for such "abstraction" to take place in the process of translation. Citing another example, according to Toynbee, in the case of *bossa* (a popular music genre in Brazil), translation amounts to embracing a musical culture that is "notionally Brazilian, but (immediately) comes to stand for the world, without much need for dialogue with local voices, or with subaltern interests" (ibid., 76). Again, ICMs act as harbingers for the translation instinct. Their hybrid identities represent local *notion*-ality enough to be legitimate ambassadors of indigeneity. However, what does Toynbee mean by "notionally Brazilian" and for whom might such "notion" exist?

The question, reformulated: "what can be done with the music of another when it has already been made your own?"[43] Drawing from study in the field, Toynbee writes that *boss nova* was created in the first place by Brazilian musicians "to translate a host of other musical forms from both near and far"; It was part of the "large scale cultural revolution as beat music in the UK" (ibid.). The problem according to Toynbee is that the process of "active translation" yielded to "coagulation, the fixing of the world in a *bossa* structure of feeling, rather than any interrogation of it" (ibid.). In other words, as I understand it, the idea of what is "Brazilian" itself was abstracted in the process.

Active translation of music is properly the work of a hermeneutical community. In the context of mission, it is a holy task. ICMs carry capacity to initiate and facilitate such a process. For example, in our opening scenario, FP was inviting participants in the musical presentation to engage in a process of active and collective translation in specific ways, such as, the collective renegotiation of religious/cultural identity—how can a Catholic priest sing praise songs to Allah and Hindu gods? This displays vulnerability on FP's part. It also appears to draw people into a safe zone for open conversation. The historical particularity of Carnatic music and its Hindu moorings along with the prevailing notion of Christianity as a "Western" phenomenon (reinforced by the garb of a Roman Catholic

---

42. Bediako, *Christianity in Africa*, 119.
43. Toynbee, *Migrating Musics*, 76.

priest in this case) is an invitation to participate in a mutual enactment/ construction of collective identity.

Active translation is also a process of mimesis. Done right, it should resist "coagulation." In other words, musical mimesis provides cultural musical cosmopolitanism a distinct flavor in terms of a postcolonial response to the colonial encounter and neocolonialism. It challenges/"interrogates" the binaries implied within dominant hegemonic discourses.[44] The "extreme ambivalence manifested in mimicry," (ibid, 24) challenges essentializing notions of indigeneity (example, Hindutva ideologies as tantamount to what it means to be Hindu or Indian, and Christianity as Western).

The space occupied by ICMs is a place between binaries, for example, of colonizer/ colonized, national/foreigner, stranger/ally, and friend/enemy. Mimetic exchange opposes the civilizing dynamic of binaries imposed by imperialistic tendencies. For example, the whole notion of "Indianness" as embodied in the identity of ML challenges the binary of national/foreign or Indian/Western. It draws the categorization of notions such as national identity into the arena of ambivalence. Recollecting Ashcroft *et al*, whether a person is Indian or not, need not be played out in terms of dominant markers that tend to "lock the project of resistance into the semiotic opposition set up by imperial discourse" (2000, 26).

The encouragement to adopt or "mimic" the cultural patterns and values of the colonizer is "never a simple reproduction of those traits" (ibid.). The result is often a "'blurred copy' of the colonizer that can be threatening" (ibid.). ML, however, presents a much needed ambivalence as a response to the already Westernized/compromised artistic ego of those who call themselves Indian but, and especially so for many Christians in the Indian subcontinent, are essentially mimicking (or at least accused of) Western standardizations of Christianity. This is not so problematic if it were not for the popular notion amongst many of the conflation of Christianity with Westernization.[45]

---

44. Ashcroft et al., *Postcolonial Studies*, 25. According to Ashcroft et al.: "The binary structure, with its various articulations of the underlying binary, accommodates such fundamental binary impulses within imperialism as the impulse to 'exploit' and the impulse to 'civilize.'"

45. Please see Oddie, "Constructing 'Hinduism,'" 155–82. From a Gal 3:28 perspective, ICMs in mission break down or deconstruct the binarism that the apostle Paul sought to avoid—the isolationism and segregation brought about by strict demarcations of national and even sexual binaries brought about by dominant perspectives. In context, it is not that these labels have no relevance, but the categories in and of themselves need redeeming from being "under sin" (Gal 3:22), in the light of the promise in Christ (cf. Gal 3:26–29). This is the task of ICMs in mission.

More specifically, in the context of "Indianness," ML's stance is a welcome opposite/response to the collective historical consciousness tampered by imperialistic hegemony. Ashcroft *et al* recollect Lord Macaulay's 1835 Minute to Parliament that disparaged Indian art and learning systems. Macaulay sought to reproduce English art and learning amongst a "'class of interpreters between us and the millions whom we govern—a class of persons Indian in blood and colour, but English in tastes, opinions, in morals, and in intellect'" (2000, 136). According to Homi K. Bhabha, the agenda of colonial mimicry is "the desire for a reformed, recognizable Other, as a subject of a difference that is almost the same, but not quite."[46]

The posturing of ML as a measure[47] of the space that he occupies between binaries invites the application of a somewhat similar logic to Bhabha's above. It shares with the colonial motive in that it is a transitory and contested "third space" that invites others to join for the bringing about of a collective identity.[48] Dialogue for mutual transformation, however, is not the intention of the colonizer. Where ML's enactment departs from a colonial intent is that the Gospel causes ML to become "all things to all people." To engage in creative construction is to earn the realization that "They love you because they feel you love them."[49]

According to Homi K. Bhabha, it is in the "emergence of the interstices—the overlap and displacement of domains of difference—that the intersubjective and collective experiences of nationness, community interest, or cultural value are negotiated" (1994, 2). ICMs embody and negotiate such creative tension in the context of mission.

The Creative Edge: "There Is Something Within Them"

Do certain persons have an edge over others when it comes to creative construction? From a *creatio Dei* perspective, all are creative equally, in the

---

46. Please see Bhabha, *Location of Culture*, loc. 2391.

47. The idea of identity as a measuring rod of space is evident through the interrogative and illuminative stance of ML's role and purpose in the *creatio Dei*. Arguing in the context of complex systems, according to Glover, the unit of measurement is the interaction and relationships between the subsystems (cf. "Compatibility or Incommensurability").

48. Bhabha, *Location of Culture*, 2. What is important is the "need to think beyond narratives of originary and initial subjectivities and to focus on those moments or processes that are produced in the articulation of cultural differences. These 'inbetween' spaces provide the terrain for elaborating strategies of selfhood—singular or communal—that initiate new signs of identity, and innovate sites of collaboration, and contestation, in the act of defining the idea of society itself."

49. Schrag, "Love Motive," 193.

imago Dei. However, some differ with this perspective. In a discussion of the Hindu belief of music as a gift to Brahmins from the gods, a key informant who performs and teaches on several continents comments that just as the "Jews believe that they are the chosen people, Brahmins too believe that god has given them these talents." He further cites the instance of how a teacher of music in the West found that Jewish kids learned a piece of music much faster than a Chinese or an Indian. For this key informant, Brahmins in India "shine" more than people from other castes since "there is something within them." He goes on to say, "God has blessed them with such wisdom and with such gifts and talents." I asked him as to how he reconciles his approach with an understanding of God who created all and who gave his life for all people. His answer caught me quite by surprise:

> I understand that. What can we say—(laughs) we are clay in his hands. We can't ask him, "Why you have given so much to them and you have given very little to us; you have created so beautifully." Sometimes when I watch TV, when I see the Israeli people, they are so handsome, so fair, with good features. But here, when you see our people here they are so puny, dark, small made people with bad features.

He goes on regarding the task of musicianship as a God-given faculty:

> But at least we should be happy that we are able to understand him. And . . . the gift of music that he has given us, at least we are able to work hard on that and do something for him through this music. So that way we have to be grateful to him.

In addition, he links such aesthetic with notions of purity that view Brahmins as having a spiritual "edge over people." He says, "You don't see much violence in the places where they live. Even when they talk, they don't use filthy language—largely speaking, most of them don't." He goes on, "But when it comes to our community people" according to this key informant, "they are at the lower level basically. This is why missionaries those days came to India to educate these people. People like me are the few lucky ones to come up in life. We should be grateful to those missionaries and for Christianity, for what Christianity has done in society."

From the diatribe above, ML as a Caucasian missionary could also be perceived as a threat amongst a portion of his audience simply because he embodies the best of the other—the Westerner that the Indian looks up to. From a pessimistic point of view, he is not only representing the other, whom the Indian national is trying to mimic, but is mimicking the Indian. This may not be a problem. But in doing so in his identity as a

Westerner he is actually setting (imposing?) a standard for the Indian in terms of his own Indianness. A perceived need to adjust to his standards of Indianness plays upon imperialized psychological sentiments. It causes within the Indian a resentment of what ML mediates because the Indian realizes that "I can never be what he is—white and Indian—the best of both worlds. I will always be 'Indian' Indian." The problem is highlighted in the context of the commodification of Christian music (CCM mainly), where indigenous artists are glossed over in preference for representatives of neoliberal hegemonic music culture.[50]

THE POETIC PALETTE

I asked ML, "In what sense do you relate to the mytho-poetic structure and backdrop of your audiences (Hindu, New Age, Indian Christians)?" For ML, it is a matter of expanding one's creative "palette." He responded: "Like a palette, a painter has colors; writers have words." According to him, "Rahman in Jai Ho uses Spanish words—Crazy idea!" He goes on: "So the palette has increased. I just think the Indian Christians need to increase their palette. Their palette is boring! Their palette is only the Bible words, the biblical words." For ML, neither the English Bible nor William Carey's translation of it in Hindi needs to be the only "palette" that Indian Christians need to use. For him, "a poet is always giving meaning to his poetry. You read and you don't understand."

For ML, meaning is not necessarily contained only or primarily in verbal language. He refers to how Jesus's disciples were constantly seeking to understand what Jesus meant. According to ML, "there is nothing wrong with being a poet that writes poetry that sounds confusing, or rails you up, makes you angry, makes you confused." He goes on, "you throw "OM" in the beginning of your poem and it makes you [the audience] confused. So, that's a poet's job to shake you up, make you confused and then drive home the point. So, that's what you do with a palette."

Mythologies could provide a way to expand the poetic palette of Christian creativity with a view to expanding the circle of participation—remythologization is a collective task. Craig Proulx notes how indigenous cosmopolitans maintain and sustain their identities via "in-reach" (targeting fellow group members) and "out-reach" (targeting non-indigenous peoples).

50. Apart from the Indian scenario, given the overwhelming participation of African Americans in "Gospel" music in the US and of white Americans in "CCM," the following questions have been raised: "If the principles within the music are the same, then why is there such an overwhelming difference in racial representation? Further, how might these differences influence the message content in the music?" Banjo and Morant, "House Divided? Christian Music in Black and White."

They exemplify "the arts of the re-mix" through the mixing of tradition with modernities while remaining indigenous.[51] Proulx notes that:

> Young people make and re-make culture through appropriating the cultural 'raw materials' of life to construct meaning in their own specific cultural localities. In a sense they are "sampling" from broader popular culture and re-working what they can take into their own specific local cultures. That is, the ways that young people sample drum rhythms and vocal segments from songs may be thought of as analogous to the ways they sample from broader cultures (such as styles from USA hip hop cultures), modify, or restructure it in some meaningful ways and re-work the 'compositions' of their own daily lives including notions of identity (2010, 59).

Several ICMs that I interviewed reveal a process of sampling from multiple musical sounds and cultures in order to construct music that represents their cultural mosaic. Hybridity tends to blur the distinctives between the different types of agency within the context of musical cosmopolitanism. Neoliberalism uses this to its advantage (for example, World Music as commodification of "rest for the West"). Critical translatability, however, pays attention to the intentionality of processes of mimesis and could make a difference.[52]

Laudan Nooshin illustrates a way in which ICMs in their role as critical translators within a context may in some way soften what may be perceived as "foreign" in the course of contextualization by appealing to the poetics of the wider culture. Nooshin's research among rappers in Tehran revealed that most did not regard hip-hop as foreign at all. Rap music utilized traditional poetic influences and music. Nooshin observes that rather than as "adoption" of distant culture Rap is regarded as the "extension" of the centrality of poetry to Iranian culture generally, and specifically, the use of such poetry as a tool for social commentary.[53] Nooshin goes on to write:

> Moreover, just as rock musicians—through their musical choices—problematize accepted notions of belonging and what it means to be Iranian in the global context of the twenty-first century ... so, through the adoption of this migrating style, hip-hop artists assert new and complex identities that are both rooted locally and shaped by a broader global consciousness (ibid., emphasis added).

51. Proulx, "Aboriginal Hip Hoppers," 58.
52. Toynbee, *Migrating Musics*, 77.
53. Nooshin, "Hip-hop Tehran," 107.

Similarly, in Brazilian music (*barquinho*), musical indigenous cosmopolitanism may be seen as an instance of "globalization-as-hybridization" that includes the influence of the capital economy ("globalization-as-capitalism") but uses "pastiche-as-mixture" or elite hybridity to "draw upon" and "disseminate" "a fantasy of global presence and power" through the simultaneity of global technologies.[54]

NEGOTIATING IDENTITIES

The negotiation of multiple identities amid a plethora of pluralities is a skill that ICMs learn in the course of mission. In doing so, ICMs mediate a "conversation between the local and the global"[55] as well as translocal. Speaking to the issue of the negotiation of multiple identities and influences that played a part in his transformative journey, JB offers the following recollection:

> In Nagaland, I had my Nagaland identity, which was so Westernized. In Pune, I had to have my North Indian, Hindi-speaking [identity]. I had to put on that hat because my dad was there. I learned Hindi in Pune ... But at times I would visit my relatives in NDA [the National Defence Academy], where they had a Hindustani Covenant Church [HCC] where all the worship was in Hindi. But even in that setting it had this flavor of "Indian Christian" that was completely different from a Hindu type of worship.

JB is not referring to theological content here but to the cultural patterns adopted by the community—a mix of Western and Indian. JB further describes the HCC church in comparison with the church in Nagaland:

> Just like in Nagaland they [the Hindustani Covenant Church] had the Westernization with hymns translated ... they had translated all the *zamoors* or the Psalms into Hindi—it was four verses, the whole structure thing.

For JB, translation of hymns from the West amounted to a departure from what may have appeared a more indigenous approach. It amounted to a choice: to divorce oneself from one narrative (Indian culture) in order to be married into another, which for JB was a watered-down narrative that had strayed from its Gospel emphasis. As far as instrumentation goes,

---

54. Some of this "global present" in bossa nova, as a "hybridized universal sound," (Keightley 2011, 123) might also be found in the Bollywood music in India.

55. Papastergiadis, *Cosmopolitanism and Culture*, 9.

according to JB, it was "*dholak*, harmonium, *chimta* [hand symbol]" But this came across as a façade. He goes on to say:

> It was another Christian bubble. In other words, anything that had to do with Hinduism was demonic; anything that had to with outside the Christian bubble was heresy. Bollywood music was completely shunned. [In order] to prove your personal sanctification, the more holy you are the less you would watch Bollywood [film] music.

Contextualization for JB is not just about using indigenous instruments and patterns. For him, the Gospel universalizes contextualization through the proclamation of the Gospel for all people—indigenous patterns or foreign really does not matter. JB responds to such a scenario with scriptural insight. He refers to the familiar passage, Jer 29:11 to emphasize that

> God allowed Israel to go into exile. Three voices are heard: the Babylonians, the Israelites, and false prophets who say, "don't have anything to do with the Babylonians." It sounds holy but that was not the voice of God. God was saying be holy and set apart so that they will see you and they will come to know the true and living God; I have sent you to Babylon for a purpose; I have plans for you, plans for good. That was huge for me because I realized that God allows his people in his sovereign plan to be a witness. Remember, the call of the people was to be a light to the Gentiles. What I found in my Christian bubble is that we were falling in [to] that second category of saying [that] we don't want to do anything with our culture around us; we just want to be among ourselves and be happy with our songs and saying to each other "Christ is born" all through our lives rather than taking this good news to the community around us. New Life Fellowship and [the] Hindustani Covenant Church were in a bubble. They catered to different classes, New Life Fellowship to upper class, educated, Christian, even English speaking, but Hindustan Covenant Church to middle class, mainly Hindi-speaking Christian.

He adds, however: "But there were real missionaries who knew the dilemma; but they would be the ones working in the villages and tribes, the churches would be scared of them." If the complex hybridity of indigenous cosmopolitanism is not enough to upset the status quo of complacent Christianity, then the creative construction patterns of ICMs should offer radical alternatives. These radical departures from the "bubble" of structural missional inadequacy could turn ICMs for mission into a threat to ecclesial-structural forces that prefer the form/ "bubble" of Christianity but are devoid of the power of Christian mission.

A further mark of the process of creative construction is a spirit of reflective discernment. JB's musical creativity is shaped not so much by a desire to reach others, but by what appears to be a response to an inner turmoil, a self-questioning concerning one's own identity (social and religious) in relation to the other. The cosmopolitan consciousness at one level is in essence (or at least aspires to be) a reconstitution of the collective consciousness of humanity. It is about coming to terms with the reality of difference—what has the "other" to do with "I"? Concerning the search for authentic identity, Richard John Neuhaus writes:

> Only when I give up on the search for myself in abandonment to another—to the Other—is my 'I' reconstituted by the 'I' to whom I surrender. The endless rummaging through memories, the poking about in the cluttered attic of self-consciousness, the removing of layer after layer of worn-out 'identities'—none of this can produce the authentic self. The truth of the self is in the telos of the self."[56]

In the light of Neuhaus's comment we conclude that the negotiation of musical identity for mission depends upon discovery of the truth of *telos* in creative continuity with the other.[57] According to David Bosch:

> The entire history of Israel unveils the continuation of God's involvement with the nations. The God of Israel is the Creator and Lord of the whole world. For this reason Israel can comprehend its own history only in continuity with the history of the nations, not as a separate history.[58]

ICMs embody and mediate the creative tension of such history-in-the-making.

---

56. Neuhaus, *Death on a Friday Afternoon*, 134. See also Hiebert, *Transforming Worldviews*, 288.

57. Hiebert, *Missiological Implications of Epistemological Shifts*, 68–111. As such it builds upon the foundation laid by a critical realist approach: it is a collective process of reexamining and reconfiguring various complementary (synchronic/diachronic) knowledge systems that are commensurable to a better a way of life together in the light of the gospel. This means a re-cognition of differences whilst respecting the other and a commitment to resolve contradictions bearing in mind the fidelity of the gospel.

58. Bosch, *Transforming Mission*, 18, italic mine.

"Bring Them to Our Church ... Not a Biblical Way"

JB illustrates the discrepancy between evangelism as it is typically understood and in terms of his personal experience with others. He invited Mohammed Islam to church. Mohammed is a musician and immigrant to the US from Bangladesh whom JB met at an outreach at a local park. JB observed: "He came, he enjoyed the music part of it, but when it came to preaching and all the other things when we come to church, we lost him." JB learned not to invite him to church again. He said:

> That taught me a lesson: if I love bhajans from a Hindu perspective, I love the music of it. But if they call me to a temple, maybe I'd listen to it, [but] everything would be foreign, and almost uncomfortable to me, the *prasad* [the food offered to idols and then distributed amongst people], the mantras, because I just came for the bhajans, not for all the other things. Islam came to me for the music aspect of it. He was not ready for [everything else that came along with it].

JB offers a helpful critique to the evangelism strategy of many churches: "I've been taught to bring them to our church services. That's the way of evangelism that I've been taught; that's not a biblical way." JB's realization demonstrates the need: A new era calls for fresh methodologies for the construction of musical creative identity. Multitextualities, decentralized sites for transition, and the irruption of multiple centers and peripheries through ICM pathways forge fresh cartographies for mission with others.

In addition, we acknowledge, research in a context of increased mobility and globalism is complex, especially for a methodology developed initially for studying small-scale societies.[59] In rethinking "anthropological locations," Akhil Gupta and James Ferguson recollect Appadurai's concern: "What is the nature of locality, as a lived experience in a global, deterritorialized world?" (ibid.). In complexity thinking, neither the physical nor the social world is mechanical—regularities are not the sole basis for knowledge; there is no object/subject differentiation; the complex world is "unknowable" in the sense that prediction will always be undermined by uncertainty.[60] In short, a complex approach to the social world will require a profound epistemological rethinking, or perhaps

---

59. Gupta and Ferguson, "Discipline and Practice," 3.

60. Cudworth and Hobden, "Foundations of Complexity, the Complexity of Foundations," 165.

"unthinking" (ibid.).⁶¹ ICMs could play a key role in facilitating transformative thinking via creative construction.

In addition, appropriating methodologies or "models" of mission from one context to another requires care. The interpretation and translation of concepts is not always consistent from one context to another. Increased mobility and globalism accentuate the risk involved. What needs to change in the process of the translation of Christianity if JB is to meet with where Islam is—outside "church"? For one, perhaps the categories of "inside" and "outside" in relation to the Body of Christ may need to be revisited, along with the other. Determining functional substitutes for current ecclesial structures and processes—the "contextual parameters of art within a cosmopolitan frame" (Paspastergiadis 2012, 14)—is itself collective mission. Whether details are truly lost in transition or merely subsumed and disguised in alternate contextual rhetoric, creative construction takes into account the uniqueness and phenomenology of the person in mission. It attempts to trace why certain details, terms, sounds, textures are re-appropriated or re-constructed. If in some cases certain details are determined or labeled to be "lost," then the creative construction methodology needs to be flexible to probe the issue and to study reasons for the same. For example, in the case of JB, this methodology might lead us to examine more closely what dynamics may or may not have contributed to "losing" his acquaintance, Islam (cf., JB's comment: "we lost him" in reference to Islam), in the process of inviting him to church.

"Responsibility As A Poet"

When asked why those of religious persuasions other than Christianity (e.g., Rahman or Pt. Ravi Shankar) were apparently able to do seemingly effortlessly what the church could only dream about in the Indian context—bring together people from different religion, cultures, in the cause of national identity, ML remarks:

> Sadly, a majority of Christians did not approve of British departure. They thought India would be a better India if the British stay here. We have that legacy of Indian Christians, sadly. Only a few Indian Christians who stand against them (e.g., Brahmabandhab Upadhyay), whose song we are using on the album . . . . He got kicked out of the Catholic church, expelled not only

---

61. For further research it would be helpful to investigate the dynamics of complexity in terms of self-organization, non-linearity, openness, and co-evolution and how these might apply to the process of Creative Construction. See Cudworth and Hobden, "Anarchy and Anarchism," 399–416; Glover, "Compatibility or Incommensurability."

primarily because he was using Krishna and Saraswati [Hindu deities] in some of his bhajans, but with linking himself with the Bengali renaissance against Britain.

Therefore, by adapting a song written by Brahmabandhab Uphadhyay, ML has taken a bold step in identifying with a tradition of resistance within the church by association with language ideologies through the lyric of Upadhyay in his own music. Further, ML appears to take a stand against colonialism and its progeny in a neocolonial context by refusing to compromise his material to suit the needs of so-called Christian recording labels.

ML did not seek to distance himself from the Indian church. Rather, seeking its endorsement, he asked key Indian leaders regarding the use of *Narahari* (a term used in reference to Vishnu, translated "man-god."). After receiving a consensus on permission to use the phrase, ML went ahead and used the phrase in the song Jaya Deva ("victory to God"). According to a source:

> Narahari was introduced as a title for Christ by Brahmabandhab Upadhyay (1861–1907) in 1901. The title first appeared in a Sanskrit *stotra* [verse] by Upadhyay, where he describes how God reveals his love to us by becoming fully human while at the same time remaining independent and free of his creation. Upadhyay was always searching for words that sprung from the soil of India that could be used to describe various aspects of God's nature. Nara-hari means, "man-God."[62]

The use of the title, *Narahari*, was well received by most except by one person with whom ML remained in touch—an example of dialogue, where there is an agreement to disagree on the subject matter. ML refers to inclusivity as a journey that is valid in terms of being a place for creative tension, the co-existence of opposing points of view. According to ML,

> I met the guy who had a negative comment on [a song] since it had the "hari" phrase in it. *Narahari*, is traditionally the term for *narasimha* or man lion, fourth incarnation of Vishnu. But Brahmabandhab Uphadyay interprets *nar* as man, and *hari*, god or "to take away our sorrows"—*dukh harane wala* . . . . This Indian Christian wrote to me: but this *narahari* word can't be used. Later he came to Varanasi and helped me to write some songs together even though we disagree [on] some thing[s].

62. Source cannot be disclosed for reasons of security, September 4, 2013.

ML explains that sensitivity to others should not "stifle" creativity. He suggests construction bearing in mind that people will be compromising their faith; but to do this with sensitivity:

> I have my responsibility as a poet. If I am passing a temple and eat the *prasad* [food offered to idols] and my friend eats it and feels compromised, that is being insensitive. If I am making an album, 10,000 copies, I can't think in those terms [i.e., what effect it will have on each and every person].

The idea of writing with intent in order to bring about a degree of compromise in others is one that reverberates amongst other ICMs I interviewed. It is a departure from the culture that seeks acceptance rather than relevance as the primary justification for the construction of creativity. However, identifying with a tradition of resistance within a culture takes boldness. In the context of global complexity, the narratives that ICMs choose to attach themselves to and be redefined by the histories, characters, and events is a major step in defining creative construction—defining oneself in relation to the other in the context of Gospel hope. It is a juxtaposition of narratives. ML justifies himself in the use of phrases from a distinct Hindu context. He takes the chance to shape the story from inside out:

> If you take the words, they are pre-Krishna, pre some of these deities, from the *Bhagvat Purana*. He [Brahmabandhab] uses the word *Govindam* and he himself translates *Govindam* in its actual meaning. There are so many of the names, like Krishna, which means dark, they are all adjectives. So, it's like saying, "the lion." And we are saying, we can't use "the lion" because "lion" means Vishnu or Jesus. So, many words for Krishna are like that.

ML goes on to explain the rationale for his adaptation of certain indigenous phrases over others as he wrestles with multiple meanings for diverse contexts in the construction of his music:

> For example, *nandala* specifically means the "son of Nand," who is Krishna; but you could use *Shyam*, another name for Krishna. Others like "*Govindam*"—go is "cow," *govindam* is "the tender of cows," the cowherd or shepherd. He [Upadhyay] translates it as "god is the one who tends us" he is the *palanahar*, which is the caretaker of us. That's his meaning for *govindam*; he is not using it to refer to Krishna. So, that's the problem with a word like *govindam*—it is Krishna, *Govinda* or *govindam* (Sanskrit). So, the Catholics have left the rest of the poem, but have changed the word *govindam* to one that does not relate so closely to Krishna. So, does that compromise Brahmanbandhab's poetry? [It is] those kinds of things [that] I wrestle with now—what is [it that I

am] communicating. I am a communicator. I am not simply trying to make a point. I want to communicate bhakti [devotion] and help people to worship (emphasis implied).

ML's discourse brings together the identity of the musician and the creative expression of such identity—the primary "responsibility" of the "poet" in mission is to guard and sustain the integrity of one's own identity and purpose in the context of the *creatio Dei*. Jesus Christ epitomizes the juxtaposition of identity and integrity. The Person is the Text. We will return to this claim in the final chapter. Similarly, when it comes to translating Christianity through the construction of music, the lifestyle and habitus of the musician are key motifs. But how is such identity to be parsed in the context of multiculturalism?

ML has in mind his three key audiences—"white American Christian, Indian Christian, and New Age/ Hindu." He finds the task "very difficult." He asks, "How do you increase your audience and your palette at the same time?" For ML "it is a journey that is valid—how to be inclusive—[and] not anything that should be considered unusual." The "cosmopolitan imaginary" is what Papastergiadis refers to as "a restless and dynamic form of mobility that gathers momentum from, rather than settles into, clusters of like-minded elements" (2012, 14). ML's stance is one that challenges the commodification of music, even though his music would fit within the World Music category. As in the case with other ICMs that I interviewed, ML has chosen to publish and distribute most of his music privately and not use any of the major Christian labels currently in the West. My sense is that ML would hesitate to align himself with the dominant streams of distribution and be labeled, "Christian." His desire is to create an environment that is safe and interactive for the participation of all peoples. This coheres with Papastergiadis's thesis that cosmopolitan artists "represent the condition of the world" as well as "enable an alternative way of imagining our participation in the world" (Papastergiadis 2012, 14).

For ML, the wider audience and calling to serve the larger community are crucial factors in order to be faithful to his mission in the context of globalization. In the context of being inclusive, I asked ML (paraphrase): "How do you reconcile caste and Christianity in Hindustani music? In some ways you seem to be reiterating the caste factor since the genre of Hindustani music is not the music of the Dalit." He answered: "We play for villages too . . . . I play a few songs on the sitar, then change my style totally—pull out the harmonium; I localize it."

With regard to identifying with a tradition of resistance, representing authority, and ushering change, the ICMs that I worked with constantly distinguish between styles, genres, instruments, and sounds. Among other questions regarding contextualization, they might ask:

Which [elements] subordinate other musical elements to it? Which are deformed to fit a new musical environment? Which elements mark cultural difference and which signify or engage modernity? Which elements blend seamlessly, and which generate difference?[63]

Hybridizing strategies betray an elitist rather than subaltern dynamic.[64] However, the degree to which hybrid strategies betray elitist rather than subaltern realities might depend on who is doing the hybridizing. For example, when Sony-BMG does a "mix" using folk and tribal sounds, then there is an element of power and elitism if profits and advantage go to producers at the cost of instrumentalists and others involved in the chain of the production of meaning.

Concerning the responsibility of the poet in the process of creative construction, according to a major film music composer of Indian origin that I interviewed, writing commercial music includes sacrifice. I paraphrase his comment, "It is not about producing what I feel like doing; I have to cater to the needs of the larger community." He is a convert to Islam, from Hinduism. The danger of compromise or negative syncretism is a reality regardless of spiritual affiliation. Yet, for ICMs in mission a poetic ethos of accountability to the larger community reveals a genuine intent to be inclusive for the sake of the Gospel, which by nature is also uncompromisingly exclusive (cf. Rom 10:9–13).

In this chapter, we learned that Creative Construction is a process of knowledge generation. Although the negotiation of ICM identity is associated with a blurring of boundaries, ICMs hold potential to facilitate a critical translatability through their creativity. Creative construction is a social process, a collective engagement, and an opportunity to dialogue. It is a process for re-historicizing tradition as well as a way for the abstraction and active reconstruction of identity in the wake of colonialism. It is a matter of conscience, a basis for establishing authenticity and difference, and a process for the translation of the Gospel. It represents an intentionality, a way to align with a tradition of resistance for justice, a process for self-reflection with the other, an opportunity for the reconstitution of the collective consciousness of humanity, and a poetic responsibility for the retelling and creative interweaving of diverse and multiple narratives for the participation of others in the mission of God.

---

63. Stokes, "Music and the Global Order," 59.
64. Stokes, "Music and the Global Order," 61.

7

Creative Performance: Expression

IN THIS CHAPTER WE explore the performative discourse of ICMs in mission in the light of the concept of creative performance outlined earlier from several sources.[1] In the context of the epistemological captivity of creativity, the non-representational character of music disqualifies it "as an emotional luxury which has not attained the seriousness of real thinking and praxis."[2] Yet, musical creativity echoes throughout Scripture in the well-known songs and hymns of the Bible and in the history of the church.[3] The dynamics of new spaces as described earlier form a ripe arena for the mediation of unique "ontological alternatives" (Jørgensen 2011, 207) through the creative performance of ICMs in mission.

---

1. Ezek 47. See also Osumare, "Global Breakdancing and the Intercultural Body"; Bevans and Schroeder, *Prophetic Dialogue*.

2. Stoltzfus, *Theology as Performance*, 169.

3. Wren, *Praying Twice*; Lockyer, *All the Music of the Bible*. For example, the song of Moses and Miriam after leading Israel through the Red Sea (Exod 15:1–18, 21), Deborah and Barak after their victory over Sisera (Judg 5:1–31), the Levitical choirs at the temple dedication (2 Chr 5:12–14), the song book of the Israelites (Psalms), Mary's song upon learning of the future virgin birth (Luke 1:46–55), Paul and Silas while in a Philippian jail (Acts 16:25), believers to praise God (Eph 5:19; Col 3:16), and Saints after their victory in tribulation (Rev 15:2–4) (Lockyer, *All the Music of the Bible*, 178). In addition, the spontaneous character of music is evident in other examples from Scripture For example, in 2 Samuel when David dances in joy before the Lord. Spontaneous song is a result of feeling joyful: "Is any merry? Let him sing psalms" (Jas 5:13) (Hunt, *Music in Missions*, 14). See also Foley, *Foundations of Christian Music*; McKinnon, *Music in Early Christian Literature*.

THE MEDIATION OF PROPHETIC PERFORMATIVE IDENTITY

ML uses the phrase "prophetic performance art" to describe the activity of the church in mediating its uniqueness in Christ to the world. ML offers a rough recollection of Ezekiel's performance in Ezekiel chapter 4:

> It's like Ezekiel walking into a church or *satsang* and lying down in a pile of poop . . . and God says now cook your food with it for the next three years right outside the temple.[4] Ezekiel was an artist whether he liked it or not. God made him be an artist even if he probably did not want to be one . . . he thought, "O my God if I am God's artist I am really in trouble."

The radical countercultural nature of creative performance is not something that is extrinsic to the creative calling and identity in Christ. We remember that as a sociocultural phenomenon, "performance is an integral component of every human being" (Gordon 2006, 4). Further, in a biblical context, to "perform" is not merely a focus on what is being presented. Rather, the general use of the word in both biblical testaments appears to emphasize the dynamic congruity between personhood and performance.[5]

ML compares an artist's life to the nature of art itself as prophetic statement:

> An artist has the privilege and blessing to let their life be a prophetic statement of all the things they are struggling with, all the anger they go through, all the problems they go through. Of course, someone working a 9–5 job also can see their life in the same way and they should; everyone should see their life as an artist.

We recollect from David Bosch, "Christian theology is a theology of dialogue" Bosch (2007, 483). Given the performative nature of events recorded in Scripture, Christian theology is a theology of performance, a dialogue that is performed together between prophet and audience. For instance, Ezekiel was not merely a prophet who spoke the word. He performed his prophetic identity. In Scripture, a prophet is one who mediates

---

4. In the Bible, we note the enactment is takes place where the Israelites were meting out their exilic existence (cf. Ezek 3:15).

5. See Ps 56:12; Gen 38:8; Lev 25:18; Ezek 12:28; Matt 5:33. Also, ultimately the full and final performance of Jesus Christ epitomized through his life, death, and resurrection where the Servant Songs of Isaiah serve to bring together the identity of the Performer as Text.

between God and humankind.⁶ There is an "intimacy" between the prophet and God; the prophet is referred to as "a man of God" (*'ish 'elohim*),⁷ as a "seer" (1 Sam 9:9), and an instrument of God's justice.⁸ Further, God brings about his purpose on earth through prophetic actions as well as prophetic words (Rev 1:3; 22:7). Music was used as a way to prophesy by the sons of Asaph (1 Chr 25:1–3).⁹

As we envision the mediation of prophetic performative identity of ICMs for mission we recognize that Ezekiel's prophetic performance mediates authentic witness in terms of "speaking forth," proclaiming God's vision and "speaking out," calling people to orient their lives to God.¹⁰ It links creative being and expression in dynamic correspondence. Prophetic performance that is interactive, collaborative, collective (tradition and habit forming),¹¹ and calls for multi-sensorial engagement between participants and cultural productions.¹²

Prophetic performance is also "performativity" since Ezekiel himself is the very metaphor through which Israel is to re-cognize its own fate. We recollect that "performativity," according to Halifu Osumare, refers to the gestures and body language expressed "literally through the muscular and skeletal structure as well as semiotically and metaphorically" (2013, 261). In the light of Korom's definition above, the real difference that ICMs mediate is in terms of their creative performativity with tangible roots to the historical tradition of Jesus Christ. In what sense does ML embody and express a prophetic creative performance?

Through a Christian friend who was actively involved in a Hindu community, ML had the opportunity to perform worship at a Hindu temple. Before the performance he was asked if his group would sing "only to Jesus or include songs to some of the Hindu deities?" ML replied that his group had a genuine love and respect for Hindu culture that they expressed through *bhakti* (loving devotion and surrender). Further, he said that Yeshu (Jesus) was their *Isht Devta* (God of choice). This was acceptable to the temple leader and they were welcomed to lead the service in the temple. According

---

6. Ezek 38:17; Ezra 9:11; Heb 1:1; Luke 1:70.
7. West, "Performance Criticism of the Narratives in the Hebrew Bible."
8. Richards, *Bible Reader's Companion*, 405.
9. Day, *Collins Thesaurus of the Bible*.
10. Bevans and Schroeder, *Prophetic Dialogue*, 40–48.
11. Brown, *Tradition and Imagination*. Ezekiel's performance is also a "traditioning" process in that it consists of codified, learned systems of movement practices.
12. Korom, *Anthropology of Performance*, 2–3.

to ML, the Hindus in the temple "were enriched by the music and message without compromising their deepest values."[13]

ML's act of loving devotion to his *Ishta Devta* resulted in a loving embrace of the Hindu community. Clearly, dialogue cannot happen while resenting the presence of the other; coexistence precedes conversion.[14] In the light of the burgeoning religious diversity in the United States,[15] ML's performance reiterates Bevans and Schroeder's insight that religious ends that "mirror the communal nature of God are more likely to constitute 'the fullest human destiny' and therefore are more worthy to pursue"[16] (2004, 383). Second, since all religions have valid religious ends, according to Bevans and Schroeder, they each need the other and therefore need to commit to dialogue.[17] Furthermore, ML's approach appears to be more a spirituality rather than a strategy.[18] The invitation to perform at the temple was preceded by a relational network, his reputation—knowledge, skill, and ability (cf. Exod 31:3), in a sense—preceded him. Learning, agreeing to disagree, and relationship building through sustained interaction are important steps to overcome barriers to dialogue. According to ML:

> We fall on both sides of the coin; it's a learning experience of listening and respecting, while at the same time disagreeing and sharing what we believe if what we believe contrasts with what we are hearing. And knowing when and how to do that, how to preserve a friendship while doing that, it's a skill that takes a lifetime . . . a skill of communication, expressing convictions . . . while at the same time showing respect by listening to their convictions about life is more tricky.

In addition, he goes on: "You are well aware that you could cause offense by rejecting those convictions where the other person might perceive that you are rejecting them as a person rather than perhaps simply rejecting their ideas." Risk-taking, conflict, humility, and vulnerability are central to the process of dialogue. ML goes on to say,

> It calls for great experimentation, patience with yourself, and learning and growing, being vulnerable, and being humble as well as being committed to speaking out about truth as you see

13. Source of publication withheld.
14. Bosch, *Transforming Mission*, 483.
15. Eck, *New Religious America*.
16. Bevans and Schroeder, *Constants in Context*.
17. Bevans and Schroeder, *Constants in Context*.
18. Bevans and Schroeder, *Prophetic Dialogue*, 2.

it when needed. And I see that many of us Christians have lost that angle of things because we have . . . been given a bad reputation of the stereotypical tele-evangelist and their convictions and their lack of sense of dialogue, their one-way street preaching, and we are on the back track of that and that's great to be able to take another approach. But the opposite approach only lasts so long before you realize that you still have convictions, beliefs, and you still need to share them.

Creative Spaces and Identities

With respect to creating spaces for encountering the other, according to JB, "knowing your audience is very important." JB's creative performance extends to the parks in and near Jackson Heights, Brooklyn, NY. However, before any such performances at the park or "a very non-Christian crowd" he studies the context beforehand. This includes studying historical and demographic information. JB's cosmopolitanism is shaped by a genuine interest in other cultures and societies. For JB, the desire to perform outside and beyond his own culture is a sign of overcoming his prejudice of the other. We recollect that, first, "our sense of attachment to a single culture, group or society must not be so strong that it precludes our engagement with other cultures, groups and societies" (Hopper 2007, 175).[19] Second, a cosmopolitan must have a genuine interest in other cultures and societies (ibid.). However, the understanding is that one need not become more empathetic by virtue of being a cosmopolitan; this will depend upon individual life experiences, predispositions, and social and educational backgrounds (ibid., 178).

JB remarks about the extent to which people have accepted or rejected him and/or his message: "Thankfully, we have not experienced rejection, so far, maybe in some church contexts, but not in a community when we go for events." Further, he adds:

> What I've experienced is everyone has a story, particular language, art, culture, a whole unique essence; as an Indian when I sing Hindi songs I get to experience all of these come together. And what I can see in their eyes that they almost see their arts, experience, culture come together in a moment of just, rejoicing.

---

19. This by itself raises important questions for how and why boundaries are constructed in society: Can one then be a Christian and a cosmopolitan at the same time? On the other hand, can one truly be Christian and not be cosmopolitan?

The "cumulative process" of cosmopolitanism is evident in creating fresh spaces for the intersection of histories. JB refers to a performance in a city in the state of New York. Several hundred South Asians (mostly Indian and Pakistani origin) attended; a majority was Hindu. The event was part of a Christmas cultural celebration with a specific focus to reach non-Christians in the area. According to JB:

> When we do the *bhangra* music I see a lot of them clapping, dancing, and having fun [refers to a song, "*rab ne bana di . . . .*"]. I thought they were . . . Christian brothers who [happen to] sing Hindi. But then I realized that they were from South India, not Hindi speakers. I even went and said: "Praise the Lord, brother." And now I have learned that even the question is terrible: "So, are you a Christian?" We are so used to asking that question in church contexts. That's not even a good question. That's like you are not even interested in the person; rather than getting to know where they were born or where they came from. That's one of the questions that I don't like to ask often. But I saw the joy that they had; that they can identify with the root music; I could use that as a platform to dialogue, start a relationship, or mess it up. Or I can just say: "Jesus is the only way, truth, and life" there and then and give them a negative view. So much responsibility is given to you at that point.

Such "responsibility" is indicative of a creativity that is not solipsistic (i.e., existing in and for itself) but contributory.[20] However, morality for JB differs fundamentally from the creative morality of creativity theorists such as Moran (2010). It is not merely a set of principles to be enacted for the common good but issues forth from a place of identification with the other in the light of the commonality of all creation having its being in the Creator God.

Creative Spaces and "Diasporic Consciousness"

For JB, creative performance goes hand in hand with community. On one occasion, Easter Sunday, he senses the need to do more than worship in church. He leads the entire congregation outside to a popular public arena in Jackson Heights. He explains the scenario:

> After Easter Sunday celebration, I said this is not it, it is wonderful, but the whole point of this is to now go out. So, we come out here to Jackson Heights in our Sunday best, ties and all.

---

20. Moran, "Role of Creativity in Society," 76.

But when we came here with guitars, dholak and singing, the whole community came out—we gathered in a meeting place that we call "Mars Hill," our place to meet people ... we just came up with that name ... but they came up with a better name that I like better: Diversity Plaza—the community came up with the official name. But when we started singing, it connected, made it accessible.

AJ, JB's co-worker, offers further insight as to why such phenomena might be "attractive" to others:

> Concerning the whole idea of marginality and place and space, the phenomenon of this kind of music and singing—I don't know how effective it would be necessarily in India itself. It takes a context like New York City where you have people in a sense who are not in their home, not in their place of origin. And that's why—with regard to South Indians and [people from] Andhra—they are connecting. They are responding to bhangra. My assumption is that if you go somewhere in India and play bhangra-inspired music, they would go: "what is this?" they are not going to respond—"this is our stuff!" And this is my experience in Africa, because when I came to America, I began to participate in and seek out experiences and things that were very Senegalese in nature. But I never did that when I was in Senegal. But it became important to me once I was removed from Senegal. And that's what we've observed here in how this impacts South Asian people—Bangladeshi, Indian, all varieties and sorts, half-Naga. But that there is something of Indianness in it, that there is something that has come out of India that is what is attractive. That is different. I don't think you would have that anywhere else.

SJ, AJ's wife, adds, "You would call that diasporic consciousness." The tendency to seek out "*bhangra*-inspired" music that is not necessarily a central linkage to one's home culture but somewhat tangential and indirect is indicative of a diasporic "structuring of the collective existence abroad."[21] In this sense, ICMs are poised uniquely to draw upon the "atopic mode" of the diasporic consciousness—"it is a space of more than a place" (ibid., 63) and defined more in terms of the dominant nature of existing networks. Music works as a uniting factor in this regard—it plays a structural role for the enmeshing of once perceived disparate identities.

---

21. Dufoix, *Diasporas*, 62–63.

On an interpersonal level, JB and his team are as much created by the community that recognizes them as creators of the community they now come to represent.[22] The interpersonal enmeshment is evident in the fact that JB has been officially approached by the members of the local community affairs to carry out events that would benefit the community. JB affirms this by saying, "If I never moved to NY I don't know where I would be—still criticizing everybody, fighting with the sub-Indian, Hindustani church, I don't know." The "diasporic consciousness" allows for a rewiring of identities as per the needs of a given context. According to AJ, "any sort of urban conglomeration of people in a place that's not their home place, it develops this consciousness and this nostalgia. It allows something like this kind of music to really impact people."

In terms of potential, JB adds, "[this is] an opportunity to grab hold of. Honestly we are not doing enough." Referring to the church in general, he says, "We've got a good team, if we can come together. But we are all caught up in the four walls. But if we were outward focused . . . [he stops]." SJ picks up where JB leaves off with respect to the inward focus of the church: "People are dealing with cultural issues, afraid of losing their identity." This no doubt serves as a fundamental insight for discerning ways in which ICMs might approach the negotiation of identity through their music. The reality of the fact is that in Christ there is certainly an anticipation of loss. However, in losing oneself, there is always the promise of a greater inheritance along with others (Mark 8:35).

Negotiating as Risk-Taking

JB's stance to go beyond the "four walls" of Christianized rhetoric and meet with the other where they are is a redeeming factor in the negotiation of identity in the context of diversity. According to JB moving beyond the "bubble" of church as-it-has-been is not merely in order to reach people:

> The ultimate cause for me to even begin to take the risk of negotiating was when by God's grace he opened my eyes to how much he negotiated with us. In the midst of the cultural background of moving (migration) the rich history that I've had, if it was not for the whole idea of the Kingdom of God, with the truth of God in Jesus, if I did not know that, I would still be stuck in my own prejudice, using music in a self-centered way. For me, that's the root issue or cause of thinking outside the box. It changed the way of thinking about church.

22. Dufoix, *Diasporas*, 73.

Continuing the conversation with regard to the state of the church in his experience, JB comments:

> I grew up in a context where the other disease was this: if you were not a Christian, you used the term "lost." But in India it was used with a sense of "too bad," almost with a karmic understanding, "you deserved it, you are lost," if you were a Hindu, Sikh etc., that was it. I did not grow up in a church culture that saw "lostness" as Scripture, as Christ sees "lostness." And so, if you are not in a church that's engaging the lost and being salt and light, what's the point of dialogue?

For JB, "dialogue, and not trying to beat down on them" paves the way for the Kingdom of God. JB's creative performance illustrates the theological principle reiterated earlier—the differentiation of the persons of the Trinity—that diversity is inherent to and a crucial ingredient for creative abundance. Theological creativity through a hermeneutic of otherness and engagement "opts for humanization and diversity."[23] Creative performance seeks to "acknowledge, respect, and engage the other" opposing implicit and explicit attempts to dominate and alienate the other.[24]

According to JB one of the most "effective ways of dialogue is music and when you sing [the] Gospel to them and they connect." JB engages in dialogue through offering music classes and collaborating with the Community Center that offers free computer and English classes. He says, "Many come, from India, Nepal, Bangladesh, Tibet . . . now we are in a place, the Learning Center—how do we take this to the next step? It is amazing how some of the leaders said: music and food!" The Learning Center is another space that illustrates a critical responsibility to learn from people of other faith orientations but with whom we are called to be in the same community. It involves the risk of submitting to the other in mutual respect; it is a sign of "authentic mission."[25]

Musical Performance: Para-Church or Church?

The creation of new places for dialogue with others as a way of being church is not merely another option for JB. At the time I met and spoke with him, he and his wife had prayerfully made the decision to leave the church where he was serving in worship on Sundays. JB now visits the Community Center during the week, where he teaches English and collaborates with

23. Brink, "In Search of the Biblical Foundations of Prophetic Dialogue," 13.
24. Brink, "In Search of the Biblical Foundations of Prophetic Dialogue," 13.
25. Bevans and Schroeder, *Prophetic Dialogue*, 59–60.

other organizations and individuals from the area as well as from across the United States to engage the community.

Among other things, the relocation of culture making from center to periphery represents a shift in perception of self—a further orienting toward the *creatio Dei*. In terms of the effectiveness of this new space to meet with others and compared to his previous "Sunday" role, JB recollects how music (by implication, its role in the formation of collective identity) and community formation were not central dimensions of what constituted "church." The main attraction, so-to-speak, was "the sermon time whenever the pastor preaches." However, in the present ecclesial form, according to JB,

> We may not even have any sermon; it may be a five-minute talk on love your family, may be not even reading from the Bible, which the church might call heresy—where is the preaching? Where is the Word, but . . . Music will be a means of dialogue.

Recollecting Stoltzfus's observation, "music has come to rival word as a location for philosophical reflection and theological construction" (2006, 242).[26] JB alludes to the so-called heresy that finds root in a neoplatonic aesthetic as differentiated from a *creatio Dei* hermeneutic. Typically, in "captivity," music is not perceived as mediating the Word, which is understood as transmitted more authentically via preaching. Leah Easley traces Augustinian theology on the arts to Plato, whereby certain dynamics have negatively contributed to Christian thought on the matter. According to Easley, Augustine's appropriation of pagan philosophy *via* Plato is evident in the diminishing of "the concrete and sensible" in that Augustine emphasized "intangible abstractions and denigrated the sensuous world in which the Logos became incarnate."[27]

Easley further speculates that an artistic-minded scholar may have rather "transformed Homer and Virgil the way St. Augustine did Plato and Plotinus; possibly the Church would discuss Jesus Christ as the fulfillment of Apollo or Dionysius as well as the Logos" (ibid.). Easley's comment is pertinent. JB resignifies the Plato-influenced Augustinian view of the role of music in mediating truth, which is often evident in the unconditional rejection of pagan art/myth and the syncretic or uncritical embrace of pagan philosophy. In doing so, JB paves a way for renewing the role of music as that which authentically bears truth as opposed to merely that which "mimics" truth.

The above discussion illustrates the dynamic relationship between theology and performance. Theologizing takes place in the act of performance.

---

26. See also Kirsh, "How to Think with Bodies and Things."
27. Easley, "St. Augustine."

Performance mediates the Word of God (but not necessarily the words of God). It is not merely "para-church" activity but it is the very becoming of the Body of Christ in substantive semiotic synergy with others. This reinforces Stoltzfus's thesis that "Music is not reducible to emotive or formal 'explanation,' since it directly mirrors and instantiates the movements of the self-conscious will that is experiencing, constructing, or indeed being 'embodied' within the music" (Stoltzfus 2006, 248).

"What Is The Church In This Community?"

Collaboration is a major part of how JB is in dialogue with others. JB partners with multiple churches and mission agencies. Several teams from churches across the United States come to visit and to share over a period of time in JB's mission in Jackson Heights. JB comments:

> AJ and SJ have come along, they live here. I think if we have likeminded brothers and sisters here who hopefully don't feel that we know more than the church but [we] truly ask the Lord, 'what is the church in this community? How can we be the church?' We can do something. I always say: We can do something!

I asked JB concerning his approach to negotiating identity—how he thinks it works. He responded:

> If I had a *"pagdi"* [turban] and was six feet tall came from Punjab and doing Christian bhangra music, maybe people would listen. But they'll be like, "this guy is Punjabi and that's his culture." But I think the other aspect that falls for my advantage is: "who's this Chinese guy singing Punjabi music and talking in Hindi a little bit?" I use that as an advantage for me. When I am talking to Nepali-Tibetan friends [I use] more of my Naga aspect. So, in some respect, to the Jew I become like the Jew, to the Greek I become like the Greek. But I think if I had my prejudice like before I would never had done that. But once again the Gospel makes you, compels you to do that.

For SJ, and the negotiation of her Korean-American identity the case is a little different. She says, "I think it's a skill, trying to relate to somebody by your comportment, the way you carry yourself." For JB, a major aspect of negotiating identity lies with learning how to relate to the host culture. He describes how he learned about "American culture":

> When I came to the US, I got into Mid America Baptist Seminary, their main campus . . . Adrian Rogers started it to refocus the church and a Naga-Indian gets tossed in there; that's where

I learned about American culture. That's where I got to learn about the American church.

He goes on to add, in a lower voice, "we use the word, 'colonial,' but obviously they had a heart to come to India, made sacrifices. However, they were not perfect. They used certain words about us; 'heathen' was just a common word." In a tone of admission, he goes on, "We were savages, but I began to understand some of the American perspectives toward India, to our tribes and so that's been very interesting." JB's learning approach facilitates a process of healing of the colonial consciousness or the captive mind as referred earlier. The process is reminiscent of Bevans and Schroeder's description of prophetic dialogue that rests upon "the beautiful but complex rhythm of dialogue and prophecy, boldness and humility, learning and teaching, letting go and speaking out" (Bevans and Schroeder 2011, 156). ICMs carry the capacity to be instruments of change in this regard. They embody the beauty of the complexity that arises from alternating ideologies seeking truth.

We recall the predicament of the Israelites in Ps.137 who had to learn the hard lesson that their identity as a people did not lie in a place, but rather as a people who live by the mercy of God and in obedience to God wherever they are (Hos 1:9, 10b; 1 Pet 2:10). However, as stated earlier, this perspective is meant to be held in tension with the idea of learning to "sing" without compromise on the truth—to sing the "Lord's song" with precision, equity, and persistence.[28]

"Will Your Churches Let My Group Come?"

It remains for us to ponder: are we (the church) ready to receive from the other? Creative Performance is not a one-way street. It requires giving to and receiving from the other as well. According to ML, with regard to mission through music amongst Hindus in North America,

> Could this loving approach to get to know and understand Hindus not be a healthy alternative to the sometimes unfortunate teachings about the Hindu world from Christian pulpits, often given by people who have not lived among them or understood the complexity of their civilization?[29]

ML and his team of performers are not received with open arms everywhere they go. ML refers to a phone conversation with the priest

---

28. Reno, "Theology's Continental Captivity."
29. Source withheld.

at a Hindu temple in California: ML introduced himself and his team of performers as those who would be performing "Yeshu Bhajans." Far from responding positively, the priest responded: "will your churches let my group come?" ML responded to the question by answering: "You'd be surprised how many churches would welcome you." While narrating the incident to me ML recollects in a lighthearted manner that he was thinking about the number of churches that had backslidden, although he did not mention this to the priest of the Hindu temple. The priest replied: "I don't think so; I have experienced it.'"

The incident did not discourage ML from forging other avenues for creative performance, such as performing at South Asian weddings, Yoga studios, and even inviting people to his home where he teaches sitar. Here we recollect Holly Kruse's thesis that the "social location" of a particular music need not mean the total "relinquishment of a world" and a full-scale "reception" of another.[30] Kruse notes how local geographical, social, and local historical networks create, transform, and sustain individual identities as well as in "opposition to other localities" (2010, 628). In much the same way, as much as ICMs seek to identify with others, they also need to learn what differentiates them from individuals and groups in various subcultures. The following episode is revealing.

"Calvary Is Not Vrindaban"

Putumayo, a global World Music record label, invited ML and his team to submit a song to be included on a Putumayo CD. ML and his team did so. However, Putumayo's Indian staff rejected it. According to ML, New York accepted it, but the Indian staff rejected it saying, "This is a Tibetan song, we don't want this." However, he recollects "it was a Nepali song actually (laughs), the album was called 'India;' but I suspect it was because the translation is very, very Christian, [a] pure Gospel song." The song is called *Na Socha*. He summarizes the song's intent, "Don't think that your life is a laughing matter, pay attention to your sins, your sins will find you out." The lyrics of the song included, in ML's translated version:

> If you are going to hide your sin; where are you going to carry the sin around your shoulders; let it down, let your sin down; where you going to go with it; the road is narrow to Calvary's hill.

For ML, it was evident: "Calvary is not Vrindavan," a place in India where the Hindu deity of Krishna is believed to have spent his childhood days. Creative performance invites people to a shared knowledge of God.

30. Kruse, "Local Identity and Independent Music Scenes, Online and Off," 625–39.

However, the rhetoric of the Gospel clearly distinguishes itself, and it should, from the ideologies of other spiritualties.[31]

No Rules, No Boundary Lines

I spoke with ML about what kind of response the church needs to have toward musicians who do appear to "cross the line" in terms of borrowing "Hindu" terms and culture to communicate Christianity (keeping in mind the construction process of the likes of FP). According to him:

> There are no rules and there are no boundary lines. There is basically the Holy Spirit who is a person living in our hearts who guides us into all truth. We have to encourage our fellow musicians to be very close to the voice of Jesus and to the Holy Spirit and to remain in fellowship with people who understand the complexities of your life.

ML's approach corroborates Bevans and Schroeder's hypothesis that the church is not the "perfect society" that is wholly identifiable with the Reign of God contra the world that is totally evil (2011, 102–3). Grace and sin are both in the church and in the world. Therefore, central to prophetic dialogue is the understanding that "The *missio Dei*, like that overflowing fountain, cannot be totally 'contained' in the church" (ibid.). However, this does not mean that boundaries do not exist. The "'places' constructed through music involve notions of difference and social boundary" (Stokes 1994, 3). The difference is that, in the context of mission, such boundaries are meant to be transgressed.

By stating, "there are no boundary lines" ML is depicting a perspective that is hinged on the very notion of "boundary-ness"—a place that emerges within the interstitial passages "in-between" postcolonial and postsecular pluralisms. It is in this place of liminality that artists learn to mediate their authentic difference. "Boundary" places are "the best places for acquiring knowledge" (Bevans and Schroeder 2011, 97). Knowledge is to be found in the boundaries between religion and culture, church and society, heteronomy and autonomy, and faith and doubt (ibid.).

According to Bhabha, "Binary divisions of social space neglect the profound temporal disjunction—the translational time and space—through which minority communities negotiate their collective identifications (1994, 331). Applying Bhabha's rhetoric to ICMs in mission, we note, "what is at issue in the discourse of minorities is the creation of agency

---

31. Cf. "Radical discontinuity," in Jørgensen, "Anthropology of Christianity and Missiology," 186–208. See also "anxious tension" in Keane, "Epilogue," 308–24.

through incommensurable (and not simply multiple) positions" (ibid.). It is through their own interstitial agency that ICMs "author" an "'interstitial' community" along with others.

Related to the idea of boundary spaces as knowledge-generating environments, I discussed with ML the potential of initiating support groups that brought together musicians from different backgrounds. For ML,

> It's not enough . . . . If you think that suddenly you can bring a bunch of musicians, one Nashville musician, one worship musician from a church in America, one guy involved in Indian classical music, and one guy in Bollywood and they're going to somehow encourage one another, that's not going to be possible until they have understood one another and their own <u>complex</u> situations. Because they will be more inclined to impose their own situation on the other, and limit the other person and say, "you can't do that, because I don't face that in Nashville" and in Nashville we only worship Jesus and you guys are struggling to be faithful to Jesus.

Boundary spaces are characterized by multiplex meaning systems. In the context of diversity, according to ML, "you are going to have the humility to listen, the humility to learn, and the humility to put aside your assumptions [regarding] what is legitimate and what is not." According to Terry Muck, listening is "a central part of developing our identity, individually and communally, and is an essential dimension of our understanding of God and the world."[32] It takes humility.

Developing a collective humility is key to authentic witness in a context of fear, prejudice, and a lack of trust. Even in the light of evolutionary approaches to creativity, wisdom entails "a sense of awe and humility" (Moran 2010, 84). Where ICMs in mission might go further is to adopt a posture of compassion in Christ. Creative performance includes compassion—"an emotional response that connects one with the object of his or her compassion."[33] Creative performance as compassion generates hope, memory, and expectation that are ultimately transformative.[34]

Picking up where he left off, I responded to ML: "It boils down to what is authentic." However, ML is not one "to present a set of rules about the situation." The reason, he says, is: "I see my primary witness not in those kind of decisions but in allowing my life to become more and more transparent to more and more people." For ML, "what I do on stage is less and less

---

32. Muck and Adeney, *Christianity Encountering World Religions*, 269.
33. Brink, "In Search of the Biblical Foundations of Prophetic Dialogue," 13.
34. Cardoza-Orlandi, "Prophetic Dialogue," 22–34.

important as to what I do in my home." Although "questions of communication (lyric, stage design etc.) through music are important, I feel that they are secondary in my witness to . . . how I live my life before God, neighbor, to what extent my life reflects selfishness versus what extent my life reflects love. These things are more important to me right now."

A New Community

In the context of his work in Jackson Heights, according to JB, "God has already blessed us with what could happen here." For JB, Jackson Heights, NY, like Ephesians, is a place for the emergence of "a new community."[35] He proceeds to explain how he was invited by a local community organization run by Pakistani immigrants to "make a difference" in the area. For JB, Mr. Aga—the president of Diversity Plaza, a community space in the middle of Jackson Heights—may be the "man of peace." JB is currently working on a plan for the transformation of Jackson Heights. He says, "I want us to really map it out and then present it to them rather than just taking it to them saying [here] we are." Looking back, according to JB, "I missed out so much of that by being secluded in that bubble." Josiah (an intern with JB's ministry) seconds the thought: "I think it's the same in America; I was so much in the bubble, I did not really know how to share, to be relevant."

JB envisions sharing in the Kingdom with others. In doing so he clearly differentiates his ministry from certain approaches to mission of the colonial era. As a few of us—JB's interns and AJ both Caucasian in origin and JB and I, of Indian origin—sat in the Learning Center sipping *chai* with the noise of the local above-the-ground train a few feet away in the background, JB said:

> The missionaries that came in the colonial time, they came with a certain baggage that we are bearing the consequences for the approach. God allowed it but I don't think it represented the Christianity of the Bible. Gandhi saw it—where the messenger and message was different. For us to be sitting here together would have been impossible fifty years ago. That for us to recognize this as God's grace; that the latter house will be more glorious than the former; so we are in good times, where God is doing something rather than us trying to make it happen.

As we looked at each other around the room there seemed to be tangible ring of truth in JB's statement. In terms of creative performance, JB

---

35. Eph 3:6, 10. He refers to John Stott's commentary on Ephesians as a motivating factor for his own ministry in Jackson Heights.

illustrates the biblical emphasis—the radical and dynamic congruity between personhood and performance (Ps 56:12; Lev 25:18). Further, concerning the bringing about of the Kingdom as a collaborative enterprise along with others, underlined the approach that the aesthetic criteria that we are concerned with is not simply "meanings and their interpretation—identity translated into discursive forms which have to be decoded—[but] mutual enactment, identity produced in performance."[36] The encounters between people of God and others who do not know the biblical God are an attested place for the saving activity of God. JB allows for the creation of such space for the exchange and the exercise of "bold humility."

Coats for Queens

JB shares an example of being the body in community with others by meeting people at a point of need. Upon invitation, he requested a church outside Jackson Heights to supply coats for the poor in the community. The church donated about 600 coats to JB for distribution. JB was anxious since they did not know what they would do with so many coats since they did not have place for storage. One cold morning, they went about setting up tables on which to display the coats at about 11am at Diversity Plaza. In JB's words:

> In less than 3 hours, all the coats were gone. *Aisa* crowd *aya* [trans. "Such a crowd came!"], the community; no advertising. The next year we wanted to connect in a tangible way. Hurricane Sandy happened, which took it to a new level. How are we going to serve the broken communities? We had 20 churches come together! We had close to 10,000 coats. We had six locations.

According to JB, once again all coats were given away. Furthermore, the event drew support from nearby stores. The nearby restaurant run by the Sikh person donated two trays of samosas. Another restaurant donated a canister of *chai*. These were offered of their own accord without any requests being made. Creative performance depends upon the rapport developed with the audience, who in this case is the very community and happens over a period of time. The varied and emergent nature of performance is evident in the interconnectedness that JB maintains with others in his community and which serves as a vital ingredient of his creative performance.

Apart from meeting a crucial need of people within the community, JB and his team invited the willing contribution of people who would not have set foot in a traditional church. The flexibility of the operative structure that allowed JB to engage in an expression of creativity sets a

---

36. Frith, *Performing Rites*, 115; Hiebert et al., *Understanding Folk Religion*, 237.

precedent for the structural efficacy of ecclesial structures in general. JB's stance to "do church" in this way is authenticated and legitimized by his leadership—the mission organization of which he is part. Such ecclesial posturing—"creativity prior to ecclesiology"—places a focus on meeting the needs and inviting contribution from others outside "the bubble" rather than primarily upon satisfying the needs of persons on the inside. In this sense, others play a central role in the enactment of the liturgy. We recollect that the *leitourgia* in terms of the public service on behalf of the people takes place not merely in the context of "worship" within the walls of the church but in public spaces with others.[37]

From a theoretical standpoint, creative performance in terms of its public interface is a "socio-analytic mediation" of creativity.[38] Creative performance as missional strategy is a tool for inviting others into the narrative of Scripture. Narrative tools (for example, "Coats for Queens") are employed to better "listen to the voices of the poor and marginalized" for redemptive engagement. As a form of hermeneutical mediation, creative performance uses Scripture to respond to injustice; practical mediation begins with "praxis as the starting point and goal of liberation theology" (Ibid.).

In addition, the agency of ICMs through creative performance as prophetic dialogue links events in time past to the eschatological present through the performance of a "new song" with others.[39] It ushers in hope. On one hand, we have the heavenly reality of cultures together before the throne of God, singing a "new song" (Rev 7:9). On the other hand, such a present and persistent reality here on earth often seems a distant possibility.[40] Creative performance becomes a place for the confrontation of otherness and the construction and exchange of difference. Further, the fact that JB can give back to the community and contribute to the overall economy of the country in which he now resides, is indicative of the operation of a creative "mechanism for nurturing a new collaborative ethos."[41] In such capacity, ICMs can and do

---

37. Hawn, *One Bread, One Body*, 5.

38. Hall, "Prophetic Dialogue," 38–39.

39. The Psalmist writes: "Shout for joy *in* the Lord, O you righteous! . . . Sing to him new song" (Ps 33:1–3). The "new song" is critically linked to the place of such expression—"in the Lord"; it is also indicative of the potential theological disposition of those in such a place, "righteous."

40. Stapert, *New Song for an Old World*, 204–6. Recollecting what we can learn from the Early Church about music, Stapert refers to how early concepts of *musica humana* (the musical harmony of the cosmos reflected in humans) and *musica mundana* (music as part of the created order of a Creator) serve to counter mechanistic claims to human identity and purpose.

41. Lamb, "Summary Analysis of Our Global Neighborhood." See also Jer 29:7.

possess the ability to build the church with others (Zech 6:15a) in the larger context of bringing about the justice of God.

Worth recollecting here is the fact that ICMs are located critically at the margins and borderlands with multiple roots and allegiances that favor the polycentric mediation of creativity away from Western-dominated global neoliberal capitalism. The places that ICMs occupy in mission are places from where they can, in Rashid Arareen's words, "re-claim their place in the history of modernism but also push this history beyond its western boundary" thereby re-signifying cultural difference, making it a place for the emergence of radical change.[42] The place for the emergence of "new song" allows the continual renewal of minds, hearts, and bodies. "New song" is a process of translation that signals the breakdown of ethnocentrisms by the theocentrism embodied and enthroned in the expression of the "new song" in a way that purposefully sustains creative diversity.[43]

On the issue of participating in the justice of God, Mark Moring draws attention to the fact that

> Artists are directly immersing themselves and their audiences in missions to hurting people, whether they are six blocks or 6,000 miles away. They are stepping to the forefront to address poverty, human trafficking, HIV/ AIDS . . . and other fatal diseases, taking personal responsibility to invest in grassroots work.[44]

Concerning the rhetorical significance of communicating reality through musical creativity, according to Moring,

> The relationship between artist and listener is closer than ever. There is greater potential for audiences to buy into the passion of the musician. Musical expression, mission, and message converge in a way that touches listeners and moves them to action. They begin seeing the artist as a credible model for activism—and realize they don't have to be a rock star to help drill a well in Africa, adopt a child from China, or simply love their next-door neighbor (ibid.).

The link between musical creativity and change is unavoidable. Where creativity is suppressed, change is absent or slow at best. Frank Fortunato of Heart Sounds International, an arm of OM fusing mission and arts, cites the response of a Wycliffe Bible Translator to a report at a gathering of Christian leaders in Pretoria, South Africa: "'In areas where translators encouraged

---

42. Arareen, "Come What May," 154–55.
43. Stapert, *New Song for an Old World*, 198–99.
44. Moring, "Songs of Justice, Missions of Mercy."

new believers to sing newly translated Scriptures, the churches grew rapidly. Where that did not happen, churches grew more slowly."[45]

Global Sound

JK founded Art and Mission, an initiative designed to provide a "safety net" for artists in mission.[46] Culture making for JK is an "incarnational" process. He used to be comfortable playing and singing music from popular CCM recording artists such as, Chris Tomlin or Matt Redman. "But now it is almost being incarnational for me to do typical praise and worship song." JK uses the word "incarnational" to mean that performing Western popular worship music would mean dying in some sense to who he truly is—the JK who now identifies with the "global sound." He goes on, "I feel more comfortable doing global sound, even with Korean people."

I responded: "You had to cross that bridge to learn that." By this I meant that JK's intentionality about paying attention to his ethnic or Korean "roots" in the context of his "shoots" or churches in America was a significant factor in his own (evolving?) sense of personhood as linked to his musical creativity. For JK, "global sound" helped to orient others to a dimension of his identity that was previously submerged; but it also facilitated the reorientation of own self in relation to others. According to JK: "Yes, but I came to the point where I feel comfortable enough to do that, comfortable enough to make people uncomfortable." I asked: "Which people?" He replied, "My people," but then quickly added:

> Or any people in general, because I believe it is almost like you are communicating to the world or the church [that] the list of songs the entire world sings should be determined by less than 10 people, 10 song writers. It is the power of globalization.

"Global sound," as per JK's use of the phrase, refers to the creative performances that characterize the fusion of life experiences through the narratives of ICMs in mission. It is a way in which ICMs respond to the issue of neoliberal market capitalism mediated through so-called Christian record companies.

Creative performance, therefore, offers a suitable probe to a dimension of the onto-epistemological captivity of creativity through Christian market

---

45. Fortunato et al., *All the World Is Singing*, xiii. See also Collard, "Promoting Arts." Importantly, however, where the Kingdom of God is pursued, there the church thrives (Krabill et al., *Worship and Mission for the Global Church*).

46. JK demonstrates a pastoral dynamic for nurturing the creative beings of the artists he works with; a place for the housing of the spiritual orphan.

capitalism—CCM (Contemporary Christian Music), which is the "global sound" that is broadly representative of Christianity in postcolonial contexts. However, creative prophetic performance challenges the hegemony of CCM as the "global sound" that represents Christianity as a homogenous Westernized phenomenon. Cardoza-Orlandi's theory of "return effects" is one of the ways in which to understand how the creative performances of ICMs might reverse the caricaturization of Christianity through the "global sound" of CCM. Cardoza-Orlandi defines return effects as:

> Ambiguous yet strong states of being and reflection generated by an encounter with something new and unexpected yet embodied in and perceived as something known. These effects challenge who we are, the way we live, and the order of our worldview and existence. Usually, return effects create a readiness for change (2013, 30).

However, for Cardoza-Orlandi, such readiness and change is often suppressed for surface-level "peace" that serves to maintain the status quo (ibid., 32). This is symptomatic of captivity. The discomfort of creative performance reverses such trend. In this way, creative performance "appreciates human reason and experience while being suspicious of human structures in church and society" (Hall 2010, 34).

DO WE NEED ANOTHER "MODEL" FOR MISSION?

JB and I along with some others who serve with JB discuss the question: "How can we best be the church in Jackson Heights, NY?" According to SJ, "we have always felt that in this particular church and community, music has been the most effective means to reach people." AJ testifies to the complexity, detail, and ever-changing context. According to him the fluid nature of the context, mainly due to migration, is "very complicated in a sense; taking [all things] into account—it's hard to foresee, to plan and to strategize." As far as he can see, "it's hard to engage a model." AJ may be facing the inevitable problem of thinking in terms of a single model to meet the needs and demands of contextual mission in this era of global complexity. In terms of a theological construct that allows for a process of simplifying multiple and complex realities, no single model will suffice.[47]

Rather than "model," AJ argues for a strategy that accounts for the complex diversity of an urban scenario, but at the same time is local and unique for a given context. Both JB and AJ seem to agree that "What does not work is taking a model and overlaying it onto your situation, changing

---

47. Bevans, *Models of Contextual Theology*, 29–33.

the way you dress, language ... but [rather] having the Word of God, the principles to bear on the questions, and for that to become the model." It might be helpful for JB and AJ to differentiate between the progressive nature of church growth rather than upon the serial nature of church growth as far as strategies for ecclesial witness.[48] Furthermore, the dynamics of global complexity tend to expose the fallacy of the "one model fits all." For further study, JB and AJ could benefit from a discussion of the various models for a contextual approach to mission when it comes to balancing Scripture, social experience, and cultural reality.

We conclude that creative performance is a spirituality to be embodied and mediated in a given context. In the light of Ezekiel's prophetic creative performance, we note that being the Body of Christ is a collective embodiment and enactment of a historical reality. It is a process of imagining along with others—a re-cognition of historical processes in the light of the Gospel that invites others to participate in the process of bringing about a new reality.

Creative performance creates the Body of Christ "on location"—multiple and diverse locations whereby the other is a crucial part of the development of the liturgy. In the context of global complexity, the need for a "new anthropology" is evident in the light of glocal connectivity, the "bio-psycho-social" process including "inner worlds and outer environments,"[49] multiple, recursive, and nonlinear linear feedback loops,[50] unpredictability, and radical interdependencies.

CREATIVE PERFORMANCE AND MISSION

According to JK and Paul Neeley, "the power of a strategic connection between worship-arts and missions has still not been realized on a practical level."[51] Due to this discrepancy, JK and Neeley see the need for Korean mission leaders to incorporate "culturally appropriate arts" into their contexts. They view some key challenges for such leaders:

> First, the relatively short history of Korean missions only focuses on the proclamation of the gospel message, rather than on building sustainable local churches with local leadership in a culturally appropriate context. Second, there are few institutions and inadequate infrastructure available to help Korean worship-artists get

48. Walls, "Mission of the Church Today in the Light of Global History," 18–19.
49. Bandy, *Christian Chaos*, 371–72.
50. Sanger and Giddings, "Teaching Note," 369–76.
51. Glocal Worship, http://glocalworship.net/2011/12/05/korean-ethnodoxology-initiative/.

theological and practical training in utilizing and contextualizing arts in missions. Third, the typical hierarchical leadership style in Korean culture hinders creative collaboration within organizations and even on the mission field (ibid.).[52]

A part of the problem may have to do with the perspective that the locus for the habitual enactment of rituals concerning "worship-arts and mission" tends to be the centralized and singular locale or central structure of the church. In terms of creative performative strategy, based upon Kirsh's (2010) study referred to earlier, creative mission is not only localized, but it is also extended and distributed. Rather than structures, however, Jesus is "the new 'place' of worship" in spirit and in truth.[53] A possible solution therefore is to emphasize discipleship initiatives that focus on equipping and empowering artists to embody and express prophetic performances in their various contexts.[54] In terms of missional posture, JK aligns his mission initiative with the 2010 Cape Town Commitment.[55]

Apart from touring extensively, both domestically and internationally, JK has enacted his mission through several platforms and events including the Urbana 12 Missions Conference (December 2013), Worship Gathering and Seminars amongst Korean Diaspora Churches in Los Angeles and Nashville, and the Calvin Symposium on Worship (January 2013), in Grand Rapids, MI.

In terms of creating a "platform" for creative performance, JK refers to a band of 20 people—Korean Americans that he started while in Dallas, TX. The gathering together of a community of people focused on using their gifts in the arts for renewal in the local church has been a rewarding experience for JK and others. In the process, he also met with Byron Spradlin, a pioneer and visionary in Christian worship arts based in the US. Spradlin runs an

52. On another dimension, for JK while there is a general recognition of the need for artists and what they may bring to a given context or mission, their contribution is generally viewed as peripheral to meeting the actual needs of a community. In order to be validated in a particular gathering and in order to be perceived as making a legitimate contribution, in JK's experience, artists would rather "be a pastor." The power associated with the titular usage of the word "pastor" is often preferred as a way to be accepted by others for the sake of making a contribution in the area of their (the artist's) gifting.

53. Piper, "Excerpt from Various Sources," 98–100.

54. Ferguson, "Bible Storying with the Creative Arts for Church Planting," 103–5.

55. Concerning posturing for Creative Performance, according to JK, the arts remains an untapped resource for mission. To counter such trend, he suggests the church must: (1) Bring the arts back into the life of the faith community as a valid and valuable component. (2) Support those with artistic gifts so that they might flourish in their work. (3) Engage the arts as a context for mission. (4) Respect cultural differences and celebrate indigenous artistic expression. Blog Post, http://glocalworship.net/2011/12/.

organization called A. C. T. Intl. (Artists in Christian Testimony International), a North American based Christian organization with headquarters in Tennessee, a commercial music hotbed in the world of music. For some key informants that I interviewed an affiliation with the "Nashville music scene" was something to be avoided as an intentional step to reverse trends in neocolonialism. For other ICMs, they felt that they simply did not "fit." However, in JK's own words, affiliation with A. C. T. Intl. has allowed him to:

> Experience more of a crosscultural ministry with my team. First, I thought of multicultural ministry, but we are a bunch of Koreans. So, right now we do cross cultural ministry. Let's interact with people from a different culture. We did a study of Korean spirituality and style of worship—mixed some traditional elements and historical elements, took some traditional music and mixed some contemporary music and took it to an American church—people love it! There is a transcultural element in worship, when people get it they [are] connected.

Interestingly, JK has arrived at this understanding after being deemed a misfit of sorts in the context of his experience as worship leader in a more traditional Korean American church. The Korean-American homogeneity or "essentializing" tendencies, as referred to earlier by SJ, play a part in the confidence with which JK approaches transcultural ministry in the United States. For JK, a multicultural context calls for a crosscultural approach. Although JK situates himself as part of a multicultural context, for him, adapting a crosscultural stance appears to be a more effective methodology to achieve his purposes.

However, "multiculturalism is not a level playing field."[56] According to Nikos Papastergiadis, recognizing difference is only one part of the solution; the other has to do with discovering "what is new in the encounter with the other" (2012, 409). Papastergiadis bases his thesis in response to the "conservative rhetoric of hostility and aversion towards multiculturalism" (ibid., 399) in Australia. Such "rhetoric" would tolerate and welcome multiculturalism only because it demonstrates an achievement of "an Australian way of doing things" (ibid.). As long as it facilitated the transformation of otherness to likeness in terms of being Australian it was something to be celebrated. In such a context, multiculturalism is tantamount to "national cohesiveness" (ibid.).

The intentional disjuncture on JK's part is predicated on his own differentiated identity as a Korean-American in a multicultural/American urban scenario. He does not see his ethnic differentiation as something of which to

---

56. Adeney, *Kingdom Without Borders*.

be ashamed. Instead of "self-alienation," he embraces his own ethnic other and leverages the same to bring about unity in a multicultural context. We noticed something similar even in JB's stance—the overcoming of prejudice by adopting bhangra music and musical culture.

As such, creative performance illustrates the Burkian principle that "extreme division gives rise to extreme identification" as well.[57] The concept of symbolic identification considers each "thing as a set of interrelated terms all conspiring to round out their identity as participants in a common substance of meaning."[58] In such a scenario, differences amongst people are central to the effectiveness of rhetoric, since, fresh connections are established in participants by bringing to their attention the relevance of new factors.[59] Furthermore, "it is when the participant brings such fresh connections "to the musical experience that the music is thus deemed persuasive" (ibid).

JK goes on to illustrate the nature of crosscultural engagement in a multicultural context:

> For example, Doxology . . . (sings the Doxology.); Western missionaries re-did it in a pentatonic scale [he proceeds to sing it in that way]. If I sing that song in an American church explaining that there was an attempt by an American missionary [who rewrote the tune for The Doxology in the context of the Korean pentatonic scale], then [in this manner] I am appreciating what they did and also affirming my culture. And it is a song they already know. That kind of thing builds a bridge—introducing Korean spirituality to non-Korean friends/people, [but] in English. It is very well received in America, because we are Korean immigrant diaspora. If my team played a bunch of Chris Tomlin songs, they [the American church] are okay, but they don't necessarily appreciate it. But if I do something Korean, <u>authentic</u> Korean, they appreciate it. When it comes out of <u>who we are</u>, then musically or artistically it has that power or energy—that art coming out from who you are—creates energy. So <u>people get it</u>.

In a sense, JK has addressed the question of "Who's the we?" that we encountered in Ps 137:4, "How shall we sing the Lord's song in a strange land?" Inasmuch as the "we" signifies the collective ingathering of the eschatological community, it also is the individual—the healthy, well-differentiated identity of the ICM along with others. The "we" in this sense is a posturing of "appreciation" of self and other in the context of creative mission. In this sense,

57. *EOR*, "Constitutive Rhetoric," 617.
58. Burke, *Grammar of Motives*, 1326.
59. Bailey, "Rhetoric of Music: A Theoretical Synthesis," 25.

therefore, there is little shame in identifying self with a colonized heritage. Rather, there is potential for healing.

Creative performance is enacted within the orb of the Creative Performance (caps intentional) of Christ, who Himself becomes the Text, a metamorphosis of the metaphor. We will explore this further in the final chapter. Attention to the details of differences is important, but imagination—"the capacity to discover something new" (Papastergiadis 2012, 409)—leads to the eruption of creativity with the other. The challenge before ICMs is to shift the collective imagination of participants in creative performance to a different sort of expectation, the eschatological expectation in Christ. This can only happen through an "incarnational relocation"[60] of creative sensibilities in order to be reshaped along with others in the light of the Gospel.

---

60. Barker, "Challenges and Possibilities," 159.

8

Theorizing ICM Identity for Mission

IN CHAPTER 1 WE began with the declaration that the God of the Jews is living, personal, and creative. The audacious implication is that the creativity of *this* God is the context for the creativity of all people. In particular, we recollect from our thesis that Christian indigenous cosmopolitan musicians for mission (ICMs) understand themselves as participating in the creativity of God, and by implication, become the channel of the creative activity of God as they embody, enact, and perform their music; they develop fresh ways to renew and to build the church for mission with others. The focus of this dissertation, therefore, has been to explore ways in which ICMs understand and practice the creativity of God as they build the church for mission in Christ. Thus far we have explored the concept of musical creativity in the context of new spaces for creative mission.

In this concluding chapter we attend to the issue of what these findings mean for the integration of a theology of creativity for mission, ecclesial presence amid global dynamics, and creative agency for mission. First, we bring together the key insights from our exploration of the understanding and practice of ICMs for mission using as lens the questions that Stephen B. Bevans (2008) raises to guide our discussion on the road to the development of a contextual theology of creativity for mission. Second, we recollect our primary research questions and summarize issues of creative understanding and practice for ICMs in mission raised in the course of responding to these questions. Third, we highlight some missiological implications for further research and mission. Fourth, we offer some final thoughts for ICM creativity for mission.

FROM CREATIVE TENSION TO CREATIVE MISSION

David Bosch signals the necessity for a theology of religion that is held together by "creative tension" rather than a simplistic dichotomization between claims to "absoluteness and arbitrary pluralism" (Bosch 2007, 483). A theology of creativity for mission in the current era of global complexity is characterized by just such a creative tension. However, it is a creative tension that arises from theological creative identity that evolves as a *process* of interactivity between musical creativity, global new spaces, and the creative mission of ICMs in Christ. The interstitial passages for the emergence of indigenous cosmopolitan creative identity amid postcolonial currents further engender such tension. Here we complete the circle: the creative tension of indigenous cosmopolitan musical creativity enlarges a space in which to engage the other within the presence of God. That is creative mission.

TOWARD A CONTEXTUAL THEOLOGY OF CREATIVITY

Stephen B. Bevans's (2008) discussion on the issues of theological method in contextual theology serves to guide our effort to summarize issues raised in theologizing not only about music but also through musical creativity for mission. Bevans raises the following questions: First, what is the form that theology should take? Second, who does theology? Third, can a "non-participant" legitimately theologize in a particular context?[1]

Bevans's questions above unite the three theoretical building blocks that form the core of this dissertation, the core concepts of *creatio Dei*, and the research questions raised earlier in this dissertation. The following table (next page) helps to visually correlate the themes running through the dissertation that help us to articulate a response to the question of "How shall we sing the Lord's song in a foreign land?"

Table: Creative Vision, Ecclesial Posturing, and Creative Agency for Mission

Research Questions	Bevans's Questions	Building Blocks	Framework: MFTC
(1) How do ICMs understand and describe their music? What affects their thinking and creative processes?	What form theology should take?	Musical Creativity: a system of knowledge	Creative Being

---

1. Bevans, *Models of Contextual Theology*, 16–21.

Research Questions	Bevans's Questions	Building Blocks	Framework: MFTC
(2) What do ICMs do as they negotiate their Christianity through the process of musical creativity in their respective contexts/global spaces?	Who does theology?	New Spaces: opportunities for a cosmopolitan collaborative creative ethos "beyond" and "in-between"	Creative Construction
(3) What kinds of theological interpretations do ICMs make that links their practices with their beliefs through the process of musical creativity?	Can a "non-participant" legitimately do theology?	Creative Mission with others	Creative Performance

What Form of Theology?

Concerning the form of a theology of creativity, there is a general acknowledgment that theologizing does not have to be verbal.[2] We have seen that musical creativity is a process for the generation of knowledge. It is a pathway for the participation of others in the creativity of God. Knowledge and truth are mediated through forms of hymns, rituals, proverbs, and works of art.[3] Both oral and literate methods are valid approaches to learning and growth.[4] There is a broad recognition of the "sacramental potential" (Blackwell 1999, 28) of music in spiritual traditions including Christianity.[5] The question is to what extent forms, and by implication, agents, of creativity are considered legitimate and authentic carriers of truth and knowledge for mission in a given cultural system.

In the course of our study we learned that relatively little attention has been paid to "the potential of music to explore theological themes" (Begbie

---

2. Bevans, *Models of Contextual Theology*, 17.

3. McKinnon, *Music in Early Christian Literature*; Bediako, *Christianity in Africa*; Moon, *African Proverbs Reveal Christianity in Culture*; Apostolos-Cappadona, *Art, Creativity, and the Sacred*.

4. Chiang and Lovejoy, *Beyond Literate Western Models*.

5. Blackwell here quotes Richard McBrien, *Catholicism*, 2:732.

2000, 3) especially in the scope of contemporary systematic theology.[6] We observed this to be the case for academic discourse within missiology as well. The amorphous nature of creativity and the ambiguity of new spaces for mission in the light of an "old anthropology" problematize the task of theological method in this era of mission.[7] Further, the cumulative influence of the epistemological captivity of creativity through the Enlightenment and sustained through the categories and structures of modern foundationalism have curtailed the freedom of the church for the wholesome engagement of its creative being for mission. The reality is that the church is not only missional by its very nature; it is also creative to its core.

In addition, when it comes to theological creativity, the issue is not solely one of epistemology but rather what we referred to earlier as the onto-epistemological captivity of creativity. From Psalm 137 we discovered that the problem was not so much that the Jews did not know "how" to "sing," but rather did not know how to sing when their *loci theologici*, Jerusalem/Zion, was in ruins and they themselves were in exile/diaspora in a foreign country. God had brought them to a place where the reconstitution of their fragmented identity was to take place on terms prescribed to them by their captors. Not only did they have to re-cognize that their identity as a people of God did not rest in their conceptualization of a nation with geographical roots in a particular place and time. In addition, amid their spatial and temporal displacement, cultural dislocation, and relational disjuncture, they had to wrestle with the axiological reality that the non-Israelites were a significant part of the plan of God for their salvation!

The predicament of the Israelites in that day prefigures the current global scenario where unsurpassed volume of transmigration, multiple and intersecting nodes of experiences, and the polycentric emergence of hybrid identities form the arena for creative mission. Today confrontation with foreignness is more often the norm rather than the exception, and this calls for the transformation of identity along with the transformation of the other. The question of what form theology should take therefore is expanded to include where should the formation of theology take place. This leads us to Bevans's next issue of "who does theology."

---

6. More recently however, there have been some notable works as pointed out by Begbie, "Future of Theology Amid the Arts," 152–54.

7. Cultural markers of ethnicity, race, and nation continue to be used as categories for the articulation of difference. Yet, as we have seen indigenous cosmopolitan identity challenges these as primary or accurate markers of cultural identity in the context of global asymmetries brought about by spatial and temporal shifts. See Levitt, "God Needs No Passport"; Cannell, *Anthropology of Christianity*.

Who Does Theology?

In the context of *creatio Dei*, creative mission amid new spaces stresses the inclusion of the other in the activity of theologizing through the construction of forms in such a way as to create room for ambivalence for mutual indwelling in the hope of the Gospel.[8] The emphasis is on a distinct embodied spirituality moving away from the concept of mission to the world to a new understanding of mission with the world. Further, we recollect that the "mission field" is not the first place to encounter the other. Rather, the holy "Other" is a core dynamic of the creative being of God.[9] Embracing diversity is a core commitment for reaping creativity. The new global proximation amid new spaces for mission creates opportunities to embrace the other and fosters a renewed search for ways of affirming our common humanity and its *telos* in Christ.[10]

Can a Non-Participant Legitimately Do Theology?

There was a time when I took lessons in Hindustani classical music. The culture prescribed bowing down to the idol of a Hindu deity before a class session. In the moment, I refused to bow down. Later, I asked myself if I was missing a deeper experience of God by not conforming to this religious practice. Had I missed an opportunity to step into the world of the other as a "participant" in the context of mission?

My situation was similar to FP's challenge to sing songs of praise to Jesus, Ganesha, and Allah. By virtue of his openness to adapt the form of the other, was he now in a position of privilege to theologize with the other? According to FP, singing songs to multiple deities is not a compromise of his faith. For him, the "essential continuity" (Walls 2006, 7) in Christ is intact. For ML, however, creating music for deities other than Christ is something that his conscience does not permit. In both cases, a deeper issue is whether the other is to be treated as a participant or non-participant? Often, in the context of religious pluralism, the other is considered a co-participant with the imposition of certain boundaries. The compartmentalization of ideologies serves as a way to legitimize understanding and practice without the express need for a theological apologetic. The following episode serves to illustrate.

---

8. Pachuau and Jørgensen, *Witnessing to Christ in a Pluralistic World*, 25–30.

9. Moltmann, *Trinity and the Kingdom*, 105–8.

10. Hiebert, "Critical Issues in the Social Sciences and Their Implications for Mission Studies," 77. See also Walls, *Cross-Cultural Process in Christian History*, 72–81.

A Christian key informant accepted a job passed on to him from a major Muslim composer. In the course of the recording, he discovered the song included a phrase ascribing worship to a popular Hindu deity. He stopped the recording and informed the Muslim composer who gave him the job that he could no longer do the work. It was discovered that the Muslim composer himself passed on the job for the very same reason.

In the context of a pre-systematic ontology of creativity, however, all people are creative. Whether or not a person is Indian or American, Hindu or Christian, Brahmin or Dalit, need not be played out in terms of dominant markers that tend to "lock the project of resistance into the semiotic opposition set up by imperial discourse" (Ashcroft 2000, 26). The dichotomy of participant versus non-participant is problematic since it presumes preexistent boundaries that call for clarification. The task of a hermeneutical community consisting of ICMs along with others must therefore wrestle with degrees of participation rather than the uncritical conceptual appropriation of the binary of participant/non-participant.

In addition, in the context of a theology of creativity, with an emphasis on understanding of the self in terms of constitution with the other[11]—a relational ontology—the question is raised as to who really is a "non-participant"? Concerning the dichotomy of participant and non-participant, we affirm that the identity of Christians is firmly rooted in Jesus Christ. The "creative tension," however, lies in the recognition of the fact that the person of Jesus Christ constitutes the mystery of communion with others across all space and time past, current, and yet to be.[12] The issue is this: are we willing to receive and learn from the indigenous/aboriginal other, Christian or not, as much as we think we may be able to contribute to the enrichment of the other through the Gospel.[13] Bevans argues that the issue is "whether a person who does not share the full experience of another can actually do authentic theology within that culture or context."[14]

SUMMARY OF CREATIVITY: UNDERSTANDING AND PRACTICE FOR MISSION

For ICMs in mission, creativity is embodied (Being), enacted (Construction), and expressed (Performance). Concerning creative being, theological creativity does not happen in a vacuum. The covenant relationship with

---

11. For Jesus Christ, "this is my body for you" is a radical definition of self in terms of the other.
12. Eph 3:6, 10. See also Walls, *Cross-Cultural Process in Christian History*, 74.
13. Pachuau and Jorgensen, *Witnessing to Christ in a Pluralistic World*, 21.
14. Bevans, *Models of Contextual Theology*, 19, italic mine.

the Creator forms the locus for the engendering of creative being. As ICMs participate in the *creatio Dei*, they extend to others the invitation to share in the *missio Dei*. *Creatio Dei* ushers a fresh discourse that deems the binary of reached/unreached as the sole purpose of the Gospel a figment of the colonial imagination. Rather, the other is someone *with* whom the church is able to create a new reality in Christ. Mission, then, is both, to reach the other and to create with the other.

Creative construction refers to the process that nurtures the emergence of indigenous cosmopolitan identity in the context of new spaces for mission. Borderlands are sites of transition and transformation. Hybridity may indeed be the new authenticity, but not without significant qualifiers that reiterate roots as well as simultaneously affirm a desire for new facets of representation located beyond previous cultural, social, and geographical markers. This contributes to the creation of new spaces for creative tension within which ICMs learn to negotiate their creative missional identities.

The construction patterns of ICMs hold potential to be poetic renditions of a new humanity in Christ. In other words, creative construction signifies a new collaborative ethic—unity and diversity, which is anchored in the life of the community of the Trinity. Authentic creative mission sustains diversity. It overcomes fear and ethnic pride. Creative construction is a social process for the gathering of multiple histories.

Creative performance is a penultimate theological expression of what is ultimately embodied, enacted, and performed in Christ.[15] It is a way for ICMs to per-form into the collective identity of humanity as expressed in the corporate personality of Jesus Christ. It is multi-sensorial as well as tradition and habit forming. Creative performance invites others to participate in actual beliefs. It entails movement. In movement, meaning is local; it is also extended and distributed. This applies as well to ideologies of power associated with place and position.

Creative performance is prophetic activity. It is truth expressed and knowledge of God mediated. Specifically, it is a hesychastic knowledge whereby theologizing in the context of *theosis* (unity of human and Divine energies in terms of Orthodoxy) is not merely theoretical, but an "experiential discipline that performs" communion with God.[16] In continuity

---

15. In a study of "theology as performance," Stoltzfus concludes, "both expressivism and formalism . . . spawn a correspondence theory of theology, and thus, from the perspective of the aesthetics of the performing arts, fail to treat theological production itself as a type of performance—as a *'praxis'* to 'create *the new*'" (*Theology as Performance*, 167).

16. Horujy, "How Exactly is the Spirit Present in Creation?," 101. In discussing the activity of the Holy Spirit in Creation, Horujy defines the Orthodox way of hesychasm

with such understanding creative performance is the unfurling of the scriptural metanarrative, a creative remythologization, and a process of traditioning that invites participation through prophetic dialogue. It offers a counterhegemonic stance to knowledge generation in captivity in that it is a place for the emergence of knowledge not merely about God, but knowledge of God.[17]

MISSIOLOGICAL IMPLICATIONS

Stephen B. Bevans and Roger P. Schroeder adapt Justo L. González's Three Types of Theology in the context of a theology of mission: saving souls and extending the Church, mission as discovery of Truth, and mission as commitment to Liberation and Transformation.[18] In the spirit of Bevans and Schroeder's typology, might we propose a theology of mission as creativity along with the other for the Kingdom? Along with the trajectory of questions that shape the six "constants in context,"[19] the nature and purpose of human creativity (theological creativity) for mission raises a seventh question: what is the nature and value of human creativity as a pre-systematic ontology for mission? The concept of theological creativity as a "seventh constant" extends Bevans and Schroeder's "Outline of Three Types of Theology" (2004, 37) as far as the inclusion of historical creative arts personages, apart from St. Francis of Assisi, from contexts around the world. Further study and research is invited on this matter.

---

in contrast with Natural Theology. Hesychasm, for Horujy, "is the school that reproduces the authentic experience of communion with Christ and union with Divine energies, and the acquisition of such experience is the aim of Christian life, in the Orthodox view" ("How Exactly Is the Spirit Present in Creation?," 95).

17. Horujy, "How Exactly Is the Spirit Present in Creation?," 100. According to Horujy, knowledge as cognitive activity is a dimension of communion with God that is indistinguishable from the "whole and nourished by it." He goes on to reason that in contrast to this, modernity specifically in the aura of Natural Theology and thereby for us, so-called knowledge in captivity, "is an isolated cognitive activity; accepting no preconditions, it disconnects itself from the economy of communion with God and tries to reach some conclusions on God by indirect ways, from knowledge of empiric phenomena. Thus, it is only some scraps of knowledge that such activity can get and they are, in addition, utterly unreliable."

18. Bevans and Schroeder, *Constants in Context*, 35–72.

19. Bevans and Schroeder, *Constants in Context*, 34. The questions are: "(1) Who is Jesus Christ and what is his meaning? (2) What is the nature of the Christian church? (3) How does the church regard its eschatological future? (4) What is nature of the salvation it preaches? (5) How does the church value the human? (6) What is the value of human culture as the context in which the gospel is preached?"

The Creative Church

What is the plan for the church to include others in the task of liturgical development, content, and strategy?[20] In reality we do know what the ultimate picture will look like (Rev 4ff.; Heb 12:22–4). The prospect of the gathering, together singing a "new song" before the throne of God (Rev 7:9) envisions a present ingathering characterized by a desire to learn to sing along with the other.[21] The diversity of such community reciprocates the creativity of the Godhead. The biblical diversity of Rev 7:9 is unified not merely by the fact that they sing a new song, but that the terms of engagement are prescribed and forged in worship of a holy God.

Congregational song[22] is a venue for celebrating the diversity of God (Rev 7:9; Heb 12:22). The cacophony of perspectives does not fade; differences are held together in a creative tension. The epiphany is this: Christ manifests, incorporates, and is formed by diversity.[23] A theology of creativity legitimizes creative expression as tantamount to the proclamation of knowledge and truth. This translates into creating contexts and experiences (i.e., doing church) for the proclamation of the Kingdom through a diversity of onto-epistemologies—movement, touch, sound, and visual imagery as primary forms for the mediation of truth along with more traditional methodologies (Sermon).

It may be worth stating that it is not merely a matter of including such elements to embellish or illustrate the "message," but employing such forms

---

20. Hunter, *Should We Change Our Game Plan?*

21. It is a journey of embracing the "insecurity" of musical identity, plotting the connections between such and other dimensions of identity, and overcoming difference and boundaries by accepting and embracing the 'other' and its 'otherness.' See Pachuau, "Engaging the 'Other' in a Pluralistic World," 72. See also Hiebert, "Critical Issues in the Social Sciences," 79, "there are no Others, only us."

22. Ingalls et al., *Christian Congregational Music*, 2–3 prefer the term, "congregational *music*" for good reason. In the context of a theology of creativity that I explore here, "congregational *song*" is broadly inclusive of the agency of humans—voices, instruments, and bodies included. This is significant especially in contexts where certain categories of instruments and ways of singing reinforce caste and class hegemonies (for example, the classical *music* system in India in general as representative of caste differentiations between people). In such contexts, "congregational song" is a venue for the voiceless, marginalized, displaced, and de-territorialized to join in heavenly song as an embodied process for the rearticulation and reinforcement of a collective human identity along with *others* in the *imago Dei*. Further, in a context of a theology of creativity, instruments are not abstracted from human embodiment, which draws parallels to certain traditions where instruments are embodied in the divinity of the deity, which provides the pattern for spiritual musical practice; resultant expressive sound, instrument, movement/behavior, and artistry are rooted in the personhood of the creator.

23. Walls, *Cross-Cultural Process in Christian History*, 77.

for actual collective participation in embodying, enacting, and expressing Truth. When it comes to the employment of the creative arts in mission, participation is not merely a theological principle, but the demonstration of actual beliefs. It subverts intellectualism.

Again, however, issues of power come into play—preaching and proclamation are not to be identified primarily with positional authority (titular application of "pastor" or "teacher") or dominant majority. For example, in the course of my research I encountered some teenage Bhutanese refugees from Nepal in a church in North America. They preferred to literally hide in the bathrooms of the church they were brought to by bus every Sunday rather than "worship" with the larger congregation. The complexity of their inclusion calls for further research in the context of what it might mean for the decolonization of Christian worship in North America as well as the decolonization of anemic copies (Taussig 1993) elsewhere.[24]

It is envisioned that in the creative church, however, without dispelling the biblical injunctions concerning the aforementioned ecclesial roles, a significant effort is made to affirm the inherent creativity of all—deaf, blind, intellectually disabled, all humans including equally, women, children, and those typically deemed "not a fit," for example, immigrants, and refugees.[25] Along with affirmation, "poetic responsibility" entails constructing opportunities for maturity in discipleship through theologizing with others. Further, this is to take place through the actual use of creativities. For example, actual creativity would mean approaching the creative arts not as hobby but as an ascetic and formative lifestyle (sodality) in Christ for the renewal of the church.[26]

---

24. For some initial thoughts, Marti, *Worship Across the Racial Divide*; Garces-Foley, *Crossing the Ethnic Divide*. Also, Jones, *Worlds Within A Congregation*.

25. There is scope to explore a theology of creativity in terms of its practical application for arts and creativity and its healing/nurturing potential for mission with the intellectually disabled (cf. some works in this direction Yong, *Bible, Disability, and the Church*; also, on *Deaf Liberation Theology*, Lewis, *Critical Examination of the Church and Deaf People*). The discussion on APEST by Allan Hirsch and others is helpful to discern directions in embracing diverse ministry styles in the context of Eph 4 (cf. "What is APEST?" https://www.theforgottenways.org/apest/.

26. Therefore, Wednesday or Thursday nights, so to speak, are not merely for "practicing" for Sunday, but a gathering of those called to *rehearse* together a lifestyle of performance in Christ. Such gathering is in essence a hermeneutical community for the proclamation of the Kingdom through the kerygmatic pronunciation and enunciation of their gifts in Christ for the building of the church for mission. In this respect, further study is invited in the role of inspiration and imagination in the context of theological creativity and how the creative intelligence of those involved in such processes may be applied toward a creative ecclesiology for mission. Revisiting the sodality of creative agency as a vital part of existing structural modalities may be a place to begin for some

In addition, in the context of appropriating the music of the other for mission, according to JB:

> Now, it is not just "come and worship" as the traditional church sees it, but bringing unity to your history, culture, language, identity. It's amazing as you sing and listen to that music; <u>there is a unity that comes together.</u> It makes you start clapping together as you would not in any other setting, moving together—a corporate setting, which can be used to make disciples, to make the Gospel clearer rather than what we have made of it for a long time. Not sure, what that is going to look like (emphasis implied).

Where is Church?

In the light of the shift from asking, "what is creativity?" to "where is creativity?" a new geo-spiritual topography ushered by global complexity offers fresh possibilities for putting into practice what is already affirmed conceptually—public liturgy.

The church is a part of a wider cultural system. ICMs are uniquely dis-placed to challenge the structural logics of modernity for the embodiment, enactment, and performative expression of congregational song. The negotiation of their identity sparks the irruption of public liturgy in terms of where it happens (i.e., where is the congregation in relation to the other?), how it transpires (in terms of formation into the common humanity in Christ), and who is included and/or excluded (who is involved in the negotiation of terms by which one is considered a "member").

The question of "where is the congregation?" is significant in terms of deterritorialized, polycentric, multitextual, asymmetrical, and asynchronous liturgical spaces. The "enactive" movement of ICMs expands and redistributes typical locations for the public performance of liturgy. Their orbital pathways amid multiple centers and peripheries could be threatening to the single-center/multisite-with-one-center model for mission. In terms of movement, ICMs meet the people where they are—developing new spheres for performativity in Christ. As such, ICMs establish a "counter-hegemonic" improvisational way of being in the "interstices" (Bhabha 1994) between current ecclesial structures and the world.

---

churches. Winter, "Two Structures of God's Redemptive Mission," 121–39.

ICMS AND CONTEMPORARY ARTISTIC PLATFORMS FOR CREATIVE DIALOGUE

The "pilgrim church" is not only missional by its very nature but is also creative to its core.[27] ICMs challenge and alter dominant discourses that shape and govern human attitudes and actions in the world. The contemporary art world offers much from which to learn. Emily Eliza Scott (2013) introduces readers to the several ways in which artists come together to address ecological issues.[28] The author draws insights from observing the practices of API (Arctic Perspectives Initiative), a social networking process comprising individuals, organizations, indigenous communities connected over extended periods of time to create "open-authored media and communication circuits" (ibid.). Several insights emerge for the creativity of ICMs for mission.

Eliza Scott observes "artist-generated" research relational networks comprised of artists who explore "complex, cross-disciplinary ecological subjects through the development of structures for sustained investigation, exchange and production," (ibid., 1). For ICMs to generate cross-structural platforms for the intermixing of histories typically separated by existing hegemonies results in the formation of new "ontological communities" (ibid., 2) for mission. Prophetic dialogue forges a basis for community; here, the generation of knowledge serves as a catalyst for further "inquiry and public discussion" (ibid., 3).

According to Scott, API creates a distinct "voice" by building upon autonomous production already in place (ibid., 8). Biological fact serves as an analogy to the fact that creativity is best forged in the context of diversity: "biological systems are strengthened by diversity" (ibid.).[29] Scott relates this scientific discovery to the actual roles of the artists who in the words of a theorist, "'don't exhaust themselves inside [the art circuit], but rather, extend elsewhere in terms of 'extradisciplinarity'" (ibid.).

Likewise, ICMs through their exposure to diverse and popular creative art forms, not typical to Christianity in a given context, expand the palette for creative expression within existing churches. Through their employment of the creative arts, they hold potential to broadcast a variety of perspectives that provoke the imagination and that usher and inspire participation for the ongoing enmeshment of local/global histories in ways that impacts

---

27. Cf. Bevans and Schroeder, *Constants in Context*, 97.

28. Scott, "Artists' Platforms for New Ecologies."

29. See also Kaufman's theory of the "Adjacent Possible" in Johnson, "Genius of the Tinkerer."

society.³⁰ The creative arts in particular create opportunity for the healing of local histories by inviting participation in the scriptural metanarrative as a "full embodied and social enterprise."³¹ This extends to the participation of institutions that results in "heightened disciplinary and institutional reflexivity" (Scott 2013, 9).

The "extradisciplinarity" of ICMs to create fresh discipleship contexts outside dominant expressions of Christianity (denominations, power struggles) can be a daunting task. According to Scott, artist led research initiatives "do not operate in an institutional vacuum. To the contrary, they reflect and produce a changed institutional habitat within and beyond the art world" (ibid.). The extent to which ICMs as creative catalysts within the body of Christ are accepted and entrusted with the vision of the church by established structures is not always clear. However, artists and academicians/pastors are to serve together in humility.³²

Scott further broaches the notions of "durability and adaptability" when it comes to transnational art-research platforms that combine the "transformatory power of art with the tangible goals of campaigning, the rigour of in-depth research with the vision to promote alternative futures" (ibid., 10).³³ Likewise, ICMs carry potential to catalyze the role of craftspersons within current ecclesial structures in creating sustainable spatial and temporal environments. Along with Christ as He builds the church (Eph 4:11), craftspersons are called to create geneplore³⁴ contexts—spaces where people can

---

30. Kelly, *Creative Confidence*, launched "openideo.com" and invited responses from people across the world to respond to a series of challenges that have emerged from issues that people have suggested, e.g., "How might we inspire young people to cultivate their creative confidence?" Creative innovation for them is a process of inspiration, missions (research), concepting (ideas for solutions), applause (shortlisting), refinement (collaborate and prototype), evaluation (rate and comment on best concepts), winning concepts (selecting diverse solutions), and realization (showcasing stories of implementation and impact). Open Ideo, "How It Works," http://www.openideo.com/how-it-works/full.html.

31. Green, "Narrative and New Testament Interpretation," 153; See also Rynkiewich, "Mission, Hermeneutics, and the Local Church," 47–60.

32. Bevans, *Models of Contextual Theology*, 21. See also Taylor, *For the Beauty of the Church*.

33. Scott offers the example of some platforms that have created a "temporality that supports a kind of deep, collective, issue-specific knowledge that is clearly unachievable over the course of one exhibition, book or symposium. It furthermore allows these groups to build wide and diverse publics, forge working protocols aligned with their core ethical values, learn from inevitable failures along the way and develop resilience against instrumentalization by the very forces and enclosures they seek to resist" ("Artists' Platforms for New Ecologies," 10).

34. Geneplore (generate + explore) refers to creativity research in the context of

generate ideas and explore their implications in the light of *creatio Dei*. These geneplore contexts are envisioned as ecclesial environs that encourage learning from others and the chance to collaborate in order to develop creative content for collectively impacting society for a new heaven and earth.

SUGGESTIONS FOR FURTHER RESEARCH AND MISSION

Based upon our study thus far we offer the following broad affirmations:

1. Creativity has its source, sustenance, and ultimate fulfillment in the Creative Being of God, the Father, the Son, and the Holy Spirit. Creativity runs concurrently with, and not in contradiction to, the mission of God.

2. Musical creativity is a primary form of participation in the ongoing Creative Construction of the revelation of God. And, thus, a different model of mission is revealed; mission as the invitation to participate in the creativity of God.

3. The embodiment, enactment, and expression of such creativity through Creative Performance opens up a place that invites others to join in a collective remaking of humanity into the fullness of Christ.

I would like to invite further research into expanding and clarifying *creatio Dei*. There is much scope for artists to work with academic theologians to further develop theological creativity as a paradigm for mission. The aspects of Creative Beauty and Creative Community deserve theological reflection in the context of missiology. There is scope to explore the dynamics of a theology of sound for mission based upon the sonic impulse of the Creator in Scripture and general revelation. Given the influence of sound in Hinduism and in shaping various New Religious Movements, a biblical theology of sound would go a long way in helping to align Christian belief with action amid new spaces for mission. Please see Appendix C for initial steps toward a sonic theology for mission.

C3M—A Suggestion for "Covenant Creative Communities for Mission" [35]

C3M is a structural innovation that applies the principles of theological creativity gleaned thus far toward an integrated approach to mission in global

---

cognitive psychology. It term refers to how people generate ideas and then proceed to explore them in a laboratory environment (Kozbelt et al., "Theories of Creativity," 32).

35. As part of the research process, this was a project undertaken in downtown Lexington, KY, where local artists and members of the church in the area were invited

new spaces with others. The context for creativity is the covenantal relationship with the Triune Creator God and through this God with all creation.³⁶ In terms of the *creatio Dei*, the agency of ICMs in mission serves to mediate the covenantal creativity generated within the Godhead with others. C3Ms are artist-generated platforms for the renewal of the church where artists as sodalities may reaffirm their calling in Christ (Eph 4:11), gather with like-minded/different others, and work out their creative mission in the context of urban and ecclesial renewal. C3M is an invitation for the development of a hermeneutical community. For further study, please see Appendix D.

MUHANA Ashram: A Suggestion for a Music Monastery

ICMs hold potential to create sustainable contexts and experiences for hope and community healing in the context of fear, insecurity, and prejudice (Haynes 2005) for urban renewal in Christ (Rev 21:22–7). A suggestion for an expression of "new song" could take the form of MUHANA, meaning "estuary" in Hindi. The word signifies the place where the prophet Ezekiel experienced the reality of "life" brought about in the flow of the River of God—abundant diversity as a breeding place for life-giving creativity (Ezek 47:1–13). Along the lines of what FP already envisions, one suggestion is to develop sites for music and meditation, a Music Monastery/Ashram for teaching and discipleship in the context of loving God, loving others, and serving the city. This could be a Christ-like parallel to the lifestyle and *habitus*-forming atmosphere of *"gharanas"* that house and develop the spiritual sensibilities for practice and performance of classical musicians in the North Indian context.³⁷ Further study is invited in this regard (Appendix E).

Creative Theological Formation

Concerning the academy, there is scope to appropriate some of the principles of theological creativity for theological formation. Within our limitations of time and space, we can only suggest a few. For example, a Community Transformation through the Arts (CTA, see Appendix F) program could be offered as a paradigm for reimagining theological formation along with existing approaches in urban anthropology and

---

to participate in the creative transformation of the city/neighborhood through creative collaboration of their stories/creativities with others in the context of the larger Story of Scripture.

36. Best, "God's Creation and Human Creativity," 13–16.

37. For further information: ITC Sangeet Research Academy, http://www.itcsra.org/sra_story/sra_story_guru/sra_story_guru_links/sra_story_guru_gharana/sra_story_guru_gharana_index.html.

theology of mission. CTA includes using creative arts as a primary strategy in human and community development. *Creating Local Arts Together: A Manual to Help Communities Reach their Kingdom Goals* (Schrag 2013) is a helpful resource for this purpose.

The idea is to create a culture of participation with others where there is relatively less opposition to creative artistic expression in the context of "civic engagement," collaboration and collective sharing of creativities, mentoring, cross-cultural exchange, affirmation of personhood as it relates to creative contribution, and in-process community formation.[38] Research has demonstrated that creativity flourishes when organizations encourage employees to pursue new ideas and they are "given the resources and opportunities needed to experiment with these new ideas."[39] Missiologically, this could imply establishing Schools for Theological Creativity that invite academics, technologists, and artisans to concretize and actualize creative intelligences through the generation of creative works in the context of a rubric that is envisioned in *creatio Dei*.

Schools for Theological Creativity (for mission) result in the need for the acquisition of a new theological skill-set and vocabulary.[40] These places/processes could be the life of a theological creative community infusing a theological vibrancy in ways not typical of captive contexts.[41]

---

38. Jenkins with Ravi Purushotama et al., "Executive Summary." Participatory culture includes Affiliations (Facebook etc.), Expression (videos, new creative forms), Collaborative problem solving (teamwork to complete tasks and develop new knowledge, reality gaming), and Circulations (shaping media flow such as blogging).

39. Burkus and G., "Noncommissioned Work," 49.

40. Jenkins et al., "Executive Summary," xiv. In the context of cultivating a participative culture, Jenkins et al. envisage the development of "new media literacies," a combination of cultural competencies and social skills. They suggest a list that includes: play, performance, simulation, appropriation (meaningful sampling and remix of media content), multitasking (ability to scan the environment and shift focus onto salient features), distributed cognition (the ability to interact meaningfully with tools that expand mental capacities), collective intelligence (ability to pool knowledge and work toward a common goal), judgment (ability to evaluate the reliability and credibility of different information sources), transmedia navigation (the ability to follow the flow of stories and information across multiple modalities), networking (searching, synthesizing, and disseminating information), negotiation (ability to travel across diverse communities whilst discerning and developing respect for alternate and multiple perspectives, and grasping and following alternative norms). With these in mind, we might propose a School of Theological Creativity that would apply these goals as strategies toward theological formation along with other existing processes.

41. The efforts of organizations such as "Sarai.net" that exist in the form of hundreds of creative "hubs" in the city of New Delhi as well as the effort of strategies employed Apple, and animators, Pixar Incorporated, appear to cast a shadow on the efforts of many churches when it comes to leveraging creative identities/approaches

Someone might argue, to the extent creative strategies remain peripheral to the embodiment of the Gospel in the course of theological education, it is a matter of wonder if it is truly the *whole Gospel* that is being taken to the whole world, where the majority does not merely *prefer* but is actively immersed in a creative world.

There is scope for rethinking goals and strategies for existing approaches to theological education—helping to incorporate creative learning strategies through the introduction of fresh technologies is one way to do this in the context of "digital immigrants."[42] However, the challenge of whether these are a matter of personal and communal preference or just a coping methodology for others are issues that requires further research.[43]

CREATIVITY, DIVERSITY, AND MISSION

The problem of indigeneity, especially when it comes to Christianity, is that there is no Christian "civilization" or "culture."[44] The dilemma of "what a Christian lifestyle looked like" that faced the Early Church is true even for the church in the current global plurality of religious-cultural expressions. For some of the Jews in Acts 15, the mark of indigeneity was evident through circumcision. However, this was not to be so for Christians.

Andrew Walls cites the example of Justin Martyr who strove to understand whether philosophers before Christ (for example, Socrates) were "totally without value. Did God have nothing to do with Socrates?" Walls explains that Justin Martyr theorized that pagan philosophers speaking in accordance to reason, the *logos*, were also speaking in accord with the *Logos*, learning to reject part of their cultural tradition, affirm part of it, and modify part of it.[45] In order for ICMs to carry out their task with theological precision, contextual sensitivity, and Kingdom-centric equity, adopting

---

for "mission." The neoliberal capitalist dimension to the equation should not be ignored. However, the principles of creativity in the context of diversity (of opinions and environments), legitimizing space to be creative and develop mutual respect and affirmation, among other things, are some ways in which the church may learn from those already "effectively" employing such strategies, albeit with different ends in mind. See also, Burkus and Oster, "Noncommissioned work," http://www.creativitypost.com/business/why_free_time_frees_creativity. Google's "free time"—non-commissioned work increases motivation and encourages risk-taking.

42. Prensky, "Digital Natives, Digital Immigrants," 3–11.

43. Personal interview with Dr. Russell West, March 5, 2014, Wilmore, Kentucky. Dr. West reviews Western literacy-contingent models and conceptualizes orality not merely as a "preference" but as an identity.

44. Walls, "Expansion of Christianity," 792–99.

45. Walls, "Expansion of Christianity," 792–99.

such a learning-on-the-way-to-prophetic posture is crucial to creativity amidst the diversity for the common humanity in Christ. Andrew Walls paints a picture of the current global scenario and the missional task at hand in the following words:

> It seems to me that now, more than at any time in history, the church looks like the great multitude described in the Book of Revelation—a multitude from every tribe and nation.
>
> Paul speaks of Jews and gentiles growing together, and he says that only when the two strands are one will they have grown into the full stature of Christ. At the time, no one had any idea how important the missions to the gentiles would prove to be. After the fall of Jerusalem, the church became as monocultural in a Hellenistic way as it had been in its earliest days in a Jewish way.
>
> We live now at a time when the church is multicultural. I think that the fullness of the stature of Christ will emerge only when Christians from all these cultures come together. If I understand what Paul says in Ephesians correctly, it is as though Christ himself is growing as the different cultures are brought together in him.[46]

In the following section we suggest a specific posture that ICMs may adopt for mission.

PERSON AS TEXT: METAMORPHOSIS OF THE METAPHOR

From an ethnomusicological standpoint, "musicking," the entire set of relationships and acts in the range of a musical performance[47] as a way of life takes us only so far. Ultimately, it is in the composite Person of Jesus Christ that the creativity of humankind finds fulfillment. In congruence with Christopher Wright's depiction of "Paul's adoption of the Servant Mission," we reiterate that participation in the form of poetic expression, per se, of the text of the so-called Servant Songs of Isaiah (52:19—53:12) is not merely a theological plausibility.[48] Christ is more than metaphor. The apostle Paul's "bold hermeneutic" in appropriating for himself the very mission of the Servant[49] demonstrates for us embodied, enacted, and performed creative mission in Christ.

46. Walls, "Expansion of Christianity."

47. Small, *Musicking*.

48. Art is indeed "theological text." Viladesau, *Theology and the Arts*, 123. But not merely.

49. Acts 13:46–47. See also Wright, *Mission of God*, 519–27.

We cannot afford to go into a detailed explanation of the significance of the text except to highlight a few dynamics as it might apply to ICMs and their ongoing creative agency for mission in Christ as a path for further study.

First, the phrase "my Servant shall act wisely" (Isa 52:13) sums up the dynamic nature of creative activity as a performative act in conjunction with the creative capacity of the Godhead through the obedience of Christ. Second, the disfiguration of Christ's human form ("had no form that we should look at him") and the negation of "aesthetics" associated with such form ("and no beauty that we should desire him") is a metaphoric posturing for mission that ICMs need to emulate (Phil 2:6–11).[50] Third, participation in the "song" is in effect a decompression of space and time enabling participation in its reality via remembrance[51] in and "beyond" the present. Fourth, the startling nature ("sprinkle," Isa 52:15) of such revelation across "many nations" is subject for imagining the scope of such revelation for mission in terms of how ICMs might continue in the traditioning[52] process of musical creativity. Fifth, the eye opening as well as ear unblocking (Isa 52:15) nature of the logical appeal of this Poet, speaks directly to the apologetic potential of the arts through the poetic personalities of ICMs in mission by virtue of their own participation in the mission of Christ.

Along the lines of St. Paul who was "provoked" in his spirit amongst the Athenians (Acts 17:16) or the prophet Ezekiel who was embittered and overwhelmed while amongst the exiles (Ezek 4:14–5), ICMs too must share a prophetic and priestly burden. Christopher Wright highlights the importance of Paul speaking of his own ministry in priestly terms; Paul speaks to the grace of God that enables him

> to be a "temple servant" [*leitourgos*] of Christ Jesus to the nations, offering the gospel of God like a priestly sacrifice [*hierourgounta*], so that the offering of the nations [*prosphora ton ethnon*] might be acceptable, having been sanctified by the Holy Spirit (Rom 15:16, author's translation) (2006, 525).

---

50. Underline mine.

51. Cf. Carlos-Orlandi, "Prophetic Dialogue." See also Robinson, "Present of Things to Come," 30–34. Music allows us to experience time differently by suggesting that music puts us "in touch with eternity by directing our attention toward that point." Robinson quotes Alex Ross according to whom the spirituality of music refers to "its ability 'to silence the noise of the mind, binding the mind to the eternal present.'" Ross, "Consolations." In this sense, therefore, musical creativity is eschatological (Leeuw *Sacred and Profane Beauty*, 331). Leeuw, *Sacred and Profane Beauty*, 331. But it is also soteriological in a very specific sense.

52. See Brown, *Tradition and Imagination*.

Such priestly service embodied in the identity of temple servants becomes the leitourgia, the public offering/liturgy enacted with others unto God. In the light of the Poet in Isaiah, the potential for a public liturgy is fulfilled in the geospatial location of the Cross of Calvary as a spectacle in the public arena. Concerning the direction of and space where the evangelistic identity of ICMs needs to be enacted, Wright's comment provides clarity: "priestly imagery is never used of ministry within the church, but Paul uses it here of his evangelistic ministry to the nations" (2006, 525).[53]

CONCLUDING THOUGHTS: ICMS AND CREATIVE MISSION

The creative mission of ICMs may be summarized in three words: creativity, diversity, and community. The context for theological creativity is the diversity of globalization that is, we recollect, "complex, heterogeneous, and plural" (Hopper 2007, 186) for the bringing about of the one interactive-participative community in Christ.[54]

The concept of indigenous cosmopolitanism is a way to theorize musical agency for mission in this age of migration and global interconnectedness. It is through the extended and distributed agency of ICMs for mission that musical creativity as a knowledge system becomes a process that challenges the strictures of modernity and anticipates the emergence of new hybrid structures for the sustenance of new creative sodalities and modalities for mission. ICMs for mission foster "global belonging" (Papastergiadis 2012, 10) and initiate a fresh relational ontology for being in the world. The non-representational and ambivalent nature of musical creativity is a natural counterpart to the hybrid nature of indigenous cosmopolitan musical identity. ICM identity emerges amid the interstitial spaces of flow and nodes of subaltern historical experiences. ICM identity is a cosmopolitan hermeneutic that resists the essentializing tendencies of neoliberal capitalist rhetoric sometimes revealed through the categories and structures/agents of World Music and CCM.

ICM creativity for mission is also a place for radical engagement with culture, a site of postcolonial resistance, and opportunity for creative collaboration with others for the bringing about of a new heaven and earth.

---

53. "If the church is to be an agent of the kingdom in the present variety of cultural and multicultural settings . . . then there must be a place and a process for Scripture to engage culture, and culture to engage Scripture." Rynkiewich, "Mission, Hermeneutics, and the Local Church," 48.

54. Walls, *Cross-Cultural Process in Christian History*, 76–78. From the creative convergence of diversities in Christ emits the spectrum of divergence with all creation for a new song that ushers hope and healing.

ICM creativity for mission is borne out of a pre-systematic ontology that deems creativity as *prior* to Christianity as an institutional construct (or for that matter any religion). As such, ICM creativity as defined here can be an effective tool for evangelism since it transcends cultural and religious essentialisms while at the same time maintains a radical continuity in terms of the *creatio Dei*. The space in-between indigeneity and cosmopolitanism offers the buffer needed for continual contestation of creative identity, differential restructuring of authenticity with the other, and the hope of the Gospel embodied in "new song" for mission as the spatial-temporal medium for the negotiation of ICM identity.

ICMs are uniquely displaced, disembedded, and dispossessed to occupy the interstices between the old and new anthropologies. As they negotiate their identities, they may:

1. Enact creative ministries as pathways to invite participation from others, engage in fruitful dialogue, and fresh research initiatives to discern the times.

2. Integrate theological creative vision, church revitalization and renewal, and specialized creative ministries.

3. Partner with local churches to form Covenant Creative Communities for mission that integrate a good "mix" between people from all walks of life for the creative transformation of the city.

Summarizing, creative mission is enlarging creative space with God. It involves extending God's invitation to others in the collaborative and collective task of God's creative remaking of the world in Christ by the power of the Holy Spirit.

As ICMs "dare to make new mistakes" (Tienou 2009, 29), as they create places for the becoming of the Body of Christ, we hear both, a call and a challenge. To evoke the imagery from Ezek 47:1–13, the call is to join in the flow of the River (the Holy Spirit) where it meets and mixes with the sea (the world) in order to create estuarine environments amid the turbulence of global complexity (See Appendix G, Estuary Cultures). The challenge, as in Ezekiel's case, is to actually get "in the water" until we can no longer "pass through" on our own (Ezek 47:5) and to collectively remember that the Creator God who brought us thus far will lead us onward in voicing a new song with others that will echo through eternity, with Christ.

APPENDIX A

Musical Creativity and Missiology

ETHNOMUSICOLOGY HAS DEMONSTRATED A link between music (as conceptualization, behavior, and resulting sound), the creation of meaning, and the shaping of identity within a group.[1] The historical relationship of the church to the arts for worship in general has been recounted elsewhere.[2] However, discourse pertaining to the formative potential of music until very recently has for most part been lacking in missiology.

It is important to establish at the outset the distinction between music, in general, and musical creativity, in the way it applies here. Previously, in academia, discussions concerning the role of music in Christianity have focused primarily on Christian worship.[3] Recently, there is significant contribution on the subject of music and theology. Again, this has been mostly in the global North.[4] In comparison, missiological reflection concerning music/arts in mission has been sparse.[5] The Fourth Edition of *Perspectives on the World Christian Movement* (Winter et al 2009)[6] contains no substantial discussion of the role of music *per se* in Christian mission. While the topic may have been broached in consultations at Edinburgh 2010,

---

1. Merriam, *Anthropology of Music*; Nettl, *Study of Ethnomusicology*; Stokes, "Introduction"; Seeger, *Why Suyá Sing*.

2. Harbison, "Redeeming the Arts."

3. Wren, *Praying Twice*; Hawn, *One Bread, One Body*; Schrag and Neeley, *All The World Will Worship*; Farhadian, *Christian Worship Worldwide*; and, more recent, Ingalls et al., *Christian Congregational Music*.

4. Notably, Begbie's *Theology, Music, and Time*; Begbie and Guthrie, *Resonant Witness*; and Guthrie's *Creator Spirit*.

5. Hunt, *Music in Missions*.

6. Winter et al., *Perspectives on the World Christian Movement*.

apparently, it was not a major theme.[7] No significant discourse or literature directly related to the subject has been generated from the event. Again, in the light of the recent focus on urban missions, the recently published *Reaching the City: Reflections on Urban Mission for the Twenty-first Century* (Casiño 2012),[8] an EMS publication, contains no article that explores music or the arts in the urban scenario.

A recent and notable exception includes Krabill *et al*'s *Worship and Mission for the Global Church* (2013). This work includes and builds upon the cumulative works of several others, most notably Brian Schrag (SIL International), Frank Fortunato (Heart Sounds International, OM, USA), Paul Neely, and Robin Harris (International Council of Ethnodoxologists).

Apparently, the dearth of missiological literature related to music is owed partly to a "opacity" of music and the arts in general (Begbie 2000, 3, 4), rather than on the actual nature or potential of music for mission. Further, there is a dearth of institutions/seminaries in the United States that have dedicated programs involving music and the arts with a specific focus on mission (an exception may be Fuller's Brehm Center in Pasadena, CA).[9] In 2008, the theme of the ASM (American Society of Missiology) conference was on music and mission. The shift in the discourse from music to the category of "arts" and mission has been helpful. It has facilitated the creation of a broader platform and greater visibility to the role of music and the arts in the context of Christianity. For example, at the recently concluded Lausanne Global Leadership Forum (LGLF) in Bangalore, India, in July 2013, there was an Arts and Mission focus group that contributed to the overall agenda at the forum.[10] On one hand, this may be seen as a step forward. On the other hand, the problem remains as to how local indigenous

---

7. "Study Themes," http://www.edinburgh2010.org/en/study-themes/main-study-themes.html.

8. Casiño et al., *Reaching the City*.

9. In the Global North, however, many programs address theology and the arts in general, e.g., Institute for Theology, Imagination, and the Arts at St. Andrews in Scotland; Theology and arts programs in Duke University (DITA) led by Dr. Jeremy Begbie, and a course to be launched in 2014 combining ethnomusicology and theology at London School of Theology. Helpfully, yet more generally, some publications have addressed the issue of music and culture (Begbie, *Resounding Truth*; Hawn, *One Bread, One Body*; and King, "Music," 584–89). Further exploration is needed for the situation in the Global South. Although, with some degree of confidence we might say that missiological literature on the subject from writers based in the Global South is relatively less compared to what is produced in the Western hemisphere and exported to the Global South.

10. Interview with ministry worker who in the past had been invited to Lausanne but chose not to attend, London, UK, July 2013. Also, such tenor is reflected in interviews with prominent indigenous scholars in the academy in North America.

agents respond to (or participate in the creation of) global manifestos proposed by organizational cultures that for most part appear anchored in power differentials and perspectives generated amongst a dominant minority (with ties) located in the global North.

APPENDIX B

Adaptation of Csikszentmihalyi's (1988, 1997, 1999) Systems Model of Creativity for ICMs in Mission

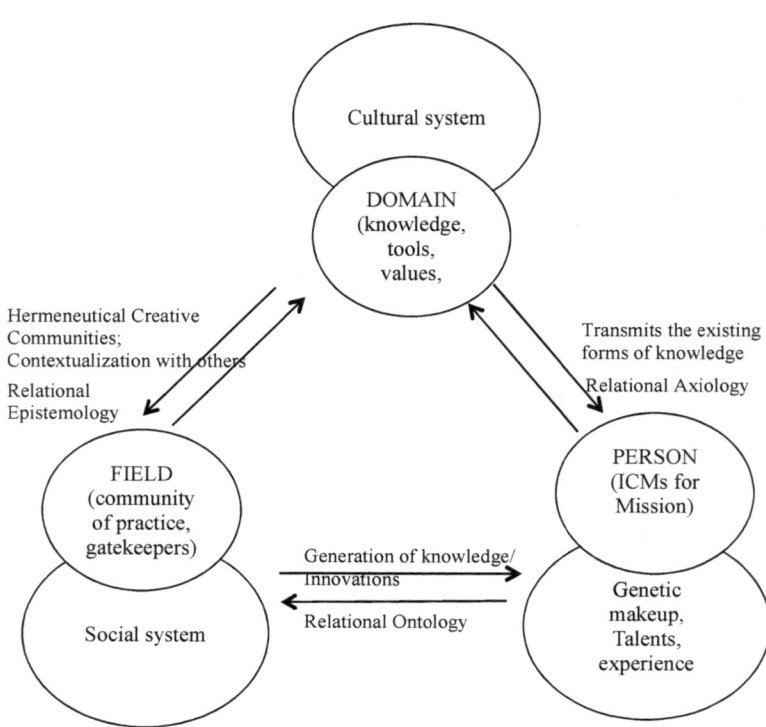

APPENDIX C

Creative Construction: Toward the Development of a Sonic Theology

THOMISTIC METAPHYSICS PROVIDES US a framework to explore the relation between form and meaning.[1] An often-neglected question concerning the nature of form has to do with what exactly does form consist of apart from the meaning assigned to it. According to Thomas Aquinas,

> A thing cannot be unless it possesses an act of being, and the thing that possesses an act of being is thereby rendered an essence/existence composite. If an essence has an act of being, the act of being is limited by that essence whose act it is.[2]

Aquinas' distinction between speculative and practical science seemed at first to succumb to a dualism between the created order (practical) and the truth (speculative) underlying it. But the distinction between "essence" and "existence" is helpful to clarify syncretistic, and avoid pantheistic, approaches to construction: it is not so much whether or not musical instruments are spiritual, but what sort of spirituality do they mediate? According to Gaven Kerr, as per Thomistic metaphysics:

1. Approaches to form differ concerning how people perceive and understand form. This is not a study of "formalism" in art for which we may need to revisit Kant's approach to form and others such as Clive Bell and his theory of "significant form." Clive Bell, *Art* (New York: Capricorn Books, 1958). Seeing things for what they are, ends in themselves and significantly so because of "God" in them. For Bell, however, God is impersonal. Guthrie draws on the work of Bell, without adopting his philosophy, and writes that "The great capacity of the artist is the ability to recognize the *significance* of 'ordinary things,' to perceive the universal in the particular, the God-in-all-things" (2011, 161).

2. Kerr, "Aquinas: Metaphysics."

In immaterial substances, essence is related to existence as potency to act. The latter follows insofar as what receives existence stands in potency to the existence that it receives. But all things receive existence from the being whose essence is its existence, in which case the existence that any one finite thing possesses is an act of existence that actuates a corresponding potency: the essence. Thomas has thus shown that immaterial substances do indeed have an element of potency, but this need not be a material potency.[3]

This naturally leads me to ask: in what sense do artists relate or interact with their materials in order to mediate and articulate power? Further, what might this imply for ways in which "sound" is constructed? In Aquinas' metaphysic, is sound "material"? If so, what is its cause? This leads us to consider Aquinas' second point in the nature of metaphysics: For Aquinas, "Insofar as essence/existence composites merely have, but are not, existence, they participate in existence in order to exist" (ibid.).[4] Materials, therefore, comprise part of the essence in which they participate. In other words, "essences exist, but they do not exist essentially, they participate in their acts of existence" (ibid.).[5]

This approach is comparable to the "Radical Orthodox Proposal" that assigns value in the transcendent because of its participation in the transcendent (Bellini 2010, 84). Peter Bellini reminds us that even Plato, in his dualism, actually celebrates physicality "in its suspension from . . . transcendence" (ibid.). From this we might ask, what is the nature of the greater "essence" that inspires persons to creativity and in which they themselves participate.

Pertinent to our discussion is Aquinas' approach to the relation between form and matter. Simply, form (for example, a statue) is made up of matter

---

3. Gaven Kerr, "Aquinas: Metaphysics." *IEP*, http://www.iep.utm.edu/aq-meta/ (accessed December 4, 2012).

4. For Aquinas, participation consists of:

   1. When something receives a specific form of what "pertains universally to another."

   2. A subject participates in the "accidents" that it has—e.g., a statue participates in the shape of the statue.

   3. An effect participates in its cause when the effect is not equal to the power of that cause. The effect particularizes and determines the scope of the cause; for the effect acts as the determinate recipient of the power of the cause (Kerr 2012, IEP, http://www.iep.utm.edu/aq-meta/).

5. "The act of existence then is individuated to the essence whose act it is, and this because the essence merely participates in, and thereby limits, the act of existence that it possesses" (Kerr 2012, IEP).

(for example, marble). From a metaphysical standpoint, form is "the principle whereby the matter has the particular structure that it has, and matter is simply that which stands to be structured in a certain way,"[6] a thing's intelligible nature. Matter therefore is a principle of potency in a thing. For Aquinas, the essence of a thing is the composition of its matter and form.[7] This does not mean a reduction to materialism but rather in the light of an "ontology of participation," it invites a "sacramental or liturgical" and even "doxological" approach to materiality and creation (cf. Bellini 2010, 84).

Interestingly, the adoption of Indian classical musical instruments (forms) as part of "Christian" worship gatherings signals a willingness on the part of the church to include and recognize the role of such musical forms in the place of Christianity. However, the question has been asked: to what extent have the underlying meanings of forms been addressed in the course of adoption? Many Indian Christians still find it difficult to participate in the instruction/discipling process related to the schooling of Indian classical music. Is there a way that a theology of form might help Christians to better negotiate their participation in musical ways of being along with musicians from other religious traditions? At an existential level the question may not seem relevant, since people appropriate classical forms and there does not seem to be any opposition to their being used in Christianity. However, from a theoretical and theological perspective, if there is meaning in form, then what meaning is being constructed and mediated? In the words of David Brown, "What matters is whether it provides the requisite signals, not its overall quality" (2012, 280).[8]

Again, a Radical Orthodox perspective is helpful since it invites a Trinitarian ontology of participation that emphasizes "peace even in difference"; dialogue is a way of being in this "differential unity" of mutual being (Bellini 2010, 85). Differential unity in this case includes mutuality in formation—the Father creates space for the Son and the operative power of the Spirit. The Incarnation of the Son is a dimension of the creativity of God. It is the place for the de-formation of Christ (the process of leaving His heavenly abode to become human in the purest form of its expression) for the sake of the re-formation of the world[9] through the Spirit, inviting

6. Kerr, "Matter and Form."
7. Kerr, "Matter and Form."
8. Brown, "Experience, Symbol, and Revelation," 280. Addressing the role of religious experience though popular art and culture, David Brown reiterates that God's power to communicate divine presence "through a gaudy statue in a church cannot be denied." They "key issue" are "what is being communicated and the strategies employed."
9. "The goodness of creation and physicality reaffirmed in the Incarnation and

humanity to join in being co-creators with God in the bringing about of a new heaven and earth.

TOWARD A SONIC THEOLOGY

However, what is the place of sound in the "ontology of participation" in God (*metousia Theou*)? We do not have the space for a full construction of a theology of sound here but this could be an area where contextualized theology needs to focus, especially when it comes to mission in the context of a Vedic, sonic Indian theology. A "sonic theology" in the context of the (Vedic) classical Indian music tradition in India assumes the primacy of sound in creative intelligence; it links sacred sound with Vedic sacrifice. According to Beck, the need of Hindu theism is "for a concept of sacred sound that was subordinate to a principal deity yet could manifest itself at random in the real world, that is, within human consciousness."[10]

What is the Matter with Sound?

What is the place of sound in Christian theology? In the context of this research, such a discussion plays a significant role in how ICMs interact with others and mediate their musical creativity. In the context of our discussion, would sound qualify as matter? The path to this answer is beyond the scope of this chapter. However, the question must be asked, especially in the light of the theistic structure of Vedic Hinduism that affects millions of people in the world and the task of mission of key informants in this study.

In addition, in the course of research I came across several Indian Christians who felt inhibited to the extent in which they could participate in the cultural musical traditions of their Hindu friends. The inability to immerse themselves in the cultural context of their "own" upbringing impeded their Christian witness. Successful compartmentalization of such experiences is a strategy that is widely employed. According to the Vedic Hindu tradition, God is sound, the primal "unstruck sound."[11] This seems suspicious to some Christians. According to one young Indian Christian musician, to sing some of the "chants" would be to worship their "gods." For another, to be in the audible range of the mantra would amount to submitting oneself to being spiritually affected by such sonic phenomena. For others, participation in

---

Resurrection anticipates an eschatological hope for an embodied existence in the new creation." Bellini, *Participation*, 85; Smith, *Introducing Radical Orthodoxy: Mapping A Post-Secular Theology*, 199.

10. Beck, *Sonic Theology*, n.p.

11. Beck, *Sonic Theology*; cf. Wulff, "On Practicing Religiously," 153.

musical activities (including schools of learning) along with Hindu others would amount to participation in Hindu rituals.

There is difference between concepts of sacred sound between Indian and Western traditions. In Christianity, Christ is the Divine logos, the embodiment and not the actual sound of the word. There tends to be a separation between the words of Christ and the person of Christ. In Hinduism, however, language or the name of the deity is a verbal formula or mantra that is considered identical with the deity itself and is never discarded (Beck 1993, 15). The sound of the God of the Bible is extremely significant not least because of the place it holds amongst the writers in causation, for example, bringing the world into being (Genesis 1:1ff.) and causing growth in nature (cf. Psalm 29; 50:1).

The sound or "voice" of the God of the Bible is always in conjunction with the Person of His Being (cf. Deuteronomy 26:14; 28:1; Jeremiah 42:6), unlike the "unstruck sound" of Vedic Hinduism. From a purely physical approach, for sound to exist (as something to be heard), it must occur in time and space. Unlike the Vedic tradition, the context for sound is the creative space (and time) of God. Sound, as that which is heard, is dependent upon matter in order for it to exist (for example, air as a medium since sound cannot exist in a vacuum).[12] To clarify, there is a context within which we experience and understand music as sound—this is true from a cultural standpoint as well as from an ontological basis: Sound is not ultimate; God is.[13]

Sound and Form

In his book, The Musical Instinct (2010), neuroscientist Philip Ball writes concerning music as a basic human instinct, "there is very little that is preordained in this palette . . . it is not determined by nature. We are free to choose the notes of music, and that's what makes the choices interesting."[14] It is crucial to distinguish between sound and God—since sound exists in God's space and time, sound can never be abstracted from him and can never become God.

---

12. According to an online source, sound is: the sensation produced by stimulation of the organs of hearing by vibrations transmitted through the air or other medium. (2) mechanical vibrations transmitted through an elastic medium, traveling in air at a speed of approximately 1087 feet (331 meters) per second at sea level (3) the particular auditory effect produced by a given cause: the sound of music (http://dictionary.reference.com/browse/sound?s=t).

13. The hesitancy to mention the name of "Yahweh" amongst believing Jews has more to do with the understanding of Yahweh's otherness or holiness rather than the equation of sound with the name of God.

14. Ball, *Music Instinct*, 33.

In terms of participation, the capacity to "hear" sound is distributed differently amongst peoples. Ball addresses the issues of "The Atoms of Music: What are musical notes and how do we decide which to use?"[15] According to him, music, in terms of sound, or more specifically as patterned or "organized sound" is a result of a "collaboration" and interaction of nature and culture, "in which the listener too plays an active part" (ibid., 33). Using a geographical metaphor, Ball suggests, music is a journey through space "that unfolds in time and the effect of which depends on how clearly we can see where we are and how well we recall where we have come from."[16]

Biologically speaking, how we "hear" music depends upon the physical construction of our ears, bodies, and somewhat generally, our location with regard to the physical environment.[17] Each human hears differently—some through ears, while others through other parts of the body.[18] Evelyn Glennie, in her lecture on "How to Truly Listen" recollects how she learned to hear subtle differences in tone through reverberations in different areas of her body. She teaches us that to truly hear we actually need more than

---

15. Ball, *Music Instinct*, 32–90.

16. Ball, *Music Instinct*, 32–90. The following questions are relevant: Are cause and effect that linear? Or is there a non-linearity, an unpredictability that grows with every sound made in a sequence? (Rynkiewich 2013, email correspondence).

17. According to the Stanford Encyclopedia of Philosophy (SEP) on "Sounds":
Indeed, the various philosophical pronouncements about the nature of sounds can be rather neatly classified according to the spatial status each of them assigns to sounds. Where are sounds? Are they anywhere? The main relevant families of answers include proximal, medial, distal, and aspatial theories. Proximal theories would claim that sounds are where the hearer is. Medial theories—exemplified by mainstream acoustics—locate sounds in the medium between the resonating object and the hearer. Distal theories consider sounds to be located at the resonating object. Finally, aspatial theories deny spatial relevance to sounds. There are significant variants of each of these. Sound theories can also be classified according to other dimensions, such as the metaphysical status they accord to sounds (for instance, as occurring events as opposed to properties or dispositions). Casati and Dokic, "Sounds," http://plato.stanford.edu/archives/sum2011/entries/sounds/>. It is to be noted, however, that "Aspatial theories deny either (i) that sounds are intrinsically spatial, or (ii) that auditory perception is intrinsically spatial." However, this is further explored based upon the Kantian notion that objective entities exist point to the fact of the existence of space. The imaginary "Hero" is proposed as a "thought-experiment" who is supposed to embody sound in terms of purely non-spatial experiences. Hypothetically, this might be a possibility, but we need to ask the question: "where is Hero?" which again brings us back to spatial notions of sound. The argument that God is not sound and specifically not "unstruck sound" is one that is beyond the scope of this project.

18. Glennie, "How to Truly Listen." Glennie uses the example of how a person laying under the marimba would experience the sound quite differently than people sitting elsewhere in the audience.

ears.[19] What is important is not merely that of "form" but the embodiment and enactment of such. Earlier, we saw how the forms that God creates are not extrinsic to His being.[20] The fact that "the earth is the Lord and its fullness thereof" (cf. Psalm 24) assigns a certain kind of sanctity to creation and all of life, because of who created it and not because of the fact of its existence. Wolfhart Pannenberg makes a point concerning Aquinas' use of the Aristotelian principle that "form gives being" whereas "the question of the essence of a thing, and the description of its essence, always presuppose its existence."[21] The worth of creation, including humanity, is derived from the fact of its Creator.[22] James K. A. Smith reasons for a "Creational Hermeneutic" and draws from Augustine according to whom:

> A corporeal object has some concord between its parts, otherwise it could not exist at all. Therefore, it was made by him who is the head of all concord. A corporeal object enjoys a certain degree of peace, due to its having form. Without that it would be nothing. Therefore he is the creator of matter, from whom all peace comes, and who is the uncreated and most perfect form. Matter participates in the something belonging to the ideal world, otherwise it would not be matter . . . . For all existence as such is good.[23]

The materials that the artist uses to construct instruments are imbued with God's goodness (Genesis1: 31). Everything that is created in God's space and time must in some sense conform to this characteristic feature of God's creation in order to fulfill God's purpose. Material forms, therefore, need to be fashioned and used in accord with God's purpose, but not necessarily to coax "meaning" out of it.[24] It is not the assigned meaning that gives vitality to the form, even though this seems to be the approach with efforts that try to redeem the created order without acknowledging the "primordial goodness of embodied human existence."[25] Further, according to James

---

19. Glennie: "What are we trying to say through music? Allow your body to be a "resonating chamber" for the music. There is a "life" of the sound. There is a journey. Experience the life of the sound after the note is struck" ("How to Truly Listen").

20. Here, I am adopting a traditional theistic view, unlike Kant who denied that God has a nature in the first place, a notion rejected by Plantinga. Carder, "Platonism and Theism."

21. Pannenberg, *Systematic Theology*, 355.

22. Wright, *Mission of God*.

23. Smith, *Fall of Interpretation*, 155.

24. Contrasted with what Guthrie suggests, Guthrie, *Creator Spirit*, 153.

25. Smith, *Fall of Interpretation*, 154.

Smith, Christian philosophy "must withdraw such an evaluation of finitude and temporality" (ibid., 155).

TOWARD A THEOLOGY OF "AUTHENTIC" FORM FOR MUSICAL CREATIVITY

The rationale that we employ here is not intended as a comprehensive approach to address a theology of authentic musical creativity. Rather, here we attempt to address the issue of authenticity of form as it pertains to musical creativity. In a manner of speaking, when (the truth of) form is violated, God is offended. A prime example of this is Eve falling prey to the Tempter in humanity's "first act of violence." The fruit of the tree of "the knowledge of good and evil" was in a sense consumed by what she "saw" as its function and perceived as its aesthetic appeal before she actually ate it (Genesis 3:6). Should we say that Eve disregarded the meaning assigned to the fruit by God and instead received the meaning assigned to it by the serpent? The interim between conceptualization or "inner-self-talk" and actual committing of the act is a significant pause in the history of the world.

In one sense, the act of eating the fruit was a willful disobedience on her part to God's commandment. At the risk of being reductionistic yet pertinent to our discussion concerning form and implications for the practice of ICMs for mission, we make the following observation. Eve's eating of the fruit radically altered her being and knowing (and so with Adam) (cf. Genesis 3:7). The moral construction of materiality is apparent in Eve's disregard of the "unseen" (yet existent) dimension of the form. From the Tempter's meaning it was something to be desired, but from God's it was something to avoid. Mark Wynn responds to David Brown's work God of Enchantment of Place (2004) and explores a "'sacramental' conception of the material world and its role in mediating, integrally and non-inferentially, various kinds of religious significance."[26] Referring to Brown, he writes, to ask whether or not a form "aids an experience of God or not" (ibid.) is not enough. The point is what sort of experience of God does it mediate—alienation or shalom?

The "disobedience" on Eve's part is something that God could have forgiven; he addresses it ultimately through Jesus Christ. Why the wait? Why did it have to take an incarnation of God? God's creativity begins with His creation of space for divine Otherness even before the creation of the world as we know it. For now, the greater problem was the disfigurement of God's handiwork: It was not merely the act of disobedience in and of itself that was the biggest problem; it was that the "likeness" of God (humanity and creation) was now corrupted; something that could only

---

26. Wynn, "Re-enchanting the World," 116.

be restored by the resurrection of God in Christ. Death had entered the "paint" and now all creation is smeared with the color of death. Further, this condition was not automatically brought about by the act of violation, but brought on by God Himself. Therefore, it is only at the altar of worship of the sacrificial atonement, ascension, and *eschaton* of Christ that all form in its material existence is entirely re-signified.[27] Nevertheless, how do we build our argument up until this point?

We notice the domino effect of sin on all creation: Genesis 3 details the pronouncement of the "curse"; it is to be noted that a direct result of the violation of God's expressive art form is the corruption of the material base—"cursed is the ground because of you."[28] Terje Stordalen's work in clarifying the role of "Mother earth in biblical and Hebrew literature" (2010) is significant in this regard. According to Stordalen, the earth is a locus for "production" and potential revivification for human beings. For ancient Hebrew imagination the grave in certain respects resembles a uterus. Further, the earth represents God's covenantal counterpart (Genesis 13:9). It is polluted when the inhabitants break this covenant (Isaiah 24:5-6). Further, the earth is bound by covenant to testify to the aberrations of its inhabitants and then to punish violators even though the sustenance of their very beings depend upon such covenant.[29] (2010, 120-125).

We notice that the pronouncement of the curse is not directly aimed at Adam and Eve (as we typically understand personhood as separate from the earth). But this does not mean that their person or being is unaffected. Rather, it is through their act of disobedience that the earth inherits the curse and the effects of the curse (Genesis 3:17; also, cf. Genesis 8:21). Therefore, Paul writes that they are not so much cursed by God but now live "under" the curse of the law (Galatians 3:10-13; 4:5). The earth needs redeeming because it has inherited the curse of God. But what about humanity? Humans need redeeming because their beings (having being made from the earth—the material substance of their individual and collective being)[30] received corruption through the disregard of God's command (Romans 5:19a). Let us explore this a little more.

---

27. Concerning the faith of figures such as Abraham and others in the context of the covenant of God ultimately fulfilled in Jesus Christ please see Wright, *Mission of God*, 325; 352.

28. "... humanity's denial of God has smeared creation at large. God's good *shalom* is spoiled." Begbie, *Resounding Truth*, 204.

29. Stordalen, "Mother Earth in Biblical Hebrew Literature," 120–25.

30. From this perspective, "creation care" is not so much because it is a mandate given to humanity by God. The fact that it is, is not disputed (Gen 1: 28). However, does the material substance from "which he was taken" (Gen 3:23) have something to

Here, we need to consider the fact that it was out of the earth that the Lord God formed man (Genesis 2:7). The substance of humanity was no longer merely the "dust of the ground" but that it was formed by God and infused with the life breath of God (Genesis 2:7b). The "breath of life" informs the material substance, "dust from the ground" (cf. ibid.). But now a part of the substance[31] of the human is cursed: the ground. The locus of "ground" as a place for the mediating of a spiritual reality may be inferred from Genesis 4:10,11: " . . . the voice of your brother's blood is crying to me from the ground. And now you are cursed from the ground . . . ."[32] This does not in any sense diminish or change the significance of the Adamic curse in Genesis 3. Several theologians endorse the redemption from this curse through Jesus Christ -the mystery of the union of humanity with the body and blood of Jesus Christ -. Prominently, from the Orthodox perspective, according to John Zizioulas:

> If soteriology means, as it was the case in the patristic period, <u>not so much a juridical reality</u> by means of which forgiveness is granted for an act of disobedience, but rather a realization of theosis, as communion of man—and through him of creation—in the very life of the Trinity, then this identification acquires existential importance: the Church's ministry realizes here and now the very saving work of Christ, which involves the very personal life and presence of the one who saves (1985, 212, underline mine).

A *creatio Dei* soteriology leans heavily on this non-juridical aspect of participation in God through Christ by the Spirit.[33] The ontology of form

---

do with how we may need to interpret the mandate of Gen 1:28? A positive response to this question may help understand why God would ask humanity to care for creation in the first place.

31. According to Zizioulas, in "Ministry and Communion," it was through the Western medieval influence and later Protestantism that the notion of "created grace" was used of "an abstraction of Christ's 'acts' or 'influence' from his person" (1985, 212n9).

32. The role of the ground could be interpreted purely metaphorically or rhetorically. However, this need not detract from the fact of its significance, even though we may not fully understand the implications of this for a Metaphysic. However, the inherent connectedness between humanity and the ground, form of expression and material substance is retained.

33. The mystery of the eucharistic encounter is much more than merely understanding how God's redeeming grace enters and transforms earthly reality. It has also to do with the substantive material dimension—the mystery of the sense in which Christ's body and blood are metaphorically substantive and adequate for the material regeneration of all humanity (cf. Rom 5) ultimately ratified through the resurrected Body of Christ, by which the presentation of our bodies becomes a living sacrifice in Christ (cf. Rom 12:1). The material existence of humanity and creation is entirely justified and

takes seriously the idea that "the divine can be mediated in our experience of material forms" (Wynn 2012, 115).[34] Mark Wynn draws on the ontology of David Brown in *God and Enchantment of Place* (2004), which is worth reproducing here:

> If the natural world is treated as an arena for 'proving' God's existence, then once such proofs are undermined, retreat would seem inevitable. But the question remains why proof should be seen as the only way of experiencing the divine impact on our world. Instead of always functioning as an inference, there was the possibility that a divine structure is already implicit in certain forms of experience of the natural world . . . . In other words, it would be a matter of an immanent given rather than of certain neutral features pointing instrumentally beyond themselves (Wynn 2012, 115).

This corroborates the hypothesis that there is more to form than meaning—especially, the social construction of meaning. Does this mean that there is a deeper and spiritual or "perfect" meaning for everything that needs to be sought out? Not necessarily; But it does mean that in deciphering or assigning meaning, God should never be left out of the picture,[35] which is the task of the hermeneutical community. How do ICMs re-signify the material significance of the forms they employ?[36] Further, how do they embody Christ as the Living Text in the negotiation of their identities? In Chapter 8 we develop the biblical metaphor of Person as Text with implications for ICMs in mission.

In "The Symbolology of Dionysius"[37] Victor Bychkov addresses the Areopagite's approach to "cataphatic symbols"—that which contains the

---

signified through the fact that "God condemns sin in the flesh of Jesus Christ" "the one true Israelite"! Dr. Timothy C. Tennent, Sermon at Asbury Theological Seminary, Wilmore, KY, on April 8, 2014.

34. In Acts 17, the problem with the materialism of the Stoics and Epicureans was that it was divorced from the Person of God. However, to do away with the significance of material forms would be to "throw the baby out with the bath water," so to speak.

35. Conversation with Dr. David Thompson on the issue in November 2012, Asbury Theological Seminary.

36. According to Begbie, "when we speak about music . . . . We turn wilderness into gardens, empty land into housing, wasteland into forests, vibrations in the air into symphonies" (*Resounding Truth*, 207). Begbie further suggests the task of vocation should include discovering, respecting, developing ("develop created realities"), healing, anticipating, together (207–9).

37. Bychkov, "Symbolology of Dionysius the Areopagite," 28–63. Bychkov studies the writings of Dionysius, an author "at the turn of the sixth century" (2012, 63n2). Dionysius differentiates broadly between two kinds of symbols: *gnoseological* and

likeness of God—that contain good, beauty, or life: it is not that these exist in God, but that "God is the Cause of all those value-related properties of being."[38] In this sense, therefore, cataphatic symbols are "completely different from the One Whom they denote" (ibid.). Symbols are *eikona* or images of their "otherworldly Archetype." They signify "the corresponding aspect of the spiritual-energetic action of God outward, into the world" (ibid., 42). Interestingly, names of God and other verbal construct "provide the impulse for a hermeneutic procedure" (ibid., 45), by which symbols correspond to and point to the personhood of God.[39] However, more than that, they allow for participation in the nature of what is being symbolized. The words of C. S. Lewis in *Mere Christianity* are relevant in terms of participating *via* construction in the Trinitarian being of God:

> The whole dance, or drama, or pattern of this three-Personal life is to be played out in each one of us; or . . . each one of us has to enter that pattern, take his place in the dance. Good things as well as bad, you know, are caught by a kind of infection. If you want to get warm you must stand near the fire; if you want to be wet you must get into the water. If you want joy, power, peace, eternal life, you must get close to, or even into, the thing that has them. If you are close to it, the spray will wet you: if you are not, you will remain dry (1960, 153; also cited in Seamands 2008, 165).

For further reflection: In this age of pluralism, how do forms of musical creativity symbolize the unique and distinct person of Christ, God's-likeness? According to Bychkov, sacred symbols "serve both to denote

---

sacral-liturgic. I appreciate these terms and their significance for music as symbol, wherein music in terms of lyrics (verbal symbols and images) are "bearers of sacred knowledge"—usually susceptible to verbal expression but not always ("Symbolology of Dionysius the Areopagite," 40). Sacral-liturgical symbols refer to "mysterious-ontological," "mystical-aesthetic" forms such as beauty, light, fragrance; it usually cannot be comprehended by the mind but is *present through communion*" (40). Gnoseological symbols can be further divided into apophatic symbols, cataphatic symbols or "like unlikeness" and "unlike likenesses" (40).

38. "God is the Cause of the [very] ability of all who partake in likeness to be alike and is the substance of likeness-in-itself" ("Symbolology of Dionysius the Areopagite," 42).

39. For example, *Seraphim* is translated as "burning ones" "indicates their ceaseless and eternal revolution about Divine Principles, their heat and keenness, the exuberance of their intense, perpetual, tireless activity, and their ability elevatively and energetically to make those below like themselves . . . ." (from Dionysius CH VII 1, in Bychkov, "Symbolology of Dionysius the Areopagite," 45). Again, regarding the sun that radiates real good to the whole earth, "It is precisely thanks to the rays of the Good that there have arisen and function all the spiritual supraworldly essence, powers, and energies — indeed, the entire Universe, including the visible sun" (43).

many phenomena of celestial space and to assist congregants in achieving real mysterial-theurgic joining to (communion with) the divine sphere" (2012, 62). In the sites of transition occupied by ICMs hold potential to be channels for the process of musical construction accomplish "the *theurgic mystery of knowledge, action* (ἐνεργείας), *and perfection* (accomplishment, τελειώσεως)" (cf. ibid., 60).

Musical Creativity as More than Sound

Musical creativity includes more than sound. The place of the human body and movement play a significant role in extending the theological parameters for the construction of a "sonic" theology. Moving beyond tone and lyrics,[40] the inherent linkage between motivation, enactment, and expression of form are inseparable and dynamically interactive. Jorgensen draws from Webb Keane to demonstrate that "language does not reveal what a person really thinks or believes but serves as verbal artistry or to demonstrate social status" (2011, 200). This is one language ideology; there are others. In the context of such an ideology, however, just because missionaries and converts use the same words they should not assume that they understand each other (ibid.). Rhetorical studies in music indicate that instrumental music conveys reality in ways that discursive forms cannot.[41] According to David Kirsh, cognitive scientist at the University of California, San Diego during a lecture on "enactive"—knowledge conveyed through action—thought at Stanford University:

> People harness materials for thought; including their bodies; their coupling is so tight the whole process is 'thinking'—a form of thinking, a coordinated system; It is more than embodied cognition, it is extended and distributed.[42]

---

40. Typical approaches for adopted for evaluation in ethnomusicology and theological evaluation of music. Woods and Walrath, *Message in the Music*; Parsons "Text, Tone, and Context."

41. In a discussion on the relation between tonal stimulation and physiological change, Leonard Meyer observes: "In the perception of music, the listener brings to the act of perception definite beliefs in the affective power of music. Even before the first sound is heard, these beliefs activate dispositions to respond in an emotional way.... And it seems more reasonable to suppose that the physiological changes observed are a response to the listener's mental set rather than to assume that tone as such can, in some mysterious and unexplained way, bring these changes about directly" (*Emotion and Meaning*, 11). I am not sure I agree with Meyer entirely—first it places the locus of transformation in the capacity of the listener's "perception"; second, it diminishes the significance of mystery; three, while it affirms the effect of thoughts on physiology, it does not consider changes in mental set as a result of physiological response.

42. Kirsh, "How to Think with Bodies and Things" (italic mine). Pertaining to the

Steven Pinker in his capacity as professor and director of the Center for Cognitive Neuroscience at MIT (Massachusetts Institute of Technology) has determined that: "Language is not a cultural artifact that we learn the way we learn to tell time or how the federal government works. Instead, it is a distinct piece of the biological makeup of our brains" (1994, 18). If we interpret music purely in terms of its role as a decipherable and meaning-making cultural artifact, then we clearly miss out on the formative role it plays in shaping who we are as human beings in the image of God. In this sense, therefore, musical creativity problematizes certain foundational tenets concerning the social construction of reality. Apparently, there is more to the process of construction than what might be gleaned through processes of ratio-cognition.

Amos Yong examines Luke's "multisensory epistemology" in order to reveal, "Spirit-inspired engagement with the world is not limited solely to that of speech (and hearing) (2011, 78). He traces the numerous instances when Jesus uses touch to communicate his presence in Luke's narrative. He concludes that "the power of touch should not be underestimated as a vehicle of the Spirit, and this is felt rather than heard or seen (ibid., italic mine). Further, "embodied and affective reason is just as important as cognitive reason" (ibid.).

What does the above mean for processes of construction through musical creativity?

First, it draws attention to the significance of being "caught up," so-to-speak, with the process of music making; it is into this constructive process that others are invited to participate. Borrowing from the field of dance, according to Karen LaMothe:

> In becoming a dancer, in learning to participate consciously in her or his own process of bodily becoming, a person is exercising and developing her or his capacity to participate in an ongoing act of creation: to let there be light by becoming that light in the world . . . becoming a dancer and manifesting light are movements in which all humans participate to some degree or another (2012, 142).

---

use of words, Kirsh quotes Ludwig Wittgenstein, who writes in Philosophical Investigations (1953): "When I think in language, there aren't 'meanings' going through my mind in addition to the verbal expressions: the language is itself the *vehicle of thought*." Also, Emilio Ribes-Inesta, "Human Behavior as Language," 109–21, suggests three dimensions of language of human behavior: as medium, instrument, and as a form of life. She bases her thesis on Wittgenstein's definition of Language Games: "Language is not limited to a psychological phenomenon, but rather it constitutes the functional dimensions under which human behavior develops and becomes meaningful."

What is striking about this last statement is that one does not merely learn to dance but what it means to become a dancer, to be the dance.[43] Furthermore, LaMothe explains how "sensory awareness" functions as a process of participation in the larger ontological reality of God and in knowledge creation. According to her, it is

> A capacity to create patterns of sensation and response that become our way of being in the world.
>
> As a need, it springs forth form our sensory awareness as an impulse to move in ways that express the careful attention to our bodily selves that we are practising.
>
> As an impulse to love, it is a capacity and need to create and become patterns of sensation and response that relate us in mutually-life-enabling ways to whatever and whomever supports our becoming (2012, 142-143, underline added).

LaMothe's explanation of "sensory awareness" through embodiment and enactment as capacity, need, and impulse to love are helpful for discerning how (and expanding ways in which) the process of musical creativity may be adapted for Christian mission. Based upon this we might ask: In what "capacity"—behavioral patterns that serve to invite others into the process of music-making—do ICMs operate as they construct their patterns of musical creativity? Further, given that the constructive process is never isolated from the creative being of the artist, how is such capacity sensationalized through the process of musical creativity? In what sense do others encounter and respond to such? Concerning need, in what sense do ICMs pay "careful attention" to their contexts and so "move in ways"- respond to the needs of the context? The idea of love as an impulse signals a primal call to ways of becoming Christ along with others.

Second, the felt power of the Spirit through the affective and embodied performativities is validated as a process of identity construction that is at least tantamount to what might be expected of ratio-cognitive processes. We arrive at this based upon the understanding that musical meaning via rational/ "intellectual" processes inherent to the context of the music itself (e.g., perceived meanings) and through so-called "extramusical" concepts (e.g., emotions and character) are not mutually exclusive (cf. Meyer 1956, 1-3).

For Roar Fotland, religion is and should be about transcendence, "the something more," and not what it is typically made out to be in the West, "the Christian Gospel as a system of ideas" (2008, 220-221). He suggests

---

43. Rynkiewich reminds us of Gary Zukov's "The Dancing Wu-li Masters: Zen Buddhism and Physics," wherein he says: "Its not the dancers, it's the dance."

the rediscovery of Christianity as a primal religion in order to restore the religious element in European Christianity.[44]

Third, musical being in essence is mediated through the physical being (embodiment and enactment, more fully articulated in Creative Performance) of the artist. The physical embodiment of creative potential and expression is consistent with God's "self-communicative presence in history" especially through the Incarnation of Jesus Christ. Further, it is Christ in whom the divine-human unity serves as a prototype, even a "promise that (by grace) other creaturely realities may be taken up into God's self-manifestation" (cf. Webster's introduction to Jüngel 2001, xvi). The material significance of the human body (cf. Romans 12:1) amplified in the resurrected body of Christ, and through Him the promise of the Resurrection for human body forms, reinforces the "primordial goodness of embodied human existence" (Smith 2012, 154). Form gives being (Aristotle, interpreted by Pannenberg 1991, 355). In this sense, musical creativity is a ministry of presence.[45]

Fourth, a theology of creativity with its valuation of the material imbues a moral value in "the particulars of the material world—cabbages and mountains, insects and rocks, songs and statues in all their concrete

---

44. Fotland refers to Harold Turner's six-feature framework for understanding primal religions as "authentically religious" and not just the epiphenomena of simple or preliterate societies as retold by Kwame Bediako, that are summarized as:
- A sense of kinship with nature (an "ecological aspect")
- A deep sense of finiteness and the need for an outside greater power
- The conviction that man is not alone in the universe (the reality of the spirit world and the assumption of intelligibility in the universe)
- The relational and interactive nature of spirit and human world
- The reality of the afterlife and the interconnectedness of "living dead" and "living living"
- The universe as sacramental—no sharp distinguishment between physical and spiritual (*Christianity in Africa*, 93–95; also cf. Fotland, "Southern Phase of Christianity," 221).

Some of these factors seem more immediately plausible amongst ICMs in mission. According to Bediako, Turner's "primal imagination" as a set of ideological constructs represents "a common religious heritage of humanity" (*Christianity in Africa*, 93–95). To what extent might these relate to processes of creative construction amongst ICMs in mission?

45. In Luke 6 we notice that after a significant time of prayer to God, Jesus is amidst the people who want to physically touch him because "power came out from him and healed them all" (vv. 12–19). More than anything else perhaps, the passage speaks to the place of prayer as communion with God in a way that facilitates the transfer of power that others may encounter, at least in the case of Jesus, and hence for Christ-followers. In what sense might ICMs be hope, healing, and comfort to those in need?

uniqueness" (cf. Seamands 2005, 122). For example, in Genesis 2:7 we observe the raw material being the dust of the earth inspired by the breath of God "and the man became a living creature." If God created the forms we have to work with in music, then the human agent/ artisan must necessarily presuppose the moral intelligibility of the Creator inherent to such basic form. To use such form in opposition to its intended use would be antithetical to its Intender.

Jeremy Montagu asks: "We know what we mean by harp and organ, but what did Moses mean by harp and organ in Genesis 4:21?" (2002, 1). Clearly context plays a large portion of how we interpret the use of instruments in the Bible. For example, in 2 Chronicles 7:6 we notice that King David makes instruments specifically for giving thanks and praise to God (also cf. 1 Chronicles 15:16; 2 Chronicles 29:26,27; Nehemiah 12:36). The fact that these were set apart for a specific purpose and not for general use ascribes a certain meaning that fuses physical/material construction and moral purpose. Could the construction of the instruments in and of themselves have symbolized a moral integrity to be maintained in how they were to be used and who used them?[46] To what extent was construction dependent upon the cultural predilections of the worshipping community is subject for further research.

The question of form and meaning is amplified in the face of the use of materials in the construction of musical instruments in certain contexts within Hinduism.[47] The divine worth of instruments is assigned by what they signify in terms of actual beliefs (cf. Beck 1993). From the point of view of a Christian doctrine of God, this is problematic since the material (matter) is itself created by God (Wright 2006, 397-420).

How might processes of the commodification of music, not excluding Contemporary Christian Music (CCM), relate to a process of theological creativity via creative construction? The material nature of the process of Creative Construction emphasizes the idea is not so much that God is real as an ontological abstraction, but whether "God is real here and now, for

---

46. Baumann, "Music and Worldview of Indian Societies in the Bolivian Andes," 101–22. In a study of Andean panpipes we discover that the "interlocking" pairs of panpipes represent a belief system where the supernatural unites with the earthly realities to represent a new "power" and "energy"—a new "bond of unity." The male and female counterparts that form the pairs of panpipes are made out of hard bamboo and wood respectively. This could suggest the separateness of the two natures (man and woman) and also points to the separate natures of creature and Creator. The instrument signifies a union between Creator and creation.

47. In Judaism, post 70 CE, the use of instruments in worship was forbidden; Jews in exile apparently "restricted their religious expression to vocalization." Levine, "Judaism and Music," 45.

me, between us, for the planet, in the world" (LaMothe 2012, 143). It is this patterning process by which musical creative construction intentionalizes space and time through action. It is in this "space" that the Logos, as being internal to God's being, becomes the "bearer of the *logoi*" generating "fresh speech-acts among his followers that become formative of God's renewed people" (Begbie 2012, 151).[48]

---

48. Begbie, "Openness and Specificity," 153, contends with Brown's suggestion that Christian revelation prevents an open and honest engagement with culture in order to "listen and learn" from it. I agree with Begbie that Christian revelation does actually or should help to be more open to God's presence in other cultures. However, I do see Brown's point that, in the past, Christianity has opted to view others through a lens that has distorted truth rather than offered a biblical perspective.

APPENDIX D

C3M—Covenant Creative Communities for Mission

THE FOLLOWING IS AN outline for embodying, enacting, and performing creativity in the context of mission. It is offered as a suggestion for initiating C3M as a movement in a given context.

Biblical References: Ezekiel 47:1-13; Exodus 31; 35:10-40:38; John 21:1-14

Metaphors—descriptive (Artisan); image (Net-Making/Net-Casting)

Description: Discipleship Networks + Creative Mission Communities

PURPOSE

C3M exists to invite people into a creative lifestyle with others. It facilitates theological thinking and critical creative expression. C3M are spaces to gather alongside others to create works that inspire and imagine a new reality in Christ. They draw on the creative potential of persons in community who are called to love God, love one another, and love the city through their creativities, arts included, and thereby to impact lives, change a city, and transform the world.

    Example: gathering together artists and others interested in participating through the creative arts in a city to collectively work on developing a series of artworks on a particular theme that addresses a need in the community (for example, human trafficking). Alternatively, artists could network with local churches and government to create a public liturgy—a series of works displayed in a city that will invite the public into imagining a better life in Christ through meditating on such artworks. Works could be displayed in stores, bus stops, or other public arenas for the purpose of initiating dialogue in the context of diversity.

C3M COVENANTAL AFFIRMATIONS (NOT A COMPREHENSIVE STATEMENT OF FAITH)

Based upon the life and teachings of Jesus Christ, we believe:

- Every person is creative—equally, in the image of God. Artisans are gifted with a unique creative intelligence to fabricate spaces for divine-human encounter (cf. Exodus 31, 36; Colossians 3:16) for God's glory.
- Every person is different. Everybody carries potential to be a significant contribution to his or her family and community. Every person is responsible to God for the use of gifts.
- Apart from tangible resources, we each need constant encouragement especially in the areas of our creative gifting and calling—to believe and to act upon it; along with this, the nurturing of our souls in order to truly create works that correspond with and heal our creative imaginations, inspire others, illuminate, and interrogate our surroundings.
- There is no substitute for individual hard work. However, we also need life-generating relationship with others to share in our passions and journey. This involves risk—opening ourselves to form relationships of trust over time by working with one another, sharing resources, learning, receiving and offering critique of another's works in an atmosphere of genuine respect and admiration.
- We need safe spaces to create where the diversity of differences in personality, race, ethnicity, sex, color, status etc., are not only places for overcoming fear, pride, and prejudices, but also, facilitate learning, growth, reconciliation, and healing.
- Specifically, we gather in order to:
- Embody the ontology (the why) of participation in Christ for the bringing about of a new heaven and earth (theological rootedness) through the creation of environments that nurture and celebrate the Creative Seed of the Gospel of Jesus Christ in every person
- (In such embodiment) Enact a critical awareness of our place and role in such participation by spiritually discerning the times in order to discern the needs of a given context, with a view to integrate into the lives of the community (contextualization)

Appendix D: C3M—Covenant Creative Communities for Mission

- (As we enact) Engage in a collective and collaborative multiplication of creativities amidst the admixture of diversities for the bringing about of godly community (creative mission). This will require confronting inherent fears and prejudices in a safe space along with others.

- (As we engage) Express works of justice, mercy, and compassion that integrate the Creative Seed of God's Word in the lives of people everywhere (e.g., neighborhoods, families, workplace etc.) that palpably address the needs of a given community.

- (As we express) Catalyze processes of change and transformation by inviting others to participate in creating works (individual and collective) that allows/ includes others to participate in tangible ways, restoring peace in households, between people, communities, and the transformation and renewal of the city (public liturgies)

- Journey with and learn from fellow creative "seed-bearers" from around the world through the mutual exchange and sharing of resources (stories, ideas, discoveries, gifts, and talents) for mutual encouragement and nurturing of creativities

- Establish sustainable partnerships with local "grass root" and indigenous artisans as well as with those around the world (global and glocal) in a way that furthers collaborative learning, socio-economic upliftment of the marginalized and poor (human and community development)

- Art As Apologetics: the proclamation of truth through the arts, addressing the condition of humanity with logical consistency, empirical adequacy, and existential relevance in the light of the everlasting Hope of the Gospel in Jesus Christ

APPENDIX E

MUHANA Ashram[1]

THE CONCEPT OF "ASHRAM" translates into the creation of places for the confluence of diversities (the mix of fresh and salt water)—to meet people where they are in order to create with them a new reality in Christ. This forms the basis for the spontaneous combustion and emergence of creativities. The ashram environment facilitates the creation of places where creativity is honed in accord with the creative vision of the Creator as exemplified through the life and teachings of Jesus Christ. What follows are some thoughts for initiating an ashram movement in a given context.

CONTEXT/ VISION

Look around. People everywhere are searching for a place to be—to create without fear, without prejudice, without insecurity. How can we create environments for hearing that is inspired, seeing that is imaginative, abiding that is restorative, and believing that brings healing?

Many spiritual traditions in the world aspire to bring about healing and harmony. Yet, clearly, in the light of the conflict, unrest, and fear that persist in cities across the world, we are far from the ideal. The Judeo Christian spiritual mythological tradition tells about a River that flows into the Sea; where this River meets the sea, the water become fresh; it is a place for vibrant creative diversity, abundant fruitfulness, and healing (Ez.47: 1-13; also, Ephesians 2:12-3). MUHANA is such a place.

---

1. The term "ashram" refers to a place of religious retreat in the context of Hinduism. The Ashram movement is popular worldwide and was used by E. Stanley Jones as a strategy to dialogue with others. For further information, please see: E. Stanley Jones Foundation, http://www.estanleyjonesfoundation.com/about-esj/history-of-the-christian-ashrams/.

SUMMARY

MUHANA—"estuary" in Hindi.

Location (for example): "The Gathering at the Bazaar" Lexington, KY

Meet time: Saturdays, 3:30pm

Purpose: Creative Arts and Healing: Creating meditative environments for Spirit-led inspiration, imagination, and introspection for individual and communal harmony.

Additionally the intention is to:

- Create space to be creative—create artworks that emerge from deep within, without the threat of having to perform for others
- Mix with others and develop friendships
- Receive instruction on living Spirit-filled lives
- Allow for and make "creative space"
- Work and learn along with others collectively on projects to impact the neighborhood
- Public Discourses/ Lectures/ Workshops may include topics such as: Am I creative? How can I tap into my creative potential? What is inspiration? Am I inspired? How can I inspire others? What is imagination? How can I use it to make a difference?

Hear—Can I really hear God's voice? See—Can I truly see God? Abide—How can I find and sustain peace in myself and with others? Believe—What do I need to believe?

MUHANA Ashram (a draft description):

- As a tool for evangelism with others, the purpose is to create room for persons to focus and learn from participation in The Creative Circle—Creative Being, Creative Construction, Creative Community, Creative Beauty, and Creative Performance.
- The rationale is that creativity is not merely something to be used, but a lifestyle of discipleship in Christ with others (6 month process or weekend retreat/s).
- The context for creativity is the diversity of the city (Community/Cultural immersion)—seeking rest and beauty in the city.

- MUHANA is a place to discern the voice of the Spirit and act upon it (Inspiration, Imagination, Illumination, Interrogation).
- MUHANA allows time for rest, reflection, and study of Scripture through a process of discerning creative gifts in alignment with personality type and how these might be used for living wholesome/integrated lifestyles.
- There is opportunity to learn collectively and to collaborate with others in the course of creating works with others Collaborative learning.
- Create: work on a project—finish writing the song or creating the artwork that is on your heart in the context of a creative community
- Related to a person's readiness, there will be opportunity to dialogue, learn, and create with persons from other faith persuasions. While MUHANA Ashram itself draws from the teachings of Jesus Christ, there is considerably much to learn from artists/creatives who may not know Christ. This creates opportunity for Creative Dialogue and reconciliation.

Rationale:
- All people are creative—equally, in the image of God
- The context for creativity is diversity—relationships with others
- Creativity does not happen in a vacuum—human creativity finds its fulfillment in the context of a covenantal relationship with God and creation through Christ

Whom Does It Involve?

People who would most likely benefit from such an immersion experience include:

- "Creatives" who are employed in producing artworks, music, dance, and other expressions/performances of creativity. This could include local artists and those in the neighborhood who wish to see their community transformed through the creative arts.
- Families with children who would like to create works, contexts, and experiences for the family/neighborhood to share in the larger "metanarrative" of life.

- Pastors, clergy, other leaders, and teams currently serving in churches. This will provide an opportunity to think out-of-the-box and brainstorm in the context of the city/glocal environments and mission
- Those working in corporates and creative agencies. to develop/enhance creativity in a way that creates a participative experience for the dissemination and accomplishment of corporate vision in the context of the city.

Related Projects:

2-day weekend "Experiencing Creativity" retreat; 6 week—community based project; 3-6 month extended stay at Ashram center in the city. Features/Learning outcomes:

- Learn to hear, see, abide, and believe, individually and collectively— Some of the biggest obstacles to creativity are fear, insecurity, and prejudice. Your greatest weakness can be your greatest strength; but without healing, little fruit is borne. MUHANA is a place to experience healing yourself, and then to extend healing to others.
- Create with a view to invite participation—Innovation and design are not ends in themselves. Do you see yourself in what/ how you create? How has this changed in your life? Do you have a vision for the way you see yourself creating? Is it realistic? In what sense does it correspond to your deepest needs and desires?
- The Journey, perspectives: learn to tell your story, with others. The greatest gift you have to offer the world is yourself, not someone else. Do you believe this? What is your story? With others, discern your role in the larger "metanarrative" of life; learn the story of your origin, meaning, purpose, and ultimate destiny. There is untold worth in your story. Join others on a similar journey.
- Share your creativity and build community in the context of diversity
- Summary benefits for participants:
- Draw out creativity that is inspired, imagined, and radical; be unique.
- Build confidence: overcome fear, insecurity, and prejudice (to take on new challenges, rebuild meaningful relationships; transform weaknesses into turning points for strengths)
- Renew the mind—bring the body in accord with your mind.
- Balance: restore individual and communal harmony

APPENDIX F

Community Transformation through the Arts (CTA)

A PROCESS OF COMMUNITY engagement is employed based upon: Hear, See, Abide, and Believe (John 5:37,38). The following strategy is suggested as a summary of a strategy for mission with others using the arts, ethnographic method, and processes of critical contextualization:

1. Discerning the SHAPE of a community (Stories, Histories, Attitudes, Perceptions, Expressions)
2. Envision Kingdom goals/values in the light of the context
3. Explore local genres/content through a process of cultural immersion and learning with/in community
4. Analyze existing works in the light of Kingdom values
5. Interpret Kingdom goals/values in local/glocal/contextually-relevant forms with a "hermeneutical community"
6. Create "new" works that integrate local talent and sustainable methods for ongoing participation and transformation in Christ

APPENDIX G

Estuary Cultures: A Way for Church Movement[1]

> "Large numbers of creatures will live where the river flows. It will have huge numbers of fish. <u>This water flows there and makes the salt water fresh</u>. So where the river flows everything will live."
>
> —Ez. 47:9, NIRV; see also, vv.8-12

CONTEXT

THE PURPOSE OF THIS document is a provide an overall vision for a way of being the body of Christ in creative ways with others for mission.

The biblical scenario: Revelation 7: 9; Hebrews 12: 22; Zephaniah 3: 9,10, the diversity of worship.

The sociocultural reality: Globalization, Migration, and Orality. The challenge is to not only to reach, but also to create with others a new reality—the Kingdom of God here on earth as it is in heaven—in Christ

---

1. Movement refers to the intense energy and organic, spontaneous-combustive activity of the Spirit resulting in an unusual love for the world, creating processes of collaboration and compassion, inspiring the Church to engage culture in Creative Dialogue, creating multiple and diverse sustainable contexts and experiences of God amongst people where they are, for the bringing about of a new heaven and earth. It also refers to the inspiration of the Spirit amongst "creative catalysts" and the unleashing of the generative capacities of artists resulting from the dynamic integration of theological creativity and vision, church vitality/ planting, and specialized ministry through the arts.

Contrary to what it might seem, the turbulence of intermingling diversities and the mixing of the currents of various ideologies present optimal, estuarine-like, conditions for the flourishing of the Body of Christ.

VISION

In Ezekiel 47, God leads the prophet through a sublime immersion experience. Where the River of God meets the sea (the world), there the salt water is healed ("fresh," v.9). Based upon the Lord's vision to Ezekiel, the church is where the River (the worshiping community) meets the sea (the world). The "mix" brought about by the meeting of river and sea creates a sustainable ecosystem for the flourishing of diversity. Abundance is a result of such dynamic and creative diversity. It is a place for the "spreading of nets" (Ez. 47:10), irruptive fruitfulness, and lasting healing (Ez. 47:12). Estuary Cultures are places for the becoming of the body of Christ.

MISSION

Estuary Cultures exists to nurture the Creative Seed in every person. Drawing from the life and teachings of Jesus Christ, EC encourages the formation of creative spaces that inspire creativity, stimulate and equip the imagination, celebrate and shape gifts, foster vibrant and transformative creative communities, and together with others, collaborate on creative projects for human and community development.

WHAT IS AN ESTUARY?[2]

An Estuary is a geographical term that refers to places along the coastline where freshwater from rivers and streams meet and mix with the salt water from the ocean. Although influenced by the tides they are protected from the full force of ocean waves, winds, and storms by landforms such as barrier reefs or islands and peninsulas.

Estuarine environments are some of the most fertile places in the world. According to the EPA (Environmental Protection Agency), they create matter that is more organic each year than comparably sized areas of forest, grassland, or agricultural land. The sheltered waters support unique communities of plants and animals especially adapted for life at the margin of the sea.

Vibrant and unique habitat types are formed in and around estuaries primarily due to the mixing of fresh and salt water. The confluence of river and sea results in a unique and rich diversity and abundance.

2. US EPA, http://water.epa.gov/type/oceb/nep/about.cfm.

II. GEOGRAPHICAL FEATURES OF AN ESTUARY

- Partially enclosed body of water
- Place of transition and movement—a place for meeting and mixing: land and ocean, freshwater and saltwater
- Highly productive—influenced by the tides, but protected by land forms
- Vibrant and unique life forms—especially adapted for life at the margin
- Diverse habitat types—marshes, rocky shores, sandy beaches, mangrove forests, sea grasses, tidal pools, deltas, peninsulas

PERTINENT CHARACTERISTICS OF CULTURE[3]

- Never static, but continually changing
- Constructed (meaning-making organisms)
- Contingent (continuity and discontinuity)
- Conflicted (negotiation and exchange of identities and ideologies)

ESTUARY CULTURES

Estuary Cultures as a way for church movement derives meaning, at least in part, from the geographical reality: a place where the River becomes a confluence of many avenues of flow resulting in a richly diverse and abundantly fertile ecosystem for the thriving of God's people.

Estuary Cultures is a dynamic, interactive, and organic environment that fosters diverse, abundant, and unique life forms, which constitute and contribute to the formation of a rich ecosystem for mutual cohabitation.[4]

The mix of River and Sea make for an estuarine ecosystem characterized by:

- Movement (asynchronous)
- Diversity ("everything"; "all kinds"; "many kinds")
- Abundance ("large" and "huge" numbers) due to diversity (an alternate discourse to quality vs./and quantity)
- Dynamic directionality ("this water goes there")

---

3. Rynkiewich "A New Heaven and a New Earth?"
4. Cf. *habitus*, habit-forming or mutually formative.

- Transformative meet and mix ("that the waters of the sea may become fresh")
- "A place for the spreading of nets" (made earlier in C3)
- The birthing of new CUPs ("swamps and marshes" as SALT communities)
- Multiplicative fruitfulness and Healing
- Nurturing the Creativity of Diversity for Community

WHERE IS CHURCH?

- The movement of the River to go beyond the limits of our current structures (church planting)
- To meet and mix with (the ocean)[5] peoples in transition—migrants and refugees in particular, also, with a focus on cities and the complex traffic in and out of urban gateways (church vitality and renewal)
- With a purpose to share the commonality of our differences in Christ (Dialogue)
- Using alternate learning behaviors, asymmetrical and asynchronous teaching environs, and creating diverse and multiple contexts and experiences of God

SIGNIFICANCE OF ESTUARIES FOR CHURCH MOVEMENT

- Meet and Mix
- Creative, interactive, and collaborative environment (Spontaneous Combustion)
- Resourceful/ Generative
- Multiplicative growth and mutual learning (the process of filtration serves to shape people where they are at rather than isolating them from their new native environments)
- Diversity and Wholeness (Ecosystem)[6]

---

5. The River of God is the worshipping community; the ocean refers to the world (book of Revelation).

6. Individual and unique identities are acknowledged in relation to the larger ecosystem (Snyder 1995).

Dynamic Directionality

Flowing with the river brings movement. The movement leads outward (directionality) from the sanctuary of God to the sea. The seawater flows inward. This mix is where salt forms (cf. Matt. 5:13). In an ideal mix,[7] the transformation of water, both fresh and salt, is so complete it is hard to tell one drop of water from the other.

Specifically, this is about facilitating such a flow between the Body of Christ and the world in order to more effectively reach those "lost in transition" where they are (migrants, refugees, and those deemed "not a fit") with an emphasis on oral learning strategies and methods.[8]

This is not in opposition to existing structures; but rather, will serve to renew the structure from within and without; it will complement what the Lord has already begun to do through the church, while inviting change via participation and immersion in fresh ways, offering opportunity to break from the negative processes of modernity.

The movement is characterized by dynamic integration of the theological creativity of people, church renewal and planting, and a commissioning and release of specialized creative ministries (e.g., arts[9] and oral-learning behaviors).

Diversity

Biodiversity is a critical component for a thriving ecosystem. The same is true when it comes to the flourishing of a Gospel ecosystem (cf. Ez.47: 7-13). Theologically speaking, the locus for creativity is the diversity of the community of the Trinity. Diversity produces abundance. Abundant numbers, while good, does not necessarily mean abundant diversity. But Christ-centered diversity[10] (beginning with the end in mind, Rev.7: 9—the creativity of the Godhead is reciprocated amidst the present diversity of the gathered community, cf. Heb. 12:22ff.)—envisions abundance.

---

7. Certain mixes are more conducive for rich diversity and wholeness than others are.

8. See, International Orality Network (ION) at http://www.oralbible.com/oral-learning/statistics-facts).

9. Major Christian movements in the past are characterized by the commissioning and explosion of indigenous creativity through the arts, e.g., Harris movement in West Africa (early twentieth century), underground church movement in China (twenty-first century), Hillsongs, Vineyard, and Methodism.

10. Not simply ethnic or racial, but all kinds—tapping into and providing for the explication of the unique *imago Dei* in every human being in our context.

This movement will provide an intentional focus on paying attention to the distinct and diverse types of "fish" and develop leaders and methods (tools and technologies) for discipleship along with them for the Kingdom.[11]

Implications for a "Creative Church"

- Reach people/migrants[12] and the marginalized where they are
- Foster relationships for sharing the Gospel
- Promote intercultural understanding and create avenues for integration and inclusion ("two-way street")
- Together with the "other," develop resources using/ through appropriate and innovative tools and technologies
- Impact lives for eternity by being a place for healing and generating Kingdom lifestyles

Suggested Strategy:

- Embody and enact creative ministries as pathways to invite participation from others, engage in fruitful dialogue, and fresh research initiatives to discern the times
- Integrate theological creative vision, church renewal and planting, and specialized creative ministries (cf. Keller 2012).
- Partner with local churches, creative, organizations to form Covenant Creative Communities within their contexts that integrate a good "mix" between people from all walks of life for renewing the life of the Body. Such C3M communities may as well as be a "tributary" to the Estuary Cultures movement for the creative transformation of the city.
- Engage and equip families/ members of a given network/neighborhood/ community for transformation and community development;

---

11. Multiculturalism is a social ideology—people do not have to give up their cultural otherness; differences become a threat if you are holding to an assimilation ideology. In Britain, multiculturalism was declared a failed policy—because they have not been able to assimilate. The same person can shift or hold more than one ideology depending upon the context, personality.

12. Broadly, "migrants" here refer to all in "movement" including people in transition, migration between cities, communities, the interchange and exchange of ideas, goods, and services, and the complex cultural situatedness (cf. displacement, disembeddedness) of various cultural groups in the context of the "intensification of interdependencies" and inequalities as a result of global processes.

Appendix G: Estuary Cultures

- Foster relationships to enable the creation of safe spaces for individual and collective flourishing of creativities through arts, media, and technologies
- Create spaces to nurture and to celebrate the creative potential of every individual exemplified through their gifts and talents
- Facilitate the mutual sharing and exchange of resources for building each other up and fostering an atmosphere of collective learning and healthy growth amongst members (dialogue, partnership, inclusion);
- Establish sustainable connections with grass-root artisans and indigenous creativities/ enterprises for social and economic betterment
- Partner with like-minded persons and churches for the development of resource pools that will be enriching within their own spheres of creativity as well as for the creation of media and technologies for human and community development

The following table helps to see the connection between Ezekiel 47:1-13 and what this implies for an embodied, enacted, and performed ecclesiology:

Estuary Ecosystem in Ezekiel 47	Estuary Cultures Body of Christ
Movement (two-way)	Treats "other" as vital
Dynamic Directionality ("this water goes there"; "wherever the river goes")	Intentional seeking out
Courageous ("enters the sea")	Dialogue—Bold Humility
Meet and Mix ("that the waters of the sea may become fresh")	Project/ Ministry oriented; creative engagement with others
"Living" to Life ("every living creature . . . will live)	Spontaneous Combustive Sprit-inspired activity
Diversity (("everything"; "all kinds"; "many kinds")	Focus on each person's unique design; individual agency
Abundance ("very many fish"; "large" and "huge" numbers)	Diversity engenders abundance
Harvest ("a place for the spreading of nets")	Shift from multisite to multi-church initiatives—what's it take to build a net? Asynchronous, Asymmetrical, multiple contexts and experiences

Appendix G: Estuary Cultures

Estuary Ecosystem in Ezekiel 47	Estuary Cultures Body of Christ
Fruitful: Abundant and Diverse ("both sides"; "all kinds"); Enduring ("will not wither, nor . . . fail"); Consistent quality ("fresh . . . every month"); Sustainable ("water . . . from the sanctuary"); Health/Wholesome and Healing ("food . . . healing")	Evidence of the Gospel as metric for church SOURCE (CUP Fellowships), FLOW (Covenant Creative Communities), MIX (space for the emergence of new CUPs)

ESTUARY CULTURES: EZ.47: 9, WHERE IS CHURCH?

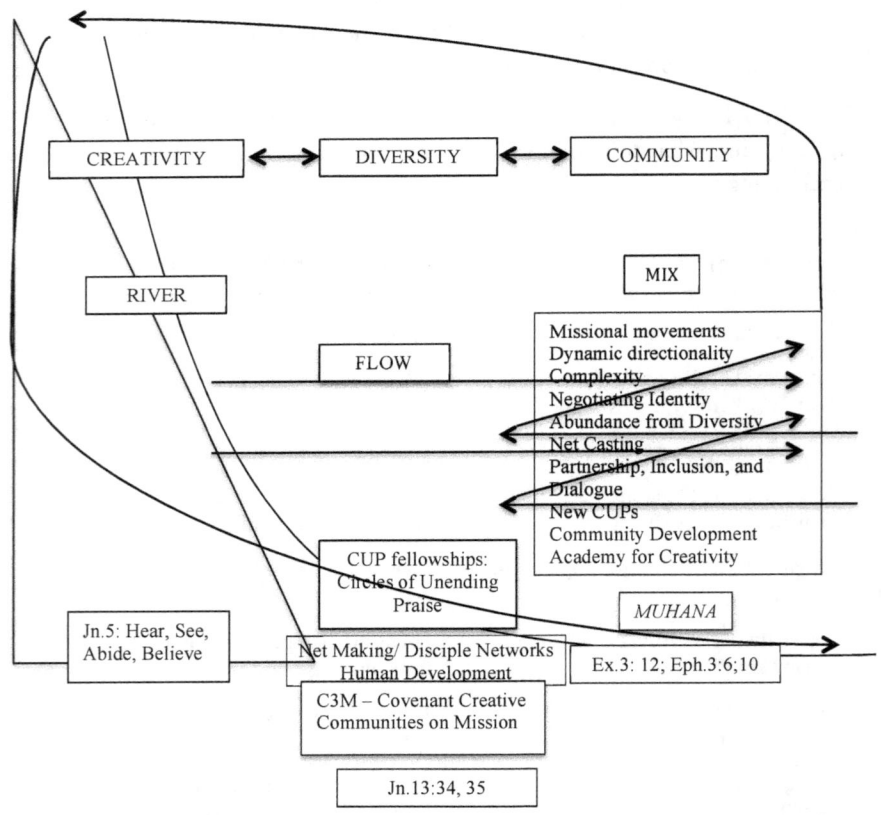

Appendix H

Questions for Witnessing Artists

THE FOLLOWING IS A condensed sample set of questions initially used for the purpose of this research amongst ICMs for mission. Actual interview questions drew from this pool, adding to and modifying depending upon context.

BACKGROUND QUESTIONS

- Who or what are some of your influences?
- How did some of these people or relationships influence your particular approach, the way you see yourself and your contribution through music?
- In what sense has others' opinions or views about you or your music shaped or changed the way you have projected yourself to others and/or your music?
- How did you become a Christian? Is there a change in your music from before to after this shift? Please explain.

Theme 1—Creative Being

1. Please describe your music? (instruments, technique, innovations, attitudes, values, knowledge)
2. In what sense does your music describe you to those whom you are trying to reach? Or, what about your music is particular to who you are or who you see yourself to be?

3. Is there a sense in which your music shapes you? Explain?
4. How would you describe your target audience/s?
5. In what ways does your music relate to people? What kinds of responses have you received to your music? Please illustrate with a few examples that would best represent this.
6. What are some of the things you hope to see your music doing in others? How do you see your music impacting or influencing others? Are there stories you can share?
7. What do you want them to experience or feel/ think after listening/ interacting to/with you? Could you please describe some instances when you have achieved this or otherwise, when this has been difficult or not possible?
8. What inspires you to create your music?
9. What barriers have you encountered that prohibit or make it difficult for you to do what you do? Could you please describe in what sense these impact you? Are there stories you can share that might best represent your experience?
10. Would you characterize your music as being "indigenous"? Why? Or why not?
11. Do you see yourself as patriotic? How does patriotism or national ideals factor in your ministry/ music?
12. How would you characterize the nature of your ministry in Christ? Is your ministry based upon a vision, dream, or any other experience?
13. What sustains you—motivates you to keep doing what you do?
14. Do you have a sense of being "called" (to lead, to be an apostle, to teach, to be Christ)? Do you expect others to follow you? Please explain.

Theme 2—Creative Construction

1. What inspires you to create?
2. What about you/ your music would you say characterizes you best? Please describe in what sense.
3. What kinds of sounds or combinations of sounds and lyrics, moods, motivations would you say characterize your music? In other words, do you prefer to combine certain words and music in specific ways? Why?

4. What mediums do you prefer to use for communicating or presenting yourself and your music? Why?
5. Do you have a "heart language" of musical expression? Please describe.
6. What indigenous languages do you speak and/ or use? What role does language have in the message you choose to communicate through your music?
7. In what sense do you relate to the poetry or musical traditions and practices of the surrounding culture/s?
8. How do you relate to Indian religious literature and/or other such forms of religious communication? What place does it hold in your theology and practice?
9. What resources (personal, technology, etc.) help you achieve what you want to achieve?
10. What kinds of innovations have you made in order to help you be more effective in your understanding?

Theme 3—Creative Community

1. Who do you work with? What role do other people play in (the process of creating) your music?
2. How do you see yourself in relation to others/ your audience/ target group?—Co-participants, passive or active listeners? In what sense?
3. How do people respond to your music? Is this in anyway different from how you would want them to respond to your music?
4. In what sense does the existing structure or religious institution of which you are part, positively contribute to using your music for effective Christian witness? (By using the word "effective" we might come up with an emic understanding of what that word means in a given cultural matrix) In what ways does it detract from effective witness?
5. What is the extent of your understanding of the background—religious, social, economic, political—of your audience? Have you knowledge of the philosophy and traditions of the country/ people (or we glean this from their answers)?
6. What role does caste, the larger religio-social structure play in how you shape your music/ ministry?

7. What aspects of the artist's experience are continuous or discontinuous with previous religio-spiritual teachings?

Theme 4—Creative Quality

1. What kinds of music, rhythms and sounds etc., seem to (effectively) communicate the message of Christianity to your audience? Please describe.
2. When it comes to your creativity in your music, what is "good"—for you? For your audience?
3. Does the music correlate/ compare/ contrast with specific spiritual and devotional practices of the culture/s? In what sense?

Theme 5—Creative Musicality

1. How have others responded to your faith in Christ?
2. In what sense does your audience seem to respond to your music—does it motivate them to Christian service in some way? Please give examples.
3. In what ways do you/ does your music contribute to make this world a "better" place—involvement in works that bring about justice, peace, and reconciliation?

Follow up questions:

1. Who else should I speak with in order to better understand you and your music?
2. Do you pray for and, in particular, with spiritual seekers?
3. Do you think I should know anything else that might help me to get a better idea of your creativity?

Bibliography

Abraham, William J. *Canon and Criterion in Christian Theology: From the Fathers to Feminism.* Oxford: Oxford University Press, 2002.

Adeney, Miriam. *Kingdom Without Borders: The Untold Story of Global Christianity.* Downers Grove, IL: IVP, 2009.

Alatas, Syed Hussain. "The Captive Mind and Creative Development." In *Indigeneity and Universality in Social Science: A South Asian Response,* edited by P. N. Mukherji and C. Sengupta, 83–98. New Delhi: Sage, 2004.

Amabile, T. M. 1999. "Consensual Assessment." In *Encyclopedia of Creativity,* edited by M. A. Runco and S. Pritzker, 346–49. San Diego: Academic.

Augustine, and W. F. Jackson Knight. *St. Augustine's De musica, a synopsis.* London: Orthological Institute, 1949.

Appingnanesi, Richard. "Introduction: 'Whose Culture' Exposing the Myth of Cultural Diversity." *Third Text: Critical Perspectives on Contemporary Art and Culture.* http://www.thirdtext.org/introcc.

Anzaldúa, Gloria. *Borderlands: the new mestiza = La frontera.* San Francisco: Spinsters/Aunt Lute, 1987.

Apostolos-Cappadona, Diane. *Art, Creativity, and the Sacred: An Anthology in Religion and Art.* New York: Crossroad, 1984.

———. "Humanity in the Arts." In *New Dictionary of the History of Ideas,* edited by Maryanne Cline Horowitz, 3:1044–61. New York: Charles Scribner's Sons, 2005.

———. "Symbols." In *Encycolpedia of Christianity,* edited by John Bowden, 1160–71. New York: Continuum, 2005.

Appadurai, Arjun. *Modernity At Large: Cultural Dimensions of Globalization.* Minneapolis: University of Minnesota Press, 1996.

Appiah, Anthony. *Cosmopolitanism: Ethics in a World of Strangers.* New York: W. W. Norton, 2006.

Arareen, Rashid. "Come What May: Beyond the Emperor's New Clothes." In *Complex Entanglements: Art, Globalisation, and Cultural Difference,* edited by Nikos Papastergiadis, 135–53. London: Rivers Oram, 2003.

———. "Ethnic Minorities, Multi-culturalism and the Celebration of the Postcolonial Other." *Third Text.* http://www.thirdtext.org.

Ashcroft, Bill, et al. *Postcolonial Studies: The Key Concepts*. London: Taylor & Francis, 2000.

———. *Postcolonial Studies: The Key Concepts*. New York: Routledge, 2013.

Attali, Jacques. *Noise: The Political Economy of Music*. Minneapolis: University of Minnesota Press, 1985.

Authentic Systems. "Motivation Research and Development." http://www.authentic-systems.com/featured-articles/difference-between-emotions-and-feelings/.

Austin, J. L. *How To Do Things With Words*. Cambridge, MA: Harvard University Press, 1962.

Bailey, Alex. "The Rhetoric of Music: A Theoretical Synthesis." *Rocky Mountain Communication Review* 3 (2006) 20–35.

Ball, Philip. *The Music Instinct: How Music Works and Why We Can't Do Without It*. New York: Oxford University Press, 2010.

Bandy, Thomas G. *Christian Chaos: Revolutionizing the Congregation*. Nashville: Abingdon, 1999.

Banjo, Omotayo, and Kesha Morant. "A House Divided? Christian Music in Black and White. Abstract." *Paper presented at the annual meeting of the International Communication Association, Suntec Singapore International Convention & Exhibition Centre, Suntec City, Singapore*, June 21, 2010. http://citation.allacademic.com/meta/p_mla_apa_research_citation/4/0/2/2/7/p402277_index.html.

Barker, Ash. "Challenges and Possibilities for a New Generation of Mission Workers." In *Living Mission: The Vision and Voices of New Friars*, edited by Scott A. Bessenecker, 156–66. Downers Grove, IL: IVP, 2010.

Barron, F. *No Rootless Flower*. Cresskill, NJ: Hampton, 1995.

Barthes, R. *Mythologies*. Translated by Annette Lavers. London: Jonathan Cape, 1973.

Baruah, Pranjal. "Music replaces sounds of bullets, bombs in Nagaland." September 4, 2012. *Times of India*. http://articles.timesofindia.indiatimes.com/2012-09-14/guwahati/33843170_1_neiphiu-rio-music-task-force-naga-musicians.

Basch, Linda G., et al. *Nations Unbound: Transnational Projects, Postcolonial Predicaments, and Deterritorialized Nation-States*. New York: Gordon and Breach. 1994.

Bass, Diana Butler. *Christianity after Religion: The End of Church and the Birth of a New Spiritual Awakening*. New York: HarperCollins, 2012.

Bauerlein, Mark. *The Digital Divide: Arguments for and Against Facebook, Google, Texting, and the Age of Social Networking*. New York: Jeremy A. Tarcher/ Penguin, 2011.

Baum, Willa K. "The Expanding Role of the Librarian in Oral History." In *Oral History: An Interdisciplinary Anthology*, edited by David K. Dunaway and Willa K. Baum, 321–40. Walnut Creek, CA: Altamira, 1984.

Baumann, Max Peter. "Music and Worldview of Indian Societies in the Bolivian Andes." In *Music in Latin America and the Caribbean: An Encyclopedic History*, edited by Malena Kuss, 101–22. Austin: University of Texas Press, 2004.

Bayazitova, Rauza. "Cultural Integration: Effect of Music on Cultures." *School of International Service, American University, Feature Edition* 2. Franklin Publishing Company, 2012.

Beale, G. K., and D. A. Carson, eds. *Commentary on the New Testament Use of the Old Testament*. Grand Rapids: Baker Academic, 2007.

Beck, Guy L. *Sacred Sound: Experiencing Music in World Religions.* Ontario, Canada: Wilfrid Laurier University, 2006.

———. *Sonic Theology: Hinduism and Sacred Sound.* Columbia, SC: University of South Carolina Press, 1993.

Beck, Ulrich. "Cosmopolitical Realism: On the Distinction Between Cosmopolitanism in Philosophy and the Social Sciences." *Global Networks* 4 (2004) 131–56.

Bediako, Kwame. *Christianity in Africa: The Renewal of a Non-Western Religion.* Edinburgh: Edinburgh University Press, 1997.

Begbie, Jeremy. "Created Beauty: The Witness of J. S. Bach." In *Resonant Witness: Conversations Between Music and Theology*, edited by Jeremy S. Begbie and Steven R. Guthrie, 83-108. Grand Rapids: Eerdmans, 2011.

———. "The Future of Theology amid the Arts." In *Christ Across the Disciplines*, edited by Roger Lundin, 152–82. Grand Rapids: Eerdmans, 2013.

———. "Openness and Specificity: A Conversation with David Brown on Theology and Classical Music." In *Theology, Aesthetics, and Culture: Responses to the Work of David Brown*, edited by Robert MacSwain and Taylor Worley, 145–56. Oxford: Oxford University Press, 2012.

———. *Resounding Truth: Christian Wisdom in the World of Music.* Grand Rapids: Baker Academic, 2007.

———. *Theology, Music and Time.* Cambridge: Cambridge University Press, 2000.

Begbie, Jeremy S., and Steven R. Guthrie, eds. *Resonant Witness: Conversations between Music and Theology.* Grand Rapids: Eerdmans, 2011.

Bell, Clive. *Art.* New York: Capricorn, 1958.

Bellini, Peter J. *Participation: Epistemology and Mission Theology.* Lexington, KY: Emeth, 2010.

Berger, Peter L., and Thomas Luckmann. *The Social Construction of Reality: A Treatise in the Sociology of Knowledge.* Garden City, NY: Anchor, 1967.

Best, Harold M. *Music Through The Eyes of Faith.* San Francisco: HarperSanFrancisco, 1993.

———. "God's Creation and Human Creativity: Seven Affirmations." In *Worship and Mission for the Global Church: An Ethnodoxology Handbook*, edited by James R. Krabill et al., 13–16. Pasadena: William Carey Library, 2013.

Bevans, Stephen. "Letting Go and Speaking Out: A Spirituality of Inculturation." In *The Healing Circle: Essays in Cross-Cultural Mission*, edited by Stephen Bevans et al., 133–46. Chicago: CCGM, 2000.

———. *Models of Contextual Theology.* Maryknoll, NY: Orbis, 2008.

Bevans, Stephen B., and Roger P. Schroeder. *Constants in Context: A Theology of Mission for Today.* Maryknoll, NY: Orbis, 2004.

———. *Prophetic Dialogue: Reflections on Christian Mission Today.* Maryknoll, NY: Orbis, 2011.

Bhabha, Homi. *The Location of Culture.* New York: Routledge, 1994. Kindle.

Bhaktin, Mikhail. Excerpt from *Marxism and the Philosophy of Language*. In *The Rhetorical Tradition: Readings from Classical Times to the Present*, edited by Patricia Bizzell and Bruce Herzberg, 1210–14. Boston/New York: Bedford/St. Martin's, 1973.

Bibeau, Gilles. Review of *Mimesis and Alterity: A Particular History of the Senses*, by Michael Taussig. *American Ethnologist* 22 (1995) 626–28.

Biddle, Ian, and Vanessa Knights. *Music, National Identity and the Politics of Location: Between the Global and the Local*. Aldershot, England: Ashgate, 2007.

Bizzell, Patricia, and Bruce Herzberg. *The Rhetorical Tradition: Readings from Classical Times to the Present*. 2nd ed. Boston/New York: Bedford/St. Martin's, 2001.

Blacking, John. *How Musical Is Man?* Seattle: University of Washington Press, 1973.

———. *How Musical Is Man?* London: Faber and Faber, 1976.

Blackwell, Albert L. *The Sacred in Music*. Louisville, KY: Westminster John Knox, 1999.

Blair, D. C. *Wittgenstein, Language and information: Back to the Rough Ground!* Information, Science, and Knowledge Management Series 10. Dordrecht: Springer, 2006.

Boff, Leonardo, and Clodovis Boff. *Introducing Liberation Theology*. Maryknoll, NY: Orbis, 1987.

Bohlman, Philip Vilas. *World Music: A Very Short Introduction*. Oxford: Oxford University Press, 2002.

Boje, David M. "Victor Turner's Postmodern Theory of Social Drama: Implications for Organization Studies." PhD diss., New Mexico State University, 2003. http://cbae.nmsu.edu/~dboje/theatrics/7/victor_turner.htm.

Boorstin, Daniel J. *The Creators*. New York: Random, 1992.

Born, Georgina, and David Hesmondhalgh. *Western Music and its Others: Difference, Representation, and Appropriation in Music*. Berkeley: University of California Press, 2000.

Born, Georgina. *Music, Sound and Space: Transformations of Public and Private Experience*. Cambridge: Cambridge University Press, 2013.

Bosch, David. J. *Transforming Mission: Paradigm Shifts in Theology of Mission*. Maryknoll, NY: Orbis, 2007.

Bowling, David. "Music Review: Simon & Garfunkel—Bridge Over Troubled Water." Monday, October 27, 2008. http://blogcritics.org/music/article/music-review-simon-garfunkel-bridge-over/.

Bradshaw, Bruce. *Bridging the Gap: Evangelism, Development, and Shalom*. Eugene, OR: Wipf and Stock, 2007.

Brand, Hillary, and Adrienne Chaplin. *Art and Soul: Signposts for Christians in the Arts*. Downers Grove, IL: IVP Academic, 2001.

Brickhouse, Thomas, and Nicholas D. Smith. "Plato (427–347 BCE)." *Internet Encyclopedia of Philosophy*. http://www.iep.utm.edu/plato.

Brink, Emily. "The Significance of Beauty and Excellence in Biblical Worship." In *Worship and Mission for the Global Church: An Ethnodoxology Handbook*, edited by James R. Krabill et al., 9–12. Pasadena: William Carey Library, 2013.

Brink, Laurie. "In Search of the Biblical Foundations of Prophetic Dialogue: Engaging a Hermeneutics of Otherness." *Missiology* 41 (2013) 9–21.

The British Geographer. "Introduction to River Processes." http://thebritishgeographer.weebly.com/river-processes.html.

Bromiley, Geoffrey W. "Evangelicals and Theological Creativity." *Themelios* 5 (1979) 4–8. http://s3.amazonaws.com/tgc-documents/journal-issues/5.1_Bromiley.pdf.

Bronowski, Jacob. *The Common Sense of Science*. London: Faber and Faber, 2011.

Brown, David. "Experience, Symbol, and Revelation: Continuing the Conversation." In *Theology, Aesthetics, and Culture: Responses to the Work of David Brown*, edited by Robert MacSwain and Taylor Worley, 265–96. Oxford: Oxford University Press, 2012.

———. *God and Enchantment of Place: Reclaiming Human Experience*. Oxford: Oxford University Press, 2004.

———. *Tradition and Imagination: Revelation and Change*. Oxford: Oxford University Press, 1999.

Brown, Frank Burch. *Aesthetics: A Theological Study of Making and Meaning*. Princeton, N.J.: Princeton University Press, 1989.

———. *Good Taste, Bad Taste, and Christian Taste Aesthetics in Religious Life*. New York: Oxford University Press, 2000.

Brown, Garrett Wallace, and David Held. *The Cosmopolitan Reader*. Cambridge, UK: Polity, 2010.

Brueggemann, Walter. *The Practice of Prophetic Imagination: Preaching an Emancipating Word*. Minneapolis: Fortress, 2012.

Bull, Michael, and Les Back. *The Auditory Culture Reader*. Oxford, UK: Berg, 2003.

Burke, Kenneth. "Excerpt from *A Grammar of Motives*." In *The Rhetorical Tradition: Readings from Classical Times to the Present*, edited by Patricia Bizzell and Bruce Herzberg, 1298–324. Boston/New York: Bedford/St. Martin's, 2001.

Burkhalter, Thomas. *Local Music Scenes and Globalization: Transnational Platforms in Beirut*. New York: Taylor & Francis, 2013.

Burkus, D., and Oster G. "Noncommissioned Work: Exploring the Influence of Structured Free Time on Creativity and Innovation." *Journal of Strategic Leadership* 4 (2012) 49–60.

———. "Why Free Time Frees Creativity." 2012, *The Creativity Post*. http://www.creativitypost.com/business/why_free_time_frees_creativity.

Burnimm, Mellonee. "The Performance of Black Gospel Music as Transformation." In *Music and the Experience of God*, edited by Mary Collins et al., 52–61. Edinburgh: T. & T. Clark, 1989.

Butler, J. *Excitable Speech: A Politics of the Performative*. London: Routledge, 1997.

Bychkov, Victor V. "The Symbololology of Dionysius the Areopagite." *Russian Studies in Philosophy* 51 (2012) 28–63.

Caccamo, James F. *The Responsorial Self: Christian Ethics and Ritual Song*. Thesis PhD thesis, Loyola University of Chicago, 2004.

Cameron, Julia. *The Artist's Way: A Spiritual Path to Higher Creativity*. Los Angeles: Jeremy P. Tarcher/Perigee, 1992.

Cannell, Fenella, ed. *The Anthropology of Christianity*. Durham: Duke University Press, 2006.

Carder, Eddie. "Platonism and Theism." http://www.iep.utm.edu/pla-thei/#SH3c.

Cardoza-Orlandi, Carlos F. "Prophetic Dialogue: a Historical Perspective Bending Time in History to Rediscover the Gospel." *Missiology: An International Review* 41 (2013) 22–34.

Carson, D. A. "Unity and Diversity in the NT: The Possibility of Systematic Theology." In *Scripture and Truth*, edited by D. A. Carson and J. D. Woodbridge, 65–95. Grand Rapids: Academie, 1983.

Casanova, José. "Human Religious Evolution and Unfinished Creation." In *The Spirit in Creation and New Creation: Science and Theology in Western and Orthodox Realms*, edited by Michael Welker, 179–91. Grand Rapids: Eerdmans, 2012.

Casati, Roberto, and Jerome Dokic. "Sounds." *The Stanford Encyclopedia of Philosophy*. http://plato.stanford.edu/archives/sum2011/entries/sounds/.

Casiño, Tereso C., et al. *Reaching the City: Reflections on Urban Mission for the Twenty-First Century*. Pasadena: William Carey Library, 2012.

Castells, Manuel. *Communication Power*. 2nd ed. Oxford: Oxford University Press, 2013.

———. *The Rise of the Network Society*. 2nd ed. Malden, MA: Blackwell, 2010.

Castleman, Dayton. "A Response to Redeeming the Arts." In *The Creative Spirit: A Journal of the Arts and* Faith, edited by Colin Harbison. Lausanne Committee for World Evangelization, 36–37. Jackson, MS: Bellhaven, 2005.

Catmull, Edwin E., and Amy Wallace. *Creativity, Inc.: Overcoming the Unseen Forces that Stand in the Way of True Inspiration*. New York: Random, 2014.

Chapell, Bryan. *Christ-Centered Worship: Letting the Gospel Shape Our Practice*. Grand Rapids: Baker Academic, 2009.

Charland, Maurice. "Constitutive Rhetoric: The Case of the People Quebecois." *Quarterly Journal of Speech* 73 (1987) 133–50.

———. 1993. Constitutive rhetoric: The case of the *Peuple Quebecois*. In *Landmark Essays on Rhetorical Criticism*, ed. T. Benson, 213–234. Davis, CA: Hermagoras.

Chaudhari, Amit. "Into the Mix. Arts & Culture." *New Statesman* 22 (2007) 38–39.

Chiang, Samuel E., and Grant Lovejoy. *Beyond Literate Western Models: Contextualizing Theological Education in Oral Contexts*. Hong Kong: International Orality Network, 2013.

Chilisa, Bagelle. *Indigenous Research Methodologies*. Thousand Oaks, CA: SAGE, 2012.

Chua, Daniel K. L. "Music as the Mouthpiece of Theology." In *Resonant Witness: Conversations Between Music and Theology*, edited by Jeremy Begbie and Steven R. Guthrie, 137–61. Grand Rapids: Eerdmans, 2011.

Clifford, James. *The Predicament of Culture: Twentieth-Century Ethnography, Literature, and Art*. Cambridge, MA: Harvard University Press, 1988.

———. *Routes: Travel and Translation in the Late Twentieth Century*. Cambridge, MA: Harvard University Press, 1997.

Collard, Dianne B. "Promoting Arts Awareness and Education in the Church." In *Worship and Mission for the Global Church: An Ethnodoxology Handbook*, edited by James R. Krabill et al., 358–63. Pasadena: William Carey Library, 1997.

Collins, Mary. "Editorial." In *Music and the Experience of God*, edited by Mary Collins et al., 3–10. Edinburgh: T. & T. Clark, 1989.

Connell, John, and Chris Gibson. "The sound and space of music." *Geodate* 16 (2003) 7–10.

———. "World Music: Deterritorializing Place and Identity." *Human Geography* 28 (2004) 342–61.

Cook, Nicholas. "Music as Performance." In *The Cultural Study of Music: A Critical Introduction*, edited by Martin Clayton et al., 204–14. New York and London: Routledge, 2003.

Coomaraswamy, Ananda K. "The Origin and Use of Images in India." In *Art, Creativity, and the Sacred*, edited by Diane Apostolos-Cappadona, 127–36. New York: Crossroad, 1984.

Cooper-White, Pamela. Review of *Translucence: Religion, the Arts, and Imagination*, edited by Carol Gilbertson and Greg Muilenberg. Minneapolis: Fortress, 2007.

Cox, C. M. *Genetic Studies of Genius: Vol. 2. The Early Mental Traits of Three Hundred Geniuses*. Stanford: Stanford University Press, 1926.

Cox, Christoph, and Daniel Warner, eds. *Audio Culture*. New York: Continuum, 2009.

Crociani-Windland, Lita. *Festivals, Affect, and Identity A Deleuzian Apprenticeship in Central Italian Communities.* London: Anthem, 2011.
Cross, Ian. "Music and Biocultural Evolution." In *The Cultural Study of Music: A Critical Introduction*, edited by Martin Clayton et al., 19–30. New York and London: Routledge, 2003.
Csikszentmihalyi. M. *Creativity: Flow and the Psychology of Discovery and Invention.* New York: Harper Perennial, 1997.
———. "Society, Culture, and Person: A Systems View of Creativity." In *The Nature of Creativity: Contemporary Psychological Perspectives*, edited by R. J. Sternberg, 325–28. New York: Cambridge University Press, 1988.
———. "Creativity." In *Handbook of Creativity*, edited by R. Sternberg, 313–35. Cambridge: Cambridge University Press, 1999. http://www.sagepub.com/upm-data/11443_01_Henry_Ch01.pdf.
Cudworth, Erika, and Stephen Hobden. "Anarchy and Anarchism: Towards a Theory of Complex International Systems." *Millennium: Journal of International Studies* 39 (2010) 399–416.
———. "The Foundations of Complexity, the Complexity of Foundations." *Philosophy of the Social Sciences* 42 (2012) 163–87.
Damasio, Antonio. *The Feeling of What Happens: Body and Emotion in the Making of Consciousness.* New York: Harcourt Brace, 1999.
Darwin, Charles. *The Descent of Man.* 2nd ed. N.d.: N.d., 2014. Kindle.
Das, Samir Kumar. *Conflict and Peace in India's Northeast: The Role of Civil Society.* Washington: East-West Center, 2007.
Davies, Stephen. *Musical Understandings: And Other Essays on the Philosophy of Music.* Oxford: Oxford University Press, 2011.
Day, Colin A. *Collins Thesaurus of the Bible.* Bellingham, WA: Logos Bible Software, 2009.
Deflem, Mathieu. "Ritual, Anti-Structure, and Religion: A Discussion of Victor Turner's Processual Symbolic Analysis." *Journal for the Scientific Study of Religion* 30 (1991) 1–25. http://www.cas.sc.edu/socy/faculty/deflem/zturn.htm.
Dennett, D. C. *Darwin's Dangerous Idea.* New York: Touchstone, 1995.
Derrida, Jacques. Excerpt from "Signature Event Context." In *The Rhetorical Tradition: Readings from Classical Times to the Present*, edited by Patricia Bizzell and Bruce Herzberg 1475–90. Boston/New York: Bedford/St. Martin's, 2001.
———. *Margins of Philosophy.* Translated by Alan Bass. Chicago: University of Chicago Press, 1982.
Detweilier, Craig, and Barry Taylor. *Matrix of Meanings: Finding God in Pop Culture.* Grand Rapids: Baker, 2003.
Dickerson, Matthew, T. *The Mind and the Machine: What It Means to be Human and Why it Matters.* Grand Rapids: Brazos, 2011.
Dueck, Byron. "Part 1 Introduction." In *Migrating Music*, edited by Jason Toynbee and Byron Dueck, 21–27. New York: Routledge, 2011.
Dufoix, Stéphane. *Diasporas.* Berkeley: University of California Press, 2008.
Dunn, J. D. G. *Unity and Diversity in the NT: An Inquiry in the Character of Earliest Christianity.* Philadelphia: Trinity, 1990.
Durham, John I. *Exodus.* Word Biblical Commentary 3. Columbia: Word, 1987.

Easley, Leah. "St. Augustine: Theologian of the Arts. The All Saints' Center for Theology: Thinking through the critical issues facing the Anglican church in North America, Summer." 2011. http://www.allsaintscenterfortheology.org/site/St._Augustine__Theologian_of_Art.html.

Eck, Diana. *A New Religious America: How a "Christian Country" Has Become the World's Most Religiously Diverse Nation*. San Francisco: Harper, 2001.

Eisner, Elliot. "Art and Knowledge." In *A Handbook of the Arts in Qualitative Research*, edited by J. Knowles and Andra L. Cole, 3–12. London: SAGE, 2008.

Eliade, Mircea. *The Sacred and the Profane: The Nature of Religion*. San Diego: Harcourt, 1987.

———. *Symbolism, the Sacred, and the Arts*. Edited by Diane Apostolos-Cappadona. New York: Crossroad, 1985.

Encyclopaedia Brittanica. http://www.britannica.com/EBchecked/topic/42902/Saint-Augustine.

Entman, R. M. "Framing: Toward Clarification of a Fractured Paradigm." *Journal of Communication* 43 (1993) 51–58.

Erol, Ayhan. "Understanding the Diversity of Islamic Identity in Turkey through Popular Music: The Global/Local Nexus." *Social Compass* 58 (2011) 187–202.

Ewing, Katherine Pratt. "Between Cinema and Social Work: Diasporic Muslim Women and the (Dis)pleasures of Hybridity." *Cultural Anthropology* 21 (2006) 265–94.

Ezzarqui, Leila. "Research Paper on Migration. Alliance of Civilizations Secretariat." 2012. http://www.unaoc.org/ibis/wp-content/uploads/2010/05/UNAoC-Background-Research-Paper-on-Migration-and-Integration.pdf.

Fairclough, N. *Critical Discourse Analysis*. Harlow: Pearson Education, 1995.

Farhadian, Charles E. *Christian Worship Worldwide: Expanding Horizons, Deepening Practices*. Grand Rapids: Eerdmans, 2007.

Faulkner, Quentin. *Wiser Than Despair: The Evolution of Ideas in the Relationship of Music and the Christian Church*. Westport, CN: Greenwood, 1996.

Feist, G. J., and F. X. Barron. "Predicting Creativity From Early to Late Adulthood: Intellect, Potential, and Personality." *Journal of Research in Personality* 37 (2003) 62–88.

Feld, Steven. "The Poetics and Politics of Pygmy Pop." In *Western Music and Its Others: Difference, Representation, and Appropriation in Music*, edited by Georgina Born and David Hesmondhalgh, 254–79. Berkeley: University of California Press, 2000.

Ferguson, Tom. "Bible Storying with the Creative Arts for Church Planting." In *Worship and Mission for the Global Church: An Ethnodoxology Handbook*, edited by James R. Krabill et al., 103–5. Pasadena: William Carey Library, 2013.

Finnegan, Ruth. "What Migrates and Who Does It? A Mini Case Study from Fiji." In *Migrating Music*, edited by Jason Toynbee and Byron Dueck, 135–49. New York: Routledge, 2011.

Foley, Edward. *Foundations of Christian Music: The Music of Pre-Constantinian Christianity*. Collegeville, MN: Liturgical, 1996.

Ford, David. *The Future of Christian Theology*. Oxford: Wiley-Blackwell, 2011.

Ford, David, et al. *The Modern Theologians Reader*. Chichester, West Sussex: Wiley-Blackwell, 2011.

The Forgotten Ways. "Developing Apostolic Imagination and Practice in Western Contexts." https://www.theforgottenways.org/apest/.

Forte, Maximilian Christian. *Indigenous Cosmopolitans: Transnational and Transcultural Indigeneity in the Twenty-First Century*. New York: Peter Lang, 2010.

Fortunato, Frank, et al. *All the World is Singing: Glorifying God through the Worship Music of the Nations*. Tyrone, GA: Authentic, 2006.

Fotland, Roar G. "The Southern Phase of Christianity: The Contribution of the Global South to the Church in the Global North." In *Mission to the World: Communicating the Gospel in the 21st Century: Essays in Honour of Knud Jørgensen*, edited by Knud Jørgensen and Tormod Engelsviken, 215–29. Oxford: Regnum, 2008.

Foucault, Michel. *The Order of Things: An Archaeology of the Human Science*. Translated by A. Sheridan. Repr. London: Routledge, 2002.

———. "Excerpt from *The Archaeology of Knowledge*." In *The Rhetorical Tradition: Readings from Classical Times to the Present*, edited by Patricia Bizzell and Bruce Herzberg, 1436–60. New York: Bedford/St. Martin's, 1969.

Foulger, David. "Models of the Communication Process." 2004. http://davis.foulger.info/research/unifiedModelOfCommunication.htm.

Frith, Simon. "The Discourse of World Music." In *Western Music and Its Others: Difference, Representation, and Appropriation in Music*, edited by Georgina Born and David Hesmondhalgh, 305–22. Los Angeles: University of California Press, 2000.

———. *Performing Rites: On the Value of Popular Music*. Cambridge, MA: Harvard University Press, 1996.

Gabora, Liane, and Scott Barry Kaufman. "Evolutionary Approaches to Creativity." In *The Cambridge Handbook of Creativity*, edited by James C. Kaufman and Robert J. Sternberg, 279–300. Cambridge: Cambridge University Press, 2010.

Galton, F. *English Men of Science: Their Nature and Nurture*. London, MacMillan, 1874.

———. *Inquiries into Human Faculty*. London, MacMillan, 1883.

Gamson, W. *Talking Politics*. Cambridge: Cambridge University Press, 1992.

Garces-Foley, Kathleen. *Crossing the Ethnic Divide: The Multiethnic Church on a Mission*. New York: Oxford University Press, 2007.

García-Rivera, Alejandro. *The Community of the Beautiful: A Theological Aesthetics*. Collegeville, MN: Liturgical, 1999.

Gardner, Howard. *Creating Minds: An Anatomy of Creativity Seen Through the Lives of Freud, Einstein, Picasso, Stravinsky, Eliot, Graham, and Gandhi*. New York: BasicBooks, 1993.

Geertz, Clifford. "Art as a Cultural System." *MLN* 91 (1976) 1473–99.

———. "Shifting Aims, Moving Targets: On The Anthropology of Religion." *Journal of the Royal Anthropological Institute* 11 (2005) 1–15.

Glennie, Evelyn. "How to Truly Listen." TEDTalk, 2007. http://www.youtube.com/watch?v=IU3V6zNER4g.

Glover, Robert W. "Compatibility or Incommensurability: International Relations Theory and Complex Systems Analysis." https://www.academia.edu/1785370/Compatibility_or_Incommensurability_International_Relations_Theory_and_Complex_Systems_Analysis.

Goffman, E. *Frame Analysis: An Essay on the Organization of Experience*. New York: Harper and Row, 1974.

Goldwater, Robert John, and Marco Treves. *Artists on Art: From the 14th to the 20th Century*. London: J. Murray, 1976.

Gordon, Stewart. *Mastering the Art of Performance: A Primer for Musicians.* New York: Oxford University Press, 2006.

Gormly, Eric. "Evangelizing Through Appropriation: Toward a Cultural Theory on the Growth of Contemporary Christian Music." *Journal of Media and Religion* 2 (2003) 251–65.

Gouzouasis, Peter, and Karen V. Lee. "Sticky Knot Danish." In *Creating Scholartistry: Imagining the Arts-informed Thesis or Dissertation*, edited by J. G. Knowles et al., 4:15–25. Toronto, ON: Backalong Books and The Centre for Arts-informed Research, 2008.

Green, Joel B. "Narrative and New Testament Interpretation: Reflections on the State of the Art." *LTQ* 20 (2005) 153–66.

Grenz, Stanley J. *The Social God and the Relational Self: A Trinitarian Theology of the Imago Dei.* Louisville, KY: Westminster John Knox, 2001.

Griffith, Ralph T. H. *The Hymns of the Rig-Veda, Volume 2.* Benares: E. J. Lazarus, 1920.

Gunton, Colin. E., ed. *The Doctrine of Creation: Essays in Dogmatics, History, and Philosophy.* London: T. & T. Clark International, 2004.

Gupta, Akhil, and James Ferguson. "Beyond 'culture': space, identity, and the politics of difference." *Cultural Anthropology* 7 (1992) 6–23.

———. "Discipline and Practice: 'The Field' as Site, Method, and Location." In *Anthropological Locations: Boundaries and Grounds of a Field Science*, 1–46. Berkeley: University of California Press, 1997.

Guthrie, Steven R. *Creator Spirit: The Holy Spirit and the Art of Becoming Human.* Grand Rapids: Baker, 2011.

Hale, Susan Elizabeth. *Sacred Space, Sacred Sound: The Acoustic Mysteries of Holy Places.* Wheaton, IL: Quest, 2007.

Hall, Gerard. "Prophetic Dialogue: A Foundational Category for Practical Theology." *IJPT* 14 (2010) 34–46.

Hamilton, Victor P. *The Book of Genesis: Chapters 1–17.* Grand Rapids: Eerdmans, 1990.

Hanson, James S. "Faith Comes From What Is Heard: Oral Performance of Scripture." In *Translucence: Religion, the Arts, and Imagination*, edited by Carol Gilbertson and Greg Muilenberg, 152–84. Minneapolis: Fortress, 2004.

Harbison, Colin. "Redeeming the Arts." https://www.colinharbinson.com/teaching/redeemingarts3.html.

Harris, Robin P. "The Great Misconception: Why Music Is Not a Universal Language." In *Worship and Mission for the Global Church: An Ethnodoxology Handbook*, edited by James R. Krabill, Frank Fortunato, Robin P. Harris, and Brian Schrag, 82-9. Pasadena: William Carey Library, 2013.

Hart, David Bentley. *The Beauty of the Infinite: The Aesthetics of Christian Truth.* Grand Rapids: Eerdmans, 2003.

Hatcher, Mark J. "Poetry, Singing, and Contextualization." *Missiology: An International Review* 29 (2001) 475–87.

Haught, John. "Excerpt from *God After Darwin*." In *The Modern Theologians Reader*, edited by David F. Ford and Mike Higton, 220–24. Malden, MA: Wiley-Blackwell, 2007.

Hawn, Michael C. "Christian Global Hymnody: An Overview." In *Music and Mission: Toward a Theology and Practice of Global Song*, edited by S. T. Kimbrough, 23–40. New York: General Board of Global Ministries, GBGMusik, The United Methodist Church, 2006.

———. *One Bread, One Body: Exploring Cultural Diversity in Worship*. Bethesda, MD: Alban Institute, 2003.

Haynes, Jo. "World Music and the Search for Difference." *Ethnicities* 5 (2005) 365–85.

Hays, Christopher B. "How Shall We Sing? Psalm 137 in Historical and Canonical Context." *Horizons in Biblical Theology* 27 (2005) 35–55.

Headland, Thomas N., and Lawrence A. Reid. "Hunter-Gatherers and Their Neighbors from Prehistory to the Present." *Cultural Anthropology* 30 (1989) 43–66.

Heath, Joanna. "Lengkhawm Zai: A Singing Tradition of Mizo Christianity in Northeast India, Durham theses, Durham University." 2013. http://etheses.dur.ac.uk/6376.

Hebdige, Dick. *Cut 'n' Mix: Culture, Identity, and Caribbean Music*. London: Methuen, 1987.

Hedlund, Roger E. *Quest for Identity: India's Churches of Indigenous Origin: The "Little Tradition" in Indian Christianity*. New Delhi, ISPCK, 2000.

Heidegger, Martin. *Poetry, Language, Thought*. New York: Harper & Row, 1971.

Held, David, and Anthony McGrew. *Globalization/Anti-Globalization: Beyond the Great Divide*. Cambridge: Polity, 2008.

Helson, R. "Personality of Women with Imaginative and Artistic Interests: The Role of Masculinity, Originality, and Other Characteristics in Their Creativity." *Journal of Creative Behavior* 6 (1972) 295–300.

Heneise, Michael T. "Bel Canto in India's Northeast: Young Naga Artists Fuse Opera, Rockabilly, and their Faith." In *Worship and Mission for the Global Church: An Ethnodoxology Handbook*, edited by James R. Krabill et al., 298–300. Pasadena: William Carey Library, 2013.

Hiebert, P. G. "Critical Issues in the Social Sciences and Their Implications for Mission Studies." *Missiology* 24 (1996) 65–82.

———. "The Flaw of the Excluded Middle." *Missiology: An International Review* 10 (1982) 35–47.

———. *The Missiological Implications of Epistemological Shifts: Affirming Truth in a Modern/Postmodern World*. Harrisburg, PA: Trinity Press International, 1999.

———. *Transforming Worldviews: An Anthropological Understanding of How People Change*. Grand Rapids: Baker, 2008.

Hiebert, Paul G., et al. *Understanding Folk Religion: A Christian Response to Popular Beliefs and Practices*. Grand Rapids: Baker, 1999.

Hoffman, Lawrence A. "Musical Traditions and Tensions in the American Synagogue." In *Music and the Experience of God*, edited by Mary Collins et al., 30–40. Edinburgh: T. & T. Clark, 1989.

Holladay, William. *The Psalms through Three Thousand Years: Prayerbook of a Cloud of Witnesses*. Minneapolis: Augsberg Fortress, 1996.

Hopper, Paul. *Understanding Cultural Globalization*. Cambridge, UK: Polity, 2007.

Horujy, Sergey. "How Exactly Is the Spirit Present in Creation? The Hesychast Reception of Natural Theology and Its Modern Implications." In *The Spirit in Creation and New Creation: Science and Theology in Western and Orthodox Realms*, edited by Michael Welker, 95–110. Grand Rapids: Eerdmans, 2012.

Howes, David. "Sensory Formations." In *The Auditory Culture Reader*, edited by Michael Bull and Les Back. Oxford, UK: Berg, 2003.

Hunt, T. W. *Music in Missions: Discipling Through Music*. Nashville: Broadman, 1987.

Hunter, George G., III. *The Celtic Way of Evangelism: How Christianity Can Reach the West . . . Again*. Nashville: Abingdon, 2000.

———. *Should We Change Our Game Plan?: From Traditional or Contemporary to Missional and Strategic*. Nashville: Abingdon, 2013.

Indira Gandhi National Centre for the Arts. http://ignca.nic.in/craft002.htm.

Ingalls, Monique Marie, et al. *Christian Congregational Music: Performance, Identity and Experience*. Burlington, VT: Ashgate, 2013.

Institute for Studies in Psychotherapy and Emotional Body-work (ISPEB). http://cirrie.buffalo.edu/encyclopedia/en/article/139/consumer.

International Council of Ethnodoxologists: A Network for Culturally Appropriate Christian Worship. http://worldofworship.org/.

Internet Encyclopedia of Philosophy. http://www.iep.utm.edu/pla-thei/#SH3b.

Irving, D. R. M. *Colonial Counterpoint: Music in Early Modern Manila*. Oxford: Oxford University Press, 2010.

Irwin, Joyce. "'So Faith Comes from What is Heard': The Relationship between Music and God's Word in the First Two Centuries of German Lutheranism." In *Resonant Witness: Conversations between Music and Theology*, edited by Jeremy S. Begbie and Steven R. Guthrie, 65–82. Grand Rapids: Eerdmans, 2011.

Jaggi, Maya. "No Barriers. Interview with Nitin Sawhney in *The Guardian*." 2006. http://www.guardian.co.uk/music/2006/apr/01/popandrock.

Jameson, Fredric. *Postmodernism, or, The Cultural Logic of Late Capitalism*. Durham: Duke University Press, 1991.

Jenkins, Henry with Ravi Purushotama, et al. "Executive Summary." In *Confronting the Challenges of Participatory Culture: Media Education for the 21st Century*, xi–xv. Cambridge, MA: MIT Press, 2009. http://mitpress.mit.edu/sites/default/files/titles/free_download/9780262513623_Confronting_the_Challenges.pdf.

Johnson, David. "Canon and Criterion: Synopsis and Critique." *Didaskalia* 14 (2003) 1–12.

Johnson, Steve. "The Genius of the Tinkerer." *Wall Street Journal*, September 25, 2010. http://online.wsj.com/news/articles/SB10001424052748703989304575503730101860838?mod=WSJ_hp_mostpop_read&mg=reno64-wsj&url=http%3A%2F%2Fonline.wsj.com%2Farticle%2FSB10001424052748703989304575503730101860838.html%3Fmod%3DWSJ_hp_mostpop_read.

Jones, W. Paul. *Worlds Within A Congregation: Dealing With Theological Diversity* Nashville: Abingdon, 2000.

Jørgensen, Adelin Jonas. "Anthropology of Christianity and Missiology: Disciplinary Contexts, Converging Themes, and Future Tasks of Mission Studies." *Mission Studies* 28 (2011) 186–208.

Jüngel, Eberhard, and J. B. Webster. *God's Being Is in Becoming: The Trinitarian Being of God in the Theology of Karl Barth*. Edinburgh: T. & T. Clark, 2001.

Kaufman, James C., and Robert J. Sternberg. *The Cambridge Handbook of Creativity*. Cambridge: Cambridge University Press, 2010.

Keane, Webb. "Epilogue: Anxious Transcendence." In *The Anthropology of Christianity*. edited by Fenella Cannell, 308–24. Durham: Duke University Press, 2006.

Keightley, Keir. "*Un voyage via barquinho*: Global Circulation, Musical Hybridization, and Adult Modernity, 1961–9." In *Migrating Music*, edited by Jason Toynbee and Byron Dueck, 112–26. New York: Routledge, 2011.

Keller, Timothy. *Center Church: Doing Balanced, Gospel-Centered Ministry in Your City*. Grand Rapids: Zondervan, 2012.

Kelly, Tom, and David Kelly. *Creative Confidence: Unleashing the Creative Potential Within Us All.* New York: Random, 2013.

———. "Reclaim Your Creative Confidence." *The Harvard Business Review*, 2012. http://hbr.org/2012/12/reclaim-your-creative-confidence.

Kerr, Gaven. "Aquinas: Metaphysics." *IEP*, 2012. http://www.iep.utm.edu/aq-meta/.

———. "Matter and Form." *IEP*, http://www.iep.utm.edu/aq-meta/.

Kim, Kyung Hee, et al. "The Relationship between Creativity and Intelligence." In *The Cambridge Handbook of Creativity*, edited by James C. Kaufman and Robert J. Sternberg, 395–412. Cambridge: Cambridge University Press, 2010.

Kimbrough, S. T., Jr. *The Lyrical Theology of Charles Wesley: A Reader.* Eugene, OR: Cascade, 2013.

King, Roberta R. "Music." In *Global Dictionary of Theology*, edited by William A. Dyrness and Veli-Matti Kärkkäinen, 584–89. Downer's Grove, IL: IVP, 2008.

———. "Negotiating the Gospel cross-Culturally." In *Paradigm Shifts in Christian Witness: Insights from Anthropology, Communication, and Spiritual Power*, edited by Charles E. Van Engen et al., 66–75. Maryknoll, NY: Orbis, 2008.

———. *Pathways in Christian Music Communication: The Case of the Senufo of Cote D'Ivoire.* American Society of Missiology Monograph. Eugene, OR: Pickwick, 2009.

King, Roberta R., et al. *Music in the Life of the African Church.* Waco, TX: Baylor University Press, 2008.

Kirsh, David. "How to Think with Bodies and Things." Lecture at Stanford University, May 7, 2010. http://www.youtube.com/watch?v=Vhcubboog6c.

Kittel, Gerhard, et al., eds. *Theological Dictionary of the New Testament*, vol. 7. Grand Rapids: Eerdmans, 1971.

———. "Word of God in the OT and NT." In *Theological Dictionary of the New Testament*, 1:506–15. Grand Rapids: Eerdmans, 1985.

Klayman, Alison, dir. *Ai Weiwei: Never Sorry.* United Media Presentation, 2012.

Knowles, J. Gary, and Ardra L. Cole. *Handbook of the Arts in Qualitative Research: Perspectives, Methodologies, Examples, and Issues.* Los Angeles: Sage, 2008.

Knowles, J. Gary, and Sara Promislow. "Using An Arts Methodology To Create A Thesis Or Dissertation." In *Handbook of the Arts in Qualitative Research: Perspectives, Methodologies, Examples, and Issues*, edited by J. Gary Knowles and Ardra L. Cole, 511–26. Los Angeles: Sage, 2008.

Korom, Frank J. *The Anthropology of Performance: A Reader.* Chichester, West Sussex: Wiley-Blackwell, 2013.

Kozbelt, Aaron, et al. "Theories of Creativity." In *The Cambridge Handbook of Creativity*, Cambridge Handbooks in Psychology, edited by James C. Kaufman and Robert Sternberg, 20–47. Cambridge: Cambridge University Press, 2010.

Krabill, James R. *The Hymnody of the Harrist Church among the Dida of South-Central Ivory Coast (1913–1949): A Historico-Religious Study.* Frankfurt am Main: P. Lang, 1995.

Krabill, James R., et al., eds. *Worship and Mission for the Global Church: An Ethnodoxology Handbook.* International Council of Ethnodoxologists (ICE). Pasadena: William Carey Library, 2013.

Kruse, Holly. "Local Identity and Independent Music Scenes, Online and Off." *Popular Music and Society* 33 (2010) 625–39.

Kumar, Raj. *Essays on Indian Music.* Daryaganj, New Delhi: Discovery, 2003.

Laenui, Poka. "Processes of Decolonization." In *Reclaiming Indigenous Voice and Vision*, edited by M. Battiste, 150–60. Toronto: UBC, 2000.

Lamb, Henry. "Summary Analysis of 'Our Global Neighborhood.' Report of the Commission on Global Governance." 1995. http://humanbeingsfirst.files.wordpress.com/2009/10/cacheof-pdf-our-global-neighborhood-from-sovereignty-net.pdf.

LaMothe, Kimerer, L. "'I am the Dance': Towards an Earthed Christianity." In *Theology, Aesthetics, and Culture*, edited by Robert MacSwain and Taylore Worely, 131–44. Great Britain: Oxford University Press, 2012.

Langer, Suzanne. *Philosophy in a New Key: A Study in the Symbolism of Reason, Rite, and Art*. Cambridge, MA: Harvard University Press, 1957.

Langton, Marcia. "Dreaming Art." In *Complex Entanglements: Art, Globalisation, and Cultural Difference*, edited by Nikos Papastergiadis, 42–56. London: Rivers Oram, 2003.

The Lausanne Movement / WEA Consultation on Arts in Mission. http://www.lausanne.org/en/gatherings/event/61-consultation-on-arts-in-mission.html.

Lee, Moonjang. "Reading the Bible in the Non-Western Church." In *Mission in the Twenty-First Century: Exploring the Five Marks of Global Mission*, edited by Andrew F. Walls and Cathy Ross, 148–56. Maryknoll, NY: Orbis, 2008.

Leeuw, G. van der. *Sacred and Profane Beauty: The Holy in Art*. New York: Holt, Rinehart and Winston, 1963.

Levine, Joseph A. "Judaism and Music." In *Sacred Sound: Experiencing Music in World Religions*, edited by Guy L. Beck, 29–59. Waterloo, ON: Wilfrid Laurier University, 2006.

Levitin, Daniel J. *This is Your Brain on Music: The Science of a Human Observation*. New York: Plume, 2007.

———. *The World in Six Songs: How the Musical Brain Created Human Nature*. New York: Plume, 2008.

Levitt, Peggy. "God Needs No Passport: Trying to Define the Boundaries of Belonging." *Harvard Divinity Bulletin* 34 (2006). http://www.hds.harvard.edu/news-events/harvard-divinity-bulletin/articles/god-needs-no-passport.

Lewellen, Ted C. *The Anthropology of Globalization: Cultural Anthropology Enters the 21st Century*. Westport, CN: Bergin & Garvey, 2002.

Lewis, C. S. *Mere Christianity*. New York: Macmillan, 1960.

Lewis, Hannah Margaret. *A Critical Examination of the Church and Deaf People: Toward a Deaf Liberation Theology*. Birmingham: University of Birmingham, 2002.

Lewis, Mark W. *The Diffusion of Black Gospel Music in Postmodern Denmark: How Mission and Music Are Combining to Affect Christian Renewal*. The Asbury Theological Seminary Series in World Christian Revitalization Movements in Intercultural Studies 3. Lexington, KY: Emeth, 2010.

Limón, J. E., and M. J. Young. "Frontiers, Settlements, and Development in Folklore Studies, 1972–1985." *Annual Review of Anthropology* 15 (1986) 437–60.

Lippman, W. *Public Opinion*. New York: Courier Dove, 2004.

Lipsitz, George. *Dangerous Crossroads: Popular Music, Postmodernism, and the Poetics of Place*. London: Verso, 1994.

Lockyer, Herbert, Jr. *All the Music of the Bible*. Peabody, MA: Hendrickson, 2004.

Lopes de Mello, Lucce. "Psychosomatic Disorders." 2010. http://cirrie.buffalo.edu/encyclopedia/en/article/139.

Louw, Johannes P., and Eugene Albert Nida. "Psychological Faculties (Domain 26)." *Greek-English Lexicon of the New Testament: Based on Semantic Domains*, 1–16. 2nd ed. Minneapolis: Fortress, 1996.

Lovejoy, Grant. "The Extent of Orality: 2012 Update." *Orality Journal: the Word Became Fresh* 1 (2012) 11–40.

Lynch, Gordon. "The Role of Popular Music in the Construction of Alternative Spiritual Identities and Ideologies." *Journal for the Scientific Study of Religion* 45 (2006) 481–88.

Mach, Zdislaw. "National Anthems: The Case of Chopin as a National Composer." In *Ethnicity, Identity, and Music: The Musical Construction of Place*, edited by Martin Stokes, 45–60. Oxford/ New York: Berg, 1994.

Mackellar, Calum. "Creation, Co-creation and the Ethics of Pro-creative Cloning." The Scottish Order of Christian Unity, 2000. http://www.socu.org.uk/Creation%20 and%20Cloning.pdf.

Mahmadalli, Hassan. "Breaking the Code: New Approaches to Diversity and Equality in the Arts." In *Third Text: Critical Perspectives in Contemporary Art and Culture*. 2011. http://thirdtext.creativecase.org.uk/?location_id=465.

Makoto Fujimura. http://www.makotofujimura.com/four-holy-gospels/.

Manuel, Peter. *Cassette Culture: Popular Music and Technology in North India*. Chicago: University of Chicago Press, 1993.

Maritain, Jacques, et al. *The Degrees of Knowledge*. London: G. Bles, The Centenary, 1937.

Marti, Gerardo. *Worship Across the Racial Divide: Religious Music and the Multiracial Congregation*. New York: Oxford University Press, 2012.

Mascall, E. L. *He Who Is: A Study in Traditional Theism*. London: Longmans, Green, 1962.

Matsue, Jennifer Milioto. "Stars to the State and Beyond: Globalization, Identity, and Asian Popular Music." *The Journal of Asian Studies: Review of Eastern and Southern Asia and the Adjacent Pacific Islands* 72 (2013) 5–20.

Maurer, Christian. "Sunoida, Suneidesis." *Theological Dictionary of the New Testament*, edited by Gerhard Kittel et al., 900–14. Minneapolis: Fortress, 1964.

Mazzola, G., et al. *Musical Creativity: Strategies and Tools in Composition and Improvisation*. Berlin: Springer, 2012.

McBrien, Richard. *Catholicism, Volume 2*. London: G. Chapman, 1980.

Mccomiskey, Thomas E. "278 בָּרָא." In *Theological Wordbook of the Old Testament*, edited by R. Laird Harris et al., 127. Chicago: Moody, 1999.

McCurdy, David W., et al. *The Cultural Experience: Ethnography in Complex Society*. Long Grove, IL: Waveland, 2005.

McGann, Mary E. *Exploring Music as Worship and Theology: Research in Liturgical Practice*. Collegeville, MN: Liturgical, 2002.

McGavran, Donald A. *The Bridges of God: A Study in the Strategy of Missions*. New York: Friendship, 1955.

McGee, Annie. "El Condor Pasa." *Audio Sparx*. http://www.audiosparx.com/sa/summary/play.cfm/crumb.1024/crumc.0/sound_iid.428201.

McLuhan, Marshall, et al. *The Medium is the Massage*. New York: Bantam, 1967.

McKinnon, James W. *Music in Early Christian Literature*. Cambridge: Cambridge University Press, 1987.

McNeill, William Hardy. *Polyethnicity and National Unity in World History.* Toronto: University of Toronto Press, 1986.

Mednick, S. A. "The Associative Basis of the Creative Process." *Psychological Review* 69 (1962) 220–32.

Mehrlander, Ursula, et al. "Changing City Spaces: Challenges to European Cultural Policy." EU funded project. In *Research Paper on Migration*, Conducted by Leila Ezzarqui, Senior Research Officer, Alliance of Civilizations Secretariat, United Nations, New York, 2006. https://www.unitar.org/ny/sites/unitar.org.ny/files/thematic_migration.pdf.

Memmi, Albert. *The Colonizer and the Colonized.* New York: Orion, 1965.

Merriam, Alan P. *The Anthropology of Music.* Evanston: Northwestern University Press, 1964.

Meyer, Leonard B. *Emotion and Meaning in Music.* Chicago and London: University of Chicago Press, 1956.

Middleton, Richard. "Musical Belongings: Western Music and Its Low-Other." In *Western Music and Its Others: Difference, Representation, and Appropriation in Music,* edited by Georgina Born and David Hesmondhalgh, 59–85. Los Angeles: University of California Press, 2000.

Miles, Margaret. "The Resurrection of Body: Re-imagining Human Personhood in Christian Tradition." In *Theology, Aesthetics, and Culture: Responses to the Work of David Brown,* edited by Robert MacSwain and Taylor Worley, 42–52. Oxford: Oxford University Press, 2012.

Mintz, Sidney W. "The Localization of Anthropological Practice: From Area Studies to Transnationalism." *Critique of Anthropology* 18 (1998) 117–33.

Moberg, Marcus. "Religion in Popular Music or Popular Music as Religion? A Critical Review of Scholarly Writing on the Place of Religion in Metal Music and Culture." *Popular Music and Society* 35 (2012) 113–30.

Mobley, Greg. "EthicsDaily Weblog. The Prophets—Performing Artists, Not Authors." http://ethicsdaily.com/the-prophets-performing-artists-not-authors-cms-20807#sthash.ponfmhud.dpuf.

Moltmann, Jürgen. "Excerpt from *The Crucified God: The Cross of Christ as the Foundation and Criticism of Christian Theology.*" In *The Modern Theologians Reader,* edited by David F. Ford and Mike Higton, 90–95. Malden, MA: Wiley-Blackwell, 1967.

———. *God in Creation: A New Theology of Creation and the Spirit of God.* Translated by Margaret Kohl. Minneapolis: Fortress, 1993.

———. *The Trinity and the Kingdom: The Doctrine of God.* Minneapolis: Fortress, 1993.

Moon, Walter Jay. *African Proverbs Reveal Christianity in Culture: a Narrative Portrayal of Builsa Proverbs Contextualizing Christianity in Ghana.* Eugene, OR: Pickwick, 2009.

———. "Teaching Oral Learners in Institutional Settings." In *Beyond Literate Western Models: Contextualizing Theological Education in Oral Contexts,* edited by Samuel E. Chiang and Grant Lovejoy, 143–52. Hong Kong: International Orality Network, 2013.

———. *Using Proverbs to Contextualize Christianity in the Builsa Culture of Ghana, West Africa.* PhD diss., Asbury Theological Seminary, 2005.

Montagu, Jeremy. *Musical Instruments of the Bible.* Lanham, MD: Scarecrow, 2002.

Monti, Anthony. *A Natural Theology of the Arts: Imprint of the Spirit*. Aldershot, Hampshire: Ashgate, 2003.

Moran, Seana. "The Role of Creativity in Society." In *The Cambridge Handbook of Creativity*, edited by James C. Kaufman and Robert J. Sternberg, 74–92. New York: Cambridge University Press, 2010.

Morcom, Anna. *Hindi Film Songs and the Cinema*. Aldershot, Hampshire: Ashgate, 2007.

Moring, Mark. "Songs of Justice, Missions of Mercy: Why Christian Musicians Are Embarking on a Different Kind of World Tour." *Christianity Today*, November 13, 2009. http://www.christianitytoday.com/ct/2009/november/19.30.html.

Mosquera, Gerardo. "Alien-Own/ Own Alien: Notes on Globalisation and Cultural Difference." In *Complex Entanglements: Art, Globalisation, and Cultural Difference*, edited by Nikos Papastergiadis, 18–29. London: Rivers Oram, 2003.

Moustakas, Clark. *Heuristic Research: Design, Methdology, and Applications*. Newbury Park, CA: Sage, 1990.

Muck, Terry C., and Frances S. Adeney. *Christianity Encountering World Religions: the Practice of Mission in the Twenty-First Century*. Grand Rapids: Baker Academic, 2009.

Multicultural Worship Leaders Network. http://multiculturalworship.org/a-multi-ethnic-worship-leader-has-conviction-by-jaewoo-kim.

Mungazi, Dickson A. "Application of Memmi's Theory of the Colonizer and the Colonized to the Conflicts in Zimbabwe." *The Journal of Negro Education* 55 (1986) 518–34.

Myers, Allen C. *The Eerdmans Bible Dictionary*. Grand Rapids: Eerdmans, 1987.

Nadel, S. F. "The Origins of Music." In *Readings in Ethnomusicology*, edited by David P. McAllester, 277–91. New York: Johnson Reprint, 1971.

Nandhivarman, N. *The Nagaland Struggle: Nagas and Dravidians*. 2010. http://www.scribd.com/doc/32363297/The-Nagaland-Struggle.

Nealon, Jeffrey, T. *Post-Postmodernism, or, The Logic of Just-in-Time Capitalism*. Stanford: Stanford University Press, 2012.

Nettl, Bruno. *Eight Urban Musical Cultures: Tradition and Change*. Urbana: University of Illinois Press, 1978.

———. *The Study of Ethnomusicology: Thirty-one Issues and Concepts*. Urbana: University of Illinois Press, 2005.

Neuhaus, Richard John. *Death on a Friday Afternoon: Meditations on the Last Words of Jesus from the Cross*. New York: Basic, 2000.

Neuman, Daniel L. "Indian Music as a Cultural System." *Asian Music* 17 (1985) 98–113.

Newbigin, Leslie. *The Gospel in a Pluralist Society*. Grand Rapids: Eerdmans, 1989.

———. *The Open Secret: An Introduction to the Theology of Mission*. Rev. ed. Grand Rapids: Eerdmans, 1995.

Nida, Eugene A. *Message and Mission: the Communication of the Christian Faith*. Pasadena: William Carey Library, 1990.

Nketia, Kwabena J. H. "The Aesthetic Dimension in Ethnomusicological Studies." *World Music* 24 (1984) 3–24.

———. "Musical Interaction in Ritual Events." In *Music and the Experience of God*, edited by Mary Collins et al., 111–26. Edinburgh: T. & T. Clark, 1989.

Nocent, Adrien. "Words and Music in the Liturgy." In *Music and the Experience of God*, edited by Mary Collins et al., 127–34. Edinburgh: T. & T. Clark, 1989.

Nooshin, Laudan. "Hip-Hop Tehran: Migrating Styles, Musical Hybridization, and Adult Modernity, 1961–9." In *Migrating Musics*, edited by Jason Toynbee and Byron Dueck, 92–111. New York: Routledge, 2011.

Norman, H. Joy. *The Bhajan: Christian Devotional Music in the Indian Diaspora*. Cambridgeshire, UK: Melrose, 2008.

Oddie, Geoffrey. "Constructing 'Hinduism': The Impact of the Protestant Missionary Movement on Hindu Self-Understanding." In *Christians and Missionaries in India: Cross-Cultural Communication since 1500*, edited by Robert Eric Frykenberg, 155–82. Grand Rapids: Eerdmans, 2003.

O'Donnell, Lawrence. "Music and the Brain." 1999. http://www.cerebromente.org.br/n15/mente/musica.html.

Ong, Walter J. *Orality and literacy: The Technologizing of the Word*. London: Methuen, 1989.

Osumare, Halifu. "Global Breakdancing and the Intercultural Body." In *The Anthropology of Performance A Reader*, edited by Frank J. Korom, 260–72. Chichester, West Sussex: Wiley-Blackwell, 2013.

Pachuau, Lalsangkima. "Engaging the 'Other' in a Pluralistic World: Toward a Subaltern Hermeneutics of Christian Mission." *Studies in World Christianity* 8 (2002) 63–80.

———. *Ethnic Identity and Christianity: A Socio-Historical and Missiological Study of Christianity in Northeast India with Special Reference to Mizoram*. Frankfurt am Main: P. Lang, 2002.

Pachuau, Lalsangkima, and Knud Jørgensen, eds. *Witnessing to Christ in a Pluralistic World: Christian Mission Among Other Faiths*. Eugene, OR: Wipf and Stock, 2011.

Pang, Laikwan. *Creativity and Its Discontents: China's Creative Industries and Intellectual Property Rights Offenses*. Durham, NC: Duke University Press, 2012.

Pannenberg, Wolfhart. *Systematic Theology, Volume 1*. Grand Rapids: Eerdmans, 1991.

Papastergiadis, Nikos. *Art and Cultural Difference: Hybrids and Cultures*. London: Oxford University Press, 1995.

———. *Cosmopolitanism and Culture*. Cambridge: Polity, 2012.

Parsons, Mark David. "Text, Tone, and Context: A Methodological Prolegomenon for a Theology of Liturgical Song." *Worship* 79 (2005).

Patel, Aniruddh D. *Music, Language, and the Brain*. Oxford: Oxford University Press, 2008.

Paul Simon. http://www.paulsimon.com/us/music/paul-simon-concert-live-rhymin/el-condor-pasa-if-i-could.

Pinker, Steven. *The Language Instinct: The New Science of Language and Mind*. London: Penguin, 1995.

Piper, John. "Excerpt from Various Sources." In *Worship and Mission for the Global Church: An Ethnodoxology Handbook*, edited by James R. Krabill et al., 96–102. Pasadena: William Carey Library, 2013.

Plsek, Paul E. "Working Paper: Models for the Creative Process." 1996. http://www.directedcreativity.com/pages/WPModels.html#TorranceCite.

Plucker, J. A., et al. "Why Isn't Creativity More Important to Educational Psychologists? Potential, Pitfalls, and Future Directions in Creativity Research." *Educational Psychologist* 39 (2004) 83–96.

Polkinghorn, John. "The Hidden Work of the Spirit in Creation." In *The Spirit in Creation and New Creation: Science and Theology in Western and Orthodox Realms*, edited by Michael Welker, 3–10. Grand Rapids: Eerdmans, 2012.

Prensky, Mark. "Digital Natives, Digital Immigrants." In *The Digital Divide: Arguments for and Against Facebook, Google, Texting, and the Age of Social Networking*, edited by Mark Bauerlein, 3–11. New York: Jeremy A. Tarcher/ Penguin, 2011.

———. "Do They Really Think Differently." In *The Digital Divide: Arguments for and Against Facebook, Google, Texting, and the Age of Social Networking*, edited by Mark Bauerlein, 12–25. New York: Jeremy A. Tarcher/ Penguin, 2011.

Prickett, Stephen. *Origins of Narrative: The Romantic Appropriation of the Bible*. New York: Cambridge University Press, 1996.

Proulx, Craig. "Aboriginal Hip Hoppers: Representin' Aboriginality in Cosmopolitan Worlds." In *Indigenous Cosmopolitans: Transnational and Transcultural Indigeneity in the Twenty-First Century*, edited by Maximilian C. Forte, 39–62. New York: Peter Lang, 2010.

Rantanen, Terhi. "A Transnational Cosmopolitan: An Interview with Ulf Hannerz." *Global Media and Communication* 3 (2007) 11–27.

Rap Basement. http://lyrics.rapbasement.com/Jay%20Z_Party%20Life_lyrics_1784.html.

Reidemann, Mark von. "Nagaland: a Tribal Church: Interview with a Bishop from Most Catholic Spot in India." 2010. http://www.zenit.org/en/articles/nagaland-a-tribal-church.

Reno, R. R. "Theology's Continental Captivity." *First Things*, April 2006. http://www.firstthings.com/article/2007/01/theology8217s-continental-captivity—-18.

Research Centre for Transnational Art. Identity. Nation (TrAIN). http://www.transnational.org.uk/.

Reynolds, Jack. "Metaphysics of Presence/ Logocentrism." *Internet Encyclopedia of Philosophy*. 2013. http://www.iep.utm.edu/derrida.

Ribes-Inesta, Emilio. "Human Behavior as Language: Some Thoughts on Wittgenstein." *Behavior and Philosophy* 34 (2006) 109–21.

Richard, H. L. *Following Jesus in the Hindu Context: The Intriguing Implications of N.V. Tilak's Life and Thought*. Pasadena: W. Carey Library, 1998.

Richards, Lawrence O. *The Bible Reader's Companion*. Wheaton: Victor, 1991.

Robertson, Roland. "Globalisation as a Problem." In *The Globalization Reader*, edited by Frank J. Lechner and John Boli, 87–94. Oxford: Blackwell, 2009.

Robey, David. "Introduction." In *Umberto Eco: The Open Work*. Translated by Anna Cancogni. Cambridge, MA: Harvard University Press, 1989.

Robins, Kevin. "Migrating music and good-enough cosmopolitanism: encounter with Robin Denselow and Charlie Gillett." In *Migrating Music*, edited by Jason Toynbee, 150–64. New York: Routledge, 2011.

Robinson, Ken. *Out of Our Minds: Learning To Be Creative*. Oxford: Capstone, 2001.

Rock, Judith, and Norman Mealy. *Performer as Priest and Prophet: Restoring the Intuitive in Worship through Music and Dance*. San Francisco: Harpercollins, 1988.

Rofel, Lisa. "Rethinking Modernity: Space and Factory Discipline in China". *Cultural Anthropology* 7 (1992) 93–114.

Romanow, Rebecca. "But . . . Can the Subaltern Sing?" *CLCWeb: Comparative Literature and Culture* 7 (2005) 2.

Romanowski, William D. *Eyes Wide Open: Looking for God in Popular Culture*. Grand Rapids: Brazos, 2001.

Ruiz, David. "Global shift from North to South." In *Worship and Mission for the Global Church: An Ethnodoxology Handbook*, edited by Frank Fortunato et al., 43–45. International Council of Ethnodoxologists (ICE). Pasadena: William Carey Library, 2013.

Runco, Mark A., and Robert S. Albert. "Creativity Research: A Historical View." In *The Cambridge Handbook of Creativity*, edited by James C. Kaufman and Robert J. Sternberg, 3–19. New York: Cambridge University Press, 2010.

Runco Mark A., and I. Chand. "Cognition and Creativity." *Educational Psychology Review* 7 (1995) 243–67.

Rynkiewich, Michael A. *Soul, Self, and Society: A Postmodern Anthropology for Mission in a Postcolonial World*. Eugene, OR: Cascade, 2011.

———. "A New Heaven and a New Earth? The Future of Missiological Anthropology." In *Paradigm Shifts in Christian Witness: Insights from Anthropology, Communication, and Spiritual Power: Essays in Honor of Charles H. Kraft*, edited by Charles H., 33–46. Maryknoll, NY: Orbis, 2008.

———. "Mission, Hermeneutics, and the Local Church." *Journal of Theological Interpretation* 1 (2007) 47–60.

Saliers, Don. *Music and Theology*. Nashville: Abingdon, 2007.

Sanger, Michael, and Martha M. Giddings. "Teaching Note: A Simple Approach to Complexity Theory." *Journal of Social Work Education* 48 (2012) 369–76.

Sapir, Edward. *Language: An Introduction to the Study of Speech*. New York: Harcourt, Brace, 1949.

Sartre, Jean Paul. "Introduction." In *The Colonizer and the Colonized*, edited by Albert Memmi, 17–25. Boston: Beacon, 1965.

Sawyer, R. K. *Explaining Creativity: The Science of Human Innovation*. New York: Oxford University Press, 2006.

Saayman, Willem, and Klippies Kritzinger, eds. *Mission in Bold Humility: David Bosch's Work Considered*. Maryknoll, NY: Orbis, 1997.

Schrag, Brian. *Creating Local Arts Together: A Manual to Help Communities Reach Their Kingdom Goals*, edited by James R. Krabill. Pasadena: William Carey Library, 2013.

———. "Excerpt from 'Why Local Arts Are Central to Mission.'" In *International Journal of Frontier Missiology* 24 (2007) 199–202.

———. "The Love Motive." In *Worship and Mission for the Global Church: An Ethnodoxology Handbook*, edited by James R. Krabill et al., 192–93. Pasadena: William Carey Library, 2013.

Schrag, Brian, and Paul Neeley. *All The World Will Worship: Helps for Developing Indigenous Hymns*. 3rd ed. Duncanville, Tex: EthnoDoxology, 2005.

Schuster, Jürgen. "Karl Hartenstein: Mission with a Focus on the End." *Mission Studies* 19 (2002) 53–81.

Schwarzstein, Dora. "Oral History in Latin America." In *Oral History: An Interdisciplinary Anthology*, edited by David K. Dunaway and Willa K. Baum, 417–24. Walnut Creek, CA: Altamira, 1996.

Scott, Emily Eliza. "Artists' Platforms for New Ecologies." *Third Text*. 2013. http://www.thirdtext.org/artists'-platforms-for-new-ecologies-arc.

Scruton, Roger. "Music and Morality." *American Spectator* 43 (February) 42–45.

Seamands, Stephen. *Ministry in the Image of God: The Trinitarian Shape of Christian Service*. Downer's Grove, IL: InterVarsity, 2005.

Seeger, Anthony. *Why Suyá Sing: A Musical Anthropology of an Amazonian People*. Cambridge: Cambridge University Press, 1987.

———. *Why Suyá Sing: A Musical Anthropology of an Amazonian People*. Urbana: University of Illinois Press, 2004.

Segovia, Fernando S. "Towards a Hermeneutics of the Diaspora." In *The Modern Theologians Reader*, edited by David F. Ford and Mike Higton, 325–29. Malden, MA: Wiley-Blackwell, 2011.

Shenk, Wilbert R. *Changing Frontiers of Mission*. American Society of Missiology Series 28. Maryknoll, NY: Orbis, 1999.

———. "New Wineskins for New Wine: Toward a Post-Christendom Ecclesiology." *IBMR* 29 (2005) 73–79.

Sherinian, Zoe. "Dalit Theology in Tamil Christian Folk Music: A Transformative Liturgy by James Theophilus Appavoo." In *Popular Christianity in India: Riting between the Lines*, edited by Selva J. Raj and Corinne G. Dempsey, 233–54. Albany: State University of New York Press, 2002.

Sherwood, Yvonne M. "Prophetic Scatology: Prophecy and the Art of Sensation." *Semeia Studies* 82 (2000) 183–224.

Siapera, Eugenia. *Cultural Diversity and Global Media: The Mediation of Difference*. Chichester, West Sussex, UK: Wiley-Blackwell, 2010.

Simonton, D. K. "Creative Productivity: A Predictive and Explanatory Model of Career Landmarks and Trajectories." *Psychological Review* 104 (1997) 66–89.

———. "Eminence, Creativity, and Geographic Marginality: A Recursive Structural Equation Model." *Journal of Personality and Social Psychology* 35 (1977) 805–16.

———. *Genius, Creativity, and Leadership*. Cambridge, MA: Harvard University Press, 1984.

———. *Origins of Genius: Darwinian Perspectives on Creativity*. New York: Oxford University Press, 1999.

———. *Scientific Genius*. New York: Cambridge University Press, 1988.

Singh, Manpreet. "The Soul Hunters of Central Asia." *Christianity Today*, 2006. http://www.christianitytoday.com/ct/2006/february/38.51.html.

Sirota, Victoria. "An Exploration of Music As Theology." *Arts in Religion and Theological Studies* 5 (1993) 24–28.

Small, Christopher. *Musicking: The Meanings of Performing and Listening*. Hanover: University Press of New England, 2011.

Smith, Boynton Henry, and James Manning Sherwood, eds. "Inspiration." *The American Presbyterian and Theological Review*, 2:312–49. New York: Somers, 1864.

Smith, James K. A. *Desiring the Kingdom: Worship, Worldview, and Cultural Formation*. Grand Rapids: Baker Academic, 2009.

———. *The Fall of Interpretation: Philosophical Foundations for a Creational Hermeneutic*. Grand Rapids: Baker Academic, 2012.

———. *Introducing Radical Orthodoxy: Mapping a Post-Secular Theology*. Grand Rapids: Baker Academic, 2004.

Smith-Christopher, Daniel L. *A Biblical Theology of Exile*. Minneapolis: Fortress, 2002.

Sohngen, Oskar. "Music and Theology: A Systematic Approach." In *Sacred Sound: Music in Religious Thought and Practice*, edited by Joyce Irwin, 1–19. Chico, CA: Scholars, 1983.

Staebler, Stephen De, and Diana Apostolos-Cappadona. "Reflections on Art and the Spirit." In *Art, Creativity, and the Sacred*, edited by Diana Apostolos-Cappadona, 24–33. New York: Crossroad, 1984.

Stapert, Calvin R. *A New Song for an Old World: Musical Thought in the Early Church*. Grand Rapids: Eerdmans, 2007.

Steiner, George. *Errata: An Examined Life*. New Haven, CT: Yale University Press, 1998.

Stewart, Charles, and Rosalind Shaw, eds. *Syncretism/Anti-Syncretism: the Politics of Religious Synthesis*. London: Routledge, 1994.
Stokes, Martin, ed. "Introduction." In *Ethnicity, Identity and Music: The Musical Construction of Place*, 1–28. New York: Berg, 1997.
———. "Migrant/Migrating Music and the Mediterranean." In *Migrating Music*, edited by Jason Toynbee and Byron Dueck, 28–37. New York: Routledge, 2011.
———. "Music and the Global Order." *Annual Review of Anthropology* 33 (2004) 47–72.
———. "On Musical Cosmopolitanism." EMacalester International Roundtable Paper 3. 2007. http://digitalcommons.macalester.edu/intlrdtable/3.
Stoltzfus, Philip E. *Theology as Performance: Music, Aesthetics, and God in Western Theology*. New York: T. & T. Clark, 2006.
Stordalen, Terje. "Mother Earth in Biblical Hebrew Literature." In *The Centre and the Periphery: A European Tribute to Walter Brueggemann*, edited by Jill Anne Middlemans et al., 113–29. Sheffield: Sheffield Phoenix, 2010.
Streng, Frederick J. *Understanding Religious Man*. Belmont, CA: Dickenson, 1969.
Stringer, Martin. *A Sociological History of Christian Worship*. Cambridge, UK: Cambridge University Press, 2005.
Sugirtharajah, R. S. "The Bible and Its Asian Readers." *Biblical Interpretation* 1 (1993) 54–66.
———. "Postcolonial and Biblical Interpretation: The Next Phase." In *A Postcolonial Commentary on the New Testament Writings*, edited by Fernando F. Segovia and R. S. Sugirtharajah, 455–61. London: T. & T. Clark, 2007.
Swanson, James A., and Orville Nave. *Zion*. Oak Harbor, WA: Logos Research Systems, 1994.
Sylvan, Robin. *Traces Of The Spirit: The Religious Dimensions of Popular Music*. New York: New York University Press, 2002.
Tajfel, H. *Human Groups and Social Categories: Studies in Social Psychology*. Cambridge: Cambridge University Press, 1981.
Talukdar, Sushanta. "Who failed the Nagas? Book Review of *The Naga Story: First Armed Struggle in India* by Harish Chandola." *The Hindu*, July 8, 2013. http://www.thehindu.com/books/books-reviews/who-failed-the-nagas/article4895341.ece.
Taussig, Michael T. *Mimesis and Alterity: A Particular History of the Senses*. New York: Routledge, 1993.
Taylor, Barry. *Entertainment Theology: New-Edge Spirituality in a Digital Democracy*. Grand Rapids: Baker Academic, 2008.
Taylor, J. B. "Word." In *New Bible Dictionary*, edited by D. R. W. Wood et al., 1247. Leicester, England; Downers Grove, IL: InterVarsity, 1996.
Taylor, Timothy D. *Beyond Exoticism: Western Music and the World*. Durham: Duke University Press, 2007.
———. "'Strategic Inauthenticity.' Excerpt from *Global Pop: World Music, World Markets*, 127-30, 134-5, 142-3." In *The Globalization Reader*, edited by Frank J. Lechner and John Boli, 151–55. Malden, MA: Blackwell, 2009.
Taylor, W. David O. *For the Beauty of the Church: Casting a Vision for the Arts*. Grand Rapids: Baker, 2010.
Tennent, Timothy C. *Invitation to World Missions: A Trinitarian Missiology for the Twenty-First Century*. Grand Rapids: Kregel, 2010.

Tienou, Tite. "Dare to Make New Mistakes: Doing Christian Mission Without Historical Guilt." *Touchstone* (2010) 19–29.
Till, Rupert. *Pop Cult: Religion and Popular Music*. New York: Continuum, 2010.
Tillich, Paul. *Dynamics of Faith*. New York: Harper Torchbooks, 1958.
Times of India. http://articles.timesofindia.indiatimes.com/2011-04-06/gurgaon/29387845_1_literacy-rate-female-population-census-officials.
Torrance, Thomas F. "Excerpt from *The Knowledge of God*." In *The Modern Theologians Reader*, edited by David F. Ford and Mike Higton, 101–3. Malden, MA: Wiley-Blackwell, 1965.
Toynbee, Jason. "Introduction to Part 2: Translations." In *Migrating Music*, edited by Jason Toynbee and Byron Dueck, 73–78. Abingdon, NY: 2011.
Toynbee, Jason, and Byron Dueck. *Migrating Musics*. New York: Routledge, 2011.
Turner, Victor. *The Ritual Process: Structure and Anti-Structure*. Chicago: Aldine, 1969.
Vanhoozer, Kevin J. *Is There a Meaning in This Text?: The Bible, the Reader, and the Morality of Literary Knowledge*. Grand Rapids: Zondervan, 1998.
Viladesau, Richard. *Theology and the Arts: Encountering God Through Music, Art, and Rhetoric*. New York: Paulist, 2000.
Von Balthasar, Hans urs. "Excerpt from *Theo-Drama: Theological Dramatic Theory, Vol. III. The Dramatis Personae: The Person in Christ*, trans. Graham Harrison." In *The Modern Theologians* Reader, edited by David F. Ford and Mike Higton, 64–68. Malden, MA: Wiley-Blackwell, 1992.
———. "Excerpt from *Theo-Drama: Theological Dramatic Theory, Vol. IV. The Action*, trans. Graham Harrison." In *The Modern Theologians* Reader, edited by David F. Ford and Mike Higton, 68–72. Malden, MA: Wiley-Blackwell, 1994.
Wade, Bonnie. *Music in India: The Classical Traditions*. Englewood Cliffs, NJ: Prentice-Hall, 1979.
Wallas, Graham. *The Art of Thought*. New York: Harcourt, Brace, 1926.
Walls, Andrew. F. *The Cross-Cultural Process in Christian History*. Maryknoll, NY: Orbis, 2002.
———. "The Expansion of Christianity: An Interview with Andrew Walls." *The Christian Century*, August 2–9, 2000. http://www.religion-online.org/showarticle.asp?title=2052.
———. "The Mission of the Church Today in the Light of Global History." *Word and World* 20 (2000) 17–21.
———. *The Missionary Movement in Christian History: Studies in the Transmission of Faith*. Mary Knoll, NY: Orbis, 2006.
Weber, William. "Cosmopolitan, National, And Regional Identities in Eighteenth-Century European Musical Life." In *The Oxford Handbook of the New Cultural History of Music*, edited by Jane F. Fulcher, 209–27. Oxford: Oxford University Press, 2011.
Weisberg, R. W. "On Structure in the Creative Process: A Quantitative Case-Study of the Creation of Picasso's Guernica." *Empirical Studies of the Arts* 22 (2004) 23–54.
Welker, Michael. *The Spirit in Creation and New Creation: Science and Theology in Western and Orthodox Realms*. Grand Rapids: Eerdmans, 2012.
Werbner, Pnina. *Anthropology and the New Cosmopolitanism: Rooted, Feminist and Vernacular Perspectives*. Oxford: Berg, 2008. http://public.eblib.com/EBLPublic/PublicView.do?ptiID=452588.

West, Travis. "Performance Criticism of the Narratives in the Hebrew Bible. ThM Thesis, Western Theological Seminary." 2009. http://www.biblicalperformancecriticism.org/index.php/component/content/article/20-full-text-articles/244-performance-criticism-of-the-narratives-in-the-hebrew-bible.

White, Bob W. *Music and Globalization: Critical Encounters*. Bloomington: Indiana University Press, 2012.

Winslow, J. C. *Narayan Vaman Tilak: The Christian Poet of Maharashtra*. Calcutta: Association, 1923.

Winter, Ralph D. *The Two Structures of God's Redemptive Mission*. South Pasadena, CA: William Carey Library, 1974.

Winter, Ralph D., et al. *Perspectives on the World Christian Movement: A Reader*. Pasadena: William Carey Library, 2009.

Witherington, Ben. *New Testament Rhetoric: An Introductory Guide to the Art of Persuasion in and of the New Testament*. Eugene, OR: Cascade, 2009.

Wittgenstein, Ludwig. *Philosophical investigations*. New York: Macmillan, 1953.

Wood, Laurence W. *God and History: The Dialectical Tension of Faith and History in Modern Thought*. Lexington, KY: Emeth, 2005.

———. *Theology as History and Hermeneutics: A Post-Critical Conversation with Contemporary Theology*. Lexington, KY: Emeth, 2005.

Woods, Robert, and Brian Walrath. *The Message in the Music: Studying Contemporary Praise and Worship*. Nashville: Abingdon, 2007.

Wren, Brian A. *Praying Twice: the Music and Words of Congregational Song*. Louisville: Westminster John Knox, 2000.

Wright, Christopher J. H. *The Mission of God: Unlocking the Bible's Grand Narrative*. Downers Grove, IL: IVP Academic, 2006.

Wulff, Donna Marie. "On Practicing Religiously: Music as Sacred in India." In *Sacred Sound: Music in Religious Thought and Practice*, edited by Joyce Irwin, 149–72. Chico, CA: Scholars, 1983.

Wynn, Mark. "Re-enchanting the World: the Possibility of Materially Mediated Religious Experience." In *Theology, Aesthetics, and Culture: Responses to the Work of David Brown*, edited by Robert MacSwain and Taylor Worley, 115–30. Oxford: Oxford University Press, 2012.

Ybarrola, Steve. "Social Ideologues." Excerpt from forthcoming book.

Yong, Amos. *The Bible, Disability, and the Church: A New Vision of the People of God*. Grand Rapids: Eerdmans, 2011.

Young, Robert. *Postcolonialism: A Very Short Introduction*. Oxford: Oxford University Press, 2003.

Zacharias, Ravi. "What Are the Boundaries of Beauty?" 2007. http://www.youtube.com/watch?v=2y5Jbi1hz7k&list=PL96410657385C3B4F.

Zizioulas, John D. *Being as Communion: Studies in Personhood and the Church*. Crestwood, NY: Saint Vladimirs Seminary, 1985.

———. *Being as Communion: Studies in Personhood and the Church*. Crestwood, NY: St Valadimir's Seminary, 1997.

Subject Index

ability, 11, 17, 31, 35, 42, 114, 149n95, 156, 188, 203, 226n40, 229n51, 237n1, 248nn38–39
aboriginal, 9n37, 66–67, 74, 175n51, 216
abstraction, 73, 162n29, 170, 184, 246n31, 253
abundance, 193, 264–65, 267, 269–70
aesthetic, 5, 31n24, 34n39, 38n57, 42n69, 47, 96, 113, 137, 148–49, 173, 194, 201, 244, 248n37
aesthetics, ix, 31, 43n69, 89n13, 96–97, 130n51, 217n15, 229
alternate, 3, 7n29, 8, 15, 26, 76, 123, 137, 142, 180, 226n40, 265–66
ambiguity, 3, 23, 33, 40, 106n71, 111, 113, 162, 164, 168–69, 214
ambivalence, 8n32, 62–63, 116, 122, 171, 215
American, ii, 17, 19, 41n65, 66, 67n58, 70, 75–76, 80n106, 81, 90, 110, 116, 124, 125, 131n52, 134, 135n63, 136n65, 142–43, 147n90, 148, 149n95, 151, 157, 170, 183, 195, 196, 208–9, 216, 234
appropriation, 10n43, 17, 67, 73–74, 77, 85, 88n11, 90, 111n10, 132–33, 149n95, 151n98, 156n14, 160, 194, 216, 226n40
Aquinas, 59n18, 237–39, 243
Asian, 15n52, 18, 69, 96n40, 111, 122–23, 131n52, 135, 191, 197
Augustine, 37n54, 41n65, 48n92, 59n18, 194, 243
authentic, xvi, 1, 3, 7, 11, 27, 33–34, 39n61, 40n64, 73, 75, 82, 84, 86–87, 99–100, 112n11, 113–16, 121, 131, 137–38, 145, 146n88, 155, 164, 166, 178, 187, 193, 198–99, 209, 213, 216, 217, 218n16, 244
authenticity, x, xvi, 4, 7, 11, 13, 33, 45, 55, 61, 70, 73–77, 79, 81–82, 110, 112, 114, 116, 121, 128, 131, 142–143n84, 165–66, 168–69, 184, 217, 231, 244
axiology, 44, 50, 65, 98n45, 168, 236
axiological, 50, 214

Babylon, 51–52, 56–57n2, 107, 109, 177
band, 17–18, 56n1, 110, 115, 122, 207
Bezalel, v, 10–11
Bhabha, Homi, 8, 57n4, 61n28, 61nn32–33, 62, 65, 71, 72n80, 95, 106, 109, 111n7, 155, 172, 198, 221
bhajan, 17–18, 117–18

Subject Index

bhajans, 117, 125, 179, 181, 197
biblical, 10, 11n45, 14, 15n52, 26, 47, 51, 52n106, 56, 89n13, 98, 103–5, 107, 142, 161, 174, 179, 186, 193nn23–24, 199n33, 201, 219–20, 224, 245, 247, 254n48, 255, 263
binary, 13, 122, 137, 145, 171, 198, 216
binaries, xi, 8, 61–62, 95, 122–23, 171–72
black, 7n25, 31n23, 38n59, 75, 81, 87n44, 124, 164, 174n50,
body, 7, 10–11, 18, 21, 25, 32–33, 37–38, 41n65, 43, 49, 54n110, 69, 95, 97n42, 102–3, 105, 112, 116, 118, 120, 137n69, 180, 185n1, 187, 195, 201–2, 206, 216n11, 223, 231, 233n3, 234, 242, 243n19, 246, 249, 252, 261, 263–65, 267–70
boundary, xvi, 1, 6n21, 28n5, 62, 64, 106, 198–99, 203
boundaries, x, xi, 6, 36, 51, 53, 57, 58, 62, 65, 82, 107n73, 119, 133, 145, 148, 155, 184, 189n19, 198, 215–16, 219n21
bounded, 22, 58, 135n62
bubble, 128, 131, 138, 177–78, 192, 200, 202

capitalism, xvi, 6, 9n37, 22n71, 60, 150, 166, 176, 203–5
captive, 4, 8n36, 69, 88n12, 109, 116, 119–20, 135n61, 196, 226
catalepsy, 105
cataphatic, 247–48
Catholic, 20, 41n65, 106n73, 119n30, 154, 158, 170, 180
cause, 39, 47, 61n28, 85n2, 98n45, 122, 146, 180, 188, 192, 238, 241n12, 242, 248
Christianity, ix–x, xvi–xvii, 1–3, 5–7, 10, 13, 15–16, 24, 27, 29, 31n24, 36n48, 37n56, 39n61, 47, 48n92, 53–55, 85n5, 94n31, 96n39, 111, 117–21, 123, 131–34, 136, 139, 142–43, 146, 150, 152, 155–56, 157n16, 158–59, 165, 166n35, 167, 168n40, 169–71, 173, 177–78, 180, 183, 198, 199n32, 200, 205, 213, 214n7, 222–23, 227, 228n46, 230, 233–34, 239, 241, 248, 252, 254n48, 274
colonial, xi, 5, 8, 40n64, 52n104, 57n2, 61n28, 69, 71, 74, 79–81, 88, 93 (colonial unconscious), 96, 111n8, 122, 132–33, 138n72, 146, 148n92, 171, 196, 200, 217
community, ii, vii, x, xiv, xvi–xvii, 5, 10, 18, 31n24, 33n33, 38n59, 47, 51, 54, 59n18, 61, 66n57, 67, 74, 87, 88n10, 89n15, 91n24, 94nn30–31, 95, 96n39, 118, 121l, 123, 128, 130n51, 131–33, 137n69, 138, 150–51, 154–55, 156n15, 162, 169–70, 172–73, 176–77, 183–84, 187–95, 199–202, 205, 207, 209, 216–17, 219, 220n26, 222, 224–26, 230, 236, 247, 253 255–57, 259–62, 264, 266–70, 273
constitutive rhetoric, 5n17, 9, 31n23, 42n66, 57n3, 97n44, 115n21, 209n57
covenant, vii, 1n1, 47, 52n104, 53, 92, 128, 176–77, 216, 224, 231, 245, 255, 268, 270
creatio, v, xvi, 4, 10, 14, 23, 25, 48, 54, 83–85, 87–88, 89n13, 90, 92–94, 96, 107, 172, 183, 194, 212, 215, 217, 224–26, 231, 246
creation, ix, 6, 15, 19, 28, 30–31, 37n53, 39n60, 41n65, 44n72, 47–48, 57, 62–63, 85, 88, 88n11, 89n13, 90, 91nn22–23, 92, 93, 93n28, 95n35, 96n39, 97, 99n46, 100, 111, 112n11, 113, 130n51, 143, 159–60, 167, 169, 181, 190, 193, 198, 201, 217, 217n16, 218n17, 225, 230n54, 233–35, 239, 239n9, 243–45, 245n28, 245n30, 246, 246n30, 246n33, 250–51, 253n56, 256, 258, 260, 269
creative mission, ix, xi–xii, xv, xvii, 2, 4–5, 10–11, 26, 27, 51–52, 60, 72–73, 83, 84–87, 91, 93, 94–95,

Subject Index   3

97, 107–8 (Ch 4), 115, 139, 207, 209, 211–15, 217, 225, 228, 230–31, 255, 257
crosscultural, 116, 208, 219
cultural, ii, xi, xv, 6, 7nn24–25, 8–9, 10n40, 12n48, 15, 21–22, 24, 28–29, 31n25, 36, 42n69, 43n69, 44n75, 47, 49n97, 51, 55, 57, 58n8, 60nn21–22, 61–65, 67–68, 70–74, 76–77, 81–82, 84, 95n35, 96n39, 100, 102, 106, 109–111, 112n12, 115n20, 116, 118n27, 121–22, 127, 132, 133, 137, 142, 143n84, 144n86, 146, 148, 153, 155n12, 157, 159, 161–63, 165, 170–72, 175–76, 184, 187, 190, 192, 203, 206, 207n55, 208, 213–14, 215n10, 216n12, 217, 219n23, 221, 226–27, 230nn53–54, 231, 236, 240–41, 250, 253, 259, 262, 268nn11–12, 273,
culture, x, 3, 7n30, 8, 15n52, 16, 22, 24, 27–28, 33, 34n41, 36n50, 40, 43n69, 46, 48n90, 49n95, 57–58, 60n21, 61n28, 61nn32–33, 62nn35–38, 63n40, 64–66, 68, 70–71, 72nn79–80, 73, 77, 79, 81, 95, 106, 107n73, 109, 110n4, 111n7, 116, 118–19, 120n36, 121, 126, 127n49, 129, 130n51, 133n58, 135–37, 139, 141–44, 150, 151n98, 158–59, 160n22, 161, 162n28, 165–66, 170, 172n46, 172n48, 174–77, 182, 187, 189, 191, 193–96, 198, 204, 207–9, 213n3, 215–16 218n19, 221, 226–27, 230, 234n9, 239n8, 242, 254n48, 263n1, 273–74

dance, 33n33, 40n63, 81, 102, 119, 133, 148, 150, 151, 160
dialogue, xvi, 5, 15, 21, 82, 90n19–20, 97, 99, 99n50, 100, 106n73, 115n20, 120n38, 123, 158, 160, 170, 172, 181, 184, 185n1, 186–187n10, 188–90, 193–96, 198–99, 202, 218, 222, 229n51, 231, 239, 256, 258, 260, 263n1, 266, 268–70
diaspora, ix, x, 6n22, 18, 58, 66n57, 117n24, 122–23, 131–132n53, 135, 207, 209, 214
diasporic, x, xvi, 58, 70, 126, 132, 135, 135, 190–92
digital, 7n24, 227
difference, xvi, 8, 12n48, 34, 51, 54n110, 55, 61–62, 67n57, 70–73, 76–77, 82, 84, 95, 104, 111n9, 112n12, 113n17, 116, 123, 124, 125, 136n65, 141–42, 144n86, 145, 162, 164, 172, 174n50, 175, 178, 184, 187, 198, 200, 202–3, 208, 214n7, 219n21, 239, 241, 259
differences, 7, 33n34, 49, 71n77, 72n80, 74, 106, 124, 161, 163, 166, 172n48, 174n50, 178n57, 207n55, 209–210, 219, 242, 256, 266, 268n11
diverse, 6, 15n52, 17–18, 58, 61, 71n77, 81–82, 84, 115n20, 120–21, 125, 143n84, 160, 184, 206, 220n25, 222, 223n30, 221n33, 226n40, 263n1, 265–66, 268, 270
diversity, xvii, 5, 7, 12n48, 17–18, 47n87, 50, 55, 58n8, 62n39, 64, 70–72, 74, 77, 78nn97–98, 79n100, 82, 92, 95, 97, 120–21, 125, 128, 131–32, 137, 144n86, 146n88, 147, 153, 161, 188, 191–93, 199–201, 203, 205, 215, 217, 219, 222, 225, 227–28, 230, 256, 258–61, 263–67, 269–70
domain, 16, 27, 38, 49–50, 236
dualism, 30, 37, 40, 41n65, 89n14, 237–38

earth, ix, 1 3n10, 5, 27n1, 28n2, 49, 54, 76, 89, 90, 93, 107, 153, 187, 202, 224, 230, 240, 243, 245–46, 248n39, 253, 256, 263, 265
ecclesial, xvi, 4, 10, 40n63, 100, 135n61, 178, 180, 194, 202, 206, 211–12, 220–21, 223–25
ecclesiology, 202, 220n26, 269
ecological, 94n31, 100, 122, 152n44

Subject Index

economic, ii, 49n94, 58, 71, 73, 100, 121n42, 128, 142–43, 166, 257, 269, 273

ecosystem, 264–67, 269

emergence, xvi, 2, 6, 13, 55–58, 60–62, 64–65, 67–68, 70, 72, 85n4, 92, 107, 119, 132n53, 145, 148, 151–52, 172, 200, 203, 212, 214, 217–18, 230, 258, 270

embodied, 1, 13, 15, 33, 79, 91, 95, 97, 103–4, 110, 122, 151, 171, 195, 203, 205–6, 215–17, 219n22, 223, 228, 230–31, 240, 243, 249, 250–52, 269

enactment, vii, xii, xvi, 12, 26, 31n24, 33, 55, 69–70, 76, 82, 84, 94–95, 97, 102, 203n63, 104, 107, 110, 112n11, 113n14, 130n51, 142, 144, 152, 154, 156, 164–65, 171–72, 186n4, 201–2, 206–7, 221, 224, 243, 249, 251–52

engagement, 8n32, 10, 40n63, 46, 63, 93, 95, 102, 110, 121, 133, 184, 187, 189, 193, 202, 209, 214, 219, 226, 230, 250, 254n48, 262, 269

English, 18, 47n87, 48n91, 126, 128n50, 130, 135n62, 140n77, 141, 144–45, 146n88, 147, 172, 174, 177, 193, 209

embodiment, vii, 7n29, 11–12, 31n24, 33n34, 51, 54n110, 55, 95, 97, 101, 103–7, 109, 113, 142, 155, 165, 206, 209n22, 221, 224, 227, 241, 243, 251–52, 256

embody, 5, 13, 28, 33, 64, 82–83, 93n29, 106, 120n37 121, 161, 172, 178, 187, 196, 207, 211, 242n17, 247, 256

epistemic, 43–44, 52, 89, 120, 153, 161,

epistemological captivity, 4, 27, 33, 38–40, 42, 52n103, 87, 120, 185, 204, 214

era, xiii, xv, xvii, 2, 5, 7, 26, 43–44, 46–47, 50, 57, 63, 71, 95n35, 96, 107, 132, 152, 179, 200, 205, 212, 214

European, 8n36, 56n1, 60n26, 71n77, 136n65, 252

eschatological, 90, 93, 99n46, 107, 158, 202, 209–210, 218n19, 229n51, 240n9

essence, 9, 33n33, 36n49, 37, 45, 79, 91, 178, 189, 220n26, 237–39, 243, 248, 252

estuary, vii, 225, 231, 259, 263–70,

ethnic, 8, 18, 61, 67–68, 71n77, 76, 81, 115, 127, 131n52, 132nn55–57, 142–44, 146n88, 147, 148n92, 168n40. 204, 208–9, 217, 220n24, 267n10

ethnicity, xi, 8, 22, 24n79, 45, 53, 58, 123, 137, 142, 214n7, 256

Ethnodoxology, 206n51

ethnomusicology, 16, 20–21, 28–29, 43, 57, 102, 135, 146n88, 233, 234n9, 249n40

evangelism, ix, xiii, 15, 20, 154, 179, 231, 259

evangelicals, 22n69, 86, 151n98

expression, vii, ix, 4, 9n37, 12, 31, 37n53, 42n69, 43, 47, 73, 88–89, 94–95, 100, 112, 115–16, 118, 132, 143, 148, 150, 160n22, 167, 169, 183, 185, 187, 201, 202n39, 203, 207n55, 217, 219, 221–22, 224–26, 228, 239, 246n32, 248n37, 249, 252, 253n47, 255, 273

Ezekiel, 37n55, 97, 101, 103–5, 107, 186–87, 225, 229, 255, 264, 269, 270

faith, 3n7, 11n44, 37n53, 41n65, 81n106, 89, 100, 107nn73–75, 122, 132, 134, 144, 146n89, 159n19, 182, 193, 198, 207n55, 215, 245n27, 256, 260, 274

Father/father, v, 9n39, 19, 21, 30n15, 91–92, 95, 97n42, 99n45, 120n35, 125–26, 128, 224, 239

fear, xvi, 6, 74, 104n65, 112n11, 119, 123, 125, 131, 142, 199, 217, 225, 256, 258, 261

feel, 6, 16, 76, 92n27, 100n52, 113–15, 124–25, 130–31, 172, 184, 195, 200, 204, 272

field, ii, 12, 16, 25, 27, 49, 50, 70n71, 85, 146n88, 170, 207–8, 215, 236, 250
form, ix, 1–2, 5, 7n29, 12–14, 18, 23n75, 26–27, 31–35, 40n64, 43, 51, 54–55, 57–58, 64, 70, 71n77, 73–74, 76, 86n8, 89n13, 90n18, 93, 95, 97, 105, 111–12, 116, 117n24, 140n76, 141–42, 144, 157–58, 163, 169–70, 178, 183, 185, 194, 202, 212–15, 217, 224–25, 226n41, 228–29, 231, 237–39, 241, 243–47, 249–53, 256, 268
formation, 8, 9n40, 15n52, 27, 36–37, 40, 42–43, 51, 64, 66, 109, 112, 132, 136n64, 145, 194, 214, 221–22, 225–26, 239, 264–65
formations, 42, 152–53
formative, 6, 12, 31, 41n65, 43, 102, 154, 220, 233, 250, 254, 265n4,
framework, xii, xvi, 10–11, 12n48, 23, 25–26, 31n24, 42–44, 46, 49, 51, 54, 65, 70, 83–84, 87–89, 96n39, 106n71, 107, 117, 158, 212–13, 237, 252n44
fresh, xi, xvii, 6, 15n53, 17, 23, 63, 85, 126, 132n53, 152–53, 179, 190, 209, 211, 217, 221, 223, 227, 230–31, 254, 258, 263–64, 266–70
fusion, xvi, 9, 18, 58, 62, 66, 68, 81, 110–12, 118, 123, 130, 136, 146, 166, 167n38, 169, 204
future, 27, 42, 47, 52, 61, 85n5, 90, 97n41, 133, 158, 185n3, 214, 218n19

Gandhi, 18n58, 200
Ganesh/Ganapati, 154, 159–60, 163, 215
gatekeepers, 50, 69, 153, 236
generation, xvi, 7, 16, 51, 76, 81, 133n58, 152, 160n22, 169, 184, 213, 218, 222, 226, 236
generative, 28, 30, 43, 49, 263n1, 266
gospel, ix, x, 3, 7n25, 16, 30n19, 31n23, 35n45, 38n59, 39 42, 50, 53, 55, 59n18, 62, 64, 72, 82, 97n44, 99n50, 100, 111, 114, 117–18, 129, 143–44, 172, 174n50, 176–77, 178n57, 182, 184, 193, 195, 197–98, 206, 210, 215–17, 218n92, 221, 227, 229, 231, 251, 256, 257, 267–68, 270

healing, 6, 21, 59n18, 99, 144, 165n31, 196, 210, 220n25, 223, 225, 230n54, 247n36, 252n45, 256, 258–59, 261, 264, 266, 268, 270
heart, x, 37n56, 110, 112n11, 128–29, 130n50, 137, 143n84, 161n23, 163, 167, 196, 203, 234, 260, 273
hegemonic, x, 3, 12n48, 21, 52n104, 57n2, 68, 74–75, 97, 171, 174
hegemonies, xv, xvi, 5, 219n22, 222
hegemony, 5, 43n69, 44, 63, 69, 88, 112, 146, 172, 205
historical, ii, 15n52, 28, 41n65, 61, 65, 74, 90, 106, 122, 126, 133, 135n61, 138–39, 143n82–83, 145, 158, 165–66, 170, 172, 187, 189, 197, 206, 208, 218, 230, 233
histories, 15n52, 27, 40, 62, 64, 66, 70–73, 77, 79–82, 88n12, 111, 122, 130n51, 134, 137, 140, 143, 162, 169, 182, 190, 217, 222–23
history, ii, 1, 4n13, 7n29, 10n40, 15n53, 19, 30nn15–16, 30n21, 31n23, 39n61, 40n65, 42, 43n69, 47, 49, 54nn109–111, 57n3, 66–67, 68n65, 70–71, 79–80, 90, 96n40, 97n44, 100n52, 110, 114, 118, 125–26, 132, 135, 140n76, 144, 148n93, 155, 158, 159n19, 169, 178, 185, 192, 203, 206, 215n10, 216n12, 219n23, 221, 228, 230n54, 244, 252, 258n1
hip hoppers, 9n37, 66–67, 175n51
hope, 6, 21, 26, 52n104, 57n2, 62–63, 65, 81n106, 90, 112, 117, 129, 156n15, 158, 182, 199, 202, 215, 225, 230n54, 231, 240n9, 252n45, 257, 272

Subject Index

home, x, 18, 20, 57, 69n71, 76, 81, 100n52, 115–16, 117n24, 124, 130n51, 149n94, 164, 174, 191–92, 197
human(s), 1, 4, 11n44, 12, 14, 29–30, 36, 39, 41n65, 42, 44–46, 48–49, 52n103, 55, 59, 61, 69, 84, 86, 89, 91n22, 92, 93n29, 94n31, 95, 100, 101–3, 113n14, 115, 118, 122, 130n51, 143, 153n4, 158n17, 181, 186, 188, 202n40, 202n40, 203, 205, 217–18, 219n22, 220, 222, 225n36, 226, 229, 239–43, 245–46, 249–50, 252, 253, 255, 257, 260, 264, 267n10, 269–70
humanity, x, 1, 4–5, 9n40, 39n60, 89n13, 91, 155n9, 158, 178, 184, 215, 217, 221, 224, 228, 240, 243–46, 252, 257
humility, 99, 100n50, 188, 196, 199, 201, 223, 269
hybrid, 6, 8–9, 45n76, 58, 61–62, 66, 82, 110, 151, 155, 166, 170, 184, 214, 230
hybridities, 63n42, 152
hybridity, xi, 7n27, 8, 61–64, 75–76, 82, 109, 129–30, 167, 169, 175–77, 217
hymn(s), ix, 85n4, 117, 118n27, 120, 133, 140, 142, 147, 156n15, 176, 185, 213
hymnody, x, 6n22, 136, 137n66–67, 138n72, 145–47

identity, vii, xi, xiii, xv, xvi, 2–4, 8–9, 11–13, 14n49, 15–17, 19, 22n71, 23–25, 27, 29–31, 34, 40, 42–43, 45, 51–53, 55, 56n1, 57–67, 69, 72–73, 76–78, 79n100, 82, 84, 88n10, 91–92, 94n31, 97, 98n45, 99n45, 103, 107, 109–112, 114–15, 117–18, 121–27, 130–34, 135n62, 136n64, 139, 141, 144–45, 146n88, 148, 151, 152n1, 154–57, 159, 167, 168n40, 169–73, 175–76, 178–79, 180, 183–84, 186, 187, 192, 194–96, 197n30, 199, 201, 202n40, 204, 208–9, 211–12, 214, 216–17, 219nn21–22, 221, 227n43, 230–31, 233, 251, 270
identities, xi, xvi, 5–8, 9n37, 10, 12n48, 17, 28, 32, 36, 51, 57–58, 60–62, 64, 68, 70, 72, 77, 111–12, 121, 130, 132n53, 136n64, 145, 151–53, 155, 170, 174–76, 178, 189, 191–92, 197, 214, 217, 226n41, 231, 247, 265, 266n6
image, 9n40, 44, 88n10, 89, 94n33, 103n63, 112–13, 116, 149n94, 150n96, 250, 255–56, 260
imagination, 47, 69, 78, 86n8, 89n15, 90n15, 91n22, 95, 107n76, 145, 148, 158n17, 159n21, 187n11, 210, 217, 220n26, 222, 229n52, 234n9, 245, 252n44, 259, 216, 264
immigrant(s), 18, 56, 70n75, 125–26, 179, 200, 209, 220, 227
indigenous cosmopolitanism, xi, xv, 5, 8–9n37, 58, 65–67, 159, 176–77, 230
indigeneity, 8, 57, 61, 65, 67, 73, 82, 84, 85, 92, 137, 155, 159, 167–71, 227, 231, 275
Israelites, 51–53, 55, 98n45, 109, 177, 185n3, 186n4, 196, 214

Jew(s), 1, 51–54, 56, 72–73, 107, 109, 173, 195, 211, 214, 227–28, 241n13, 253n57
justice, xvi, 6, 10, 53, 94n31, 100, 129, 184, 187, 203, 257, 274

kingdom, 17, 49, 88n11, 90n17–18, 92nn26–27, 99, 149n95, 192–93, 200–201, 204n45, 208n56, 215n9, 218–19, 220n26, 226–27, 230n53, 262–63, 268
Korean(s), 19, 127, 134, 135, 142–43, 150, 195, 204, 206–9

language, ix–x, 14n49, 15, 20, 22n71, 26, 28–30n15, 30n20, 34–35, 37, 45, 46n80, 47n87, 51, 52n103,

74–76, 97, 102–3, 110, 118, 127, 135n62, 140n77, 141–42, 144, 154, 159–60, 166, 168, 173, 174, 181, 187, 189, 206, 221, 241, 249–50, 273
learning, 5, 8, 52–53, 60, 69n71, 82, 106, 109, 130, 134, 140, 143, 162, 172, 185n3, 188, 193, 195–96, 200, 213, 224, 227–28, 241, 250, 256–57, 260–62, 266–67, 269
lived experience, xv, 8, 73, 179
local, ix-xi, 5, 9, 22n73, 24n78, 28, 57, 60n23, 63, 69n71, 73, 75, 77–78, 110, 119n33, 120, 136, 139, 141, 147, 149n94, 150, 153, 156n13, 162, 166, 170, 175–76, 179, 192, 197, 200, 205–7, 217, 222–23, 224n35, 226, 230n53, 231, 234, 255, 257, 260, 262, 268,
locality, 66, 73, 76, 78, 82, 110, 130n51, 179
location, 7n30, 8n35, 18, 22n71, 53, 57n4, 61n28, 61nn32–33, 62n35–38, 72n80, 93, 95, 106, 111n7, 116, 121, 157n16, 159, 172n46, 172n48, 194, 197, 206, 230, 242, 259

media, 3, 7, 12, 20, 29, 58, 60, 62, 70–71, 135, 144, 148, 150nn97–151n98, 153, 222, 226n38, 226n40, 269
mediation, 2–3, 5, 7, 17, 24, 27, 29, 40, 55, 70, 79, 81–82, 85, 111, 113, 116, 119–21, 125, 152–53, 185–87, 202–3, 219
mediate, xi, 11–12, 40, 53, 72, 82, 84, 107, 176, 178, 187, 198, 225, 237–38, 240, 244
metaphor, 66, 72, 101, 105–6, 187, 210, 228, 242
mind, 2, 7, 8n36, 25, 29, 30n19, 32n26, 39, 42, 54n110, 69, 79, 88n12, 103, 105n66, 139n75, 141, 143n84, 150, 158, 163, 178n57, 182–83, 196, 198, 226n40, 227n41, 229n51, 248n37, 250n42, 261, 267

missiological, xii, xvi–xvii, 2n4, 10, 12, 23, 25–27, 43, 46, 50n101, 54, 84–85, 87–88, 93, 107, 110, 133, 161n26, 178n57, 211, 218, 233–34
missiology, 6, 16, 25–26, 165–66n35, 198n31, 214, 224, 233–34
missional, xiii, 3, 6n22, 11, 13, 19, 52, 100, 117, 177, 202, 207, 214, 217, 222, 228, 270
missionary, 3, 6, 9, 17, 19–20, 42, 91, 99, 100n52, 107, 110, 126, 133, 138, 142–43, 146, 173, 209
modern, 4, 26, 30n15, 39n61, 40, 75, 78–79, 85n2, 92n27, 94n31, 120, 145, 156n13, 158, 169, 214
modernity, 5, 7n24, 8, 15n53, 37, 40n65, 61, 63, 68, 71, 72, 75, 111–12, 132n53, 167n38, 184, 118n17, 121, 130, 167
musical creativity, xv–xvi, 2–6n20, 12–16, 21–23, 25–26, 27–42 (Ch2), 43n70, 46n80, 50–51, 55, 57, 58–59, 62–64, 67, 69–70, 76, 79, 81–84, 87, 89, 90, 97, 102, 108, 113–14, 116, 119–20, 122, 125, 130n51, 134, 136, 138–39, 142, 144, 153, 155, 155n12, 157–59, 160n22, 161–62, 164–65, 178, 185, 203–4, 211–13, 224, 229, 229n51–230, 233, 240, 244, 248–52
multicultural, 19, 74, 144, 162, 208–9, 228, 230
myth (ologies), 119, 123, 153n4, 174, 194, 218, 258

neoliberal, xv, xvi, 5, 9n37, 34, 51, 56–57, 59, 63, 67–69, 71, 75, 82, 123, 166, 174, 203–4, 227n41, 230
new spaces, xi–xii, xv, 2–3, 5–8, 12–13, 25–27, 44, 51, 55–59, 61–64, 67, 70–72, 76–79, 82–85, 97, 107–9, 116, 166, 185, 211–15, 217, 224–25

Subject Index

outside, ix, 18, 49, 57, 66n,57 74, 90, 91n23, 100, 137, 147, 157n16, 177, 180, 186, 189–90, 192, 201–2, 223, 252
outward, 9n38, 41n65, 88, 93, 192, 248, 267

participation, xi, xvi, 2, 5, 10, 13–16, 28, 30, 31n24, 35, 38, 42, 44n70, 49, 74, 76, 88n10, 93, 95, 96n39, 99, 101–2, 108, 116, 120, 130n51, 137, 141–42, 144, 152, 162, 167, 169, 174, 183–84, 213, 216, 218, 220, 222–24, 226, 228–29, 231, 238–39, 240–42, 246, 248, 251, 256 259, 261–62, 267–68
perform, 12–13, 83, 98n45, 99n45, 112, 118, 186–89, 211, 259
performance, vii, x, xii, xvi, 10, 12–13, 17, 23, 29n12, 31n24, 33n33, 38n59, 40n63, 54–55, 87, 97–99, 101–8, 113, 122, 137n69, 150–51, 166, 185–90, 193–97, 199–202, 204–7, 209–10, 213, 216–18, 220n26, 221, 224–25, 226n40, 252, 259
performative, xvi, 14, 28, 35, 112, 185–87, 207, 221, 229
performativity, 4, 62, 102–3, 106, 187, 221
performing, 10, 18, 28n7, 31n24, 34n38, 76, 98n45, 99, 102, 129, 155, 197, 201n36, 204, 217n15, 255
postcolonial, xi, xv–xvi, 2–3, 6–8, 13–15, 21, 23, 26, 34, 44, 51, 55, 57, 60–64, 69, 71, 77–79, 81–82, 84–85, 88, 90, 92, 95–97, 105, 111n88, 122n44, 141, 147, 153, 155, 165–66, 168, 171, 198, 205, 212, 230
postcolonialism, 6n22, 7n27, 9n37, 24, 61n28, 146, 168
postmodern, 7n25, 31n23, 35n44, 53, 61, 97n44, 111n10, 160n22, 165
popular, xv, 18, 36, 43, 44n72, 45, 56, 58, 63n42, 66, 71, 77–78, 88, 115, 117, 118n27, 123, 127, 128n50, 130n51, 134, 136, 141, 144, 150, 151n98, 154–56, 158n17, 164n31, 170–71, 175, 190, 204, 216, 222, 239n8, 258n1
potential, 6, 11–12, 14, 33n34, 36, 37n54, 38n57, 40n65, 41n65, 42–46, 55, 63, 73–74, 80, 82, 85, 116–18, 119n30, 121, 123, 129, 139, 141, 154, 184, 192, 199, 202n39, 203, 210, 213, 217, 220n25, 222–23, 225, 229–30, 233–34, 245, 249, 252, 255–56, 259, 269
power, xi, 1–3, 5, 6n22, 7–8, 24, 31, 45, 46n80, 47, 54, 58, 60n27, 62, 68, 73, 77, 79–81, 91–92, 95, 101, 111–12, 121n42, 135n62, 147n91, 148–49, 162, 165n31, 166, 176, 178, 184, 204, 206, 207n52, 209, 217, 220, 223, 231, 235, 238–39, 248, 249n41, 250–52, 253n46
public, xvi, 35, 38, 63–64, 97, 102, 106, 108, 153n4, 190, 202, 221, 222, 230, 255–57, 259

radical, xi, 40, 64, 98–99, 104, 106, 120, 133, 148, 165, 177, 186, 198n31, 201, 203, 206, 216n11, 230–31, 238–39, 240n9, 261
rap, 55n16, 73, 136, 170, 175
rational, 12, 30, 31n21, 33, 38–39, 41n65, 95, 102, 161, 251
rationalism, 39n61, 40, 48
religious, 6n21, 15, 20, 22n71, 33, 36, 41n65, 43, 47n87, 52n104, 55, 56n1, 58, 85, 86n8, 94n31, 104, 117n24, 119n29, 146n88, 151, 155–56, 158–58, 162, 165–66, 170, 178, 180, 188, 215, 224, 227, 231, 239, 244, 252, 253n47, 258n1, 273
representation, 1n1, 5, 8, 12, 23n75, 58, 75, 77, 103, 110, 111n10, 112, 132, 141, 144, 153, 155, 161–62, 164, 174n50, 217
rhetoric, ix, xiii, 5, 12n48, 31n23, 42n66, 52, 57n3, 60, 62, 68–69, 74, 78,

Subject Index 9

97n44, 111, 115, 134, 151n98, 166, 180, 192, 198, 208–9, 230
rhizomic, 65, 66, 82, 167n38,

sacred, 6n19, 32, 33n36, 35n45, 36, 37nn53–54, 38n57, 40n65, 41n65, 74, 85, 89n14, 90, 119, 120n37, 137n66, 151, 164, 213n3, 229n51, 240–41, 248
sacramental, 38n57, 213, 239, 244, 252
secular, 14, 16, 28n5, 36, 42, 85, 89n14, 90, 149–51, 155, 161, 164, 240n9
sing, 5, 20, 28n5, 31n25, 32n32, 51–54, 56nn1–2, 67n61, 72–73, 82, 84, 99, 109, 130, 140, 150, 154, 156n15, 161, 163, 170, 185n3, 187, 189, 190, 193, 196, 202n39, 204, 209, 212, 214, 215, 219, 221, 233n1, 240
singing, 5, 20, 21, 41n65, 52n103, 78, 99n46, 117–18, 127, 129–30, 138nn71–72, 140n76, 150, 154, 159–60, 163–64, 167, 191, 195, 202, 204, 215, 219
social, ii, xvi, 4n12, 6, 9n40, 10, 21–22, 24, 28–29, 35nn44–45, 41n65, 42n69, 44n72, 44n75, 46–47, 49n97, 50–51, 56n1, 58–60, 62–64, 69n71, 70n75, 79–80, 103, 106, 111, 119, 150n97, 153n4, 155, 159–60, 166, 175, 178–79, 184, 189, 197–98, 206, 215n10, 217, 219n21, 222–23, 226n40, 236, 247, 249–50, 268n11, 269, 273
sociocultural, 29, 33n36, 43, 49, 51, 53, 55, 94, 145, 186, 263
sound, 5, 6n19, 17, 23, 25–26, 28, 32, 33n33, 33n36, 34, 36, 37n53, 41n65, 67n62, 68n63, 68n67, 81, 85, 110, 111n8, 113n15, 115n20, 119n32, 120n37, 128, 144, 146n89, 153, 176n54, 204–5, 219, 224, 233, 238, 240–42, 243n19, 249,
song, x, 5, 20, 37n55, 51–54, 56, 62, 67, 72–73, 76, 79–81, 84, 99, 114, 116n2, 119n31, 126, 129, 150, 154, 156n14, 157, 160, 163, 168, 180–81, 185n3, 190, 196–97, 202–4, 209, 212, 216, 219n22, 221, 225, 229, 230n54, 231, 260
sonic, vii, 26, 32–33, 36n49, 85, 93n29, 94–95, 97, 110, 112, 118, 120, 154n6, 124, 137, 140, 149
subaltern, 14, 23–24, 76n71, 96–97, 107, 143, 170, 184, 230
substance, 88n10, 94, 113n16, 115, 209, 245–46, 248n38

tension(s), x, xvi, 8, 9n37, 12n48, 37n53, 41n65, 45n77, 53, 71n77, 126, 130–31, 144, 163, 172, 178, 181, 196, 188n31, 212, 216–17, 219
text, 1n1, 14–15, 28n8, 31–32, 34–35, 37, 41n65, 63n40, 85, 95n35, 107, 113, 142, 154n8, 158n17, 183, 186n5, 210, 228–29, 247, 249n40
transcultural, 9, 17, 43, 50–51, 111, 208
transnational, xi, 6n21, 9, 13, 36, 50, 56–57, 59–61, 63–65, 67, 69–70, 78, 82, 111, 116, 166, 223
transnationalism, 57–58, 122,

value, 8, 30, 33, 39n60, 40, 47, 61, 76, 80, 84–85, 89n13, 94n33, 104, 116, 129, 134, 144n86, 146–47, 149, 155, 172, 218, 227, 238, 248, 252
verbal, 13–14, 21, 26, 37, 103, 162, 174, 213, 241, 248–49, 250n42
vision, 40n63, 43n69, 53, 72, 100, 104, 187, 212, 223, 231, 258, 261, 263–64, 268, 272
voice(s), 8n36, 25, 40n63, 51, 67n61, 90, 91n24, 143, 160–61, 170, 177, 196, 198, 202, 219n22, 222, 241, 246, 249, 260
vulnerability, 100–111, 125, 170, 188
vulnerable, 24, 92n27, 153, 188

water, 80, 81n106, 101–2, 105, 124, 167, 231, 247n34, 248, 258, 263–65, 267, 269–70

Subject Index

West, 3, 18, 24n78, 32, 37, 46–47, 56, 61, 67–69, 71–72, 75–76, 78, 85, 94n31, 96, 101n55, 120, 124, 126, 134, 141–43, 145n86, 146n88, 147–48, 149n94, 150, 157, 173, 175–76, 183, 187n7, 227n43, 251, 267

Western, x, 3, 5, 7, 8n34, 12, 15n52, 18 24n78, 26, 34–36, 39n61, 40n65, 41n65, 47, 54, 67n61–62, 68n65, 69, 70n71, 71, 75–76, 79, 81, 90, 94, 96–97, 105, 110–11, 113n17, 116, 118, 120n35, 122–23, 127, 129, 133n58, 134, 136, 140, 142–43, 145–46, 148, 150, 152n1, 155, 162n29, 165–66, 169–71, 176, 203–4, 209, 2213n4, 227n43, 234n9, 241, 246n31

Westernization, 32, 79, 136–37, 139–40, 155, 156n13, 171, 176

Westernized, 5, 14, 40, 61, 78–79, 87, 96–97, 112, 120, 126, 128n50, 130, 135–36, 138, 150, 171, 176, 205

witness, 17, 37n53, 53, 99–100, 121, 165, 177, 187, 199–200, 206, 233n4, 240, 273

worship, ix–x, xiii–xiv, xvi, 7, 10, 11n45, 19–20, 22, 24–25, 33n33, 36, 37nn55–56, 38n58, 40n64, 41n65, 52n104, 54, 94n34, 97n44, 100, 104, 109, 116–17, 119n31, 128–30, 132, 136–138n72, 143, 146–50, 155, 157, 163, 169, 176, 183, 187, 190, 193, 199, 202, 204, 206–8, 216, 219–21, 233–34, 239–40, 245, 253n47, 263

work, ii, xiv, xvi, 11, 17–18, 22, 23n75, 31, 41n65, 46, 50n99, 67, 89n15, 99, 100n50, 102, 103n63, 105n66, 121n42, 131, 138, 142, 148, 170, 173, 175, 200, 203, 205, 207n55, 216, 224–25, 226nn39–40, 227n41, 234, 237n1, 244–46, 253, 255–56, 259–60, 273

www.ingramcontent.com/pod-product-compliance
Lightning Source LLC
Chambersburg PA
CBHW050619300426
44112CB00012B/1567